RENEWALS 458-4574

DATE DUE			
GAYLORD			PRINTED IN U.S.A.

Expert .NET
Micro Framework

■ ■ ■

Jens Kühner

Apress®

Expert .NET Micro Framework

Copyright © 2008 by Jens Kühner

ISBN-13: 978-1-59059-973-0

ISBN-10: 1-59059-973-X

ISBN-13 (electronic): 978-1-4302-0608-8

ISBN-10 (electronic): 1-4302-0608-X

Printed and bound in the United States of America 9 8 7 6 5 4 3 2 1

Distributed to the book trade worldwide by Springer-Verlag New York, Inc., 233 Spring Street, 6th Floor, New York, NY 10013. Phone 1-800-SPRINGER, fax 201-348-4505, e-mail orders-ny@springer-sbm.com, or visit http://www.springeronline.com.

For information on translations, please contact Apress directly at 2855 Telegraph Avenue, Suite 600, Berkeley, CA 94705. Phone 510-549-5930, fax 510-549-5939, e-mail info@apress.com, or visit http://www.apress.com.

Apress and friends of ED books may be purchased in bulk for academic, corporate, or promotional use. eBook versions and licenses are also available for most titles. For more information, reference our Special Bulk Sales—eBook Licensing web page at http://www.apress.com/info/bulksales.

The source code for this book is available to readers at http://www.apress.com. You may need to answer questions pertaining to this book in order to successfully download the code.

To my wonderful son Marek and beautiful wife Iryna: you have added a wonderful new dimension to my life that I didn't even know I was missing.

Contents at a Glance

Contents

■CHAPTER 3 Getting Started

■CHAPTER 4 Introducing the .NET Micro Framework Base Class Library

About the Author

JENS KÜHNER works as principal software engineer for Vallon GmbH in Germany, a company that develops and manufactures metal detectors and ferrous locators. He creates software for data acquisition and evaluation using the .NET Framework and .NET Compact Framework. Since this software must be incorporated closely with the detectors' hardware, an interest in embedded systems was only natural.

Jens has been involved with the .NET Micro Framework from the very start, when he saw it presented at MEDC Europe. Since then, he's been an active beta tester of the technology and a regular contributor to the .NET Micro Framework forum.

You can reach him through his blog at http://bloggingabout.net/blogs/jens.

About the Technical Reviewer

■**FABIO CLAUDIO FERRACCHIATI** is a senior consultant and a senior analyst/developer using Microsoft technologies. He works for Brain Force (http://www.brainforce.com) at its Italian branch (http://www.brainforce.it). He is a Microsoft Certified Solution Developer for .NET, a Microsoft Certified Application Developer for .NET, a Microsoft Certified Professional, and a prolific author and technical reviewer. Over the past ten years, he's written articles for Italian and international magazines and coauthored more than ten books on a variety of computer topics. You can read his LINQ blog at http://www.ferracchiati.com.

Acknowledgments

Writing this book was fun and immensely rewarding, but it took a great deal of effort and time to write. I would like to thank a number of individuals for supporting me and making this book possible.

First, I want to thank my wife, Iryna, and my son, Marek, who suffered most from my absence, for their love, tolerance, and patience. Iryna took care of so many things in order to make my life frictionless while I was writing. Without her active and emotional support, this project would never have gotten completed.

Thanks a lot to my parents, Bärbel and Helmut, for buying me my first computer. They always supported me and believed in me without knowing where these endless hours in front of the screen would end up, and they shaped me to be the person I am.

I'd like to thank the entire .NET Micro Framework team for developing this great technology and especially Zach Libby, Jonathan Kagle, Jim Mateer, and Lorenzo Tessiore for providing me beta bits as well as their advice, feedback, and support. I was very happy that Microsoft and Digi International provided me modules and development kits. Thanks to Frank Prengel (embedded developer evangelist at Microsoft) for providing me photographs and illustrations.

Next, a special mention goes to my boss at Vallon GmbH for believing in and supporting innovative ideas and for letting me always use the latest tools and technologies.

Finally, thanks to my technical reviewer Fabio Ferracchiati for his great suggestions to improve the overall quality of this book. I am deeply indebted to the whole Apress team, especially copy editor Heather Lang and production editor Elizabeth Berry for making my words easier to read.

Introduction

It all started at Microsoft's European Mobile and Embedded Developers Conference (MEDC Europe) 2006 in Nice, France. At this event, I saw the .NET Micro Framework presented for the first time in a session by Jonathan Kagle and Lorenzo Tessiore. As a .NET programmer for desktop and smart device applications, I was very impressed by the idea of being able to program embedded microcontrollers with my everyday development tool and programming language: Microsoft Visual Studio and C#.

I got a CD with the not-yet-released .NET Micro Framework SDK 1.0 from Lorenzo after the presentation; the emulator it included was not customizable and was specially built for the Sumo Robot contest that took place at the conference. The contest's goal was to program a Sumo robot (a small robot supporting the .NET Micro Framework) with Visual Studio and C# so that it was intelligent enough to react to sensor input and push an enemy from the battlefield.

Instead of going to the beach in Nice in the evening, I stayed in my hotel room and tweaked the software development kit's (SDK's) emulation mechanism to launch my own emulator. My first emulator just indicated the activity of a general purpose input/output (GPIO) port on the emulator's user interface using a check box. This allowed me to write my first .NET Micro Framework application that toggled a GPIO port and run it on my first emulator.

Since then, I have been an active beta tester of this technology and a regular contributor to the .NET Micro Framework forums. This passion, combined with the lack of good documentation and practical samples and the users' questions in the forum, motivated me to write this book for you.

What makes a developer productive and efficient? It is the combination of the right tools and the knowledge and skills to use them. When you use .NET Micro Framework devices, the extensible emulator, and the base class library with Visual Studio and the C# programming language, you're using powerful and modern tools. To improve your knowledge of and skill in efficiently using these tools, this book has the ambitious goal of being the best tutorial and reference available for programming with the .NET Micro Framework. Many books just scratch the surface instead of diving deeply into a topic and providing practical samples; those books are over when the fun is just beginning. I know this book is different, and I hope you find plenty of information in it that you can use to create many powerful and effective embedded applications.

■ ■ ■

CHAPTER 1

Introducing the .NET Micro Framework

This chapter introduces the .NET Micro Framework; we will discuss its history, motivation, goals, and architecture. We will have a look at where the .NET Micro Framework fits in the story of Microsoft's offerings for embedded development, and you will learn about the benefits and limitations of the .NET Micro Framework. Finally, the chapter provides a technical overview of the .NET Micro Framework.

What Is the .NET Micro Framework?

The Microsoft .NET Micro Framework is a small and efficient .NET runtime environment used to run managed code on devices that are too small and resource constrained for Windows CE and the .NET Compact Framework.

The .NET Micro Framework enables you to write embedded applications for small, connected, embedded devices with Visual Studio and C#. That means you can now use the same development tools and language that you use to build desktop and smart device (PDA and smartphone) applications to develop applications for microcontrollers. The .NET Micro Framework also provides an extensible hardware emulator for rapid prototyping and debugging.

The .NET Micro Framework requires no underlying operating system. A scaled-down version of the Common Language Runtime (TinyCLR) sits directly on the hardware, so the framework is often called a bootable runtime. The runtime has a small footprint; it uses only a few hundred kilobytes of RAM and does not require the processor to have a memory management unit (MMU). Therefore, the .NET Micro Framework can run on small and inexpensive 32-bit processors without consuming a lot of power.

.NET Micro Framework History

Let's take a look at the history and versions of the .NET Micro Framework:

- Smart Personal Object Technology (SPOT) started at Microsoft Research in 2001. David Massarenti developed the first proof-of-concept version of a scaled-down and ECMA-compliant CLR, the TinyCLR.

- Smart watches first shipped in 2004 (see Figure 1-1) and Microsoft TV set top boxes in 2005.

- The .NET Micro Framework 1.0 on Sumo robots (see Figure 1-2), which included a Sumo robot emulator, was presented at the 2006 Mobile and Embedded Developers Conference (MEDC); the conference also featured a Sumo robot contest.

- In February 2007, the .NET Micro Framework 2.0, with a customizable emulator, was released. Some development boards (see Figure 1-3) and devices (see Figure 1-4) were available, and others followed in 2007. You will learn more about the available development boards and hardware platforms in the next chapter.

- In 2007, Microsoft presented Windows SideShow, which is based on the .NET Micro Framework, and hardware manufacturers started shipping Windows SideShow-capable devices (see Figure 1-5).

- Later in 2007, Service Pack 1 for the .NET Micro Framework 2.0 was released.

- In February 2008, Microsoft released the .NET Micro Framework 2.5.

Figure 1-1. *A smart watch*

Figure 1-2. *A Sumo robot*

Figure 1-3. *A .NET Micro Framework development board (copyright of Freescale Semiconductor, Inc. 2008, used by permission)*

Figure 1-4. *A .NET Micro Framework network-enabled device*

Figure 1-5. *A notebook with an integrated display utilizing SideShow*

Motivation

This section describes why Microsoft developed the .NET Micro Framework and the benefits of using managed code on devices.

Embedded Development in the Past

Developing an embedded device from scratch and programming it with C++, C, or even assembly language can be challenging. Embedded developers are used to writing code that directly interfaces with the hardware. Running the software written for one controller on another platform will not work, even if the CPU core is the same. Every board has different buses, interrupt controllers, memory, and I/O interfaces.

The tools and development environments for embedded development are not very comfortable and complete even today. Also, every CPU vendor provides its own compiler and development tools, and simulating hardware and debugging embedded applications on your development PC is hard.

A Different Approach

Standard hardware platforms with the .NET Micro Framework already on board provide a different approach. The .NET Micro Framework hardware features ready-to-use single-board computers (see Chapter 2) with common hardware components such as memory, general purpose input/output (GPIO) ports, serial ports, and a display on board. The code to interface with the hardware components is already complete. You just need to write your application, and you can focus on domain-specific problems.

The .NET Micro Framework abstracts hardware access through its base class library and treats hardware components as objects. That enables you to program hardware components in an object-orientated way. Instead of dealing with hardware details and setting bit masks to configure peripheral hardware, you just need to set the properties of an object. This approach is also referred to as *managed drivers* and will help make your embedded application independent from a particular platform.

.NET Micro Framework applications can be programmed using Visual Studio and C#. Visual Studio is a widespread and state-of-the-art development tool. If you are already programming .NET applications for the desktop, smartphones, or PDAs, you can continue using your everyday development tool. C# is a modern high-level programming language that allows you to write clear and reusable object-orientated code. With the .NET Micro Framework, every developer familiar with .NET can also be an embedded developer!

Like the full .NET Framework and the .NET Compact Framework, the .NET Micro Framework runs managed code. The C# compiler generates a processor-independent intermediate language that TinyCLR executes on the device. The next section describes the benefits of managed code.

Benefits of Managed Code

As stated earlier, the .NET Micro Framework contains the TinyCLR. Code that targets the CLR is referred to as *managed code*, whereas code that does not target the CLR is known as *unmanaged (native) code*. The CLR executes intermediate-language code and provides the following core services and benefits:

- Automatic memory management using a garbage collector

- Thread management and synchronization

- Exception handling

- Strict type safety

- Secure and robust managed code

- Debugging services

The CLR uses a garbage collector that automatically frees unused memory blocks and manages threads by providing time slices to the individual threads and methods to synchronize access to shared resources. Since managed code is executed under the control of the CLR, which takes care of references to objects, you do not have to deal with the unsafe pointers that are common with native programming. With managed code, you can't access memory blocks once they've been disposed of, because the CLR frees objects only when they are not referenced anymore. It also enforces strict type safety, and the TinyCLR prevents execution of unsafe, custom, native code. Together with exception handling, a modern way to handle errors, managed code enables secure and robust applications.

Managed code assemblies contain much information (metadata). Therefore, using managed code also allows you to use static code analysis tools like FxCop to detect and enforce the following to write better code:

- Enforcing consistent naming of classes and methods
- Detecting unused code
- Detecting performance issues
- Detecting design issues

Where the .NET Micro Framework Fits

Now that we have discussed the benefits of managed code, let's look at where the .NET Micro Framework fits in the story of Microsoft's offerings (see Figure 1-6). Windows XP, Windows XP Embedded, and Windows Vista support the full .NET Framework, while Windows CE supports the .NET Compact Framework. There may be an overlap among the offerings, so two systems may fit well and be good choices for one application.

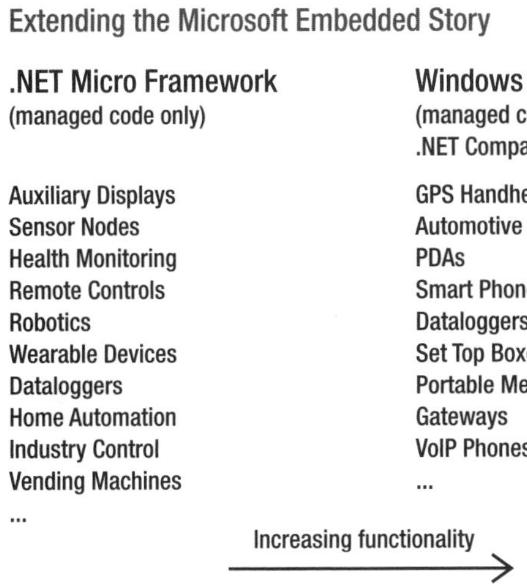

Extending the Microsoft Embedded Story

.NET Micro Framework (managed code only)	Windows Embedded CE (managed code with the .NET Compact Framework)	Windows XP Embedded (managed code with the full .NET Framework)
Auxiliary Displays	GPS Handhelds	Retail Point-of-Sale
Sensor Nodes	Automotive	Windows-based Terminals
Health Monitoring	PDAs	Medical devices
Remote Controls	Smart Phones	Entertainment devices
Robotics	Dataloggers	Kiosks
Wearable Devices	Set Top Boxes	...
Dataloggers	Portable Media Players	
Home Automation	Gateways	
Industry Control	VoIP Phones	
Vending Machines	...	
...		

Increasing functionality →

Figure 1-6. *Microsoft's embedded offerings*

The .NET Micro Framework is the smallest .NET platform to date and provides only a subset of the full .NET Framework and .NET Compact Framework. While Windows CE configurations supporting managed code with the.NET Compact Framework require at least 12MB of RAM, the .NET Micro Framework running directly on the hardware requires only about 300KB of RAM. The smart watches, for example, came with an ARM7 chipset clocked with 27 MHz and having 384KB RAM and 1MB flash memory (a suggested minimal configuration). The currently available .NET Micro Framework devices start at 55 MHz and require 8MB of RAM and 1MB of flash memory.

The .NET Micro Framework requires a 32-bit processor. Although common embedded programming in assembly language or C still takes place on 16-bit or even 8-bit processors, improved production techniques have reduced the manufacturing costs and power requirements of 32-bit processors. However, since the .NET Micro Framework does not require an MMU, it can run on less expensive processors than Windows CE can.

What the Framework Is Not

The .NET Micro Framework is not a real-time system. Although it is very fast and suitable for most applications, do not expect real-time deterministic behavior. A timer event may not be triggered exactly after the specified amount of time (varying by some milliseconds), or the runtime environment may take a few milliseconds to react to an interruption by calling the interrupt service routine.

In addition, the garbage collector will run to free unused memory when memory gets low. Garbage collection might block all threads for a few milliseconds.

Also, executing managed code is a bit slower than executing native code. With the .NET Micro Framework, all managed code will be interpreted. There is no just-in-time compiler that compiles managed code parts to native machine code on the first execution as there is for the full .NET Framework and .NET Compact Framework.

Licensing

The .NET Micro Framework SDK is available for download at no cost. To develop for the .NET Micro Framework, you need Visual Studio 2005 Standard Edition or better (not Express Edition). A fee is charged for each device containing the .NET Micro Framework, but the fee is lower than the one for Windows CE. Also, you are not required to pay the fee directly. When you buy ready-to-use prebuilt modules or development boards containing the .NET Micro Framework, the license fee has already been paid to Microsoft.

Benefits of the .NET Micro Framework

For embedded development, the advantages of the .NET Micro Framework can be summarized as follows:

- Lower development costs than other embedded platforms

- Faster time to market than other embedded platforms

- Lower hardware costs than other managed platforms

- Smaller hardware size than other managed platforms

- Lower power consumption than other managed platforms

- Not bound to a specific chipset or board vendor

- Important part of Microsoft's embedded strategy

The following features of the .NET Micro Framework allow you to reduce development costs and bring your products to market faster in comparison to other traditional embedded platforms:

- Managed code

- Modern language with Visual C#

- Rich base class library (a subset of common .NET and extensions for embedded development)

- Ability to touch the hardware with managed drivers

- Integration with Visual Studio, a first-class and widespread development tool

- Many .NET developers available

- Sharing code with existing solutions

- Rapid prototyping and debugging using the extensible emulator

- Live debugging on devices

The .NET Micro Framework and Windows SideShow

You often hear about Microsoft Windows SideShow together with the .NET Micro Framework. SideShow is an environment based on the .NET Micro Framework that runs on devices containing the framework; it can get content from a host computer and display that content on small devices (see Figure 1-7). SideShow-enabled devices can be permanently connected to a computer, or you can use them independently of the host computer that provides the content. For example, a SideShow-enabled auxiliary display on a notebook cover enables you to browse your appointments or read e-mail while your notebook is turned off (see Figure 1-5). The next time the notebook is turned on, the two devices synchronize.

Figure 1-7. *SideShow screen*

Devices enabled to use SideShow include the following:

- An auxiliary display for a PC or notebook (see Figure 1-5)

- A remote control with a display (see Figure 1-8)

- A designer bag with a built-in display (see Figure 1-9)

- A cordless phone

- A picture frame

- A portable media player

You can see more SideShow-enabled devices at www.SideShowDevices.com.

Figure 1-8. *A SideShow-capable remote control*

The content displayed by SideShow-enabled devices is described in the Simple Content Format (SCF), which is based on XML. You can create a custom gadget application for Side-Show in native or managed code that runs on your Windows host computer and provides SCF content to a connected SideShow-enabled device. The device's SideShow-enabled environment, which is written with the .NET Micro Framework, shows the SCF content as well as supporting interaction, like menu navigation and responding to other user input.

The SideShow-enabled environment on the devices could theoretically be ported to platforms other than the .NET Micro Framework. However, no other port is available now, and the .NET Micro Framework does the job well.

Microsoft provides a Windows SideShow Device SDK for the .NET Micro Framework that allows original equipment manufacturers (OEMs) to write built-in applications with the .NET Micro Framework and install them on their SideShow-enabled devices (see Figure 1-10).

Figure 1-9. *Designer bag with a built-in display using SideShow*

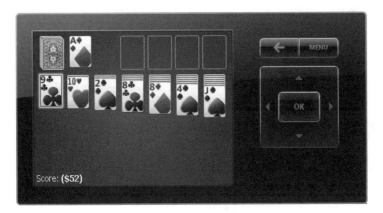

Figure 1-10. *A built-in application using SideShow written with the .NET Micro Framework*

Technical Overview

Now that you know why Microsoft developed the .NET Micro Framework, let's take a look at how it works.

Introducing the Bootable Runtime Environment

The .NET Micro Framework does not require an underlying operating system and can run directly on the hardware. It provides the following services that are usually provided by an operating system:

- Boot code
- Code execution

- Thread management

- Memory management

- Hardware I/O

However, the .NET Micro Framework is not a full-featured operating system; it's a bootable runtime environment tailored for embedded development. That's how the .NET Micro Framework can run directly on the hardware without an underlying operating system. However, the .NET Micro Framework can still use an underlying operating system and its services; the extensible emulator running on Windows is an example of that.

Architecture

As I said, the .NET Micro Framework is not a full-featured operating system but a bootable runtime environment tailored for embedded development; it consists of the four layers shown in Figure 1-11.

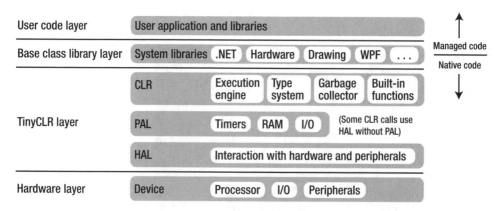

Figure 1-11. *Layered architecture of the .NET Micro Framework*

User Code Layer

The topmost layer is the user code layer. This layer consists of your managed application written in C#. Your application may use your reusable class libraries shared with other projects.

Base Class Library Layer

The next layer is the .NET Micro base class library layer, which provides a subset of the common .NET libraries and domain-specific extensions, such as libraries for touching the hardware, simple drawing, complex graphical user interfaces, and networking.

The .NET Micro Framework provides a subset of the full .NET Framework base class library (BCL). Microsoft tried to stay in line with the full .NET Framework class library wherever possible. If the functionality or interface of a class deviates from the full .NET Framework, that class or interface was moved to the new namespace `Microsoft.SPOT`.

The .NET Micro Framework base class libraries use a mix of managed and native code. The class libraries do not contain native code. The native methods are built into the runtime environment and are used to perform time-critical tasks or access hardware.

TinyCLR

The TinyCLR layer consists of the following three components:

- *Hardware abstraction layer (HAL)*: The HAL is tightly coupled to the hardware and provides functions to access the hardware and peripherals. When running on an operating system, the HAL provides functionality by using the services of the underlying OS.

- *Platform abstraction layer (PAL)*: The PAL provides additional abstractions of the HAL, such as timers and memory blocks.

- *.NET Micro Framework CLR*: The CLR consists of the execution engine that manages code at execution time. The managed type system ensures strict type safety. The CLR also contains the garbage collector, which is responsible for automatically freeing unused memory blocks, and the internal native methods called by the base class library. In addition, there is a boot loader that loads and starts the TinyCLR.

Hardware Layer

The hardware layer consists of the actual hardware platform. This is either the target device (microprocessor and peripheral) or the hardware emulator running on a windows PC.

Compiling for the .NET Micro Framework

In .NET, compilers, such as the C# compiler, transform the source code to assemblies—executables (.exe files) and libraries (.dll files)—containing the common intermediate language and metadata for a self-describing code. The CLR then executes the managed code.

The .NET Micro Framework uses a special intermediate language representation optimized for size. A global, shared string table for text and metadata such as type, method, and field names is used to reduce ROM and RAM usage on the devices.

Therefore, the .NET Micro Framework metadata processor tool generates the optimized pe-files to be deployed out of the managed .NET assemblies. Visual Studio and the .NET Micro Framework plug-in hide all these steps from you (see Figure 1-12). You will not see that the metadata processor is used, but you should know that Visual Studio actually deploys special optimized assemblies that the .NET Micro Framework CLR will interpret.

Currently, the .NET Micro Framework supports only Visual C#. Theoretically, every .NET language compiler could be supported, since the metadata processor parses common .NET assemblies that each .NET compiler should be able to generate. In practice, Visual Basic uses a special Visual Basic runtime library that has not yet been ported to the .NET Micro Framework.

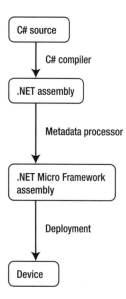

Figure 1-12. *Compiling for the .NET Micro Framework*

Target platforms

Currently, the .NET Micro Framework runs on ARM7 and ARM9 chipsets. Support has been announced for the Blackfin processor, from Analog Devices. The extensible emulator is another port of the CLR on X86 processors; it uses an underlying operating system, such as Windows XP or Vista.

Platform Porting

The .NET Micro Framework separates all code that interfaces with the hardware in the hardware and platform abstraction layers (HAL and PAL). Theoretically, porting to a new platform seems like it ought to be an easy task, but it is complex and requires a complete understanding of the hardware being used. In practice, a full porting effort will be done by hardware platform vendors rather than by individual embedded developers.

Microsoft provides a porting kit and porting workshops. The porting kit includes the source code for a reference HAL and PAL implementation. The porting kit requires a porting agreement along with payment of an associated fee.

The chipset itself is not so important when programming with the .NET Micro Framework, since the code is processor independent. There are several platforms available that provide all the peripheral hardware supported by the .NET Micro Framework. The devices just vary in display and networking support. This is an active area of development, and we will certainly see interesting new platforms in the future. The next chapter presents available modules and development boards supporting the .NET Micro Framework.

Links for Further Information

For further general information, visit the following web sites:

- *Official .NET Micro Framework site*: The official .NET Micro Framework site at the Microsoft Developer Network (MSDN) contains news such as porting announcements, the download link for the latest SDK, and a link to the .NET Micro Framework newsgroups at MSDN: `www.microsoft.com/netmf`.

- *.NET Micro Framework team blog*: The blog of the .NET Micro Framework team can be found here: `http://blogs.msdn.com/netmfteam`.

- Here are some .NET Micro Framework–related pages and blogs:

  - *Jan Kuera's web site*: `www.microframework.eu`

  - *Pavel Bánský's blog*: `http://bansky.net/blog`

  - *Sean Liming's web page*: `www.seanliming.com/NETMicroFramework.html`

  - *My blog*: `http://bloggingabout.net/blogs/jens`

- *Windows SideShow–related pages*: For more information on Widows SideShow, visit the following web pages:

  - *Windows SideShow team blog*: `http://blogs.msdn.com/sideshow`

  - *Windows SideShow development forum*: `http://forums.microsoft.com/MSDN/ShowForum.aspx?ForumID=1296&SiteID=1`

  - *Windows SideShow devices examples*: `www.SideShowDevices.com`

Summary

Now you know what the .NET Micro Framework is. This chapter discussed the history and background of the framework, including the motivation that led to its creation.

This chapter also illustrated how the .NET Micro Framework fits into the story of Microsoft's offerings for embedded development. We discussed the benefits of the .NET Micro Framework compared to other managed embedded options and to traditional embedded development. You learned about the benefits of managed code in general and the limitations of managed code on devices. This chapter also provided a technical overview of the .NET Micro Framework, as well as a description of its architecture.

Regardless of whether you are a .NET developer or a traditional embedded developer, after reading this chapter, you should understand the benefits that the .NET Micro Framework provides. Now that your interest in learning more about this different embedded development approach is piqued, let's continue the tour in the next chapter, which presents all the currently available .NET Micro Framework devices.

CHAPTER 2

■■■

Devices

This chapter presents you with some of the available .NET Micro Framework devices and development boards. It will give you a sense of the current possibilities before we dig into concrete programming in later chapters and will help you select the right device for your project.

The list of embedded development devices for the .NET Micro Framework is rapidly changing and growing. Therefore, the information provided in this chapter is naturally only a snapshot at the time of this writing. Please see the official .NET Micro Framework and manufacturer pages (provided later in this chapter) to get the latest information.

Freescale i.MXS Development Kit

The Freescale i.MXS Development Kit (see Figure 2-1) enables developers to quickly create applications for the .NET Micro Framework and Windows SideShow, for which it is the reference platform.

The major features of the i.MXS reference board follow:

- Freescale i.MXS 100-MHz (ARM920T) processor

- 32MB of SDRAM

- 8MB of flash memory

- 2.5-inch QVGA (320 × 240 × 16 bpp) TFT LCD panel

- Ten general purpose input/output (GPIO) ports

- One on-board RS232 Universal Asynchronous Receiver Transmitter (UART) serial port

- One UART serial port available with an extension card

- A serial peripheral interface (SPI) bus

- An inter-integrated circuit (I²C) bus

- One USB port for debugging and deploying applications

- 5V input power supply

- Can be powered by USB or power jack

Figure 2-1. *Freescale i.MXS Development Kit (Copyright of Freescale Semiconductor, Inc. 2008, Used by Permission)*

The development board includes an on-board LCD display and is available for approximately $500.

You can find further product information at `www.freescale.com/imx`. At this web site, you can also download the contents of the Development Kit for free. It includes an SDK with the emulator for the i.MXS board shown in Figure 2-2.

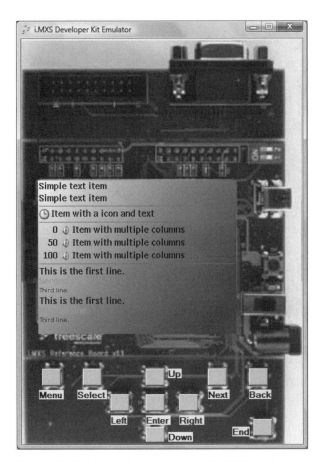

Figure 2-2. *Emulator for the Freescale i.MXS board*

Device Solutions Meridian and Tahoe

This section presents the Meridian CPU and the Tahoe development kit from Device Solutions (which acquired EmbeddedFusion). The Meridian CPU is designed for high production volume and is targeted at devices utilizing the graphics and user interface capabilities of the .NET Micro Framework. Although not supported with the .NET Micro Framework, you can use the built-in pulse width modulation (PWM) with the Meridian module and Tahoe board.

The development kit provides an SDK with lots of samples, extensions (e.g., PWM), and an emulator for the Tahoe development board. You can find further product information and separately download the latest SDK for free from the Device Solutions web site at `www.DeviceSolutions.net`. In addition, the guys from Device Solutions are frequently present in the .NET Micro Framework newsgroups.

Meridian CPU

The Meridian CPU integrates a Freescale i.MXS processor, RAM, flash memory, and a power supply into a 35-mm × 35-mm surface-mounted component (see Figure 2-3).

Figure 2-3. *Meridian CPU*

The major features of the Meridian CPU follow:

- Freescale i.MXS 100-MHz (ARM920T) processor

- 8MB of SDRAM

- 4MB of flash memory

- A connector for a 2.7-inch QVGA (320 × 240 × 16 bpp) TFT LCD panel

- 16 to 32 GPIO ports

- Two RS232 UART serial ports

- An SPI bus

- An I²C bus

- One PWM channel

- One USB port for debugging and deploying applications

- 5V input power supply

- Can be powered by USB

- 3.3-V output capacity for peripherals

In addition, the Meridian CPU enables you to use its on-board pulse width modulator with managed drivers, although PWM is currently not supported by the .NET Micro Framework.

Tahoe Development Kit

The Tahoe development kit includes a development board (see Figure 2-4) featuring a Meridian CPU and on-board LCD display. All available peripherals including SPI, I²C, and UART ports, are exposed. It is available for approximately $300.

Figure 2-4. *The Tahoe development board*

Digi International's Embedded Development Products

The following sections highlight the principal .NET Micro Framework–compatible devices from Digi International.

You can find the latest information about Digi Connect's .NET Micro Framework products at www.digi.com/dotnet.

Digi Connect ME

This section presents the Digi Connect ME module and development kit. Digi Connect ME devices are designed to utilize the network (Ethernet local area network [LAN] and wireless local area network [WLAN]) capabilities of the .NET Micro Framework.

The Digi Connect Module

The Digi Connect ME device was the first .NET Micro Framework device with an Ethernet network adapter and TCP/IP (Transmission Control Protocol/Internet Protocol) stack on board (see Figure 2-5).

The Digi Connect Wi-ME (see Figure 2-6) is the current wireless model supporting 802.11b WLAN. The next-generation product Digi Connect Wi-ME 9210 will support 802.11b/g, and support for .NET Micro Framework is expected in late 2008. The Digi Connect Wi-ME 9210 module is built on a 32-bit ARM9-based Digi NS9210 processor running at 75 MHz with integrated 10/100 Mb/s Ethernet interface, on-chip AES accelerator, Flexible Interface Modules (FIMs), and power management capabilities. The module will also support up to ten shared GPIOs, external interrupt requests (IRQs), SPI, and I²C.

The next-generation version of the Digi Connect ME, called Digi Connect ME 9210, is based on the same Digi NS9210 processor and will support the same peripheral interfaces as the Digi Connect Wi-ME 9210. Support for the .NET Micro Framework is expected in late 2008 as well.

All Digi Connect ME family modules are pin compatible and can be plugged onto a single development board and/or the customer's carrier board. In addition, there are several Digi Connect EM variants, but these are not shipped with the .NET Micro Framework on board.

Figure 2-5. *Digi Connect ME*

Figure 2-6. *Digi Connect Wi-ME*

The key features of the Digi Connect ME module follow:

- 55-MHz ARM7 (Digi NS7520) processor

- 8MB of SDRAM

- 2MB of flash memory

- Five GPIO ports

- One RS232 UART serial port

- An integrated 10/100 Mb/s Ethernet adapter

- 3.3V input power supply

Debugging and deploying a .NET Micro Framework application takes place over a network connection, which means a .NET Micro Framework application can use the serial port of a device.

The Digi Connect ME with Ethernet operates in a temperature range from –40 to 85°C. Figure 2-7 illustrates the dimensions of the Digi Connect ME module. Pricing starts at approximately $50.

Figure 2-7. *Dimensions of the Digi Connect ME*

Development Kit

The Digi JumpStart Kit for the Microsoft .NET Micro Framework provides a complete and easy-to-use solution for embedded development. The kit includes a Digi Connect ME embedded module, a development board (see Figure 2-8) with a power supply, sample code, and user documentation. The included Microsoft .NET Micro Framework SDK and the fully functional 90-day trial of Microsoft Visual Studio 2005 allow professional embedded C# development right out of the box. The kit is available for approximately $250.

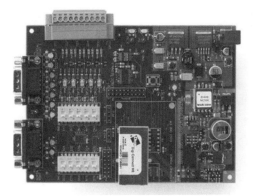

Figure 2-8. *Development board for the Digi Connect ME and Wi-ME*

Digi ConnectCore 9P 9215

The ConnectCore 9P 9215 module (see Figure 2-9) is another embedded device from Digi International, and it delivers a powerful network-enabled core processor solution with a rich set of peripherals and flexibility.

.NET Micro Framework support for the ConnectCore 9P 9215 with Ethernet should be available by June 2008, and support for the wireless variant ConnectCore Wi-9P 9215 is expected toward the end of 2008.

At the heart of the 5-cm × 5-cm ConnectCore 9P 9215 module is a 32-bit ARM-based Digi NS9215 processor running at 150 MHz. The Digi ARM processor on the 9P 9215 family of modules does not provide an on-chip LCD controller. However, as part of the .NET Micro Framework implementation for the ConnectCore 9P 9215 family, the module will fully support an external Epson LCD controller, and customers will be able to tie that controller to the module's memory bus. The advantage of that specific Epson controller is that a customer has two options for using it: with direct component integration on an existing carrier board (the lowest cost option) or by simply purchasing the pretty cost-effective and widely available off-the-shelf LCD modules for design integration.

Figure 2-9. *Digi ConnectCore 9P 9215 module*

The ConnectCore 9P 9215 hardware provides the following key features and benefits:

- Digi NS9215 150-MHz processor (with an ARM926EJ-S core)

- Up to 16MB of SDRAM (8MB by default)

- Up to 16MB of flash memory (4MB by default)

- An on-board 10/100 Mb/s Ethernet adapter (or 802.11b/g WLAN)

- Up to 64 shared GPIO ports

- Four serial ports (one RS232/422/485, one RS232, and two transistor-transistor level [TTL] ports)

- An I^{2}C bus

- An SPI bus

- Support for an external Epson LCD controller

- An on-board real-time clock with battery backup

- Five PWM channels

- Two DRPIC165x-based, on-chip FIMs

- An eight-channel 12-bit analog-to-digital converter

SJJ Embedded Micro Solutions Embedded Development Kit

SJJ's first .NET Micro Framework platform is the Embedded Development Kit (EDK) for the Microsoft .NET Micro Framework (see Figure 2-10). The EDK provides the core hardware and training materials necessary to get started using the .NET Micro Framework and is ideal for engineering students, hobbyists, and professional engineers who are learning to write code for embedded systems or looking to develop small-footprint devices.

Figure 2-10. *SJJ's Embedded Development Kit (EDK)*

The EDK features a special version of EMAC's iPac-9302 single-board computer (SBC) that supports the .NET Micro Framework.

The major features of the EDK platform follow:

- Cirrus Logic EP9302 ARM9 processor at 200 MHz

- 8MB of flash memory

- 8MB of SDRAM

- 16 GPIO ports

- An SPI bus

- One RS232 serial port for debugging and deploying applications

- Internal real-time clock (no battery backup)

- A 10/100 Mb/s Ethernet adapter on-board

- Two PWM channels

- A five-channel 12-bit analog-to-digital converter

- Two USB 2.0 host ports

- One SD/MMC hot swap card socket

- Dimensions of 96 × 90 mm (PC/104 size)

- 5V power supply

- A 9-pin ribbon cable and a null modem cable

There is an EDKplus available that has an additional serial port for use with your applications and a battery-backed real-time clock.

The EDK includes an iPac-9302, a CD with a step-by-step development guide, example applications, and utilities. It is available for less than $200.

You can find the web site for the Microsoft .NET Micro Framework EDK at www.sjjmicro.com. The first version of the *EDK Step-By-Step Guide* is available at no cost at www.sjjmicro.com/ Docs/EDK_Step_By_Step_Guide.pdf, and additional information and white papers can be found at www.seanliming.com/NETMicroFramework.html.

Crossbow Imote2.NET Edition

This section presents the Crossbow Technology Imote2.NET Edition products including the module, sensor board, and development kit. The Imote2 platform brings a new level of performance and capacity to the processor and radio platform for wireless sensor networks. The Imote2 platform achieves this level of performance by overcoming computational and memory limitations of current platforms to enable low-power operation for battery-powered, data-rich sensor network applications where there is a need for both high performance and high bandwidth.

You can find further information about Crossbow's wireless sensor network products at www.xbow.com.

Module

The Imote2.NET Edition is an advanced wireless sensor node platform (see Figure 2-11). It is built around the low-power PXA271 XScale processor and integrates an 802.15.4 radio with a built-in 2.4-GHz antenna. The Imote2.NET Edition is a modular stackable platform and can be expanded with extension boards to customize the system to a specific application. Through extension board connectors, sensor boards can provide specific analog or digital interfaces. System power can be provided by a connected battery board or from a USB port. The module is factory configured to run the .NET Micro Framework and sold as part of the Imote2.Builder kit.

Figure 2-11. *The Crossbow Imote2.NET module*

The main features and benefits of the Imote2.NET module follow:

- A Marvell PXA271 416-MHz XScale processor
- A Marvell Wireless MMX DSP coprocessor
- 256KB of SRAM
- 32MB of SDRAM
- 32MB of flash memory
- GPIO ports
- Three RS232 UART serial ports
- Two SPI busses
- An I²C bus
- An SDIO card interface
- An integrated 802.15.4 radio module (Wireless Personal Area Network)
- An integrated 2.4-GHz antenna (optional external connector)
- USB host and USB device capable
- Dimensions of 36 × 48 × 9 mm

Multisensor Board

The Crossbow multisensor board allows developers to start working with actual sensors right from the beginning of the development cycle. It contains digital, calibrated environmental sensors for light, humidity, and temperature. In addition, this board features a low-noise, digital three-axis accelerometer, which can be used for tilt angle and motion detection.

Furthermore, an external connector provides four external 0V to 3V analog channels with 12-bit resolution and an I^2C bus for adding digital sensors. This unique and versatile sensor board plugs into the extension board connectors on the Imote2 platform.

The multisensor board features include the following:

- Sensirion SHT15 dual temperature and humidity sensor

- Texas Instruments TMP175 digital temperature sensor

- TAOS TSL265 light sensor for visible and infrared light

- ST Micro LISL02DQ three-axis accelerometer

- Maxim MAX1363 analog-to-digital converter

- An I^2C bus interface to connect peripheral hardware

Development Kit

The Imote2.Builder development kit (see Figure 2-12) from Crossbow Technology simplifies and accelerates the design of wireless sensor applications. The development kit is priced at $990.

Figure 2-12. *Imote2.Builder*

Imote2.Builder includes the following features:

- Three Imote2 modules (IPR2410CA with the .NET Micro Framework on board)

- Two Imote2 battery boards (IBB2400)

- Two Imote2 sensor boards (ITS400CA)

- A CD containing both the .NET Micro Framework and Crossbow SDKs

- An evaluation copy of Microsoft Visual Studio 2005 on CD

The Crossbow SDK for the .NET Micro Framework offers the following software extensions:

- Drivers for operating all of the sensors and interfaces on the ITS400 multisensor board

- Wireless networking support for a star network topology to enable clusters of Imote2 modules to form an ad-hoc wireless network

- Support for the Imote2 module to serve as a USB-based gateway for pulling rich data from one Imote2 module or clusters of modules, via the 802.15.4 radio, into a PC

- Advanced power-management software embedded on the Imote2 to increase battery life

Adeneo Ports

Adeneo is a leading designer of complete hardware and custom software. Adeneo offers a complete turnkey solution for embedded markets including the medical, avionic, transportation, retail, and industrial control markets. With nine years' experience in Windows Embedded CE, and thanks to its partnerships with both hardware vendors and Microsoft, Adeneo is the key partner for complete hardware and software designs targeting rich-featured high-end products.

Adeneo is the Microsoft porting partner that ported the .NET Micro Framework to support NXP Semiconductors's popular ARM9-based NXP LPC3180 microcontroller and to the Atmel AT91SAM9261 ARM-9-based processor.

For more information on Adeneo, please visit www.adeneo-embedded.com. From their FTP server, you can download a custom emulator with a sample application for each development board.

PHYTEC phyCORE-LPC3180

Adeneo has ported the .NET Micro Framework to the phyCORE-LPC3180 hardware that belongs to PHYTEC's phyCORE single-board computer module family, which integrates all core elements of a microcontroller system on a subminiature board and is designed to ensure easy expansion and embedding in peripheral hardware. The phyCORE-LPC3180 insert-ready single-board computer is populated with the NXP Semiconductors (founded by Philips) LPC3180 microcontroller.

The phyCORE-LPC3180 hardware offers the following key features:

- NXP Semiconductors LPC3180 208-MHz ARM9 microcontroller

- Up to 128MB of flash memory (32MB by default)

- Up to 128MB of SDRAM

- Subminiature (60 × 53 mm) single-board computer

- Improved interference safety, achieved through multilayer printed circuit board (PCB) technology and dedicated ground pins

- GPIO ports

- Seven UART serial ports (three RS232-level and four TTL ports)

- A battery buffered real-time clock

- Two SPI busses

- Two I²C busses

- One 32-KB I²C EEPROM

- Two PWM channels

- Keyboard support for up to 64 keys in an 8 × 8 matrix

- An SD/MMC card interface

- A USB on-the-go (OTG) interface

- One high-speed capture port

PHYTEC offers the development board for the PHYTEC phyCORE-LPC3180 shown in Figure 2-13.

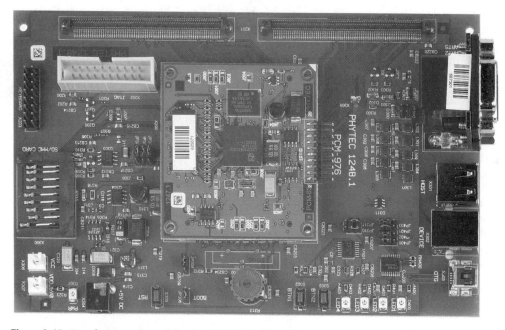

Figure 2-13. *Development board for the PHYTEC phyCORE-LPC3180*

You can find more product information about the PHYTEC phyCORE-LPC3180 at www.phytec.com.

Atmel AT91SAM9261

The AT91SAM9261, another hardware component to which Adeneo has ported the .NET Micro Framework, is a complete system-on-chip built around the ARM926EJ-S ARM Thumb Processor. The AT91SAM9261 is an optimized ARM9-based host processor for applications with an LCD display.

The AT91SAM9261 hardware's key features include the following:

- 200-MHz ARM9-based ARM926EJ processor

- LCD controller for a QVGA (320 × 240 × 16 bpp) LCD panel

- GPIO ports

- Three RS232 USART serial ports

- Two SPI busses

- 10/100 Mb/s Ethernet capabilities

- One USB port for debugging and deploying applications

- A USB device port

- One PWM channel

- An SD/MMC card interface

Figure 2-14 shows the Atmel development board for the AT91SAM9261 module with the LCD display on board.

Figure 2-14. *Development board for the AT91SAM9261 module*

You can find more information about the AT91SAM9261 module at `www.atmel.com/products/at91` under the AT91SAM9 series; this page describes only the general hardware. For .NET Micro Framework–related information, please visit Adeneo's (the porting partner's) page at `www.adeneo-embedded.com`.

GHI Electronics Embedded Master

This section presents the Embedded Master Module and development kit from GHI Electronics. Embedded Master is the first and only device that combines the benefits of the .NET Micro Framework with FAT file system and USB hosting capabilities, as well as providing support for PWM and the controller area network (CAN), which are not supported directly by the .NET Micro Framework.

You can find the latest information about Embedded Master products at `www.ghielectronics.com` and `www.EmbeddedMaster.com`, where you can also find the latest firmware with native drivers and the Embedded Master library with the managed wrappers.

The Embedded Master Module

GHI Electronics Embedded Master implements Microsoft's .NET Micro Framework on a very small (1.55-inch × 1.55-inch) OEM module (see Figure 2-15). On top of the many benefits that the .NET Micro Framework has, Embedded Master adds many other software and hardware features.

Embedded Master is the first and only .NET Micro Framework OEM device to add FAT file system support (through a subset of System.IO classes) and USB hosting capabilities to allow managed-code access files on SD/MMC cards and on USB memory devices, such as thumb drives and hard drives. Also, with the embedded USB host/device stacks, you can use other USB devices like mice, keyboards, joysticks, printers, and Bluetooth dongles.

Also added natively are other peripherals' libraries, such as those for analog inputs (analog-to-digital converters), analog outputs (digital-to-analog converters), PWM, CAN bus, and more. All libraries are written below the CLR, in the HAL layer, and none are managed libraries, which lets them run much faster. Above the CLR, managed wrappers allow users to access the unmanaged libraries.

The Embedded Master hardware offers the following key features:

- LPC2468 72-MHz ARM7 processor

- Up to 64MB of SDRAM (8MB by default)

- 4.5MB of flash memory

- One dedicated SPI port for the graphical LCD

- 45 GPIO ports (30 can be used as interrupt ports)

- An SPI bus

- An I²C bus

- 4 UART TTL serial ports

- 10/100 Mb/s Ethernet capabilities

- An on-board real-time clock with battery backup

- A hardware-based monotone generator (Piezo)

- USB host and USB device capable

- Two CAN channels

- A four-channel 10-bit analog-to-digital converter

- A 10-bit digital-to-analog converter

- One SD/MMC card interface

- Three PWM channels

- A –40° to 85° industrial temperature grade

Figure 2-15. *The Embedded Master Module*

Development Kit

The development system combines an Embedded Master Module with a full-featured mother board (see Figure 2-16). All available peripherals, including SPI, I²C, and UART ports, are exposed.

The key features of the Embedded Master development kit include the following:

- Embedded Master Module on board

- On-board 128 × 64 pixel display (displays 16 shades of yellow)

- A connector for a 128 × 128 pixel color display

- An on-board 10/100 Mb/s Ethernet adapter

- A USB host port

- Two USB device ports (one is used for application debugging and deploying and the other can be accessed as virtual COM1 from the embedded application)

- An RS232 serial port with RTC and CTS

- A CAN connector

- An SD/MMC card connector

- A Piezo speaker

- Seven user buttons and a reset button

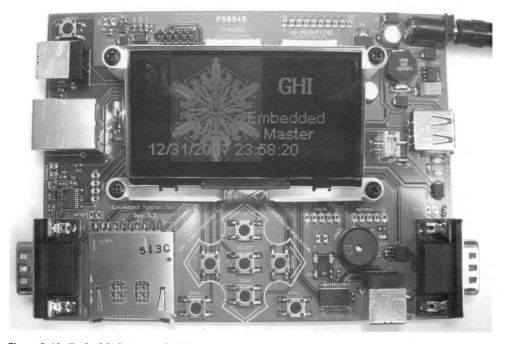

Figure 2-16. *Embedded Master development kit*

emtrion HiCO.ARM9

This section presents the ARM9-based HiCO.ARM9-Core module and HiCO.ARM9-SBC development kit from emtrion. For more information, visit `www.emtrion.com/hicoarm9_core_en.php`.

The HiCO.ARM9-Core Module

emtrion's HiCO.ARM9-Core module (see Figure 2-17) provides the following major hardware features:

- 180-MHz ATMEL AT91RM9200 ARM9 processor
- Up to 64MB of SDRAM
- Up to 32MB of flash memory
- A QVGA (320 × 240 × 16 bpp) TFT LCD panel with touch support
- Four UART serial ports (one RS232 and three TTL ports)
- GPIO ports
- An SPI bus
- An I²C bus
- A 10/100 Mb/s Ethernet adapter on-board
- A battery-buffered real-time clock
- Application debugging and deploying using a serial port
- USB host and USB device capable
- An SD/MMC card interface
- 5V input power supply

Figure 2-17. *HiCO.ARM9-Core module*

Development Kit

The development board HiCO.ARM9-SBC (Figure 2-18) is a single board computer with a HiCO.ARM9-Core module and connector on board.

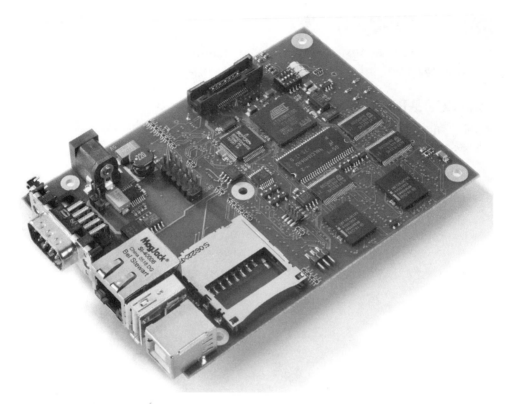

Figure 2-18. *HiCO.ARM9-SBC*

Summary

Now, you have an idea of the devices that can be used for programming with the .NET Micro Framework and their capabilities. Though you might already have selected (or even ordered) a development board for your application, you can use the .NET Micro Framework without real hardware at all, using the extensible hardware emulator. In any case, knowing the features and capabilities of available devices is a great benefit.

It is time now to write our first .NET Micro Framework application. In the next chapter, which tours the .NET Micro Framework SDK, tools, and development environment, you will learn how to write, compile, deploy, execute, and debug your first .NET Micro Framework application.

CHAPTER 3

■■■

Getting Started

In this chapter, you'll get started using the .NET Micro Framework and create your first application with it. This chapter covers the system requirements for developing with the .NET Micro Framework and introduces Visual Studio, explaining how the .NET Micro Framework extensions are integrated and can be used with it. This chapter also gives you an overview of the files and tools in the .NET Micro Framework SDK.

Getting Your System Ready

Follow the steps in this section to get your system set up to create your .NET Micro Framework applications.

System Requirements

Developing for the .NET Micro Framework requires the following:

- Microsoft Windows XP or Vista

- Microsoft Visual Studio 2005 Standard Edition or better, with Service Pack 1

- .NET Micro Framework SDK version 2 with Service Pack 1 or version 2.5

The free Express editions of Visual Studio cannot be used with the .NET Micro Framework, because they do not allow installing extensions at all. Do not forget to install Visual Studio 2005 Service Pack 1.

■**Note** Although the .NET Micro Framework 2.5 SDK was released months after Visual Studio 2008, the SDK targets only Visual Studio 2005. That is because the integration mechanism has significantly changed in Visual Studio 2008. Microsoft decided to give the Visual Studio 2008 support a lower priority than other features, since Visual Studio 2005 and 2008 can be installed side by side on the same machine.

Installing the .NET Micro Framework SDK

After you have set up your development PC and installed Visual Studio, you're ready to install the .NET Micro Framework SDK. You can find a link to the latest SDK on the official MSDN .NET Micro Framework page at www.microsoft.com/netmf.

Using Visual Studio and the .NET Micro Framework

In this section, you learn to work with Visual Studio in order to build, deploy, execute, and debug your first .NET Micro Framework application.

Creating a New Project

After installing Visual Studio and the .NET Micro Framework SDK, you can start Visual Studio and create a new .NET Micro Framework project. Selecting File ➤ New ➤ Project will open a dialog box in which you can enter project details (see Figure 3-1). This dialog box allows you to enter the project type, name, and location.

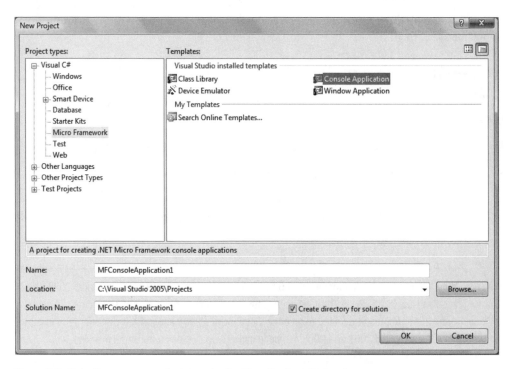

Figure 3-1. *Selecting a new project type in the New Project dialog box*

The .NET Micro Framework SDK integrates the Micro Framework project type under Visual C#. You can choose among four .NET Micro Framework–related project templates:

- *Class Library*: For grouping and sharing code

- *Console Application*: An application with core libraries

- *Window Application*: An application with a graphical user interface using a special version of Windows Presentation Foundation (WPF)

- *Device Emulator*: A custom device emulator

Your First .NET Micro Framework Application

Now, it is time to create your first .NET Micro Framework application; we will create a .NET Micro Framework console application, as described in the previous section.

A new console application created with the wizard contains a C# source file (see Listing 3-1) that contains the application's main entry point. The code in the Program.cs file just prints the text "Hello World!" to the Visual Studio Output window.

Listing 3-1. *Default C# Code for a New Console Application*

```
using System;
using Microsoft.SPOT;

namespace MFConsoleApplication1
{
    public class Program
    {
        public static void Main()
        {
            Debug.Print(
                Resources.GetString(Resources.StringResources.String1));
        }

    }
}
```

A fresh console application contains references to the core mscorlib.dll and Microsoft.SPOT.dll libraries. You can reference further class libraries with Project ➤ Add Reference.

The Print method of the Debug class accepts text to print to the Output window. You will learn more about this class in the next chapter.

The Resources.GetString method call takes the string to print from the embedded resources of the application. You will learn more about resources in Chapter 8. The template default C# code does the same as Debug.Print("Hello World!");.

The Visual Studio Workspace

The Visual Studio workspace (see Figure 3-2) contains several child windows, including the following:

- The source code editor window
- The Solution Explorer window
- The Error List window
- The Output window

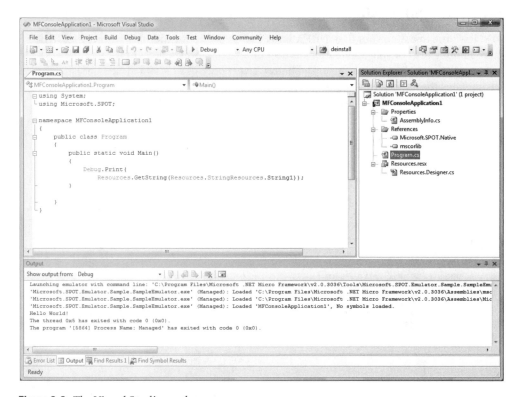

Figure 3-2. *The Visual Studio workspace*

Figure 3-2 shows our first .NET Micro Framework project in the Visual Studio Integrated Development Environment (IDE). The Solution Explorer provides a hierarchical view of the files of a project. The References subitem shows all referenced class library assemblies. Right-clicking the References subitem will open the dialog box to add further references (see Figure 3-3).

In the Output window, you can see the text "Hello World!" printed when you execute your first application using Debug mode (by pressing F5).

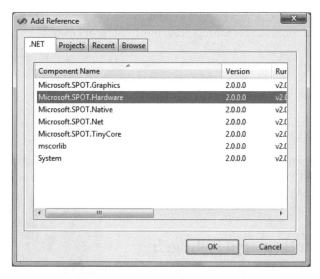

Figure 3-3. *Adding class library references*

Setting Project Properties

The .NET Micro Framework SDK installs a new page called Micro Framework within the project settings (see Figure 3-4) that allows you to configure .NET Micro Framework–specific settings such as the deployment. In the Solution Explorer, right-click your project item, and select Properties to show the configuration details.

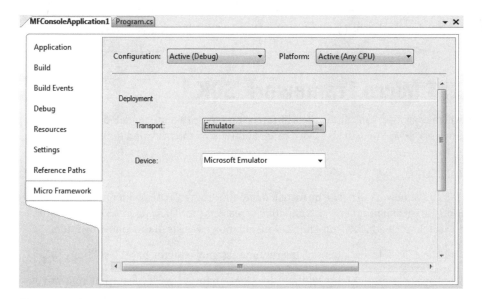

Figure 3-4. *The .NET Micro Framework project settings*

The page in Figure 3-4 allows you to select a target device or emulator to deploy your application. The Transport drop-down list is comprised of the following transport mechanisms:

- Emulator

- USB

- Serial

- TCP/IP

Depending on your Transport selection, you can select a device, emulator, or COM-Port from the Device drop-down list. The .NET Micro Framework provides a default emulator called Microsoft Emulator. For our first sample, make sure Transport is set to Emulator, and Microsoft Emulator is selected for Device.

Building, Deploying, Executing, and Debugging

Now that we have explored the development environment and created our first .NET Micro Framework application, it is time to run it. Press F5 or select Debug ➤ Start Debugging to run and debug your application. Actually, this command will build, deploy, execute, and debug your application on an emulator or device.

To set a breakpoint, go to the desired source code line, and press F9 or select Debug ➤ Toggle Breakpoint. After execution stops at a breakpoint, you can use the mouse to hover over a variable or other identifier to get the value or other information. To continue execution, press F5 again. To step to the next statement, press F10 or select Debug ➤ Step Over.

■**Note** Breakpoints will not work if you have selected to build the Release version.

The .NET Micro Framework SDK

Now, we will take a closer look at the files, libraries, and tools that are installed with the .NET Micro Framework SDK. You will also learn more about using the provided tools.

File Structure

The .NET Micro Framework SDK will be installed into the Program Files folder in a subdirectory depending on the version number. For compatibility reasons the SDK version 2.5 uses the same subfolder as version 2.0 (v2.0.3036). The SDK installation consists of the following folders:

- Assemblies: This folder contains all the runtime assemblies of the base class library (BCL).

- Fonts: The Fonts subdirectory contains two fonts in the .tinyfnt file format, ready to use with the .NET Micro Framework.

- `Tools`: This folder contains the default emulator, shared emulator libraries, and the MFDeploy and TFConvert tools. The `Tools` folder also contains a `Fonts` subfolder with several TrueType sample fonts to convert with TFConvert.

- `Documentation`: The .NET Micro Framework help files, which are integrated into and available via the common Visual Studio documentation, are stored in this folder.

The .NET Micro Framework SDK installation also provides some sample projects in the `Documents` folder in the `Micro Framework` subfolder.

The Base Class Library Runtime Assemblies

The runtime libraries that you can find in the `Assemblies` subdirectory of your .NET Micro Framework installation include the following:

- `Mscorlib.dll`: A subset of the core .NET classes.

- `System.dll`: Only the `System.Net` namespace.

- `System.Xml.dll`: A subset of the core .NET XML classes necessary to read XML files.

- `Microsoft.SPOT.Native.dll`: Core .NET Micro Framework classes.

- `Microsoft.SPOT.Hardware.dll`: Managed hardware drivers.

- `Microsoft.SPOT.Graphics.dll`: Low-level graphics classes.

- `Microsoft.SPOT.TinyCore.dll`: User interface elements for complex WPF GUIs.

- `Microsoft.SPOT.Net.dll`: Internal socket drivers. When using network sockets, you need to include `System.dll` and `Microsoft.SPOT.Net.dll`.

Further assemblies for the Device Profile for Web Services (DPWS) stack are also included. Although provided with the .NET Micro Framework 2.5 SDK release, the implementation of the DPWS stack is still in beta, and therefore, the DPWS libraries are not installed by default with the .NET Micro Framework SDK. When installing the SDK you need to choose either the Install All option or the Custom Installation option with DPWS selected.

The MFDeploy Tool

The .NET Micro Framework provides the .NET Micro Framework Deployment Tool (MFDeploy), which you can find in the `Tools` subfolder of the SDK. The primary purpose of MFDeploy is to copy your application to devices. MFDeploy provides a GUI (see Figure 3-5), can be invoked from the command line, and provides a .NET API, and thus allows you to use MFDeploy in your production environment to replicate a standard deployment on your devices without Visual Studio.

The features of MFDeploy include the following:

- Discovering and pinging devices to test if they are responsive

- Creating a standard deployment from a master device

- Copying your application to the device

- Upgrading firmware

- Creating and updating device keys

- Signing code

- Setting network parameters and USB names

- Use via a UI or automatically via the command line or programmatically

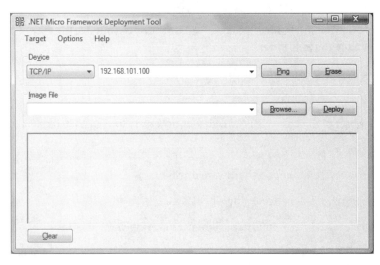

Figure 3-5. *The MFDeploy tool*

A more detailed description of this tool can be found in the MFDeploy help file.

Deploying with MFDeploy

When you use MFDeploy to copy your application to a device, the managed assemblies and .pe files are not copied directly to the device. Instead, you need to deploy your application to a master device with Visual Studio first. After that, you can create an application deployment image file from that master device with the MFDeploy tool (using the Target ➤ Application Deployment ➤ Create Application Deployment menu command). Once you have this standard application deployment, in the form of an image file on your hard disk, you can replicate it on multiple devices (by entering the file path into the Image File field and clicking the Deploy button).

To upgrade the .NET Micro Framework firmware, you need to obtain the image files from Microsoft or your hardware platform vendor.

Image files need to be in the Motorola S-record (SREC) format, which are in .hex format, and can contain your application and libraries or the .NET Micro Framework firmware. When installing an image file, MFDeploy will directly update the deployment sectors in the device's flash memory according to the image file.

You can install multiple image files to a device. All image files that contain an application have an entry point that describes where to start executing your application code.

Signing Code

Manufacturers might want to prevent others from installing unauthorized code on their devices after they are available on the market, so MFDeploy provides a means to sign code to verify its creator.

You can store up to two public keys on a device: one for the firmware and one for your application. Once the keys are assigned, you can update the firmware or application image only on a device that was digitally signed with the right private key. If there is no firmware key on the device, you can install any firmware. If there is no application key, you can install any application.

You can create a key pair with Target ➤ Manage Device Keys ➤ Create Key Pair and sign an image file with Target ➤ Application Deployment ➤ Sign Deployment File.

You can also update or remove your device keys with Target ➤ Manage Device Keys ➤ Update Device Keys. Doing so requires you to have the private key, as you must with signing.

■**Note** Once you have stored an application key on your device, you cannot deploy with Visual Studio anymore. Visual Studio does not provide a way to specify a key with the project settings, so you cannot use Visual Studio for devices containing a locked application. To continue deploying and debugging with Visual Studio, you need to remove the key first.

Automating MFDeploy

The MFDeploy tool can be automated programmatically, which allows you greater flexibility in your production environment than even the command-line interface does.

In order to automate MFDeploy, you need to create a Windows console or Windows GUI application project. You need to add a reference to the `MFDeployEngine.dll` assembly to your project; you can find this assembly in the `Tools` subdirectory of your .NET Micro Framework installation.

The following code line allows you to obtain all .NET Micro Framework devices connected to your PC via USB ports:

```
IList<MFPortDefinition> portDefs = deploy.EnumPorts(TransportType.USB);
```

In addition to `USB`, there are the `Serial` and `TCPIP` transport types.

Once you have discovered a device, you can connect to it. The following code will connect to the first device that was found:

```
MFDevice device = deploy.Connect(portDefs[0]);
```

The `Deploy` method will deploy an image file to a connected device. The method accepts a deployment image file path. You can create an image file using the MFDeploy GUI, as described earlier in this chapter. You have the option to specify a path to a signature file if you have signed the image file, and you can create a signature file by signing an image using the MFDeploy GUI, also described earlier in this chapter.

```
if (device.Deploy("c:\\myapp.hex", // deployment image
                  "c:\\myapp.sig", // signature file (optional)
                  ref entryPoint // return the app's entry point
                  ))
```

The Deploy method returns the entry point of the deployment image file. This entry point can be used to execute the deployed application:

```
device.Execute(entryPoint);
```

The code in Listing 3-2 will obtain and list all devices connected to a USB port. If at least one device is found, the application deploys a signed deployment image to the first available device and executes the deployed code on the device.

Listing 3-2. *Automating the .NET Micro Framework Deployment Tool*

```
using System;
using Microsoft.NetMicroFramework.Tools.MFDeployTool.Engine;
using System.Collections.Generic;

namespace MFDeployAutomation
{
    class Program
    {
        static void Main(string[] args)
        {
            using (MFDeploy deploy = new MFDeploy())
            {
                // Obtain devices connected to USB port
                IList<MFPortDefinition> portDefs =
                                        deploy.EnumPorts(TransportType.USB);

                // List devices
                Console.WriteLine("USB Devices:");
                foreach (MFPortDefinition portDef in portDefs)
                {
                    Console.WriteLine(portDef.Name);
                }

                // Return if no device was found
                if (portDefs.Count == 0)
                {
                    Console.WriteLine("No device.");
                    return;
                }
```

```
// Connect to first device that was found
using (MFDevice device = deploy.Connect(portDefs[0]))
{
    uint entryPoint = 0;
    if (device.Deploy(
                    "c:\\myapp.hex", // deployment image
                    "c:\\myapp.sig", // signature file (optional)
                     ref entryPoint // return app's entry point
                       ))
    {
        Console.WriteLine("Deploying succeded.");

        if (entryPoint != 0) // check if image has an entry point
        {
            Console.WriteLine("Executing application.");
            device.Execute(entryPoint);
        }
    }
    else
        Console.WriteLine("Deploying failed.");
}
```

The TFConvert Tool

The .NET Micro Framework uses the `.tinyfnt` file format to work with fonts. This special format uses fixed size bitmaps for a simpler way to render fonts. Two sample `.tinyfnt` fonts are included in the `Fonts` subdirectory of your .NET Micro Framework installation. To create other fonts in the size, style, and language tailored to your application, you can use the TFConvert tool to create a `.tinyfnt` font from TrueType or OpenType font files. That enables you to select character sets and even create fonts for displaying Cyrillic and Chinese characters.

In the `Tools\Fonts` subdirectory, you can find some sample TrueType fonts from Ascender Corporation, which you can convert to meet your needs. These free sample fonts provide a reduced character set; the full versions can be purchased from the company.

The TFConvert command line tool is located in the `Tools` subdirectory of your .NET Micro Framework installation. TFConvert accepts a path to a font definition file that describes the font's size, style, and characters to convert.

The system tool character map (`charmap.exe`) provided with your Windows installation can help you determine which characters or character ranges to convert.

To get more information about creating `.tinyfnt` fonts with the TFConvert tool, please see the .NET Micro Framework SDK documentation, where this is described in detail.

In addition, on the SJJ Embedded Micro Solutions web site, you can find a great article that describes how to convert fonts with TFConvert (`www.sjjmicro.com/SJJ_Articles.html`).

On the web site of a Czech .NET Micro Framework enthusiast, Jan Kucera, at `www.microframework.eu`, you can find the Tiny Font Tool GUI. This tool provides a graphical user interface that assists you in creating the font definition files.

Summary

This chapter provided you an overview of .NET Micro Framework SDK installation, runtime assemblies, and Visual Studio integration. You wrote, deployed, and executed your first .NET Micro Framework application. You learned how to select an emulator or target device to run your application, and how to use the MFDeploy and TFConvert tools.

You are now prepared to go on to the next chapter, where we start to explore the .NET Micro Framework BCL.

■ ■ ■

Introducing the .NET Micro Framework Base Class Library

This chapter gives you an overview of the basic features and classes of the .NET Micro Framework. The .NET Micro Framework is a subset of the full .NET Framework, but it also provides new namespaces and classes. This chapter considers the differences between the full .NET and .NET Micro Framework, so you will see what is possible and what features are not supported with the .NET Micro Framework. We will examine how you can output text for diagnostics, pause the program execution, and use timers. Further, you will learn how to effectively use strings, numbers, arrays, and lists. Finally, this chapter shows you how to handle exceptions.

Text Output for Diagnostics

Since the .NET Micro Framework will run on many devices with no display, having the option to output text for debugging and tracing is enormously important. Probably the most frequently used method is to output text via the `Print` method of the `Debug` class from the `Microsoft.SPOT` namespace.

■Tip If you have no experience with .NET, you can write either `Microsoft.SPOT.Debug.Print("Hello world")`—where `Microsoft.SPOT` is the namespace, `Debug` the class name, and `Print` the method—or just `Print("Hello world")`. The namespace does not have to be placed at the beginning of the command if the namespace is given to the compiler with the line `using Microsoft.SPOT;` at the beginning of a file. The `Print` method of the `Debug` class is declared as static; that's why a method call without previous creation of an instance of the `Debug` class is possible.

With Visual Studio, it is possible to compile a project once as a debug version and again as a release version. The debug version is not optimized by the compiler. For example, no unnecessary assignments on local variables are removed; otherwise, their values would not be visible in the debugger.

With the full .NET Framework and .NET Compact Framework conditional compilation will include all debug code to the debug versions since the `DEBUG` compiler constant is defined.

The `System.Diagnostics.Debug.WriteLine` method that's used to output debug messages with the full .NET and .NET Compact Frameworks isn't available in the .NET Micro Framework. Here, we output debug messages in both the debug and release version of an application, which is also a reason why the `Debug` class is placed in a different namespace in the .NET Micro Framework.

The `Microsoft.SPOT.Trace.Print` method offers a similar text-output functionality for diagnostic purposes in Visual Studio. The method is deactivated by default and will only be compiled into the program if the compiler constant `TINYCLR_TRACE` is defined. The constant is not set automatically in either the debug or release version and, therefore, must be declared manually in the project properties on the `Build` page (see Figure 4-1). The `Trace` class has no other properties and only one other method in the .NET Micro Framework—the `Print` method (see Listing 4-1).

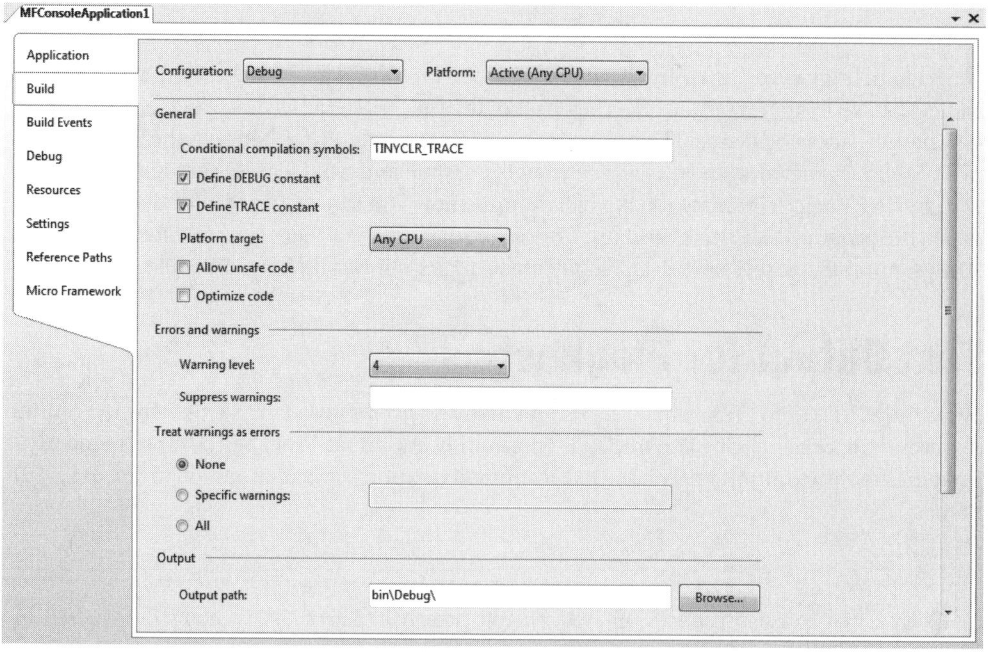

Figure 4-1. *Enabling trace output via the compiler constant in the project's properties*

Listing 4-1. *The Microsoft.SPOT.Trace Class*

```
public static class Trace
{
    [Conditional("TINYCLR_TRACE")]
    public static void Print(string text);
}
```

The `Debug` class, provided in Listing 4-2, offers some additional methods.

Listing 4-2. *The Microsoft.SPOT.Debug Class*

```
public static class Debug
{
    [Conditional("DEBUG")]
    public static void Assert(bool condition);
    [Conditional("DEBUG")]
    public static void Assert(bool condition, string message);
    [Conditional("DEBUG")]
    public static void Assert(bool condition, string message,
                             string detailedMessage);
    public static extern uint GC(bool force);
    public static extern void Print(string text);
    public static extern void DumpBuffer(byte[] buf, bool fCRC, bool fOffset);
    public static extern void DumpHeap();
    public static extern void DumpPerfCounters();
    public static extern void DumpStack();
}
```

There are three overloaded Assert methods to guarantee certain assertions. For example, the instruction Debug.Assert(myVar != null); verifies that the myVar variable is not null. If this is not the case, the debugger will stop there. Assert methods are compiled only into the debug version.

The DumpXXX methods are for Microsoft's for internal use. They show information about the managed heap and stack. They are available only in special debug versions of the .NET Micro Framework runtime environment for devices and the emulator. In the official release versions of the runtime environment, you can call the methods, but nothing will be output.

■**Note** The two classes Microsoft.SPOT.Debug and Microsoft.SPOT.Trace are in the assembly Microsoft.SPOT.Native.dll. If you create a new .NET Micro Framework project, a reference to this assembly is added automatically to the project.

Pausing Program Execution

Even if programs are executed relatively slowly on microprocessors, in comparison to those run on a PC, you may have the need to let the program execution pause for a certain amount of time nevertheless. You can do this by calling the static method Sleep of the Thread class from the System.Threading namespace (see Listing 4-3). The method expects the number of milliseconds to pause as parameter.

Listing 4-3. *Pausing Program Execution One Second*

```
using System;
using System.Threading;
using Microsoft.SPOT;
```

```
namespace SleepSample
{
    public class Program
    {
        public static void Main()
        {
            while (true)
            {
                Debug.Print("Hello World!");
                Thread.Sleep(1000); //1000  milliseconds = wait 1 second
            }
        }
    }
}
```

To pause a program an infinite amount of time, in this case until the battery is dead, you can call the method Sleep by passing the constant System.Threading.Timeout.Infinite, which represents the value –1.

This program would require some minor changes to the text output methods to work as a console application with the full .NET Framework on a PC and with the .NET Compact Framework on a Pocket PC or smartphone.

Note The classes Thread and Timeout are in the mscorlib.dll assembly, just like in the larger frameworks. A reference to that assembly is also added automatically to a new .NET Micro Framework project, like the Microsoft.SPOT.Native.dll assembly.

Setting and Getting the System Time and Time Zone

You can query for the local system time and time zone information in the .NET Micro Framework similar to the way you can in the full .NET Framework. Additionally, you are able to set the local system time and time zone with the .NET Micro Framework. With the full .NET Framework running on Windows, on the other hand, you cannot set them, because the time is changed under the Windows shell.

You can change the local system time in a .NET Micro Framework application with the SetLocalTime method of the Utility class from the Microsoft.SPOT.Hardware namespace and set the time zone with the ExtendedTimeZone class from the Microsoft.SPOT namespace. The class Microsoft.SPOT.ExtendedTimeZone inherits from the class System.TimeZone.

To change the time zone, the new time zone is specified by the Microsoft.SPOT.TimeZoneId enumeration.

All these classes—Microsoft.SPOT.Hardware.Utility, Microsoft.SPOT.ExtendedTimeZone, and Microsoft.SPOT.TimeZoneId—are located in the Microsoft.SPOT.Native.dll assembly.

The .NET Micro Framework application in Listing 4-4 demonstrates the possibilities.

Listing 4-4. *Working with System Time and Time Zones*

```
using System;
using Microsoft.SPOT;
using Microsoft.SPOT.Hardware;

namespace LocalTimeSample
{
    public class Program
    {
        public static void Main()
        {
            Debug.Print("Local Time: " + DateTime.Now.ToString());
            DateTime newLocalTime = new DateTime(2007, 1, 2, 3, 4, 5);
            Utility.SetLocalTime(newLocalTime);
            Debug.Print("New Local Time: " + DateTime.Now.ToString());
            Debug.Print("Time Zone: " + TimeZone.CurrentTimeZone.StandardName);
            Debug.Print("Local Time: " + DateTime.Now.ToString());
            ExtendedTimeZone.SetTimeZone(TimeZoneId.Berlin);
            Debug.Print("New Time Zone: " + TimeZone.CurrentTimeZone.StandardName);
            Debug.Print("Local Time: " + DateTime.Now.ToString());
        }
    }
}
```

The following output in the debug window of Visual Studio 2005 is produced by the application in Listing 4-4:

```
Local Time: 01/07/2007 20:20:34
New Local Time: 01/02/2007 03:04:05
Time Zone: Pacific-US
Local Time: 01/02/2007 03:04:05
New Time Zone: Berlin,Rome
Local Time: 01/02/2007 12:04:05
```

■**Note** So that the changes on the system time remain after power cycling a .NET Micro Framework device, the device must naturally have a built-in back-up battery clock.

Using Timers

With timers, you have the possibility of executing methods in certain time intervals. In the .NET Micro Framework, two timer classes are available: System.Threading.Timer, which is also available in the full .NET Framework, and Microsoft.SPOT.ExtendedTimer, which is unique to the .NET Micro Framework. You can see the members of the Timer class in Listing 4-5.

Listing 4-5. *The System.Threading.Timer Class*

```
namespace System.Threading
{
    public sealed class Timer : MarshalByRefObject, IDisposable
    {
        public Timer(TimerCallback callback, object state, int dueTime, int period);
        public Timer(TimerCallback callback, object state, TimeSpan dueTime,
                    TimeSpan period);

        public bool Change(int dueTime, int period);
        public bool Change(TimeSpan dueTime, TimeSpan period);
        public void Dispose();
    }
}
```

When creating a timer, the timer callback method is passed via the callback parameter. Using the state parameter, you can pass any object that holds additional information or data. The object is handed over to the callback method when it is called. If you do not need this functionality, simply specify null.

The class has two constructors, which differ in the way the time span is specified. The first possibility is to pass the time interval directly as number of milliseconds. Alternatively, you can pass the time interval as an instance of the System.TimeSpan class, which describes an interval also.

The parameter dueTime describes the delay to the first call of the timer callback method. A value of 0 milliseconds, or TimeSpan.Zero, causes the timer method to start immediately. The value –1, or new TimeSpan(-1), deactivates the Timer class instance. That means the method will never be executed.

The period parameter indicates on what time interval the method is to be called again and whether the call is repetitive. A value of –1 milliseconds, or new TimeSpan(-1), causes the method to be called only once.

The timer method is not executed from the same thread in which the timer was created and started. It is executed from a thread in the thread pool. Calling the Dispose method will stop a timer and free its reserved resources, for example, the used thread from the thread pool, for other usage.

The code example in Listing 4-6 creates a timer that calls the OnTimer method immediately after creation and then calls it every 500 milliseconds. Between the calls of the OnTimer method, the program, or more exactly the microcontroller, is in sleep mode and uses nearly no energy.

Listing 4-6. *Using Timers*

```
using System;
using Microsoft.SPOT;
using System.Threading;

namespace TimerSample
{
```

```
    public class Program
    {
        public static void Main()
        {
            Debug.Print("Start");
            System.Threading.Timer timer =
                new System.Threading.Timer(new TimerCallback(OnTimer), null, 0, 500);
            Thread.Sleep(Timeout.Infinite);
        }

        private static void OnTimer(object state)
        {
            Debug.Print("Timer");
        }
    }
}
```

The second timer class, `Microsoft.SPOT.ExtendedTimer` (see Listing 4-7), adds to the functionality of the `System.Threading.Timer` class. First, it allows the timer method to be executed one time or repeatedly starting on a certain date. This can be used, for example, to create an alarm or reminder feature.

In addition, the `ExtendedTimer` class offers the possibility to call the timer method for certain time events, like a new second, minute, hour, or day, as well as after changing the time (using the `SetTime` method) or changing the time zone.

Listing 4-7. *The Microsoft.SPOT.ExtendedTimer Class*

```
namespace Microsoft.SPOT
{
    public sealed class ExtendedTimer : IDisposable
    {
        public ExtendedTimer(TimerCallback callback, object state,
                            ExtendedTimer.TimeEvents ev);
        public ExtendedTimer(TimerCallback callback, object state, DateTime dueTime,
                            TimeSpan period);
        public ExtendedTimer(TimerCallback callback, object state, int dueTime,
                            int period);
        public ExtendedTimer(TimerCallback callback, object state, TimeSpan dueTime,
                            TimeSpan period);

        public void Change(DateTime dueTime, TimeSpan period);
        public void Change(int dueTime, int period);
        public void Change(TimeSpan dueTime, TimeSpan period);
        public void Dispose();

        public TimeSpan LastExpiration { get; }
```

```
    public enum TimeEvents
    {
        Second = 0,
        Minute = 1,
        Hour = 2,
        Day = 3,
        TimeZone = 4,
        SetTime = 5,
    }
  }
}
```

An `ExtendedTimer` can be triggered by exactly one time event. You cannot combine the values of the enumeration `TimeEvents`, and the callback method is always a `TimerCallback` delegate with only the `state` parameter of the `object` type. An `ExtendedTimer` that reacts to changes to the time zone follows:

```
ExtendedTimer timer = new ExtendedTimer(new TimerCallback(OnTimer), null,
                                ExtendedTimer.TimeEvents.TimeZone);
```

■**Note** The class `TimeEvents` is an inner class of the `ExtendedTimer` class; therefore, you must prefix it with the outside class, `ExtendedTimer`.

Using Strings

Nearly every application uses strings, which can stress the garbage collector if not used correctly. The following sections show you how to use strings and encodings effectively.

The System.String Class

Strings are represented in all .NET Frameworks by the `System.String` class. Strings are stored internally by the .NET Micro Framework runtime environment in the UTF-8 format. But the `String` class makes strings available to you in the Unicode format, like they are in the .NET Micro Framework.

■**Note** The keyword `string` of the C# language is an alias of `System.String`.

Listing 4-8 shows the methods and properties of the `String` class. Most members from the full .NET Framework are likewise available in the .NET Micro Framework.

Listing 4-8. *The System.String Class*

```
namespace System
{
    [Serializable]
    public sealed class String
    {
        public static readonly string Empty;

        public String(char[] value);
        public String(char c, int count);
        public String(char[] value, int startIndex, int length);

        public static bool operator !=(string a, string b);
        public static bool operator ==(string a, string b);

        public int Length { get; }

        public char this[int index] { get; }

        public static int Compare(string strA, string strB);
        public int CompareTo(object value);
        public int CompareTo(string strB);
        public static string Concat(object arg0);
        public static string Concat(params object[] args);
        public static string Concat(params string[] values);
        public static string Concat(object arg0, object arg1);
        public static string Concat(string str0, string str1);
        public static string Concat(object arg0, object arg1, object arg2);
        public static string Concat(string str0, string str1, string str2);
        public static string Concat(string str0, string str1, string str2,
                            string str3);
        public static bool Equals(string a, string b);
        public int IndexOf(char value);
        public int IndexOf(string value);
        public int IndexOf(char value, int startIndex);
        public int IndexOf(string value, int startIndex);
        public int IndexOf(char value, int startIndex, int count);
        public int IndexOf(string value, int startIndex, int count);
        public int IndexOfAny(char[] anyOf);
        public int IndexOfAny(char[] anyOf, int startIndex);
        public int IndexOfAny(char[] anyOf, int startIndex, int count);
        public static string Intern(string str);
        public static string IsInterned(string str);
        public int LastIndexOf(char value);
        public int LastIndexOf(string value);
        public int LastIndexOf(char value, int startIndex);
        public int LastIndexOf(string value, int startIndex);
```

```
        public int LastIndexOf(char value, int startIndex, int count);
        public int LastIndexOf(string value, int startIndex, int count);
        public int LastIndexOfAny(char[] anyOf);
        public int LastIndexOfAny(char[] anyOf, int startIndex);
        public int LastIndexOfAny(char[] anyOf, int startIndex, int count);
        public string[] Split(params char[] separator);
        public string[] Split(char[] separator, int count);
        public string Substring(int startIndex);
        public string Substring(int startIndex, int length);
        public char[] ToCharArray();
        public char[] ToCharArray(int startIndex, int length);
        public string ToLower();
        public override string ToString();
        public string ToUpper();
        public string Trim();
        public string Trim(params char[] trimChars);
        public string TrimEnd(params char[] trimChars);
        public string TrimStart(params char[] trimChars);
    }
}
```

Concatenating Strings

If you create one string out of several substrings, as can happen in a loop, then with each run, a new String instance is created. To avoid this, you can use the System.Text.StringBuilder class in the full .NET Framework to build strings. But the StringBuilder class is not available in the .NET Micro Framework.

To use strings efficiently, you should consider this way of concatenating code:

```
string s = a + b + c;
```

The previous line of code is translated by the compiler to the following code:

```
string s = String.Concat(a, b, c);
```

The static method Concat of the class String concatenates up to four substrings into one and returns the new string. The following code creates exactly the same string as the first sample; however, the compiled code is less efficient:

```
string s = a;
s += b;
s += c;
```

The previous instructions are compiled to the following code:

```
string s = a;
s = String.Concat(s, b);
s = String.Concat(s, c);
```

So please avoid assigning an intermediate result if possible.

Encoding Strings

You may want to convert strings into an array of bytes, or the other way around, to read from a stream or serial port, for example. You can do the conversion with the System.Text.Encoding class, as shown in Listing 4-9. In the .NET Micro Framework, only UTF-8 encoding is available, implemented by the UTF8Encoding class. The static property UTF8 of the Encoding class supplies an instance of the UTF8Encoding class.

■**Tip** If needed, further encodings can be added by deriving your own class from the abstract class Encoding.

Listing 4-9. *The System.Text.Encoding Class*

```
namespace System.Text
{
    [Serializable]
    public abstract class Encoding
    {
        protected Encoding();

        public static Encoding UTF8 { get; }

        public virtual byte[] GetBytes(string s);
        public virtual char[] GetChars(byte[] bytes);
    }
}
```

Listing 4-10 demonstrates the usage of the Encoding class. Encoding does not own a method to convert a byte array directly to a string; it has only one method, for converting a byte array into a character array. The String class, however, has a constructor that takes a character array to create a string instance of it.

Listing 4-10. *Using System.Text.Encoding*

```
string text = "Hello World";
byte[] bytes = Encoding.UTF8.GetBytes(text);
string restoredText = new string(Encoding.UTF8.GetChars(bytes));
Debug.Print(restoredText);
```

Using Arrays

The following sections demonstrate how to use arrays efficiently.

Multidimensional Arrays

In C#, there are two kinds of multidimensional arrays. On the one hand, there are rectangular arrays, which are defined as shown in Listing 4-11.

Listing 4-11. *A Rectangular Array*

```
byte[,] rectArray = new byte[10, 3];
```

On the other hand, there are jagged arrays, which are arrays with elements that are arrays themselves. The subarrays can be of different lengths. The declaration and initialization of a jagged array is show in Listing 4-12.

Listing 4-12. *A Jagged Array*

```
byte[][] jaggedArray = new byte[10][];
for (int i = 0; i < jaggedArray.Length; ++i)
    jaggedArray[i] = new byte[3];
```

■**Caution** With the .NET Micro Framework, you can use *only* jagged arrays.

Combining Byte Arrays

Often, you may need to copy or join arrays when working on a hardware-dependent platform. Since byte arrays are probably most frequently used to exchange data over streams or to access hardware components, the .NET Micro Framework delivers auxiliary functions particularly optimized for byte arrays. It is always more efficient to use these already implemented system methods of the base class library, instead of copying the data manually in a loop, since these built-in routines execute optimized native code on the microprocessor.

In the Utility class in the Microsoft.SPOT.Hardware namespace in the Microsoft.SPOT. Native.dll assembly, you can find the CombineArrays method, a special method for combining byte arrays. There are two overloads of the method. One is for joining two complete arrays, and one combines subranges. Listing 4-13 demonstrates the usage of the utility methods for joining byte arrays.

Listing 4-13. *Using the Microsoft.SPOT.Hardware.Utility Class to Combine Byte Arrays*

```
using System;
using Microsoft.SPOT.Hardware;

namespace ArraySample
{
```

```
public class Class1
{
    public static void Main()
    {
        //combining two byte arrays
        byte[] byteArray1 = new byte[] { 0, 1, 2, 3, 4, 5, 6, 7 };
        byte[] byteArray2 = new byte[] { 8, 9, 10, 11, 12, 13, 14, 15 };
        byte[] byteArray3 = Utility.CombineArrays(byteArray1, byteArray2);
        byte[] byteArray4 = Utility.CombineArrays(byteArray1, //array 1
                                        2, //start index 1
                                        3, //number of elements in 1
                                        byteArray2, //array 2
                                        5, //start index 2
                                        2); //number of elements in 2
    }
}
}
```

After all statements are executed, byteArray3 contains the eight bytes from 0 to 15, and byteArray4 consists of the five values 2, 3, 4, 13, 14.

Extracting Ranges from Arrays

You can find a method in the Utility class for extracting a partial array from a total array. The method can only be used for byte arrays and has the following signature:

```
public static byte[] ExtractRangeFromArray(byte[] data, int offset, int count);
```

The method creates a new byte array with count elements and copies count elements, starting from the position offset, from the total array into the new array. Here again, native machine code is executed, and therefore, this approach is much more efficient than manually creating a new array and copying the elements in a loop.

Combining and Copying Nonbyte Arrays

You can use the Copy method of the Array class to copy any array in the .NET Micro Framework, exactly as in the full .NET Framework. For example, in Listing 4-14, two character arrays are combined using two copying operations. This approach requires you to create a target array first. The array items unnecessarily are initialized automatically with zero values; they are over-written immediately thereafter by the copying operations

Listing 4-14. *Combining Nonbyte Arrays with the Array.Copy method*

```
using System;
namespace ArraySample
{
    public class Program
    {
```

```
public static void Main()
{
    //concatenate two arbitrary arrays
    char[] charArray1 = new char[] { 'A', 'B', 'C', 'D' };
    char[] charArray2 = new char[] { 'E', 'F', 'G', 'H' };
    char[] charArray3 = new char[charArray1.Length + charArray2.Length];
    Array.Copy(charArray1, 0, charArray3, 0, charArray1.Length);
    Array.Copy(charArray2, 0, charArray3, charArray1.Length,
               charArray2.Length);
}
}
}
```

Integer and Byte Arrays

The already mentioned Utility class allows you to insert the individual bytes of an unsigned 8-, 16-, or 32-bit integer into a byte array as well as to copy or extract an integer value from an array of bytes.

Inserting a byte or a 16- or 32-bit integer into an array is done with the following method:

```
public static void InsertValueIntoArray(byte[] data, int pos, int size, uint val);
```

You need to specify the target array, the start index in the target array, the size of the integer value, and the value itself. Valid sizes are 1, 2, or 4 bytes. The sequence of the bytes depends on the processor used by the .NET Micro Framework platform. Some processors handle data as Little Endian and others as Big Endian. With Little Endian processors, the least significant byte is stored first, and thus at the lowest memory address. With Big Endian byte order, the most significant byte comes first. When running an application on the emulator, the data, like with all Windows PCs with X86 compatible processors, is stored in the Little Endian format. Likewise, all currently available .NET Micro Framework devices have Little Endian processors, but others (Big Endian processors) may come available later. Because this method relies on the processor's byte order, you need to consider it.

You must consider the byte order when exchanging data with other devices. If the data is stored and used only locally, then this method offers a comfortable way for copying an integer value into a byte array.

The reverse is also possible. With the ExtractValueFromArray method, an unsigned integer can be extracted from an array of bytes. The same order of bytes and integer sizes are valid as with InsertValueIntoArray.

```
public static uint ExtractValueFromArray(byte[] data, int pos, int size);
```

With the help of the methods InsertValueIntoArray or ExtractValueFromArray, you are able to determine, at runtime, whether the platform on which your .NET Micro Framework application is running uses a Little or Big Endian byte order:

```
bool isLittleEndian =
        Utility.ExtractValueFromArray(new byte[] { 0xAA, 0xBB }, 0, 2) == 0xBBAA;
```

Using Collections

The following sections demonstrate how to use the ArrayList class to manage collections.

Understanding the ArrayList Class

Arrays can be used, if you know in advance the number of items and if the number of items will not change. However, you may need more flexibility; for example, you may want the storage size to grow as more items are added to a collection.

Exactly for this purpose, .NET provides the ArrayList class (see Listing 4-15) in the System. Collections namespace. An ArrayList object increases its storage capacity when necessary.

An ArrayList holds elements of the type object. Since the type object is the base of all data types, an ArrayList can contain any element types, including items of various different types.

Listing 4-15. *The ArrayList Class*

```
using System;
using System.Diagnostics;
using System.Reflection;

namespace System.Collections
{
    [Serializable]
    [DebuggerDisplay("Count = {Count}")]
    public class ArrayList : IList, ICollection, IEnumerable, ICloneable
    {
        public ArrayList();

        public virtual int Capacity { get; set; }
        public virtual int Count { get; }
        public virtual bool IsFixedSize { get; }
        public virtual bool IsReadOnly { get; }
        public virtual bool IsSynchronized { get; }
        public virtual object SyncRoot { get; }

        public virtual object this[int index] { get; set; }

        public virtual int Add(object value);
        public virtual int BinarySearch(object value, IComparer comparer);
        public virtual void Clear();
        public virtual object Clone();
        public virtual bool Contains(object item);
        public virtual void CopyTo(Array array);
        public virtual void CopyTo(Array array, int arrayIndex);
        public virtual IEnumerator GetEnumerator();
        public virtual int IndexOf(object value);
        public virtual int IndexOf(object value, int startIndex);
```

```
        public virtual int IndexOf(object value, int startIndex, int count);
        public virtual void Insert(int index, object value);
        public virtual void Remove(object obj);
        public virtual void RemoveAt(int index);
        public virtual object[] ToArray();
        public virtual Array ToArray(Type type);
    }
}
```

Note The use of the ArrayList class occurs similarly to the full .NET Framework. The ArrayList class is, however, the only class in the .NET Micro Framework for managing collections. The generic versions are not available, since generics are not available at all in the .NET Micro Framework.

Using the ArrayList Class

You can create a list as follows:

```
ArrayList myList = new ArrayList();
```

After that, you can add items to the list by calling the Add method:

```
myList.Add(1);
myList.Add("Item");
```

The items can be addressed via the indexer, which begins counting at zero. The indexer always returns an object element. Therefore, you must cast an item to its appropriate data type before assignment and usage.

```
int i = (int)myList[0];
string s = (string)myList[1];
```

The Count property gives you the number of items stored in a list. Using a for loop, you can walk through the list and retrieve all items. It is assumed here that all items in the list are of the type int.

```
for(int i = 0; i < myList.Count; ++i)
{
    int item = (int)myList[i];
    Debug.Print(item.ToString());
}
```

The ArrayList class implements the ICollection interface from the System.Collections namespace; that's why you are able to iterate through the list with a foreach loop.

```
foreach(int item in myList)
{
    Debug.Print(item.ToString());
}
```

■**Tip** It is good practice to avoid `foreach` loops if possible, because they degrade performance. Iterating through items with a `foreach` loop requires additional method calls.

Working with Numbers

Each application needs to process numbers. The following sections will explore limitations with the .NET Micro Framework and demonstrate how to output and parse numbers.

Real Decimal Numbers

The number type `decimal` is not available in the .NET Micro Framework. With this type, in the full .NET and .NET Compact Framework, you can calculate with decimal floating point numbers without rounding errors. With `float` and `double` numbers, rounding errors can occur when converting between the decimal and binary system. In addition, real decimal numbers are not natively supported on a PC by the processor; they're only emulated. Emulating real decimal operations on a .NET Micro Framework system would make excessive demands of performance and create a too-large memory footprint. That's why Microsoft decided to omit the `decimal` type.

■**Note** The C# keyword `decimal` is an alias of the Common Language Runtime (CLR) type `System.Decimal`; also, `float` stands for `System.Single`, and `double` can be used for `System.Double` in C#.

Hexadecimal Number Output

You might encounter the need to convert integers into hexadecimal quite often when programming for hardware-dependent platforms, especially for diagnostic output. The .NET Micro Framework does not give you a possibility to convert these by using the "X" format with the `ToString` method.

The following code snippet, which works fine with the full .NET Framework, would cause an `ArgumentException` when calling the `ToString` method with "X" or "X8" for the `format` parameter:

```
int i = 16;
string hex = i.ToString("X");
```

With the .NET Micro Framework, you need to implement this functionality by yourself. The method in Listing 4-16 shows how to convert a byte value into a hexadecimal string.

Listing 4-16. *Converting a Byte Value into a Hexadecimal String*

```
public static string ByteToHex(byte b)
{
    const string hex = "0123456789ABCDEF";
    int lowNibble  = b & 0x0F;
    int highNibble = (b & 0xF0) >> 4;
    string s = new string(new char[] { hex[highNibble], hex[lowNibble] });
    return s;
}
```

Parsing Numbers

In the .NET Micro Framework, simple numeric data types, such as integers and floating point numbers, do not have Parse methods to parse numbers from strings. Therefore, I implemented a custom NumberParser class with the methods ParseInt64, ParseUInt64, ParseUInt64Hex, and ParseDouble—as well as a TryParse variant for each of these. The code base has its origin in the DotGNU project (an open source port of the .NET Framework to Linux similar to the Mono project). When I ported it to the .NET Micro Framework, I simplified and optimized it too.

The NumberParsingSample project (see Listing 4-17) demonstrates the possibilities.

Listing 4-17. *Parsing Numbers with the Kuehner.NumberParser Class*

```
using System;
using Microsoft.SPOT;
using Kuehner;

namespace NumberParsingSample
{
    public class Program
    {
        public static void Main()
        {
            Debug.Print(NumberParser.ParseInt64("1234").ToString());
            Debug.Print(NumberParser.ParseInt64("-1234").ToString());
            Debug.Print(NumberParser.ParseUInt64("1234").ToString());
            Debug.Print(NumberParser.ParseUInt64Hex("FF").ToString());
            Debug.Print(NumberParser.ParseDouble("1234.56").ToString());
            Debug.Print(NumberParser.ParseDouble("-1234.56").ToString());
            Debug.Print(NumberParser.ParseDouble("+1234.56").ToString());
            Debug.Print(NumberParser.ParseDouble("1,234.56").ToString());
```

```
Debug.Print(NumberParser.ParseDouble("1.23e2").ToString());
Debug.Print(NumberParser.ParseDouble("1.23e-2").ToString());
Debug.Print(NumberParser.ParseDouble("123e+2").ToString());
double result;
if (NumberParser.TryParseDouble("1234.56a", out result))
    Debug.Print(result.ToString());
else
    Debug.Print("1234.56a is not a valid number.");


        }
    }
}
```

■**Note** You can find the source code of the NumberParser class in the NumberParsingSample project in the directory for Chapter 4, available from the Source Code page on the Apress web site.

The NumberParser class can deal with floating point numbers with thousand separators and can handle scientific notation (exponents). The following static methods are exposed by the class:

- bool TryParseInt64(string str, out long result)

- long ParseInt64(string str)

- bool TryParseUInt64(string str, out ulong result)

- ulong ParseUInt64(string str)

- bool TryParseUInt64Hex(string str, out ulong result)

- ulong ParseUInt64Hex(string str)

- bool TryParseDouble(string str, out double result)

- double ParseDouble(string str)

■**Tip** Conditional compilation allows you to include or exclude code parts. Undefining the compiler constant SUPPORT_FLOATINGPOINT_NUMERICS will exclude support for floating point number parsing to reduce the footprint of the deployed code on the device.

Mathematical Functions

Mathematical functions are implemented in the .NET Micro Framework in the same way as in the full .NET Framework—in the System.Math class. This class was substantially trimmed, however, for the .NET Micro Framework (see Listing 4-18). For example, for the methods Abs, Min, and Max, only the integer overloads are available. Floating point numbers such as float and double lack support, and trigonometric functions like the computation of sine and cosine were completely eliminated from the class.

Listing 4-18. *The System.Math Class*

```
namespace System
{
    public static class Math
    {
        public const double E = 2.71828;
        public const double PI = 3.14159;

        public static int Abs(int val);
        public static int Min(int val1, int val2);
        public static int Max(int val1, int val2);
        public static double Round(double a);
        public static double Ceiling(double a);
        public static double Floor(double d);
        public static double Pow(double x, double y);
    }
}
```

In addition to System.Math, there is a .NET Micro Framework–specific Math class, located in the Microsoft.SPOT namespace (see Listing 4-19). The Microsoft.SPOT.Math class exposes methods for the calculation of sine and cosine as well as for generating random numbers.

Listing 4-19. *The Microsoft.SPOT.Math Class*

```
namespace Microsoft.SPOT
{
    public static class Math
    {
        public static int Sin(int angle);
        public static int Cos(int angle);
        public static void Randomize();
        public static int Random(int modulo);
    }
}
```

Why did Microsoft create two Math classes? If you look carefully at the sine and cosine functions, you recognize that the method signatures are different from the methods in the full .NET Framework. In the full .NET Framework, the sine and cosine methods expect a radian angle as a floating point number and return a double value between –1 and 1. On the other hand, the .NET Micro Framework versions of the sine and cosine functions expect an integer angle in degrees and return an integer value between –1000 and 1000.

Random numbers are generated not by the System.Math class in the full .NET Framework but by a separate System.Random class with extended functionality. In the .NET Micro Framework, only two methods are available: Randomize for initializing the random number generator and Random for generating the random numbers. The Random method returns a random integer value. The generated number is greater or equal to zero and less than the modulo value.

■**Note** Microsoft could have assembled all mathematical functions in one class with the .NET Micro Framework. However, in the .NET Micro Framework, properties, methods, classes, or namespaces of the .NET base class library were just trimmed, but nothing new was added or modified. The .NET Compact Framework already uses this approach in the same way. The .NET Compact Framework for Windows CE is, likewise, a subset of the full .NET Framework for Windows. Microsoft uses this model consistently and selected it so that applications remain compatible to the full .NET Framework. If a method or property from the full .NET Framework was thus maintained, you can rely on the fact that it is compatible to the original of the full .NET Framework. As an example consider, as previously mentioned, the Debug class for the output of diagnostic messages.

Exception Handling

An exception is thrown in when an error occurs. The .NET Framework uses exceptions to signal an unwanted event, instead of using return values as was common practice in previous times. If an error occurs, the normal program flow is interrupted, and an instance of an exception is thrown to describe the error situation. The exception is passed on until it is caught and handled by an exception handler. If no exception handler exists, the exception is caught and handled by the operating system or, in the case of the .NET Micro Framework, by the runtime system. That means that the program is terminated when an exception is not caught.

A .NET Micro Framework application running on a microcontroller should never be terminated. The only cause to stop an embedded application should be switching off the device. Because of that, you should provide proper exception handling in your application.

All exceptions are subclasses of the System.Exception class. The exceptions that are available in the base class library of the .NET Micro Framework are shown in Figure 4-2. But you are free to derive your own custom exception classes from the Exception class or from any other existing exception.

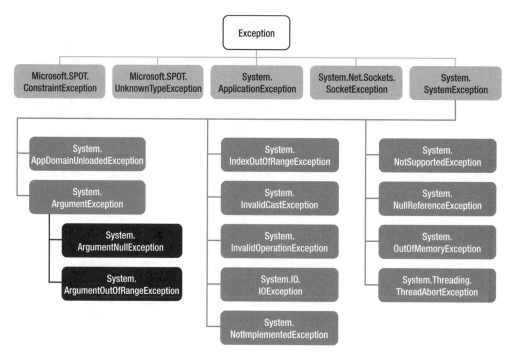

Figure 4-2. *Hierarchy of the base class library exceptions in the .NET Micro Framework*

Throwing Exceptions

An exception is thrown by using the `throw` keyword. A message can be passed to describe the error situation:

```
throw new Exception("Text to describe the error situation.");
```

■**Note** In the base class library of the .NET Micro Framework, all exceptions are thrown without passing an error message to the constructor, which keeps the runtime footprint small. When handling exceptions, they can be distinguished only by data type, so it is up to you to specify an error message, if necessary, when you throw exceptions.

Here's another example of throwing exceptions:

```
public MyClass(string str, int count)
{
    if(str == null)
        throw new ArgumentNullException("str");
    if(count <= 0)
        throw new ArgumentOutOfRangeException("count", "Count must be positive.");
}
```

You can use exceptions to check the parameters passed to your method. If they are invalid, the method or constructor throws an exception. Therefore, your method can never be called with invalid arguments. For throwing an exception because of an invalid argument, you should use ArgumentException or one of its subclasses (see Figure 4-2).

Note Exceptions should be used rarely. Never use exceptions for controlling the execution flow (e.g., instead of an if statement). It is good practice to use exceptions when you cannot solve the problem by requesting invalid data again or when resources are missing.

Catching an Exception

If an exception is thrown in a method, the exception bubbles up to the nearest exception handler. If there is no exception handler, the exception is handled by the runtime environment. If an exception is caught at runtime, the thread in which the method was called is terminated. If the throwing method was in an application's main thread, the application is terminated.

If you want to catch an exception, you enclose the critical code in a try-catch block combination. To catch all types of exceptions, you can write something like the following:

```
try
{
    int a = 1;
    int b = 0;
    int c = a / b; //division by zero will throw an exception here
}
catch
{
    Debug.Print("Division failed.");
}
```

The division fails, because a is divided by zero.

The previous code is similar to the next code snippet:

```
try
{
    ...
}
catch(Exception)
{
    ...
}
```

Both samples will catch any exception type.

As soon as an exception occurs, the remaining code in the try block is ignored, and the catch block is executed. If no execution occurs, the program will never branch to the catch block, and the try block is executed completely.

The finally Block

Sometimes, you have a code block that must be executed both after error-free execution and in an error situation. An example of this would be freeing a hardware component's resources for use later on or in other parts of a program. You accomplish this with the `finally` block:

```
try
{
    //using resources
}
catch
{
    //handling exceptions
}
finally
{
    //freeing resources
}
```

Even if you exit a method with the `return` keyword within a `try` block, the code in the `finally` block is executed before leaving the method.

You should protect the code in a `finally` block (e.g. freeing resources) with a `try-catch` construct if the code may throw exceptions too.

Handling Multiple Exception Types

You can implement different `catch` blocks to handle different exception types separately:

```
try
{
    ...
}
catch(IOException)
{
    ...
}
catch(NotSupportedException)
{
    ...
}
catch(Exception)
{
    ...
}
```

Make sure that the `catch` block for the most general exception comes at the end; otherwise, the special `catch` blocks are never executed. The catch blocks will be checked in the order of appearance, and as soon as one block applies, the others are ignored. In the preceding example, the first `catch` block will handle all exceptions that derive from `IOException`. Placing the catch(Exception) block first would make the other blocks useless, because all exceptions are derived from Exception, and therefore, this block will be executed whenever an execution is thrown.

Getting Information from an Exception

Instead of just catching an exception, you can inspect it and get more details about the error cause and information about where the exception occurs.

```
try
{
    throw new Exception("Text to describe the error situation.");
}
catch(Exception ex)
{
    Debug.Print("Message: " + ex.Message);
    Debug.Print("Stack Trace: " + ex.StackTrace);
}
```

Every exception has a Message property, but if the exception is thrown by a method of the .NET Micro Framework runtime library, an error message is not passed to the constructor of an exception.

The StackTrace property provides useful information about where the exception was thrown.

Rethrowing Exceptions

After you have caught an exception in a handler and some handling code in a catch block was executed, you can rethrow this exception to pass it to another exception handler and inform other parts of the code about the error.

```
try
{
    ...
}
catch(Exception)
{
    //special treatment code
    throw; //rethrow it by keeping the stack trace
}
```

It is even possible to catch an exception of a certain type and then rethrow it as an exception of another type. In the following sample, all types of exceptions are caught and thrown again as IOException instances.

```
try
{
    //e.g. send data to hardware component
}
catch(Exception) //catch all exceptions
{
    throw new IOException("Sending data failed."); //throw some special exception
}
```

Summary

This chapter covered tracing techniques to debug your application, and you learned how to effectively use timers, numbers, arrays, lists, and exceptions. In doing so, this chapter compared the .NET Micro Framework to the full .NET Framework and explained why some types were moved to the specific namespace Microsoft.SPOT. You saw that you can use your existing .NET knowhow to program with the .NET Micro Framework.

You are all set now to start learning how to interface with the various hardware components. See you in the next chapter.

CHAPTER 5

■ ■ ■

Accessing Hardware

To be truly useful, an embedded device must be able to interface with hardware components. This chapter describes how you can access general purpose input/output (GPIO) ports, transfer data with the RS232 serial port, and interface with devices on the inter-integrated circuit (I²C) and serial peripheral interface (SPI) busses. Further, you will learn how to obtain information about the charging state, processor speed, and system identification.

What Are GPIO Ports?

General purpose input/output (GPIO) ports are probably the most frequently used way for a microcontroller to contact its environment. A GPIO port can be initialized and used either as an input or output line. A typical example of an output line is one to control a light-emitting diode (LED). Monitoring a push button or a switch is the function of an input line.

A GPIO port can have either a low (0 volts) or high (a positive voltage, usually 3.3 volts) status. In the .NET Micro Framework, the status of a GPIO port is represented as a Boolean value. The value `false` corresponds to low status and `true` to high.

■Note Setting a GPIO output port to logical low will usually provide 0 volts at the GPIO pin and 3.3 volts for high. An input voltage of less than one volt at a GPIO input pin will usually be interpreted as logical low and voltages between 1.7 and 5.5 volts represent logical high. Input voltages above 5.5 volts might damage your hardware.

The GPIO sample code in this section is written particularly for the `GpioPortSampleEmulator` emulator, which is shown in Figure 5-1; you can find the source code in the directory for Chapter 13.

■Note To get the examples in this chapter running on real hardware, you need to change the pin numbers in the code according to the device's pin set. You can find the pin numbers in the documentation of your development board.

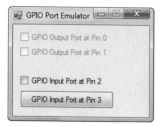

Figure 5-1. *The GPIO port emulator*

Output Ports

Within the Microsoft.SPOT.Hardware namespace resides the OutputPort class, which represents a GPIO output port. OutputPort inherits from Microsoft.SPOT.Hardware.Port, the general base class for GPIO ports.

So that the class can be used, you need to add a reference to the Microsoft.SPOT. Hardware.dll assembly to your project. New projects will only reference the Microsoft.SPOT. Native.dll assembly.

Listing 5-1 demonstrates how to configure the first line of your CPU as a GPIO output port and how to toggle the output port twice a second in an infinite loop. Figure 5-2 shows the schematic of a lamp that is connected to and driven by a GPIO output port. The lamp is wired between the ground and the GPIO pin. If you write false to the output port, the lamp gets 0 volts from the GPIO pin. If you write true, the output pin provides a positive supply voltage (referred as VCC+), for example, 3.3 volts to drive the lamp.

Listing 5-1. *Toggling a GPIO Output Port*

```
using System;
using System.Threading;
using Microsoft.SPOT.Hardware;

namespace GpioOutputPortSample
{
    public class Program
    {
        public static void Main()
        {
            OutputPort outputPort = new OutputPort(Cpu.Pin.GPIO_Pin0, true);
            while (true)
            {
                Thread.Sleep(500);
                outputPort.Write(!outputPort.Read()); //toggle port
            }
        }
    }
}
```

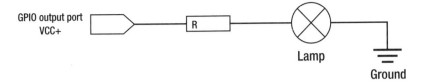

Figure 5-2. *A lamp or LED driven by a GPIO output port*

The constructor of OutputPort follows:

```
public OutputPort(Cpu.Pin portId, bool initialState);
```

It expects the port's ID and initial state, where true represents high and false low.

■**Note** Please consider that the port ID addresses the pin of a CPU line of your device. However, a micro-controller has not only GPIO lines but also other lines such as the transmission and receipt lines for serial interfaces and control lines for the SPI and I²C busses. Pin 0, therefore, does not necessarily correspond to the first GPIO port. The correspondence depends on the hardware you are using and is described in the documentation of your development board.

The port ID is not an integer value; it's of the enumeration type Cpu.Pin, which provides GPIO_NONE with the value –1 and 16 predefined pins with the names GPIO_Pin0 to GPIO_Pin15, as shown in Listing 5-2.

Listing 5-2. *The Enumeration Microsoft.SPOT.Hardware.Cpu.Pin to Specify Pin Numbers of I/O Lines*

```
namespace Microsoft.SPOT.Hardware
{
    public static class Cpu
    {
        public enum Pin
        {
            GPIO_NONE = -1,
            GPIO_Pin0 = 0,
            GPIO_Pin1 = 1,
            GPIO_Pin2 = 2,
            GPIO_Pin3 = 3,
            GPIO_Pin4 = 4,
            GPIO_Pin5 = 5,
            GPIO_Pin6 = 6,
            GPIO_Pin7 = 7,
            GPIO_Pin8 = 8,
            GPIO_Pin9 = 9,
            GPIO_Pin10 = 10,
```

```
                GPIO_Pin11 = 11,
                GPIO_Pin12 = 12,
                GPIO_Pin13 = 13,
                GPIO_Pin14 = 14,
                GPIO_Pin15 = 15
         }
     }
}
```

It is good practice to create a custom class with constants for the different control lines, as shown in Listing 5-3, so that a .NET Micro Framework application can be adapted better for different .NET Micro Framework hardware. This class with the separated pin definitions can be easily exchanged for the different platforms. For example, you have a status LED that is wired on one platform to pin 0 and on another to pin 3. If you use MyPins.StatusLED in your program code to address your LED, then you have to change only the value in the MyPins class to adapt your application to other platforms. Other parts of your application code do not need to be touched.

Listing 5-3. *A Class for Separating the Pin Definition*

```
public static class MyPins
{
    public const Cpu.Pin StatusLED = Cpu.Pin.GPIO_Pin0;
    public const Cpu.Pin UpButton = Cpu.Pin.GPIO_Pin1;
    public const Cpu.Pin DowButton = Cpu.Pin.GPIO_Pin2;

    public const Cpu.Pin Ser1Rx = Cpu.Pin. GPIO_Pin9;
    public const Cpu.Pin Ser1Tx = Cpu.Pin. GPIO_Pin10;
}
```

For example, instead of passing the GPIO pin directly to the constructor of OutputPort, you should use the pin definition class that maps your device's user interface to the pin definitions of your platform. Each platform may have its own pin layout. The first GPIO pin might be on one platform at pin 0 and on a different platform at a different pin (e.g., pin 3). The constructor of OutputPort accepts the pin number as Cpu.Pin. The MyPins class allows you to change the pin numbers at a central place, so you can reuse your code for different hardware platforms:

```
OutputPort outputPort = new OutputPort(Cpu.Pin.GPIO_Pin0, true); // bad
OutputPort outputPort = new OutputPort(MyPins.StatusLED, true);  // good
```

The most important methods of OutputPort are Write and Read. The Write method controls the port state, and Read returns the current state, which is the state that was last set.

The Port class implements the IDisposable interface with the Dispose method. Since the OutputPort class inherits from Port, you can manually free the resources that were allocated for a port by calling the Dispose method, without waiting for the garbage collector to call the finalizer when freeing the object. The garbage collector disposes of the object only if the object is no longer referenced from any part of your code.

Input Ports

Input ports are addressed in the .NET Micro Framework via the `Microsoft.SPOT.Hardware.InputPort` class. `InputPort` inherits, likewise, from the `Microsoft.SPOT.Hardware.Port` base class. It resides, like `OutputPort`, in the `Microsoft.SPOT.Hardware.dll` assembly.

Listing 5-4 shows how the CPU line of the microcontroller is configured as a GPIO input port and the state is read continuously in an infinite loop. Reading a state, in this case the state of the GPIO input port, is called polling.

Listing 5-4. *Polling a GPIO Input Port*

```
using System;
using System.Threading;
using Microsoft.SPOT;
using Microsoft.SPOT.Hardware;

namespace GpioInputPortSample
{
    public class Program
    {
        public static void Main()
        {
            InputPort inputPort = new InputPort(Cpu.Pin.GPIO_Pin2,
                                        false,
                                        Port.ResistorMode.PullDown);
            while (true)
            {
                bool state = inputPort.Read(); //polling of port state
                Debug.Print("GPIO input port at pin " + inputPort.Id +
                            " is " + (state ? "high" : "low"));

                //enable device to sleep or emulator to react to Visual Studio
                Thread.Sleep(10);
            }
        }
    }
}
```

The `InputPort` class's constructor expects the following parameters:

```
public InputPort(Cpu.Pin portId, bool glitchFilter, Port.ResistorMode resistor);
```

When creating a new `InputPort` object, you pass the hardware pin of the port as the first parameter, `portId`.

The second parameter, `glitchFilter`, indicates whether bouncing (which causes noise) in the input signal is to be ignored. Bouncing causes glitches, but sometimes, having a bouncing push button is unavoidable. Mechanical switches and buttons can bounce—a single press of your button can produce multiple pulses. A glitch filter removes immediate successive changes between high and low state. You can define the intensity of the glitch filter's operation with the GlitchFilterTime static property of the Microsoft.SPOT.Hardware.Cpu class. This property is a time span: all signal changes within the indicated time span are ignored. By default, GlitchFilterTime equals 0 seconds, that is, nothing will be filtered.

With the following line of code, you can set the time span for the glitch filter to 5 milliseconds:

```
Cpu.GlitchFilterTime = new TimeSpan(0, 0, 0, 0, 5);
```

The last constructor parameter indicates the resistor mode. A simple switch can be either open or closed. A microcontroller requires a defined input voltage, which should be either high (3.3 volts) or low (0 volts) at the digital GPIO inputs. For a switch, you need to add either a pull-up or pull-down resistor, so that the microcontroller gets a defined voltage (remaining either high or low, nothing in between). If no resistor is added, the input signal is undefined if the switch is opened. An undefined input signal is floating—due to external electrical interference, a noise on the line might occur, since the line can work like an antenna.

Whether a resistor is a pull-up or pull-down resistor depends on where it is wired (see Figure 5-3). A resistor placed between 3.3 volts (VCC+) and the GPIO line is a pull-up resistor. A resistor between the ground and the GPIO pin against it is a pull-down resistor.

A switch that is placed between 3.3 volts (VCC+) and the GPIO input port (see the pull-down configuration in Figure 5-3) will set the GPIO line on 3.3 volts when it is closed. That means the voltage at the GPIO input line is 0 volts (low) if the switch is opened and 3.3 volts (high) when it is closed. With a push button, you will read logical high (true) when the button is pressed.

If a push button is wired with a pull-up resistor, the logic levels will be inverted. That means you will read a high state (true) when the button is not pressed and low (false) when it is pressed.

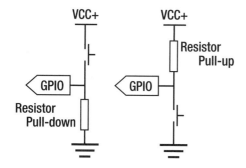

Figure 5-3. *Pull-down and pull-up schematics*

The enumerating Port.ResistorMode provides the following modes:

```
public enum ResistorMode
{
    Disabled,
    PullDown,
    PullUp
}
```

The indication of the resistor mode is actually relevant only for the emulator. With the indication of Disabled or PullDown, the port is set to low level. With PullUp, it is set to logical high. Disabled does not mean that the port is deactivated, only that there is no pull-up or pull-down resistor wired.

Interrupt Ports

In the previous section, you learned how to read the state from an input port in a continuous loop. If you want your application to wait for a key press, then using polling for that is not good practice; it's pedantic and not very efficient. For triggering a rising or falling edge of a pulse (see Figure 5-4), this approach is also unsuitable. Continuously reading a GPIO state will keep the processor busy and give it no idle time, so it can never go to low-power mode.

Interrupt ports are the keys to solving this problem; the special class called InterruptPort extends the InputPort class. Interrupts are hardware events. If the microcontroller has nothing further to do than wait for a certain GPIO event, the processor can confidently go into power-saving mode. As soon as a signal change occurs at the input pin, the microcontroller wakes up and a certain method, the interrupt service routine (ISR), will be executed.

You can configure an interrupt port to wait either for the rising edge of a pulse, falling edge of a pulse, both edges of a pulse, or for the high or low signal level in general (Figure 5-4 shows these).

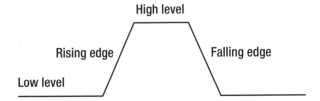

Figure 5-4. *Anatomy of a pulse*

The constructor looks like the InputPort one, but with an additional parameter interrupt of the type Port.InterrupMode.

```
public InterruptPort(Cpu.Pin portId, bool glitchFilter, Port.ResistorMode resistor,
                     Port.InterruptMode interrupt);
```

InterruptMode indicates on what you want to trigger. Figure 5-5 shows how the interrupt modes apply to a pulse.

```
public enum InterruptMode
{
        InterruptNone,          // The port is deactivated
        InterruptEdgeLow,       // falling edge (Change from high to low)
        InterruptEdgeHigh,      // rising edge (Change from low to high)
        InterruptEdgeBoth,      // both edges (Any state change)
        InterruptEdgeLevelHigh, // high
        InterruptEdgeLevelLow   // low
}
```

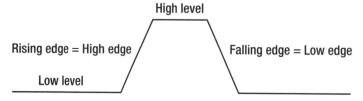

Figure 5-5. *Interrupt modes*

Triggering an Edge

The code in Listing 5-5 shows how you can trigger to both edges. The interrupt handler routine is assigned over the delegate (reference to a method) OnInterrupt. The custom interrupt handler port_OnInterrupt is then executed as soon as the state of the GPIO port changes.

Listing 5-5. *Triggering Both Edges*

```
using System;
using System.Threading;
using Microsoft.SPOT;
using Microsoft.SPOT.Hardware;

namespace GpioInterruptPortEdgeSample
{
    public class Program
    {
        public static void Main()
        {
            InterruptPort port =
                    new InterruptPort(Cpu.Pin.GPIO_Pin3,
                                      false, //no glitch filter
                                      Port.ResistorMode.PullDown,
                                      Port.InterruptMode.InterruptEdgeBoth);
            port.OnInterrupt += new GPIOInterruptEventHandler(port_OnInterrupt);

            Thread.Sleep(Timeout.Infinite);
        }

        private static void port_OnInterrupt(Cpu.Pin port,
                                             bool state,
                                             TimeSpan time)
        {
            Debug.Print("Pin=" + port + " State=" + state + " Time=" + time);
        }
    }
}
```

Triggering to a Level

If you want to wait for a certain level, either high or low, you need to pass either
`InterruptEdgeLevelHigh` or `InterruptEdgeLevelLow` as the interrupt mode. The interrupt handler
will only be called once, as soon as the port achieves the desired state. The interrupt handler will be
called again only if you clear the interrupt by calling `ClearInterrupt`. Listing 5-6 demonstrates how
to trigger to a level.

Listing 5-6. *Triggering to a Level*

```
using System;
using System.Threading;
using Microsoft.SPOT;
using Microsoft.SPOT.Hardware;

namespace GpioInterruptPortEdgeSample
{
    public class Program
    {
        private static InterruptPort interruptPort;

        public static void Main()
        {
            interruptPort =
                    new InterruptPort(Cpu.Pin.GPIO_Pin2,
                                        false, //no glitch filter
                                        Port.ResistorMode.PullUp,
                                        Port.InterruptMode.InterruptEdgeLevelLow);
            interruptPort.OnInterrupt +=
                                    new GPIOInterruptEventHandler(port_OnInterrupt);

            Thread.Sleep(Timeout.Infinite);
        }

        private static void port_OnInterrupt(Cpu.Pin port,
                                                bool state,
                                                TimeSpan time)
        {
            Debug.Print("Pin=" + port + " State=" + state + " Time=" + time);
            interruptPort.ClearInterrupt();
        }
    }
}
```

In Listing 5-6, the variable `interruptPort` cannot be declared locally in the `Main` method
like it is in Listing 5-5, because the variable needs to be addressed in the `interruptPort_`
`OnInterrupt` interrupt method. Therefore, you need to declare the variable as a static class
member.

Resources of an interrupt port can be likewise freed with the `Dispose` method. After disposing of a port, you cannot use it anymore, and the interrupt method will no longer be called. If you just want to deactivate an interrupt port temporarily, in order to reactivate it at a later time again, then you can deactivate it with this:

```
interruptPort.Interrupt = Port.InterruptMode.InterruptNone;
```

Resources will not be freed in this case; the instance remains in memory. The port can be reactivated by assigning another interrupt mode later.

Tristate Ports

Sometimes, you might need to use a GPIO port, depending on whether an input or output port is required, and your application should be able to swap the direction at runtime. To avoid having to create a new instance of `InputPort` and `OutputPort` to reconfigure the port, the .NET Micro Framework provides the `TristatePort` class (see Listing 5-7). Its `Active` property indicates the direction, thus the port will function as an input or output port. The term "tristate" can be misleading, because it does not have anything to do with a high-impedance line condition between high and low.

```
public TristatePort(Cpu.Pin portId, bool initialState, bool glitchFilter,
                    Port.ResistorMode resistor);
```

The constructor of the `TristatePort` class expects parameters that are relevant for the input and/or output mode: the `initialState` parameter is for the output mode of importance and `glitchFilter` and `resistor` for the input direction. If the `Active` property is true, the port acts as an output port; with `false`, it acts as an input port. After creating a new `TristatePort` instance the port will initially be an output port, the property `Active` thus equals to true.

Listing 5-7. *Using the TristatePort Class*

```
TristatePort tristatePort = new TristatePort(Cpu.Pin.GPIO_Pin4,
                                             false, //initial state
                                             false, //no glitch filter
                                             Port.ResistorMode.PullUp);
Debug.Print("Port is active and acts as output port.");
tristatePort.Write(true);

tristatePort.Active = false;
Debug.Print("Port is inactive and acts as input port.");
Debug.Print("Input = " + tristatePort.Read());
```

■**Caution** Please note that you cannot assign the same value to the `Active` property that it already has—only toggling the direction is possible. If `Active` is, for example, already `false` and the port acts as its input, then assigning `false` again (`tristatePort.Active = false`) will throw an exception. If `Active` is already `true`, then setting it to `true` again will also cause an exception. In order to avoid an exception, the value of `Active` can be queried before the assignment.

The RS232 Serial Port

Even though the concept of the serial interface has been around for years and USB is becoming more and more established, there are still many devices that need to be interfaced with a serial port, for example, measuring instruments and GPS receivers. In addition, the Bluetooth standard defines several protocols (profiles) to access different devices like head sets and printers, and it also has a communication profile via Bluetooth named `Serial-Port`. Some serial-to-Bluetooth adapters exist already. If such an adapter is connected to the serial interface of the microcontroller, a .NET Micro Framework application can communicate wirelessly with a PC, PDA, smartphone, or other microcontroller (see Chapter 7).

Together with the serial interface, you quite often hear the terms "UART," "USART," and "RS232." UART and USART are names for the serial hardware component, the Universal (Synchronous) Asynchronous Receiver Transmitter. The RS232 standard describes how data will be physically transferred over the cable. Further standards are RS422 and RS485.

The SerialPort Class

The serial port is addressed in the .NET Micro Framework via the `Microsoft.SPOT.Hardware.SerialPort` class. The class is not identical to the `System.IO.Ports.SerialPort` class from the full .NET Framework or .NET Compact Framework or a subset of it. The class is especially for the .NET Micro Framework and therefore resides in the `Microsoft.SPOT.Hardware` namespace.

The constructor of the `SerialPort` class expects an instance of the `SerialPort.Configuration` class. With the `Configuration` class, you specify the COM port number, the baud rate, and whether flow control (handshake) shall be used. There are several kinds of flow controls for the serial interface. The .NET Micro Framework supports only software (using XON/XOFF characters) flow control or no flow control. With the software flow control, the XOFF byte is transmitted to stop the transmission, and the XON byte to resume data transmission.

To execute the serial port samples of this chapter on an emulator, you first need to build the `SerialPortSampleEmulator` emulator shown in Figure 5-6 (the code to execute it is in the directory for Chapter 13 in this book's source code) so that you can select and use this special serial port emulator for your sample projects.

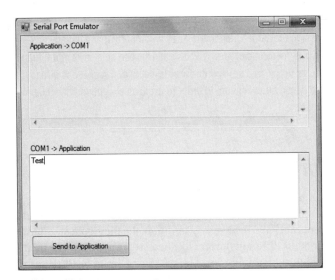

Figure 5-6. *The serial port emulator*

Listing 5-8 shows the SerialPort class with its inner Configuration class, the Serial enumeration for addressing COM ports, and the Baudrate enumeration to select a baud rate.

Listing 5-8. *The Microsoft.SPOT.Hardware.SerialPort Class*

```
using System;

namespace Microsoft.SPOT.Hardware
{
    public sealed class SerialPort : IDisposable
    {
        public SerialPort(SerialPort.Configuration config);

        public SerialPort.Configuration Config { get; set; }

        public void Dispose();
        public void Flush();
        public int Read(byte[] buffer, int offset, int count, int timeout);
        public int Write(byte[] buffer, int offset, int count);

        public enum BaudRate
        {
            Baud4800 = 4800,
            Baud9600 = 9600,
            Baud19200 = 19200,
            Baud38400 = 38400,
            Baud57600 = 57600,
            Baud115200 = 115200,
            Baud230400 = 230400,
        }
```

```
public enum Serial
{
    COM1 = 0,
    COM2 = 1,
    COM3 = 2,
    COM4 = 3,
}

public class Configuration
{
    public readonly SerialPort.Serial Com;
    public readonly bool FlowControl;
    public readonly SerialPort.BaudRate Speed;

    public Configuration(SerialPort.Serial com, SerialPort.BaudRate speed,
                         bool flowControl);
}
}
}
```

You can send data to the serial port with the Write method and receive data with the Read method. The Flush method causes all buffered input and output data to be sent immediately. Usually, you do not need to call the Flush method manually, since the buffering is handled well by the UART controller.

Sending Data

The code snippet in Listing 5-9 shows how to configure serial communication over the first COM port with 9600 baud and without any flow control. Then, a string followed by a Windows-compatible line feed is sent over the serial port.

The Write method does not have any further overload. It expects the data to be written in the form of a byte array. To write string data, you first need to convert it to a byte array. When writing a byte buffer, you also have to pass the index of the first byte in the buffer and the number of bytes to send to the Write method.

Please note that the SerialPort class in the .NET Micro Framework provides no Open method and thus cannot be opened and closed explicitly. Right after creating an instance of SerialPort, you can use the serial port. When you do not need to access a COM port anymore, the Dispose method will free all resources.

Listing 5-9. *Sending Data to a Serial Port*

```
using System;
using System.Text;
using System.Threading;
using Microsoft.SPOT;
using Microsoft.SPOT.Hardware;
```

```
namespace SerialPortWriteSample
{
    public class Program
    {
        public static void Main()
        {
            SerialPort.Configuration config =
                        new SerialPort.Configuration(SerialPort.Serial.COM1,
                                                SerialPort.BaudRate.Baud9600,
                                                false);
            SerialPort serialPort = new SerialPort(config);
            byte[] outBuffer = Encoding.UTF8.GetBytes("Hello World!\r\n");
            serialPort.Write(outBuffer, 0, outBuffer.Length);
            serialPort.Dispose();
            //keeps the emulator running to see results
            Thread.Sleep(Timeout.Infinite);
        }
    }
}
```

Receiving Data

In Listing 5-10, you can see how to receive a string and display it in the Debug window of Visual Studio. The data is read with 115200 baud.

Listing 5-10. *Receiving Data from a Serial Port*

```
using System;
using System.Text;
using System.Threading;
using Microsoft.SPOT;
using Microsoft.SPOT.Hardware;

namespace SerialPortReadSample
{
    public class Program
    {
        public static void Main()
        {
            SerialPort.Configuration config =
                        new SerialPort.Configuration(SerialPort.Serial.COM1,
                                                SerialPort.BaudRate.Baud115200,
                                                false);
            SerialPort serialPort = new SerialPort(config);
            byte[] inBuffer = new byte[32];
            while (true)
            {
                int count = serialPort.Read(inBuffer, 0, inBuffer.Length, 0);
```

```
                if (count > 0) //minimum one byte read
                {
                    char[] chars = Encoding.UTF8.GetChars(inBuffer);
                    string str = new string(chars, 0, count);
                    Debug.Print(str);
                }
                Thread.Sleep(25); //give device time to sleep
            }
        }
    }
}
```

The Request-Response Approach

The last parameter for the Read method is a read timeout, expressed in milliseconds. Calling the method results in blocking the read, and it blocks no longer than the specified timeout. The Read method resumes if all requested bytes were received or the timeout time expires. The Read method returns the number of actually received bytes, so no exception is thrown if not all bytes were received within the timeout. In the previous sample (in Listing 5-10), the timeout was zero, which caused all immediately available bytes to be returned without blocking.

Often, a microcontroller needs to communicate with a measuring instrument to fetch the measuring data over the serial interface. Therefore, the microcontroller requests the measuring results and gets the measured data provided. The measuring device requires some time to handle the request and to provide the data. Listing 5-11 demonstrates how the microcontroller sends a request and waits for the response. If the measuring device does not respond within the timeout time, the application displays an error message in the Debug window of Visual Studio.

Listing 5-11. *Sending a Request and Waiting for an Answer*

```
using System;
using System.Text;
using System.Threading;
using Microsoft.SPOT;
using Microsoft.SPOT.Hardware;

namespace SerialPortWriteReadSample
{
    public class Program
    {
        public static void Main()
        {
            SerialPort.Configuration config =
                    new SerialPort.Configuration(SerialPort.Serial.COM1,
                                                 SerialPort.BaudRate.Baud115200,
                                                 false);
            SerialPort serialPort = new SerialPort(config);
            byte[] outBuffer = Encoding.UTF8.GetBytes("All right?\r\n");
            byte[] inBuffer = new byte[2];
```

```
            while (true)
            {
                Debug.Print("Request data");
                serialPort.Write(outBuffer, 0, outBuffer.Length);
                int count = serialPort.Read(inBuffer, 0, 2, 5000);
                if (count == 2)
                {
                    Debug.Print("Received expected two bytes!");
                }
                else
                {
                    if (count == 0)
                        Debug.Print("No response!");
                    if(count == 1)
                        Debug.Print("Not enough bytes received!");
                }
                Debug.Print(string.Empty);
            }
        }
    }
}
```

Pin Usage and Reservation

This section explains why reserving pins can be helpful in making your application more robust.

Why Reserve Pins?

By reserving CPU pins, you can explicitly control the usage of the pins. By registering a hardware provider, you are able to reserve the required pins for the serial interface and the I²C and SPI busses to detect multiple usage of a pin and to avoid the resulting conflicts. The use of hardware providers is optional, but they provide simple and central management of shared pins.

The HardwareProvider Class

The Microsoft.SPOT.HardwareProvider class supplies information about the pin usage of hardware for serial communications. Serial communication includes not only the RS232 serial port but also the SPI and I²C busses. Please note that even though the HardwareProvider class is introduced in this chapter after the serial interface, it is not unique to the serial port. The HardwareProvider class possesses the methods represented in Listing 5-12.

Listing 5-12. *The Microsoft.SPOT.Hardware.HardwareProvider Class*

```
namespace Microsoft.SPOT.Hardware
{
    public class HardwareProvider
    {
```

```
        public static HardwareProvider HwProvider;

        public HardwareProvider();

        public virtual void GetI2CPins(out Cpu.Pin scl, out Cpu.Pin sda);
        public virtual void GetSerialPins(SerialPort.Serial com, out Cpu.Pin rxPin,
                                           out Cpu.Pin txPin);
        public virtual void GetSpiPins(SPI.SPI_module spi_mod, out Cpu.Pin msk,
                                        out Cpu.Pin miso, out Cpu.Pin mosi);
        public static void Register(HardwareProvider provider);
    }
}
```

A custom hardware provider must inherit from the HardwareProvider class and at least one of the virtual methods GetI2CPins, GetSerialPins, and GetSpiPins should be overwritten. Your custom hardware provider is then registered with the static Register method.

The overwritten methods return the used pin numbers of the underlying hardware. Not all methods must be overwritten. There are default implementations for all methods that return Cpu.Pin.GPIO_NONE.

Custom Hardware Providers

When creating an instance of SerialPort, the CLR checks whether a hardware provider is registered, and if it is, the required pins are determined with the registered hardware provider. These required pins are then reserved with the static ReservePin method of the Microsoft. SPOT.Hardware.Port class. If either a second instance of a serial port with the same COM port or a GPIO port with a pin that is already in use is created, an exception is thrown. When creating objects for addressing the serial port and the I²C and SPI busses, there is no constructor to pass the required pins. You can manage pin sharing in a simple and centralized way with hardware providers.

The sample code in Listing 5-13 shows a custom hardware provider with a custom implementation of the GetSerialPins method, which returns for a certain COM port number the pin numbers for the receipt (RX) and transmission (TX) lines.

Listing 5-13. *A Custom Hardware Provider for the RS232 Serial Port*

```
using System;
using Microsoft.SPOT;
using Microsoft.SPOT.Hardware;

namespace HardwareProviderSample
{
    internal sealed class MyHardwareProvider : HardwareProvider
    {
        public override void GetSerialPins(SerialPort.Serial com,
                                            out Cpu.Pin rxPin,
                                            out Cpu.Pin txPin)
        {
```

```
            switch (com)
            {
                case SerialPort.Serial.COM1:
                    rxPin = Cpu.Pin.GPIO_Pin0;
                    txPin = Cpu.Pin.GPIO_Pin1;
                    break;
                case SerialPort.Serial.COM2:
                    rxPin = Cpu.Pin.GPIO_Pin2;
                    txPin = Cpu.Pin.GPIO_Pin3;
                    break;
                default:
                    rxPin = Cpu.Pin.GPIO_NONE;
                    txPin = Cpu.Pin.GPIO_NONE;
                    break;
            }
        }
    }
}
```

You can register a custom hardware provider with the following line of code:

```
HardwareProvider.Register(new MyHardwareProvider());
```

With the preceding MyHardwareProvider hardware provider shown, the following code would cause a runtime error:

```
SerialPort.Configuration config =
                    new SerialPort.Configuration(SerialPort.Serial.COM1,
                                                 SerialPort.BaudRate.Baud9600,
                                                 false);
SerialPort serialPortA = new SerialPort(config);
SerialPort serialPortB = new SerialPort(config); //will fail
```

If the serialPortA resources were freed with the Dispose method before serialPortB was created, no exception would be thrown. The Dispose method of SerialPort frees the used resources of the serial port and releases the pin reservation.

Let's look at another sample of a pin sharing conflict:

```
SerialPort.Configuration config =
                    new SerialPort.Configuration(SerialPort.Serial.COM1,
                                                 SerialPort.BaudRate.Baud9600,
                                                 false);

SerialPort serialPortA = new SerialPort(config); //reserves Pin 0 und 1 for COM1
OutputPort outputPort = new OutputPort(Cpu.Pin.GPIO_Pin1, false);
```

When creating GPIO ports, the used pins are reserved and released with Dispose again.

Also, pins can be reserved manually with the ReservePin static method of the Port class:

```
Port.ReservePin(Cpu.Pin.GPIO_Pin1, true);
```

Release the reservation like so:

```
Port.ReservePin(Cpu.Pin.GPIO_Pin1, false);
```

The value of the second parameter indicates whether the pin is to be reserved or released.

The I²C Bus

I²C stands for inter-integrated circuit (say "I squared C"). It is used for communication between microcontrollers and hardware modules. I²C is a serial bus, and the original system was developed by Philips Semiconductors at the beginning of the 1980s. In 1992, the first specification came out. Today, the I²C bus is quasi standard.

The I²C bus is special in that it only requires two bidirectional wires and that it can access a network of hardware components. Although it is much slower than most other bus systems, I²C is ideal for peripheral devices because of its low costs. Also, during operation, components can be added to or removed from the bus, which makes the I²C bus useful for pluggable hardware.

It is used frequently for volume controls, analog-to-digital or digital-to-analog converters, real-time clocks, small nonvolatile memory, switches, and multiplexers. Many electronic sensors today already have an AD converter for I²C built in.

Over the first line, called serial data (SDA), the actual data are serially transmitted. The second wire is called serial clock (SCL); it clocks the bus.

The original specification provides a maximum bus speed of 100 kilohertz. Per clock cycle, one bit will transfer. With a 100 kilohertz bus speed, 100 kilobits per second will transfer. Since this may no longer be sufficient for today's applications, the specifications were reworked.

Each I²C module can be selected over a 7-bit address. The eighth bit of the address byte is called the read/write (R/W) bit, and it indicates whether the microcontroller wants to read or write from a module. The data bytes that follow depend on the respective hardware component. Whole bytes will be transferred always, and the most significant bit of a byte is transferred first.

Communication takes place between a master and a slave. Several masters are also possible (multimaster mode), but this will not be described here. The master first sends the start condition. After that, all slaves on the bus will listen and compare their own address with the address on the bus that the master requests. Next, the slave with the right address must send an acknowledgment to the master to confirm that it is present and ready. Now, these two devices can exchange data. After each byte, an acknowledgment will be sent, until the communication is completed and the master sends a stop condition. Once the stop condition is sent, the bus is again ready for other communications. Table 5-1 illustrates the sequence of read access to a hardware component.

Table 5-1. *Read Access*

	Address	Subaddress	R/W Bit		Data	
	Most significant bits	Least significant bits			MSB LSB	
Start condition	0100	XXX	1	Acknowledgment	XXXXXXXX	Stop condition

Some addresses are reserved to keep the bus extendable. The reserved addresses are listed in Table 5-2.

Table 5-2. *Reserved Addresses*

Address	R/W Bit	Reserved For
0000000	0	General calls
0000001	X	CBUS devices
0000010	X	Another bus format
0000011	X	Future extensions
00001XX	X	Future extensions
11111XX	X	Future extensions
11110XX	X	10-bit addressing

After omitting the reserved addresses, 112 free addresses remain that you can use with the 7-bit addressing. The first four bits depend on the respective component type and cannot be changed. The three bits following it are dependent on the component; that is, you can set a unique address as desired at the module (subaddress). In this way, you can connect eight equal components in a bus. The eighth bit (the R/W bit) in the address byte still indicates whether you want to read or write.

Since, over time, more and more I²C components were developed, 10-bit addressing was introduced. This permits up to 1024 (2^{10}) devices at a bus. Reserving the 11110XX addresses and their R/W bits, means that existing 7-bit modules at the bus will not be disturbed as the standard is extended. Table 5-3 illustrates 10-bit addressing. You can even mix up 7- and 10-bit devices at a bus.

Table 5-3. *10-Bit Addressing*

Reserved Address	First Part of Address	R/W Bit		Second Part of Address	
11110	XX	X	Acknowledgment	XXXXXXXX	Acknowledgment

First, the reserved address with the first five reserved bits, 11110, is transmitted. Thus, as already mentioned, there will be no conflict with 7-bit modules. Next, the first two bits of the actual address follow. Then comes the R/W bit. Since, in fact, several participants can react to the first part of the address, each of these participants will send an acknowledgment. After the first acknowledgement, the second part of the address, which consists of eight bits, follows. All participants that acknowledged the first part of the address will examine also the second address byte, but only one component can send an acknowledgement. After the second acknowledgment, the right module is identified, and the actual data exchange can begin.

You can obtain the maximum clock rate of a component from its manual. Communication does not need not to take place with a certain clock rate but should not be faster than what's supported by a device. You can connect and access components with different speeds at a bus.

Accessing I²C Devices with the .NET Micro Framework

Now that you have learned about the architecture and functionality of the I²C bus, you now will learn how to program the bus with the .NET Micro Framework. I²C devices are addressed with the `Microsoft.SPOT.Hardware.I2CDevice` class, represented in Listing 5-14.

Listing 5-14. *The Microsoft.SPOT.Hardware.I2CDevice Class*

```
using System;

namespace Microsoft.SPOT.Hardware
{
    public class I2CDevice
    {
        public I2CDevice.Configuration Config;

        public I2CDevice(I2CDevice.Configuration config);

        public I2CDevice.I2CReadTransaction CreateReadTransaction(byte[] buffer);
        public I2CDevice.I2CWriteTransaction CreateWriteTransaction(byte[] buffer);
        public void Dispose();
        public int Execute(I2CDevice.I2CTransaction[] xActions, int timeout);

        public class Configuration
        {
            public readonly ushort Address;
            public readonly int ClockRateKhz;

            public Configuration(ushort address, int clockRateKhz);
        }

        public sealed class I2CReadTransaction : I2CDevice.I2CTransaction
        {
        }

        public class I2CTransaction
        {
            public readonly byte[] Buffer;

            protected I2CTransaction(byte[] buffer);
        }
```

```
            public sealed class I2CWriteTransaction : I2CDevice.I2CTransaction
            {
            }
        }
    }
}
```

You need to create one instance of the I2CDevice class per peripheral device. An instance of the embedded I2CDevice.Configuration class needs to be passed to the constructor. With the Configuration class, you specify the device address and the communication speed in kilohertz.

Afterward, you need to create transaction objects for read and write access with the CreateReadTransaction and CreateWriteTransaction methods. When creating a transaction, you need to pass a buffer, which holds the data to read or that can be written. An output buffer must, naturally, be filled with data.

After that, you need to provide an array of transactions to the Execute method, and the communication will start. You can mix up read and write transactions in the array passed to the Execute method. The sequence and kind of transactions depend on the respective component that is to be addressed, as the second parameter, a timeout value, in milliseconds, needs to be passed to the method. Execute returns as soon as either all transactions are completed or the timeout has expired. The Execute method returns the total number of the actually transferred bytes (the number sent plus the number received) as a return value. The value Timeout.Infinite or –1 will block the Execute method until all transactions are completed.

The sample code in Listing 5-15 demonstrates how to address a peripheral module with the address 58, send the byte 0xAA to it, and read four bytes. The bus clocking amounts to 100 kilohertz.

Listing 5-15. *Accessing an I²C Device*

```
using System;
using Microsoft.SPOT;
using Microsoft.SPOT.Hardware;

namespace I2CSample
{
    public class Program
    {
        public static void Main()
        {
            I2CDevice.Configuration config =
                            new I2CDevice.Configuration(
                                                        58, //address
                                                        100 //clockrate in KHz
                                                    );
            I2CDevice device = new I2CDevice(config);

            //prepare buffer to write byte AA
            byte[] outBuffer = new byte[] { 0xAA };
            I2CDevice.I2CWriteTransaction writeTransaction =
                            device.CreateWriteTransaction(outBuffer);
```

```
            //prepare buffer to read four bytes
            byte[] inBuffer = new byte[4];
            I2CDevice.I2CReadTransaction readTransaction =
                                    device.CreateReadTransaction(inBuffer);

            //execute both transactions
            I2CDevice.I2CTransaction[] transactions =
                            new I2CDevice.I2CTransaction[] {
                                                    writeTransaction,
                                                    readTransaction
                                                };
            int transferred = device.Execute(
                                        transactions,
                                        100 //timeout in ms
                                    );
            //transferred bytes should be 1 + 4 = 5
        }
    }
}
```

10-Bit Addressing

The sample in Listing 5-16 shows how to address a device with the 10-bit address 129 (in binary, 1000000001), send the byte 0xAA to the device, and then read 4 bytes. For 10-bit addressing, an additional write transaction, as already described, is needed.

Listing 5-16. *10-Bit Addressing*

```
using System;
using Microsoft.SPOT;
using Microsoft.SPOT.Hardware;

namespace I2C10BitAddressSample
{
    public class Class1
    {
        public static void Main()
        {
            //our 10 bit address
            //binary 1000000001 = 129
            const ushort address10Bit = 0x1001;
            //reserved address mask 011110XX for 10 bit addressing
            const byte addressMask = 0x78;

            //first MSB part of address
            //is 7A and contains the two MSB of the 10 bit address
            ushort address1 = addressMask | (address10Bit >> 8);
            I2CDevice.Configuration config = new I2CDevice.Configuration(address1,
                                                                100);
```

```
            I2CDevice device = new I2CDevice(config);

            //second LSB part of address
            byte address2 = (byte)(address10Bit & 0xFF); //the other 8 bits (LSB)
            byte[] address2OutBuffer = new byte[] { address2 };
            I2CDevice.I2CWriteTransaction addressWriteTransaction =
                              device.CreateWriteTransaction(address2OutBuffer);

            //prepare buffer to write data
            byte[] outBuffer = new byte[] { 0xAA };
            I2CDevice.I2CWriteTransaction writeTransaction =
                                   device.CreateWriteTransaction(outBuffer);

            //prepare buffer to read data
            byte[] inBuffer = new byte[4];
            I2CDevice.I2CReadTransaction readTransaction =
                                  device.CreateReadTransaction(inBuffer);

            //execute transactions
            I2CDevice.I2CTransaction[] transactions =
                      new I2CDevice.I2CTransaction[] {
                                                 addressWriteTransaction,
                                                 writeTransaction,
                                                 readTransaction
                                                 };
            device.Execute(transactions, 100);
        }
    }
}
```

■**Note** It would be nice to be able pass a 10-bit address directly when creating an I2CDevice instance and have the .NET Micro Framework runtime build and transmit the additional sequence under the hood. However, since Microsoft's developers are of the opinion that nobody *needs* 10-bit addressing (except in cases with more than 112 devices) and since configuring 10-bit addressing is possible (though not the best option), they did not provide a comfortable way for 10-bit addressing. Therefore, the .NET Micro Framework remains lightweight and free of ballast that the majority of the developers will never require.

A Managed Driver for the TI TMP100 Temperature Sensor

This section shows you how to measure the temperature with the TMP100 temperature sensor from Texas Instruments connected to the I²C bus. This sensor can measure temperatures from –55°C to 125°C. It is possible to wire up to eight TMP100 sensors at an I²C bus. This temperature sensor can measure resolutions from 9 to 12 bits. With 12 bits, the accuracy of the measurement amounts to 0.0625°C. The sensor takes, on average, 320 milliseconds, and maximally

600 milliseconds, to convert a 12-bit temperature value. Thus, the TMP100 can provide the temperature about three times per second in a 12-bit resolution, which allows you to configure for faster conversion time or higher resolution. The sensor supports a one-shot mode, which needs to be triggered by the master and a continuous measurement. Additionally, you can configure a temperature range; exceeding the range causes the sensor to send an alert bit.

■**Tip** You can find the data sheet for the TI TMP100 on the Web at `http://focus.ti.com/lit/ds/symlink/tmp100.pdf`.

In Listing 5-17, you can see how the temperature sensor is configured for a resolution of 12 bits in one-shot mode, how conversion is triggered, and how the result is obtained over the I²C interface. This temperature sensor provides four registers: the temperature register for holding the measurement, the configuration register, and registers for the minimum and maximum temperature alert limits. A single shot is triggered by setting the one-shot/alert bit. If you set the shutdown bit in the configuration register also, the sensor will shut down as soon as the current conversion is completed to reduce current consumption. After you trigger a conversion, you need to wait the maximum conversion time the sensor requires for the temperature conversion. Then, you can read the current from the temperature register. Continuous measurement will not be described here; you can find more about it in the sensor`s data sheet.

To execute the sample in Listing 5-17 on an emulator, you need to build the `I2CTemperatureSensorSampleEmulator` emulator shown in Figure 5-7 (the code to execute it is in the directory for Chapter 13 in this book's source code) so that you can select and use this special emulator with that sample project.

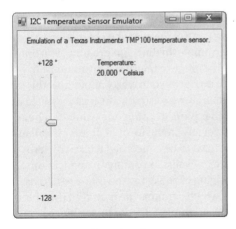

Figure 5-7. *Emulator for the temperature sensor connected to the I²C bus*

The emulator for the TI TMP100 allows you to set the current temperature of the sensor, which can be measured with a track bar control. The emulator even simulates the conversion timing of the sensor; you will obtain a measurement from the emulator component after the maximum conversion time for the resolution. You will learn more about emulating I²C devices in Chapter 13.

Listing 5-17. *Interfacing the Temperature Sensor*

```
using System;
using System.Threading;
using Microsoft.SPOT;

namespace I2CTemperatureSensorSample
{
    public class Program
    {
        private const byte sensorAddress = 72;

        public static void Main()
        {
            TMP100Sensor temperatureSensor = new TMP100Sensor(sensorAddress);
            while (true)
            {
                float temperature = temperatureSensor.Temperature();
                Debug.Print("Temperature: " + temperature.ToString("F4") +
                            " ° Celsius");
                Thread.Sleep(100);
            }
        }
    }
}
```

All hardware-dependent implementation details to control the sensor were hidden in the TMP100Sensor class, so the main program remains rather simple. In the main program, you only need to create an instance of the sensor and call the Temperature method continuously to obtain the current temperature. In the calling code, you do not need to worry about how this is done. Later, if you need to interface another type of temperature sensor for any reason, you just need to replace or modify the sensor-specific class; other parts of your code would not be affected. This approach of interacting with hardware devices in the form of objects is called managed drivers, and it's easy and flexible. You do not have to be concerned with hardware-dependent details and deal with bit patterns and control registers in your main application. Hardware components can be replaced by simply changing or replacing the managed driver.

You can see the TMP100Sensor class in Listing 5-18, which contains the managed driver for interfacing the sensor chip. The class was kept consciously simple, in order to be able to show the triggering of the measurement well. You might make the class still more configurable and add the support for 9-, 10 - and 11-bit accuracy, as well as continuous measurement. In addition, it would be more efficient to create the various arrays that hold the communication data in the constructor to avoid re-creating them for every measurement.

Listing 5-18. *A Managed Driver for the Temperature Sensor*

```
using System;
using System.Threading;
using Microsoft.SPOT;
using Microsoft.SPOT.Hardware;

namespace I2CTemperatureSensorSample
{
    /// <summary>
    /// Managed driver for the TMP100 temperature sensor chip
    /// from Texas Instruments on the I2C bus.
    /// </summary>
    public class TMP100Sensor
    {
        #region constants
        private const byte clockRateKHz = 59;

        private const byte REGISTER_Control = 0x01; //command to configure sensor
        private const byte REGISTER_Temperature = 0x00; //command to request result

        private const byte CONTROL_EnergyModeShutdown = 0x01;
        private const byte CONTROL_DataLengthTwelveBits = 0x60;
        private const byte CONTROL_OneShot = 0x80;

        //ms The maximum time needed by the sensor to convert 12 bits
        private const int conversionTime = 600;

        private const int transactionTimeout = 1000; //ms
        #endregion

        private readonly byte address;
        private readonly I2CDevice device;

        public TMP100Sensor(byte address)
        {
            this.address = address;
            I2CDevice.Configuration config =
                                        new I2CDevice.Configuration(address,
                                                                    clockRateKHz);
            this.device = new I2CDevice(config);
        }

        public float Temperature()
        {
            //write to one shot bit in control register to trigger measurement,
            //that means telling the sensor to capture the data.
```

```
    byte controlByte = CONTROL_OneShot |
                       CONTROL_DataLengthTwelveBits |
                       CONTROL_EnergyModeShutdown;
    byte[] captureData = new byte[] { REGISTER_Control, controlByte };
    WriteToDevice(captureData);

    //the conversion time is the maximum time
    //it takes the sensor to convert a physical reading to bits
    Thread.Sleep(conversionTime);

    //prepare the control byte to tell the sensor to send
    //the temperature register
    byte[] temperatureData = new byte[] { REGISTER_Temperature };
    WriteToDevice(temperatureData);

    //prepare the array of bytes that will hold the result
    //comming back from the sensor
    byte[] inputData = new byte[2];
    ReadFromDevice(inputData);

    //get raw temperature register
    short rawTemperature = (short)((inputData[0] << 8) | inputData[1]);
    //convert raw temperature register to Celsius degrees
    //the highest 12 Bits of the 16 Bit-Signed-Integer (short) are used
    //one digit is 0.0625 ° Celsius, divide by 16 to shift right 4 Bits
    //this results in a division by 256
    float temperature = rawTemperature * (1 / 256.0f);
    return temperature;
}

private void WriteToDevice(byte[] outputData)
{
    //create an I2C write transaction to be sent to the temperature sensor
    I2CDevice.I2CTransaction writeXAction =
                            device.CreateWriteTransaction(outputData);

    //the I2C data is sent here to the temperature sensor
    int transferred =
        this.device.Execute(new I2CDevice.I2CTransaction[] { writeXAction },
                        transactionTimeout);

    //make sure the data was sent
    if (transferred != outputData.Length)
        throw new Exception("Could not write to device.");
}
```

```
    private void ReadFromDevice(byte[] inputData)
    {
        //prepare a I2C read transaction to be read from the temperature sensor
        I2CDevice.I2CTransaction readXAction =
                                device.CreateReadTransaction(inputData);

        //the I2C data is received here from the temperature sensor
        int transferred =
            this.device.Execute(new I2CDevice.I2CTransaction[] { readXAction },
                        transactionTimeout);

        //make sure the data was received
        if (transferred != inputData.Length)
            throw new Exception("Could not read from device.");
    }

    public byte Address
    {
        get { return this.address; }
    }
  }
}
```

Hardware Providers for I²C

Also, for the I²C-bus, you can implement and register a device-specific custom hardware provider. The hardware provider will reserve both pins—SCL and SDA—needed for the bus to prevent other code from using them. To get this, you need to override the GetI2CPins virtual method so that it returns the pin numbers of the two lines:

```
public override void GetI2CPins(out Cpu.Pin scl, out Cpu.Pin sda)
{
    scl = Cpu.Pin.GPIO_PIN10;
    sda = Cpu.Pin.GPIO_PIN12;
}
```

The SPI Bus

Serial peripheral interface (SPI) is, like I²C, a serial bus system for interfacing peripheral components, and it was introduced by Motorola. SPI is not standardized completely. You can configure, for example, whether data is obtained at the rising or falling edge. In addition, you are able to select the idle state of the clock line and other timing settings, thus SPI is very flexible.

Motorola developed SPI further to queued serial peripheral interface (QSPI). QSPI uses a kind of queue to send and receive data and is backward compatible with SPI.

■**Note** A bus system similar to SPI was developed by National Semiconductor and is called Microwire. Microwire's components can be accessed and configured in ways that are similar to SPI. And, like SPI, it's been extended; National calls its Microwire extension simply MicrowirePLUS. MicrowirePLUS is capable of higher clock rates.

SPI requires three wires, unlike the I²C bus. One line is for clocking; one is for an input data line, and one an output data line. Thus SPI is full duplex.

These are the three bus lines:

- Serial data out (SDO), also called master out/slave in (MOSI)

- Serial data in (SDI), also called master in/slave out (MISO)

- Serial clock line (SCKL)

There is no addressing, as with the I²C bus. Each chip must be connected to the microcontroller via an individual GPIO pin. Using this line, the microcontroller signals with which device it would like to communicate. This signal is called slave select/chip select (SS/CS) or slave transmit enable (STE). The microcontroller functions as the master and provides the clock signal. The connected modules are the slaves. One bit will transfer per bus clock cycle. The transmission is done after the master sets the level of the chip select signal to the original state.

Accessing SPI Devices with the .NET Micro Framework

Now that you know how the SPI bus works, you're ready to learn how to program SPI devices with the .NET Micro Framework. SPI devices are represented by the Microsoft.SPOT.Hardware. SPI class (see Listing 5-19).

Listing 5-19. *The Microsoft.SPOT.Hardware.SPI Class*

```
using System;

namespace Microsoft.SPOT.Hardware
{
    public sealed class SPI : IDisposable
    {
        public SPI(SPI.Configuration config);

        public SPI.Configuration Config { get; set; }

        public void Dispose();
        public void Write(byte[] writeBuffer);
        public void Write(ushort[] writeBuffer);
        public void WriteRead(byte[] writeBuffer, byte[] readBuffer);
        public void WriteRead(ushort[] writeBuffer, ushort[] readBuffer);
        public void WriteRead(byte[] writeBuffer, byte[] readBuffer,
                              int readOffset);
```

```
public void WriteRead(ushort[] writeBuffer, ushort[] readBuffer,
                      int readOffset);

public enum SPI_module
{
    SPI1 = 0,
    SPI2 = 1,
    SPI3 = 2,
    SPI4 = 3,
}

public class Configuration
{
    public readonly Cpu.Pin ChipSelect_Port;
    public readonly bool ChipSelect_ActiveState;
    public readonly uint ChipSelect_SetupTime;
    public readonly uint ChipSelect_HoldTime;
    public readonly bool Clock_IdleState;
    public readonly bool Clock_Edge;
    public readonly uint Clock_RateKHz;
    public readonly SPI.SPI_module SPI_mod;

    public Configuration(Cpu.Pin ChipSelect_Port,
                         bool ChipSelect_ActiveState,
                         uint ChipSelect_SetupTime,
                         uint ChipSelect_HoldTime,
                         bool Clock_IdleState,
                         bool Clock_Edge,
                         uint Clock_RateKHz,
                         SPI.SPI_module SPI_mod);
    }
  }
}
```

For each SPI device, you need to create an instance of the SPI class. When creating an instance, you have to provide an instance of the inner class SPI.Configuration to the constructor. The Configuration class holds the configuration information, such as the GPIO pin serving as the chip select as well as the other configuration parameters for communication with the SPI component. All parameters are passed to the constructor of Configuration. Please see your SPI component's data sheet for all the configuration parameters. The following parameters can be configured and provided to the constructor of the Configuration class:

- Cpu.Pin ChipSelect_Port: This is the GPIO pin to use as the chip select for your component.

- bool ChipSelect_ActiveState: This is the state of the chip select that will choose and activate a device. With true, the chip select signal will be set to high for selecting a device. With false, the chip select will be set to low.

- uint ChipSelect_SetupTime: This parameter specifies the time, in milliseconds, that the system will wait after selecting the chip before clocking and data transfer will start.

- uint ChipSelect_HoldTime: This parameter specifies the amount of time, in milliseconds, that a chip should remain selected after data transfer.

- bool Clock_IdleState: This parameter indicates the chip's idle state; that is, it specifies whether the serial clock line (SCKL) should be set to high or low when a chip is not selected. The value true means the clock line will be set to high; otherwise, it will be set to low.

- bool Clock_Edge: This parameter describes whether data is obtained at the rising or falling edge of the serial clock line. The value true causes data to be taken at the rising edge of the clock signal; otherwise, it's taken at the falling edge.

- uint Clock_RateKHz: This is the clock rate in kilohertz.

- SPI.SPI_module SPI_mod: A device may have more than one SPI bus. This parameter lets you select the bus you want to use.

An example for an SPI configuration could look like the following:

```
SPI.Configuration config = new SPI.Configuration(
                chipSelectPin, //chip select port
                false,         //IC is accessed when chip select is low
                1,             //setup time 1 ms
                1,             //hold chip select 1 ms after transfer
                true,          //clock line is high if device is not selected
                false,         //data is sampled at falling edge of clock
                15000,         //clockrate is 15 MHz
                SPI.SPI_module //use first SPI bus
                                     );
SPI spi = new SPI(config);
```

After you have created an instance of the SPI class, the data communication can take place with both the Write and WriteRead methods. The chip select pin is automatically handled by the system. You do not need to set a GPIO port manually. There are several overloads for Write and WriteRead to provide data in the form of arrays with bytes or 16-bit values.

With the following code snippet, you can transmit a 16-bit command to a chip and read one 16-bit result value afterward:

```
ushort writeBuffer = new ushort[1] = 0xAAAA;
ushort readBuffer = new ushort[1];
spi.WriteRead(writeBuffer, readBuffer);
```

A Managed Driver for the AD124S101 AD Converter

In this section, you will learn how to measure input voltage with the four-channel 12-bit analog-to-digital converter AD124S101 from National Semiconductor at the SPI bus.

The maximum measurable voltage depends on the voltage that is supplied for the chip; the measurable range is from 0 volts to the supply voltage.

To accomplish a measurement, you need to send the number of the desired AD channel in the form of a 16-bit value to the AD converter, and you will receive the measured voltage with 12-bit resolution coded in a 16-byte value. The smallest measurable unit is 1/4096 of the supply voltage. To keep it simple, the sample in Listing 5-20 shows how to obtain the voltage from the first AD channel.

■**Tip** You can find the data sheet for the AD124S101 on the Web at www.national.com/ds/DC/ ADC124S101.pdf.

To execute the SPI sample in Listing 5-20 on an emulator, you need to select the emulator of the SpiAdConverterSampleEmulator project, which is shown in Figure 5-8 (the code to execute the emulator is in the directory for Chapter 13 in this book's source code). This emulator allows you to change the measurable voltage for the first channel of the AD converter via a track bar.

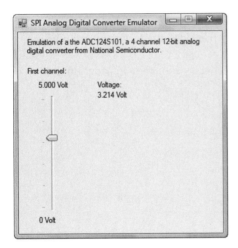

Figure 5-8. *Emulator for an AD converter at the SPI bus*

Listing 5-20. *Interfacing an AD Converter at the SPI Bus*

```
using System.Threading;
using Microsoft.SPOT;
using Microsoft.SPOT.Hardware;

namespace SpiAdConverterSample
{
    public class Program
    {
        public static void Main()
        {
```

```
            ADC124S101 adc = new ADC124S101(Cpu.Pin.GPIO_Pin10, //chip select port
                                            5,                  //supply voltage
                                            15000,              //clock rate in KHz
                                            SPI.SPI_module.SPI1 //first SPI bus
                                            );
            while (true)
            {
                float voltage = adc.GetVoltage(ADC124S101.AdcChannel.ADC1);
                Debug.Print("ADC1: " + voltage.ToString("F3") + " Volt");
                Thread.Sleep(10); //give emulator time to react to Visual Studio
            }
        }
    }
}
```

Listing 5-20 shows the main program and the main loop to read from the AD converter. All details for accessing the AD converter were hidden in a managed driver. In the main program, you just need to create an instance of the driver class, and you can obtain the voltage with GetVoltage by specifying the desired channel. If you need to replace the AD converter with another model, you just have to adapt or replace the driver class; the rest of your application does not need to be changed.

Listing 5-21 shows the ADC124S101 managed driver class with code to program the AD converter.

Listing 5-21. *Managed Driver for the AD Converter*

```
using System;
using Microsoft.SPOT;
using Microsoft.SPOT.Hardware;

namespace SpiAdConverterSample
{
    /// <summary>
    /// Managed driver for a 4 channel 12-bit analog digital converter
    /// from National Semiconductor.
    /// </summary>
    public sealed class ADC124S101
    {
        public enum AdcChannel {ADC1, ADC2, ADC3, ADC4};

        private readonly Cpu.Pin chipSelectPin;
        //the maximum input voltage depends on supply voltage,
        //so the supply voltage is needed to calculate the measured voltage
        private readonly float supplyVoltage;
        private readonly SPI spi;
        private readonly ushort[] writeBuffer = new ushort[1];
        private readonly ushort[] readBuffer = new ushort[1];
```

```
public ADC124S101(Cpu.Pin chipSelectPin,
                  float supplyVoltage,
                  uint clockRateKHz,
                  SPI.SPI_module spiModule)
{
    if (chipSelectPin == Cpu.Pin.GPIO_NONE)
        throw new ArgumentOutOfRangeException("chipSelectPin");
    if (supplyVoltage <= 0.0f)
        throw new ArgumentOutOfRangeException("supplyVoltage");
    this.chipSelectPin = chipSelectPin;
    this.supplyVoltage = supplyVoltage;

    SPI.Configuration config =
        new SPI.Configuration
                        (
                         chipSelectPin, //chip select port
                         false, //IC is accessed when chip select is low
                         1, //setup time 1 ms, is actually min 10 ns
                         1, //hold chip select 1 ms after transfer
                         true, //clock line is high if device is not selected
                         false, //data is sampled at falling edge of clock
                         clockRateKHz, //possible 10000 - 20000 KHz
                         spiModule //select SPI bus
                        );
    this.spi = new SPI(config);
}

public float GetVoltage(AdcChannel channel)
{
    this.writeBuffer[0] = (ushort)channel; //select ADC channel
    this.readBuffer[0] = 0; //reset buffer for safety
    //trigger conversion and read result
    spi.WriteRead(writeBuffer, readBuffer);
    //raw value is 12 Bit the 4 most significant bits of the ushort are zero
    ushort rawValue = readBuffer[0];
    //smallest change is 1/4096 of supply voltage
    return rawValue / 4096.0f * this.supplyVoltage;
}

public Cpu.Pin ChipSelectPin
{
    get { return this.chipSelectPin; }
}
```

```
        public float SupplyVoltage
        {
            get { return this.supplyVoltage; }
        }
    }
}
```

Hardware Providers for SPI

Also, for the SPI bus, you can implement and register a hardware provider for your platform so that the three pins necessary for the bus can be reserved and thus excluded from other usage. To do so, the virtual GetSpiPins method must be overwritten and must deliver the pin numbers of the three pins for the indicated SPI bus.

```
public override void GetSpiPins(SPI.SPI_module spi_mod,
                                out Cpu.Pin msk,
                                out Cpu.Pin miso,
                                out Cpu.Pin mosi)
{
    msk = Cpu.Pin.GPIO_Pin10;
    miso = Cpu.Pin.GPIO_Pin11;
    mosi = Cpu.Pin.GPIO_Pin12;
}
```

Here are the names of the wires:

- msk is the serial clock line.

- miso is the master in/slave out line.

- mosi is the master out/slave in line.

Other Hardware

Though the .NET Micro Framework lacks direct support for pulse-width modulation (PWM), file systems, and USB devices, you can use these features anyway, as explained in this section.

PWM

Some .NET Micro Framework modules have on-board pulse-width modulators. But currently, PWM can be used on only these few modules through special integration by device vendors. In addition, using PWM requires native and managed drivers on your platform.

Devices that support PWM through proprietary libraries include the Meridian CPU from Device Solutions, Embedded Master Module from GHI Electronics, and Embedded Development Kit (EDK) from SJJ Embedded Micro Solutions. These devices are described in greater detail in Chapter 2.

Mass Storage Devices with a File System

There is no built-in file system support with the .NET Micro Framework, but the GHI Electronics
Embedded Master Module (see Chapter 2) is the first and only .NET Micro Framework OEM
device that adds file allocation table (FAT) file system support (through a subset of the System.IO
classes). This lets managed code access files on SD/MMC cards and on USB memory devices,
such as hard drives and thumb drives.

GHI Electronics also has a product called uALFAT, which is an extension module to hold
flash memory with a FAT file system that is programmable via a serial port, SPI, or I²C. The
OEM module is available with either an SD (for SD cards) or USB (for USB dongles) connector.
Theoretically, writing a managed driver for the uALFAT component, so that you can use a FAT
file system for a .NET Micro Framework device, could be possible (though I haven't tried it).

USB

Currently, the .NET Micro Framework lacks USB support, and no USB stack has been implemented in version 2.5. Even if a device has a USB connection, it is used only for debugging and
deploying a .NET Micro Framework application.

Serial communication with other devices can take place over the RS232 serial port with an
RS232-serial-to-USB adapter or wirelessly via Wireless LAN, Bluetooth, or ZigBee as described
in Chapter 7.

The Embedded Master Module (see Chapter 2) is the first and only .NET Micro Framework
OEM device that has USB host capabilities. With its embedded USB host and device stacks,
USB devices (mice, keyboards, joysticks, printers, Bluetooth dongles, and more) can be used
with managed code.

Obtaining Power Supply and Charging State Information

The Battery class that resides in the Microsoft.SPOT.Hardware namespace provides methods
for obtaining information about your device's power supply and state of charge. The class is
presented in Listing 5-22 and contains only static methods; you do not need to create an instance
of it to use the methods.

■**Note** The Battery class of the .NET Micro Framework's base class library should be declared as static,
because it does not contain any instance members. This is, however, not the case, and you are able to create
an instance of the class. Probably Microsoft simply forgot to mark the class as static.

The StateOfCharge method returns the state of charge of the accumulator or battery cell as
a percentage. StateOfCharge is a method, like ReadVoltage, ReadTemperature, OnCharger, and
IsFullyCharged, and not a property, as you might expect.

■**Note** A rule from Microsoft's *Design Guidelines* for developing class libraries says that a property must always supply the same value for successive calls. This is not the case with the charging state, which changes constantly. Implementing StateOfCharge as a method was to clarify that calling the method twice might not return the same value. However, Microsoft does not always adhere to this rule, as you can see with System.DateTime.Now, which returns the current time. This property has existed, however, since the first version of the .NET Framework, when this rule did not exist yet. For backward compatibility reasons, the rule will not be changed again. Now, enough details about the *Design Guidelines*.

The ReadVoltage method returns the voltage in millivolts in the form of an integer.

The ReadTemperature method returns the current temperature of the accumulator pack or the battery cell. The method provides the temperature in degrees Celsius multiplied by ten. Thus the temperature's smallest unit is a tenth of a degree, without having to use a more complex floating point number.

IsFullyCharged returns true when the accumulator is properly loaded; "properly loaded" does not mean that the accumulator must be loaded to 100 percent, only that it supplies sufficient energy, starting from 40 percent of the loading capacity. If IsFullyCharged supplies the value false, the application should introduce energy-saving operations.

The OnCharger method indicates whether the equipment is connected to a battery charger.

Using the WaitForEvent method, you can let your application wait for a change in the charging state. The method expects the maximum time in milliseconds that is to be waited. The method returns as soon as either the charging state changes or the timeout time expires. The return value signals whether a change occurred or the time expired. If the value true is returned, the charging state has changed. If you specify the value System.Threading.Timeout.Infinite for the timeout parameter, the method blocks until the charging state changes.

Listing 5-22. *The Microsoft.SPOT.Hardware.Battery Class*

```
using System;

namespace Microsoft.SPOT.Hardware
{
    public sealed class Battery
    {
        public Battery();

        public static Battery.ChargerModel GetChargerModel();
        public static bool IsFullyCharged();
        public static bool OnCharger();
        public static int ReadTemperature();
        public static int ReadVoltage();
        public static int StateOfCharge();
        public static bool WaitForEvent(int timeout);
```

```
        public sealed class ChargerModel
        {
            public readonly int Charge_Full;
            public readonly int Charge_FullMin;
            public readonly int Charge_Hysteresis;
            public readonly int Charge_Low;
            public readonly int Charge_Medium;
            public readonly int Charge_Min;
            public readonly TimeSpan Timeout_Backlight;
            public readonly TimeSpan Timeout_Charged;
            public readonly TimeSpan Timeout_Charger;
            public readonly TimeSpan Timeout_Charging;
        }
    }
}
```

The GetChargerModel method supplies an instance of the Battery.ChargerModel class. This class contains information about the loading behavior of the accumulator.

The .NET Micro Framework application in Listing 5-23 prints all available information for the power supply of a device. It can be executed also on the standard .NET Micro Framework emulator or on the BatterySampleEmulator custom emulator (the code to execute the emulator is in the directory for Chapter 13 in this book's source code). The special BatterySampleEmulator emulator uses no graphical user interface and just prints the charging configuration, which you can specify in the configuration file for the emulator.

Listing 5-23. *Printing the Charge State and Other Charging Information*

```
using System;
using Microsoft.SPOT;
using Microsoft.SPOT.Hardware;
using System.Threading;

namespace BatterySample
{
    public class Program
    {
        public static void Main()
        {
            PrintBatteryInfo();
            PrintChargerModel();
            while (true)
            {
                if (Battery.WaitForEvent(Timeout.Infinite))
                    PrintBatteryInfo();
            }
        }
```

```csharp
private static void PrintBatteryInfo()
{
    Debug.Print("*** Battery Info ***");
    Debug.Print("State of Charge: " + Battery.StateOfCharge() + "%");
    Debug.Print("Is fully charged: " +
                (Battery.IsFullyCharged() ? "Yes" : "No"));
    float voltageVolt = Battery.ReadVoltage() / 1000.0f;
    Debug.Print("Voltage: " + voltageVolt.ToString("F3") + " Volt");
    float degreesCelsius = Battery.ReadTemperature() / 10.0f;
    Debug.Print("Temperature: " + degreesCelsius.ToString("F1") +
                "° Celsius");
    Debug.Print("On Charger: " + (Battery.OnCharger() ? "Yes" : "No"));
}

private static void PrintChargerModel()
{
    Battery.ChargerModel chargerModel = Battery.GetChargerModel();

    Debug.Print("*** Charger Model ***");
    Debug.Print("Charge Min: " + chargerModel.Charge_Min + "%");
    Debug.Print("Charge Low: " + chargerModel.Charge_Low + "%");
    Debug.Print("Charge Medium: " + chargerModel.Charge_Medium + "%");
    Debug.Print("Charge Full Min: " + chargerModel.Charge_FullMin + "%");
    Debug.Print("Charge Full: " + chargerModel.Charge_Full + "%");
    Debug.Print("Charge Hysteresis: " + chargerModel.Charge_Hysteresis +
                " ms");
    float timeoutChargingMinutes = chargerModel.Timeout_Charging.Ticks /
                                   (float)TimeSpan.TicksPerMinute;
    Debug.Print("Timeout Charging: " +
                timeoutChargingMinutes.ToString("F0") + " min");
    float timeoutChargedMinutes = chargerModel.Timeout_Charged.Ticks /
                                  (float)TimeSpan.TicksPerMinute;
    Debug.Print("Timeout Charged: " + timeoutChargedMinutes.ToString("F0") +
                " min");
    float timeoutChargerSec = chargerModel.Timeout_Charger.Ticks /
                              (float)TimeSpan.TicksPerSecond;
    Debug.Print("Timeout Charger: " + chargerModel.Timeout_Charger.Seconds +
                " sec");
    float timeoutBacklightSec = chargerModel.Timeout_Backlight.Ticks /
                                (float)TimeSpan.TicksPerSecond;
    Debug.Print("Timeout Backlight: " + timeoutBacklightSec.ToString("F0") +
                " sec");
    }
  }
}
```

When running the application in Listing 5-23 on the `BatterySampleEmulator` emulator, the following output will be produced:

```
*** Battery Info ***
State of Charge: 35%
Is fully charged: Yes
Voltage: 5.123 Volt
Temperature: 23.4° Celsius
On Charger: Yes
*** Charger Model ***
Charge Min: 10%
Charge Low: 20%
Charge Medium: 30%
Charge Full Min: 60%
Charge Full: 98%
Charge Hysteresis: 6 ms
Timeout Charging: 30 min
Timeout Charged: 10 min
Timeout Charger: 5 sec
Timeout Backlight: 5 sec
```

Obtaining Processor Speed Information

The `Microsoft.SPOT.Hardware.Cpu` class contains the internal `Pin` class for specifying pin numbers for GPIO ports, serial ports, and the I²C and SPI busses. In addition, it contains three further static properties: `SystemClock`, `SlowClock`, and `GlitchFilterTime`. The `SystemClock` property provides the clock rate of the system clock, and thus the speed of the processor's clock in Hertz.

The `SlowClock` property returns the clock rate of a slower but more accurate timer than the system clock in Hertz. `SlowClock` does not have anything to do with slowing the clock's rate when in energy-saving mode. `SlowClock` is used for controlling the timing of GPIO ports.

Both `SystemClock` and `SlowClock` are read-only properties.

Finally, the class `Cpu` allows you use the `GlitchFilterTime` property to specify the time within which input GPIO ports will be debounced. The value 0 means that the filter is deactivated. Details are described in this chapter's `InputPort` class section.

The members of the `Cpu` class are presented in Listing 5-24.

Listing 5-24. *The Microsoft.SPOT.Hardware.Cpu Class*

```
namespace Microsoft.SPOT.Hardware
{
    public static class Cpu
    {
        public static TimeSpan GlitchFilterTime { get; set; }
        public static uint SlowClock { get; }
        public static uint SystemClock { get; }
```

```
        public enum Pin
        {
            GPIO_NONE = -1,
            GPIO_Pin0 = 0,
            ...
            GPIO_Pin15 = 15
        }
    }
}
```

Listing 5-25 demonstrates how to use the Cpu class. First, the time for the glitch filter is set to 100 milliseconds. Next, the information about processor speed and the glitch filter are printed.

■**Tip** With the TimingServicesSampleEmulator emulator, you can change the processor speed in the configuration file. You will learn more about configuring an emulator in Chapter 13, which covers hardware emulator components.

Listing 5-25. *Using the Cpu Class*

```
using System;
using Microsoft.SPOT;
using Microsoft.SPOT.Hardware;

namespace CpuSample
{
    public class Program
    {
        public static void Main()
        {
            Cpu.GlitchFilterTime = new TimeSpan(0, 0, 0, 0, 100); //100 ms

            float systemClock = Cpu.SystemClock / 1000000.0f;
            Debug.Print("System Clock: " + systemClock.ToString("F6") + " MHz");
            float slowClock = Cpu.SlowClock / 1000000.0f;
            Debug.Print("Slow Clock: " + slowClock.ToString("F6") + " MHz");
            float glitchFilterTimeMs = Cpu.GlitchFilterTime.Ticks /
                                    (float)TimeSpan.TicksPerMillisecond;
            Debug.Print("Glitch Filter Time: " + glitchFilterTimeMs.ToString("F1") +
                        " ms");
        }
    }
}
```

Running Listing 5-25 on an emulator will give you the following results:

```
System Clock: 27.000000 MHz
Slow Clock: 0.000000 MHz
Glitch Filter Time: 100.0 ms
```

On the other hand, the Digi Connect ME hardware prints the following:

```
System Clock: 55.296000 MHz
Slow Clock: 0.001000 MHz
Glitch Filter Time: 100.0 ms
```

System Identification

You might require an application to run on various .NET Micro Framework hardware platforms. In certain parts of your application, you may need to run special hardware-dependent code. One way you can achieve this is by conditionally compiling with #if, #else, and #endif. If you take this approach, you need to recompile your application for each platform separately. Another option is to determine, at runtime, on which platform the application runs and decide then which code to execute.

Information about the platform at runtime can be determined with the Microsoft.SPOT.Hardware.SystemID class. Listing 5-26 shows the members of this class. You can find the class in the Microsoft.SPOT.Hardware namespace. However, unlike the hardware classes in the namespace that were already discussed, Microsoft.SPOT.Hardware.SystemID is not in the Microsoft.SPOT.Hardware.dll assembly. Instead, it's in the Microsoft.SPOT.Native.dll assembly. The class is defined as static and possesses only static properties. The properties provide information not in string form but as integer IDs. Each manufacturer and each hardware model has a unique number assigned.

Listing 5-26. *The Microsoft.SPOT.Hardware.SystemID Class*

```
namespace Microsoft.SPOT.Hardware
{
    public static class SystemID
    {
        public static byte Model { get; }
        public static byte OEM { get; }
        public static ushort SKU { get; }
    }
}
```

The application in Listing 5-27 prints all available system information.

Listing 5-27. *Printing System Information*

```
using System;
using Microsoft.SPOT;
using Microsoft.SPOT.Hardware;

namespace SystemIdentificationSample
{
    public class Program
    {
        public static void Main()
        {
            Debug.Print("Model: " + SystemID.Model);
            Debug.Print("Original Equipment Manufacturer (OEM): " +
                        SystemID.OEM);
            Debug.Print("Stock Keeping Unit (SKU): " + SystemID.SKU);
        }
    }
}
```

If you run Listing 5-27 on an emulator, you will get the following output:

```
Model: 2
Original Equipment Manufacturer (OEM): 1
Stock Keeping Unit (SKU): 3
```

On the other hand, with the Digi Connect ME hardware, you will get the following output:

```
Model: 0
Original Equipment Manufacturer (OEM): 255
Stock Keeping Unit (SKU): 65535
```

Summary

This chapter covered various aspects of hardware communications. Now, you know how to read and write GPIO ports and how to use interrupt and tristate ports. This chapter described how to use serial communications with the RS232 serial port. You also learned how to write managed drivers to interface with I²C and SPI hardware components. Finally, you learned how to obtain information about *your* platform.

The next chapter covers Ethernet networking and describes how you can establish connections to other network nodes to communicate with other devices.

CHAPTER 6

■■■

Networking

This chapter explores the possibilities that the .NET Micro Framework provides for programming network-enabled applications that communicate with other devices over an Ethernet network. This enables you to write Internet, local area network (LAN), and wireless local area network (WLAN) communication applications using one set of classes.

First, we will explore how to use sockets to make and accept connections and exchange data over the network. You will learn what clients and servers are and how they come together for data exchange with the Transmission Control Protocol (TCP)/Internet Protocol (IP) or User Datagram Protocol (UDP).

The second half of this chapter covers Web Services for devices. The Device Profile for Web Services (DPWS) describes a standard for finding and communicating with devices in a network. The DPWS specification defines a subset of the Web Services specification but adds a mechanism so clients can easily discover devices. You will learn how to write discoverable device applications that provide services to other communication partners and also how to discover other devices and consume their services. We'll look at the following DPWS topics:

- Architecture of the DPWS stack

- Discovering devices

- Describing devices and exchanging metadata

- Controlling devices

- Eventing

- Handling faults

- Messaging with SOAP

Although it is included with the .NET Micro Framework 2.5 SDK release, the implementation of the DPWS stack is still in beta release. Therefore, some minor breaking changes could arrive with subsequent SDK versions. The DPWS libraries are not installed by default with the .NET Micro Framework SDK. When installing the SDK, you need to choose either the Install All option or Custom Installation option with DPWS selected.

> **Note** I recommend you read the release notes (`Micro Framework Release Notes.txt`) in the .NET Micro Framework SDK installation directory. This document describes several network-related issues and resolutions for them.

Sockets

Programming applications that access a network was originally a complicated affair, but with the .NET Framework, this is no longer the case. The .NET Framework provides classes that substantially simplify complex network programming. These classes are in the `System.Net` and `System.Net.Sockets` namespaces in the `System.dll` assembly.

The most important class for network programming is `System.Net.Sockets.Socket`. The Socket class abstracts and implements the Socket API and/or Berkeley socket interface standard. The Socket API was developed at the beginning of the 1980s at the University of California, Berkeley for Berkeley Software Distribution (BSD) UNIX.

A socket is an endpoint of a connection. With sockets, you can read and send data to and from a network on both the client and server sides. To send or receive data from a socket, you need to know the IP address of the other communication partner (endpoint) and one agreed-upon port number, which can vary depending on application purposes. A client application, thus, must know the IP address of the server and connect with that server on a particular port. The server listens on the agreed port or ports and accepts incoming connections from one or more clients.

The Socket Class

Naturally, the Socket class (see Listing 6-1) in the .NET Micro Framework does not provide the complete functionality of the full .NET Framework; for example, the methods for asynchronous data exchange were omitted. However, it does have a considerable number of members.

Listing 6-1. *The System.Net.Sockets.Socket Class*

```
namespace System.Net.Sockets
{
    public class Socket : IDisposable
    {
        public Socket(AddressFamily addressFamily, SocketType socketType,
                    ProtocolType protocolType);

        public int Available { get; }
        public EndPoint LocalEndPoint { get; }
        public EndPoint RemoteEndPoint { get; }

        public Socket Accept();
        public void Bind(EndPoint localEP);
        public void Close();
        public void Connect(EndPoint remoteEP);
```

```
        protected virtual void Dispose(bool disposing);
        public object GetSocketOption(SocketOptionLevel optionLevel,
                               SocketOptionName optionName);
        public void GetSocketOption(SocketOptionLevel optionLevel,
                               SocketOptionName optionName,
                               byte[] val);
        public void Listen(int backlog);
        public bool Poll(int microSeconds, SelectMode mode);
        public int Receive(byte[] buffer);
        public int Receive(byte[] buffer, SocketFlags socketFlags);
        public int Receive(byte[] buffer, int size, SocketFlags socketFlags);
        public int Receive(byte[] buffer, int offset, int size,
                        SocketFlags socketFlags);
        public int ReceiveFrom(byte[] buffer, ref EndPoint remoteEP);
        public int ReceiveFrom(byte[] buffer, SocketFlags socketFlags,
                           ref EndPoint remoteEP);
        public int ReceiveFrom(byte[] buffer, int size, SocketFlags socketFlags,
                           ref EndPoint remoteEP);
        public int ReceiveFrom(byte[] buffer, int offset, int size,
                           SocketFlags socketFlags, ref EndPoint remoteEP);
        public int Send(byte[] buffer);
        public int Send(byte[] buffer, SocketFlags socketFlags);
        public int Send(byte[] buffer, int size, SocketFlags socketFlags);
        public int Send(byte[] buffer, int offset, int size,
                     SocketFlags socketFlags);
        public int SendTo(byte[] buffer, EndPoint remoteEP);
        public int SendTo(byte[] buffer, SocketFlags socketFlags,
                       EndPoint remoteEP);
        public int SendTo(byte[] buffer, int size, SocketFlags socketFlags,
                       EndPoint remoteEP);
        public int SendTo(byte[] buffer, int offset, int size,
                        SocketFlags socketFlags, EndPoint remoteEP);
        public void SetSocketOption(SocketOptionLevel optionLevel,
                               SocketOptionName optionName, bool optionValue);
        public void SetSocketOption(SocketOptionLevel optionLevel,
                               SocketOptionName optionName,
                               byte[] optionValue);
        public void SetSocketOption(SocketOptionLevel optionLevel,
                               SocketOptionName optionName, int optionValue);
    }
}
```

In order to instantiate a socket, you need to pass three arguments to the constructor.

The first parameter is addressFamily; it is of the AddressFamily type and describes the scheme to resolve addresses. Socket applications for the Internet or LAN need to use InterNetwork. The AddressFamily.InterNetwork value indicates that an IP version 4 address is expected when the socket connects to an endpoint. The present release of the .NET Micro Framework does not support IP version 6 addresses.

The socketType parameter of the SocketType type indicates the type of the sockets, and probably the most common socket type is Stream, which supports reliable two-way and connection-based data streams. The other possible value is Dgram for connectionless data transmission, which is unreliable but faster.

The protocolType parameter specifies the low-level protocol that the socket will use for communication. Possible values are Tcp and Udp; you will learn more about these in the following sections.

If you no longer need a socket, you should call its Close method or enclose the socket access within a using statement to free up resources.

▪ Note To use the Socket class with your .NET Micro Framework application, you need to add a reference to the System.dll and Microsoft.SPOT.Net.dll assemblies to your project.

TCP

A TCP/IP connection is the right choice when you need a reliable two-way, connection-based communication that ensures that data packets will be received in the correct order and that no data will be lost or transferred multiple times. You can create a TCP/IP socket with the following code:

```
Socket socket = new Socket(Addressfamily.InterNetwork,
                           SocketType.Stream,
                           ProtocolType.Tcp);
```

Connecting to a Server as a Client

After you have created a socket object, you are able to initiate a connection to a (remote) server with the Connect method of your socket. Your .NET Micro Framework application is thereby the client application. The connection establishment takes place synchronously, so your client application will be blocked until a connection is available.

```
public void Connect(EndPoint remoteEP);
```

Take note of the remoteEP parameter of the abstract type System.Net.EndPoint in the signature of the Connect method. For IP connections, you need to pass an instance of the System.Net.IPEndPoint class to the Connect method. IPEndPoint contains the IP address and the communication port, and it is derived from EndPoint.

You can create an IPEndPoint object with one of the following two constructors:

```
public IPEndPoint(long address, int port)
public IPEndPoint(IPAddress address, int port)
```

Addressing

An IP version 4 address is coded as 4-byte integer value but usually indicated in the more legible dotted decimal notation, for example, 192.168.101.100. When creating an instance of the IPEndPoint and IPAddress classes, you need to specify the address coded as a long value. You cannot directly parse an IP address from a string with the Parse method of IPAddress as you can with the full .NET Framework; the .NET Micro Framework does not provide a Parse method for IPAddress. You can indirectly parse using the System.Net.Dns class, but first, take a look at the following code snippet, which demonstrates how you can convert a dotted decimal IP address to an IP address of the long value type.

```
public static long DottedDecimalToIp(byte a1, byte a2, byte a3, byte a4)
{
    return (long)((ulong)a4 << 24 | (ulong)a3 << 16 | (ulong)a2 << 8 | (ulong)a1);
}
```

Using the preceding snippet, you can easily create an endpoint with legible decimal notation:

```
IPEndPoint ep = new IPEndPoint(DottedDecimalToIp(192, 168, 101, 100), 80);
```

As I said, there is a way to convert the IP address using the System.Net.Dns class, which allows you to use the Internet Domain Name System (DNS). The Dns class is responsible for resolving server names. Server addresses can be specified either in decimal notation or as a server name like www.microsoft.com. The GetHostEntry method returns a collection of the entries found in the DNS database. If you pass a particular address in decimal notation, you will always get one entry in the form of an IPAddress object:

```
IPHostEntry entry = Dns.GetHostEntry("192.168.101.100");
IPAddress ipAddr = entry.AddressList[0];
IPEndPoint ep = new IPEndPoint(ipAddr, 80);
```

Passing an empty string ("") to the GetHostEntry method will deliver the local IP address of the device.

The IPAddress class possesses two predefined static addresses properties: IPAddress.Loopback and IPAddress.Any. IPAddress.Loopback describes the address 127.0.0.1, which is used if the client and server are on the same PC or device. IPAddress.Any is 0.0.0.0 and does not have a meaning for client applications; we will discuss that parameter in detail later, with server applications.

For example, to connect with a server at the address 192.168.101.100 on the port 80, you need the following code:

```
Socket clientSocket = new Socket(Addressfamily.InterNetwork,
                                 SocketType.Stream,
                                 ProtocolType.Tcp);
IPEndPoint serverEndPoint = new IPEndPoint(DottedDecimalToIp(192, 168, 101, 100),
                                 80); // port no
clientSocket.Connect(serverEndPoint);
```

You can obtain the two endpoints of the socket when a connection is available with the RemoteEndPoint and LocalEndPoint properties. Casting these into an IPEndPoint object will make the IP address available over the Address property.

You can determine the individual bytes of an IP address with the GetAddressBytes method, which supplies a byte array. With IP version 4, GetAddressBytes returns a byte array of 4 bytes. In addition, the ToString method provides a string displaying the IP address in dotted decimal notation.

```
IPEndPoint remoteIPEndPoint = (IPEndPoint)communicationSocket.RemoteEndPoint;
byte[] addressBytes = remoteIPEndPoint.Address.GetAddressBytes();
```

Transmitting Data with a Socket

Once you have a connection, you can send data synchronously with the socket's Send method:

```
clientSocket.Send(Encoding.UTF8.GetBytes("Hello World!"));
```

And you can receive data with the Receive method. The maximum number of bytes the Receive method reads is limited by the amount the specified buffer can hold. The method returns the actual number of bytes that were read:

```
byte[] inBuffer = new byte[100];
int count = clientSocket.Receive(inBuffer);
char[] chars = Encoding.UTF8.GetChars(inBuffer);
string str = new string(chars, 0, count);
Debug.Print(str);
```

You can poll the socket to test if data has been received. The first polling parameter specifies the amount of time, in microseconds, you want your application to wait for a response. Set it to –1 or System.Threading.Timeout.Infinite to let your application to wait an infinite amount of time:

```
if (communicationSocket.Poll(-1, //timeout in microseconds (-1 = infinite)
                            SelectMode.SelectRead))
{
    ...//read data here
}
```

Using the Available property of the Socket class, you can determine the number of bytes that are available to read before receiving them, which allows you to allocate a buffer that can hold all available bytes before reading the data.

Accepting Client Connections with a Server

Now, you will learn how a .NET Micro Framework application can act as a server and accept connections from clients. Creating the socket instance is similar to setting up the client site. After creation, you need to tell the socket from which clients it should accept connections. Therefore, you must call the Bind method of the socket and pass an IPEndPoint object. The EndPoint describes which client addresses can be accepted and on which port the server socket should listen for clients. The server can listen for a client with only a particular address or for arbitrary clients. To let the server accept any client, you need to indicate IPAddress.Any as the IP address. To accept only connections from the local PC or from the same device as the server, you need to use IPAddress.Loopback and specify the particular port the server should listen on.

With the Listen method, you can set the server socket to listen mode. This method is not blocking. Afterward, you need to call the Accept method, which will block program execution until a client has connected and then return a socket object for communication with only the specified client. The Accept method can be called several times, and you must call it for each client to get a client socket instance that enables communication. The Listen method expects a further parameter, backLog. The backLog value indicates the maximum number of connection requests that should be buffered. Assuming you have used the value 1 for the backlog, and there are two or more clients that want to connect after the server has called the Listen method but before invoking the Accept method, only the first client request is buffered, and all further requests are immediately rejected. However, if an additional client request comes after the first client has been accepted and connected, this request can be accepted by a second Accept method call.

```
Socket listeningSocket = new Socket(AddressFamily.InterNetwork, SocketType.Stream,
                                    ProtocolType.Tcp);
EndPoint endPoint = new IPEndPoint(IPAddress.Any, 80);
listeningSocket.Bind(endPoint);
listeningSocket.Listen(1);
Socket communicationSocket = listeningSocket.Accept();
```

After a connection has been established, you can use the communication socket to transfer data with the Send and Receive methods of the Socket class, like you did on the client side.

TCP/IP Client and Server Samples

Listing 6-2 shows a TCP/IP client for the .NET Micro Framework, and Listing 6-3 shows a server implementation. After a connection is established, the client sends a message to the server. The server waits until a response is available and then reads it.

Listing 6-2. *A TCP/IP Client*

```
using System;
using Microsoft.SPOT;
using System.Net;
using System.Net.Sockets;
using System.Text;
using System.Threading;

namespace SocketTcpClientSample
{
    public class Program
    {
        private const string dottedServerIPAddress = "127.0.0.1";
        private const int port = 2000;

        public static void Main()
        {
            using (Socket clientSocket = new Socket(AddressFamily.InterNetwork,
                                                    SocketType.Stream,
                                                    ProtocolType.Tcp))
            {
                // Addressing
                IPHostEntry entry = Dns.GetHostEntry(dottedServerIPAddress);
                IPAddress ipAddress = entry.AddressList[0];
                IPEndPoint serverEndPoint = new IPEndPoint(ipAddress, port);
```

```
                // Connecting
                Debug.Print("Connecting to server " + serverEndPoint + ".");
                clientSocket.Connect(serverEndPoint);
                Debug.Print("Connected to server.");
                // Sending
                byte[] messageBytes = Encoding.UTF8.GetBytes("Hello World!");
                clientSocket.Send(messageBytes);
            }// the socket will be closed here
        }
    }
}
```

Listing 6-3. *A TCP/IP Server*

```
using System;
using System.Net.Sockets;
using System.Net;
using System.Text;
using Microsoft.SPOT;

namespace SocketTcpServerSample
{
    public class Program
    {
        private const int port = 2000;

        public static void Main()
        {
            using (Socket listeningSocket = new Socket(AddressFamily.InterNetwork,
                                            SocketType.Stream,
                                            ProtocolType.Tcp))
            {
                listeningSocket.Bind(new IPEndPoint(IPAddress.Any, port));
                Debug.Print("Listening for a client...");
                listeningSocket.Listen(1);
                using (Socket communicationSocket = listeningSocket.Accept())
                {
                    Debug.Print("Connected to client.");
                    //wait infinitely to get a response
                    if (communicationSocket.Poll(-1, //timeout in microseconds
                                            SelectMode.SelectRead))
                    {
                        byte[] inBuffer = new byte[communicationSocket.Available];
                        int count = communicationSocket.Receive(inBuffer);
                        string message =
                                    new string(Encoding.UTF8.GetChars(inBuffer));
                        Debug.Print("Received '" + message + "'.");
```

```
                }
              }
            }
          }
        }
}
```

The client and server code shown in Listings 6-2 and 6-3 is not specific to the .NET Micro Framework. You can use it to write a client or server for the full .NET Framework or for the .NET Compact Framework, though with these frameworks, you could also use the static `IPAddress.Parse` method to obtain an IP address object from a string that represents an IP address in dotted decimal notation.

■**Note** You can find the TCP/IP server and client sample projects in this chapter's directory in the `Sockets` subdirectory.

With the .NET Micro Framework SDK, the `SocketServer` sample project implements a simple .NET Micro Framework web server. The server is able to receive an HTTP request from an Internet browser on the client, respond, and send the appropriate site back.

The .NET Micro Framework SDK provides a sample project (`SocketClient`) for a network client. The client application requests the web page at `www.msn.com` by sending an HTTP request. In order to request a web site, you need to connect to the server that hosts the site at port 80 and send an HTTP request for a desired page that might look like this: `"GET / HTTP/1.1\r\nHost: www.apress.com\r\nConnection: Close\r\n\r\n"`.

UDP

UDP is a connectionless protocol that is lightweight and faster than TCP, but it's error prone because data can be lost in transmission or arrive more than once. UDP is used for streaming services such as Voice over IP, where real time matters but dropping packets just affects the sound quality.

One of the additional advantages of using UDP is the ability to broadcast or multicast data across a network. The DNS service to resolve Internet addresses and the discovery service of the Device Profile for Web Services use the broadcast feature of UDP.

With UDP, a client does not need to connect to a server. Connectionless transmission takes place with the `SendTo` and `ReceiveFrom` methods. `ReceiveFrom` returns an endpoint object that is populated with the actual sender information. Listing 6-4 shows a UDP client and Listing 6-5 a UDP server. They demonstrate the usage of a connectionless end-to-end transmission but are not using the broadcast feature.

If you want to send a broadcast message that theoretically all network nodes will get, you can use the IP address 255.255.255.255. There is no predefined broadcast address like `Any` or `Loopback` as there is with the full .NET Framework. You can also create a broadcast IP address object using `new IPAddress(0xFFFFFFFF);`.

Listing 6-4. *A UDP Client*

```
using System;
using Microsoft.SPOT;
using System.Net;
using System.Net.Sockets;
using System.Text;
using System.Threading;

namespace SocketUdpClientSample
{
    public class Program
    {
        private const string dottedServerIPAddress = "127.0.0.1";
        //use 255.255.255.255 for a broadcast
        private const int port = 2000;

        public static void Main()
        {
            using (Socket clientSocket = new Socket(AddressFamily.InterNetwork,
                                                    SocketType.Dgram,
                                                    ProtocolType.Udp))
            {
                // Addressing
                IPHostEntry entry = Dns.GetHostEntry dottedServerIPAddress);
                IPAddress ipAddress = entry.AddressList[0];
                IPEndPoint serverEndPoint = new IPEndPoint(ipAddress, port);

                // Sending
                byte[] messageBytes = Encoding.UTF8.GetBytes("Hello World!");
                clientSocket.SendTo(messageBytes, serverEndPoint);
            }// the socket will be closed here
        }
    }
}
```

Listing 6-5. *A UDP Server*

```
using System;
using System.Net.Sockets;
using System.Net;
using System.Text;
using Microsoft.SPOT;
```

```
namespace SocketUdpServerSample
{
    public class Program
    {
        private const int port = 2000;

        public static void Main()
        {
            using (Socket serverSocket = new Socket(AddressFamily.InterNetwork,
                                          SocketType.Dgram,
                                          ProtocolType.Udp))
            {
                EndPoint remoteEndPoint = new IPEndPoint(IPAddress.Any, port);
                serverSocket.Bind(remoteEndPoint);
                if (serverSocket.Poll(-1, //timeout in microseconds
                                SelectMode.SelectRead))
                {
                    byte[] inBuffer = new byte[serverSocket.Available];
                    int count = serverSocket.ReceiveFrom(inBuffer,
                                                ref remoteEndPoint);
                    string message = new string(Encoding.UTF8.GetChars(inBuffer));
                    Debug.Print("Received '" + message + "'.");
                }
            }
        }
    }
}
```

■**Note** You can find the UDP server and client sample projects in this chapter's directory in the `Sockets` subdirectory.

Network Configuration

This section teaches you how you can obtain information about the network capabilities of your device and configure your device programmatically.

The NetworkInterface Class

The `Microsoft.SPOT.dll` assembly provides the `NetworkInterface` class (see Listing 6-6) in the `Microsoft.SPOT.NetworkInformation` namespace. This class provides information about the networking capabilities of your device.

Listing 6-6. *The Microsoft.SPOT.Net.NetworkInformation.NetworkInterface Class*

```
using System;

namespace Microsoft.SPOT.Net.NetworkInformation
{
    public class NetworkInterface
    {
        public string[] DnsAddresses { get; }
        public string GatewayAddress { get; }
        public string IPAddress { get; }
        public bool IsDhcpEnabled { get; }
        public bool IsDynamicDnsEnabled { get; }
        public NetworkInterfaceType NetworkInterfaceType { get; }
        public byte[] PhysicalAddress { get; set; }
        public string SubnetMask { get; }

        public void EnableDhcp();
        public void EnableDynamicDns();
        public void EnableStaticDns(string[] dnsAddresses);
        public void EnableStaticIP(string ipAddress,
                                   string subnetMask,
                                   string gatewayAddress);
        public static NetworkInterface[] GetAllNetworkInterfaces();
        public void ReleaseDhcpLease();
        public void RenewDhcpLease();
    }
}
```

The static GetAllNetworkInterfaces method returns an array of all available network adapters.

The MAC Address

The Media Access Control (MAC) address is a globally unique identifier for your network adapter on its network. You can obtain it with the PhysicalAddress property of the NetworkInterface instance. Although changing the physical address is possible, you should use the unique identifier provided by default, and you should ensure that all devices on your network have a unique identifier.

Subnet Mask

A subnet is a part of the overall address space. A subnet mask indicates to which subnet a device belongs. A common subnet mask is 255.255.255.0, which indicates that the last byte of an IP address contains host information. You can obtain the actual subnet mask as a string with the read-only SubnetMask property. You can set the subnet mask explicitly with the EnableStaticIP method.

Gateway Address

When you send an IP packet to an endpoint outside of your local subnet, it must pass a gateway (typically a router). You can set the gateway address explicitly as part of an `EnableStaticIP` call or let the DHCP (Dynamic Host Configuration Protocol) service automatically configure it, as described in the next section.

DHCP

You need not set the IP address, gateway address, and subnet mask explicitly. If your local network provides a reachable DHCP service, you can let the DHCP service automatically configure these parameters. The `EnableDhcp` method enables the DHCP service, which is the default setting. Alternatively, calling `EnableStaticIP` will deactivate the usage of DHCP.

Dynamic IP addresses are assigned temporarily. You can release a dynamic IP address with `ReleaseDhcpLease` or renew it with `RenewDhcpLease`. The `IsDhcpEnabled` property indicates if DHCP is currently enabled.

DNS

The DNS is capable of translating a server name like `www.apress.com` into a real IP address, and it can be used with the .NET Micro Framework, like in the full .NET Framework, with the static `System.Net.Dns` class.

Dynamic DNS, which is enabled by default, attempts to automatically discover the DNS servers. You can verify if dynamic DNS is enabled by checking the read-only `IsDynamicDnsEnabled` property. You can also explicitly specify a list of DNS server IP addresses on your network using the `EnableStaticDns` method.

■**Caution** The `EnableDynamicDNS` method of the `NetworkInterface` class is not implemented in the current version (2.5) of the .NET Micro Framework TCP/IP stack and will cause an exception if called from a managed application. Dynamic DNS address assignment is accomplished by enabling DHCP after setting the static DNS address to 0.0.0.0. For a detailed description and resolution to this and further issues related to DNS and DHCP, have a look at the .NET Micro Framework release notes file.

Learning More About Sockets

If you'd like to learn more about using sockets to manage client and server connections, check out these resources:

- *TCP/IP Sockets in C#* by David Makofske, Michael J. Donahoo, and Kenneth L. Calvert (Morgan Kaufmann Publishers, 2004)

- *Professional .NET Network Programming* by Andrew Krowczyk, Vinod Kumar, and Nauman Laghari (Wrox Press, 2002)

- *Network Programming in .NET* by Fiach Reid (Digital Press, 2004)

Web Services for Devices

The Device Profile for Web Services (DPWS) was initially published in May 2004 by Microsoft. It implements a subset of the Web Services specifications but adds a mechanism so clients can easily discover devices. Once a device is discovered, a client can retrieve a description of services hosted on that device and use those services. Microsoft Windows Vista natively integrates DPWS with a stack called Microsoft Web Services on Devices API (WSDAPI) to use services from a device or provide services to other devices.

The DPWS focuses on Ethernet-enabled (LAN- or WLAN-enabled), resource constrained devices, and its intentions are similar to those of Universal Plug and Play (UPnP). You could look at the DPWS as a kind of USB for Ethernet, but it is fully aligned with the Web Services specification. It builds on core Web Services standards but is a lightweight protocol that supports dynamic discovery, one- and two-way control messaging, and eventing. The DPWS does not define specific application messages; these are left to the device manufacturers.

Devices are units that are attached to a network and may include zero or more services. A device can provide services for other network nodes and/or use the services of other devices. Examples are printers, scanners, projectors, cameras, and video systems.

The DPWS enables you to show a presentation on your projector using WLAN without taking care of cables. You can also think of devices within your home that would benefit from automation. The temperature level of your next generation freezer may be controlled from a remote control, PDA, mobile phone, or PC. Or a washing machine could submit its progress to your mobile phone. There are many scenarios, and this technology offers many possibilities we might not think about at the moment. The .NET Micro Framework makes the Device Profile for Web Services available to small, resource constrained devices.

Several devices already communicate with others, but their communication methods are proprietary. The DPWS defines a standard so that devices of different hardware vendors can be connected. Some of the already existing standards such as Java Intelligent Network Infrastructure (JINI), UPnP, and Home Audio/Video Interoperability (HAVi) work satisfactorily, but none can be used for multiple domains.

DPWS Architecture

Figure 6-1 illustrates the core components that build the DPWS stack. The core transport components are UDP with its multicast messages that are used for discovery and TCP/IP for data exchange. The messages are sent between a client and server with the HTTP protocol that sits on top of TCP/IP. All messages are in the Simple Object Access Protocol (SOAP) format, which is based on XML and is used for common Web Services. Next, there are some core standards from the Web Services technology like WS-Addressing, WS-Security, and WS-Policy. On top of these basic components are the standards for discovery, metadata exchange, and eventing. These components and standards provide a common communication solution flexible enough to use for multiple domains, because you are able to build your custom vendor- or domain-specific protocols.

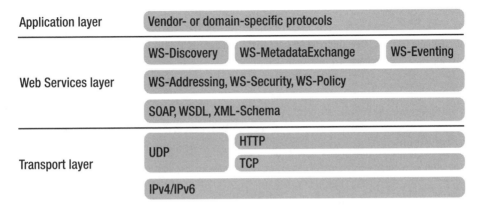

Figure 6-1. *The architecture of the DPWS stack*

The communication between a client and a service device is usually done using the following pattern:

1. Discovery

2. Description

3. Control

4. Events

Both a client and a service device need to reference the MFWsStack.dll assembly, which contains standard Web Services components.

Further, a device needs to reference the MFDpwsDevice.dll assembly, which contains DPWS-specific classes especially for devices hosting services. Clients need to use the MFDpwsClient.dll assembly, which provides classes for DPWS clients.

Further, you need to use classes from the System.Xml.dll and MFDpwsExtensions.dll when building and parsing SOAP messages.

Omitted features of the present .NET Micro Framework DPWS stack are WS-Policy, WS-Security, and support for IP version 6 (only IP version 4 is supported).

Discovery

In the following section, you will learn about dynamic discovery of devices and detecting newly available devices. This is a very important feature that the DPWS adds to the Web Services standard.

Endpoint Addresses vs. Transport Addresses

Before we explore the discovery mechanisms, you need to understand addressing and know the difference between an endpoint and transport address.

An endpoint address (also referred to as a logical address) is a unique transport-neutral mechanism to define service and message addressing, as shown in the following example:

```
urn:uuid:c5201073-fa27-c8c9-9634-0000001dd159
```

■**Tip** The endpoint address is a globally unique identifier (GUID). The .NET Micro Framework provides the `Guid` structure in the `System.Ext.Guid` namespace that resides in the `MFDpwsExtensions.dll` assembly. Invoke the static `NewGuid` method to create a new GUID.

The transport address (also referred to as the physical address) defines how to reach a device. It usually consists of the IP address, port number, and endpoint address, as shown in the following example:

```
http://192.168.0.1:8084/c5201073-fa27-c8c9-9634-0000001dd159
```

Host Services vs. Hosted Services

It is also important that you are able to differentiate between a host service and a hosted service. Each service device can have zero or one host services and zero or more hosted services. A host service can be thought of as the main service of the device and is directly associated with a device. It plays an important role in the discovery process and might be the most general service to provide basic controlling. You could further add more specific services as hosted services. If your device only provides one service, you can set it as the host service.

Hosted services are mostly functional. In addition to your custom hosted services, the DPWS standard defines a set of built-in services to manage discovery, metadata exchange, and eventing.

Later, when probing for devices that provide a particular service, whether a service is the host or is hosted doesn't matter. The only difference is that a probe match will only contain details about the host service; you will not see the hosted services. We'll discuss matches in the next section.

Probing for Devices

To find a particular device, such as a printer, the client sends a probe message over UDP's multicast feature. In the probe message, the client defines what kind of device it is looking for and contains a filter specifying the service types you need. A client filters or searches not for particular devices but for certain services that are the host service or hosted services on a device. Every device listens for probe messages, and if a device hosts a service the client is searching for, the device responds with a probe match.

A probe match contains the type name of the device, a namespace with a prefix, an endpoint address, and a transport address.

In the next section, you will learn how to build a simple device. The section after that demonstrates a simple client that probes for services; you'll learn how to dynamically discover clients with that sample client.

Building a Simple Service Device

Now, we will explore how to build a simple service device. Each device needs a unique endpoint address so that clients can identify this device. Having a logical address enables you to run several service devices on one hardware platform. You can assign a unique endpoint address to your device with the following line:

```
Device.EndpointAddress = "urn:uuid:c5201073-fa27-c8c9-9634-0000001dd159";
```

If you do not assign an endpoint address, you do not get a random address; you get the default one (e.g., `urn:uuid:3cb0d1ba-cc3a-46ce-b416-212ac2419b51`).

Next, you can set the host service. Each service needs to be derived from `DpwsHostedService`, regardless of whether it will be the host service or a hosted service. The following code will create a new functionless service without any operations and events and set it as the host service of your device:

```
DpwsHostedService service1 = new DpwsHostedService();
service1.ServiceTypeName = "SimpleServiceType1";
service1.ServiceNamespace =
                new WsXmlNamespace("simple1", // prefix
                                "http://schemas.sample.org/SimpleService1");
service1.ServiceID = "urn:uuid:cf16db78-02c9-c8ca-b37b-0000004071f6";
// Set the service as host service
Device.Host = service1;
```

You need to describe each service with a service type name, a namespace prefix, and a namespace Unique Resource Identifier (URI). These properties are used with the probing mechanism in order to filter and search for services.

To access individual services of a device, each service needs a globally unique service ID.

Finally, you need to set the service as host service by assigning it to the static `Host` property of the `Device` class.

To add a hosted service to your device, you need to create an object of the `DpwsHostedService` class or a subclass of it. The following code will create a new service without any operations and events and add it to your device as a hosted service:

```
DpwsHostedService service2 = new DpwsHostedService();
service2.ServiceTypeName = "SimpleServiceType2";
service2.ServiceNamespace =
                new WsXmlNamespace("simple2", // prefix
                                "http://schemas.sample.org/SimpleService2");
service2.ServiceID = "urn:uuid:ec499d62-02c9-c8ca-b7ee-0000000bf3dd";
// Add the service as hosted service
Device.HostedServices.Add(service2);
```

The static `HostedServices` property of the `Device` class holds a list with all the hosted services on a device.

Listing 6-7 shows a simple service device that has a simple host service (service 1) and a simple hosted service (service 2). This project requires you to include references to the `MFWsStack.dll` and `MFDpwsDevices.dll` assemblies.

Listing 6-7. *A Simple Service Device*

```
using System;
using System.Threading;
using Ws.Services.Xml;
using Ws.Services.Utilities;
using Dpws.Device;
using Dpws.Device.Services;
```

```
namespace MFSimpleDeviceSample
{
    public class Program
    {
        public static void Main()
        {
            // *** Relationship (Services) ***
            // Set a simple service without any
            // operations and event as host service
            DpwsHostedService service1 = new DpwsHostedService();
            service1.ServiceTypeName = "SimpleServiceType1";
            service1.ServiceNamespace =
                    new WsXmlNamespace("simple1", // prefix
                                    "http://schemas.sample.org/SimpleService1");
            service1.ServiceID = "urn:uuid:cf16db78-02c9-c8ca-b37b-0000004071f6";
            // Set the service as host service
            Device.Host = service1;

            // Add a second service as hosted service
            DpwsHostedService service2 = new DpwsHostedService();
            service2.ServiceTypeName = "SimpleServiceType2";
            service2.ServiceNamespace =
                    new WsXmlNamespace("simple2", // prefix
                                    "http://schemas.sample.org/SimpleService2");
            service2.ServiceID = "urn:uuid:ec499d62-02c9-c8ca-b7ee-0000000bf3dd";
            // Add the service as hosted service
            Device.HostedServices.Add(service2);

            // Let clients identify this device
            Device.EndpointAddress =
                                "urn:uuid:c5201073-fa27-c8c9-9634-0000001dd159";
            // Set this device property if you want to ignore this client's request
            Device.IgnoreLocalClientRequest = false;

            // Start the device
            Device.Start();

            // Keep the device alive
            Thread.Sleep(Timeout.Infinite);
        }
    }
}
```

To make a device available to the network, you need to start it with the static Start method of the Device class, which will start all background listeners that listen for messages and commands of clients (UDP service host, HTTP service host, and event subscription manager). To gracefully disconnect a device from the network, you need to call the Stop method.

Starting a device will multicast a "Hello" message; and stopping will send a "Bye" message. The Hello and Bye events will be discussed later in detail.

The Device class also provides the IgnoreLocalClientRequest property. Set this property to false if you need to debug a DPWS .NET Micro Framework device and a client on the same machine. Set it to true on real devices to gain a little performance boost by preventing the DPWS stack from processing its own multicast messages.

The Probing Client

Now, you will learn how to program a client that probes for devices that provide a service of the type SimpleServiceType2 (see Listing 6-7) with the http://schemas.sample.org/SimpleSevice2 namespace and simple2 prefix. To a client project, you need to add references to the MFWsStack.dll and MFDpwsClient.dll assemblies. This sample also makes use of the System.Ext.Guid class that is located in the MFDpwsExtensions.dll assembly.

First of all, you need to implement your own client that derives from the DpwsClient class, because you need to use the protected property DiscoveryClient of the DpwsClient class to get an instance of the DiscoveryClient class that is used for probing.

In order to probe for devices, you need to invoke the Probe method of the DiscoveryClient class. The Probe method accepts a list of DpwsServiceType objects that specifies the service types to look for. A device sends a probe match if its host service or one of its hosted service types (defined with the ServiceTypeName property of a service) matches to one of the requested types in the list. Probe matches are sent back directly to the sender of the probe request.

```
DpwsServiceType serviceType = new DpwsServiceType(
                        "SimpleServiceType2", // type name
                        "http://schemas.sample.org/SimpleService2"); // ns URI
DpwsServiceTypes filters = new DpwsServiceTypes();
filters.Add(serviceType);
// Probe for devices
DpwsServiceDescriptions probeMatches = this.DiscoveryClient.Probe(filters);
if (probeMatches != null)
{
...// Matches found
}
```

If you want to get all devices in your network, you need to pass null for the filter argument to the Probe method.

Listing 6-8 shows the complete client code.

Listing 6-8. *A Client That Probes for Devices*

```
using System;
using Microsoft.SPOT;
using Dpws.Client;
using Dpws.Client.Discovery;

namespace MFProbingClientSample
{
```

```
public class ProbingClient : DpwsClient
{
    public void PrintProbeMatchInfo()
    {
        Debug.Print("Discovering service devices...");
        // Define search criterias
        DpwsServiceType serviceType = new DpwsServiceType(
                        "SimpleServiceType2", // type name
                        "http://schemas.sample.org/SimpleService2"); // ns URI
        DpwsServiceTypes filters = new DpwsServiceTypes();
        filters.Add(serviceType);
        // Probe for devices
        DpwsServiceDescriptions probeMatches =
                                        this.DiscoveryClient.Probe(filters);
        if (probeMatches != null)
        {
            for (int i = 0; i < probeMatches.Count; ++i)
            {
                DpwsServiceDescription probeMatch = probeMatches[i];
                // Print probe match information
                Debug.Print("");
                Debug.Print("Probe Match:");

                Debug.Print("Endpoint Address = " +
                            probeMatch.Endpoint.Address.AbsoluteUri);

                Debug.Print("Types:");
                for (int t = 0; t < probeMatch.ServiceTypes.Count; ++t)
                {
                    DpwsServiceType matchType = probeMatch.ServiceTypes[t];
                    Debug.Print("\tName = " + matchType.TypeName);
                    Debug.Print("\tNamespace = " + matchType.NamespaceUri);
                    Debug.Print("");
                }

                Debug.Print("XAddrs:");
                foreach (string xaddr in probeMatch.XAddrs)
                    Debug.Print("\tTransport Address = " + xaddr);

                Debug.Print("Metadata Version = " + probeMatch.MetadataVersion);
            }
        }
        else
            Debug.Print("No service device found.");
    }
}
```

In the entry point of your application, you should create an instance of your client and call the `PrintProbeMatchInfo` method to see the probe matches in the Output window of Visual Studio.

```
public static void Main()
{
    using (ProbingClient client = new ProbingClient())
    {
        client.PrintProbeMatchInfo();
    }
}
```

The Probe Match

To discover a device, you need to first start the device (see Listing 6-7) and then start the probing client (see Listing 6-8). You can run both the device and client projects on an emulator from Visual Studio on your PC. Therefore, make sure that the device sets the `IgnoreLocalClientRequest` property of the `Device` class to `false`.

■**Note** You can find the simple device and probing client sample projects in this chapter's directory in the `Web Services` subdirectory.

The client prints out the following results for the probe match if it finds the device in Listing 6-7:

```
Probe Match:
Endpoint Address = urn:uuid:c5201073-fa27-c8c9-9634-0000001dd159
Types:
    Name = Device
    Prefix = wsdp
    Namespace = http://schemas.xmlsoap.org/ws/2006/02/devprof

    Name = SimpleServiceType1
    Prefix = simple1
    Namespace = http://schemas.sample.org/SimpleService1

XAddrs:
    Transport Address = http://127.0.0.1:8084/c5201073-fa27-c8c9-9634-0000001dd159
Metadata Version = 1
```

Every device has a service called `Device` that you will get with each probe match. Although we probed for a device that contains the `SimpleService2` service, the probe match contains information about the `SimpleService1` service. That is because the probe match does not contain all services of a device, only information about the host service (if the device has a host service).

This is true regardless of the service you probe for. Consider that the probe match returns the transport address of the device but not any service ID. To get a service ID of a particular service so that you can access it, you need to request the metadata of a device, as discussed later.

A device may return several transport addresses (with the XAddrs collection), because it may provide several ways to connect to it. The .NET Micro Framework only supports IP version 4 addressing. You can check if the XAddrs collection contains a valid IP version 4 transport address with the System.Ext.Uri class in the MFDpwsExtensions.dll assembly:

Listing 6-9. *Verifying the IP Version 4 Transport Address*

```
Uri uri = new Uri(xAddr);
if(uri.HostNameType == UriHostNameType.IPv4)
{
    // Valid IPv4 transport address that can be used with the .NET Micro Framework.
}
```

In the output, you can also see the metadata version number, as the Device class provides a MetadataVersion property. If you do not set the metadata version number in the code for the device, it has the value 1 by default. Whenever a device changes its metadata, you need to increase the metadata version number to prompt clients caching the metadata to refresh the description. We will discuss more ways to obtain device information in the following sections.

SOAP Messaging

You will see the actual SOAP messages that are sent between client and device in the Visual Studio Output window.

As with common Web Services, the DPWS stack uses messages in the SOAP format for communication and data exchange. The SOAP format is a protocol standard for a remote method call mechanism of the World Wide Web Consortium, or W3C (www.w3.org/TR/soap), that is based on XML and therefore is readable, flexible, open, and platform independent.

Although the.NET Micro Framework's DPWS stack does most of the work when it automatically parses and builds SOAP messages, parsing and building a SOAP message yourself is sometimes necessary. The format of a remote method call result coming from a two-way request is neither defined nor constrained, so the format is up to you as long as it is valid XML and placed in the message body. Therefore, you need to build and extract the results of a SOAP response message yourself. To that end, we will take a closer look at the SOAP messages that are sent behind the scenes through the DPWS stack.

The whole message is embedded within an Envelope root tag. Each message has at least a message header that contains address information, a unique message ID, and the purpose of the message. The unique message identifier is added so that other devices can respond and refer to exactly this message. All message addressing information is contained in the message header to decouple the message content from the transport.

The parameter data specific to a particular message and vendor- and domain-specific high-level protocol data is placed in the message body.

Using SOAP Messages for Probing

Listing 6-10 shows how a probe message may look if sent by the client in Listing 6-8 over UDP multicast. The Action tag indicates that this is a probe message. A probe message is multicast, so you will not find a physical target address in the To section. The Probe tag in the message body contains the search criteria.

Listing 6-10. *A Probe Message in the SOAP Format*

```
<?xml version='1.0' encoding='UTF-8' ?>
<soap:Envelope xmlns:soap="http://www.w3.org/2003/05/soap-envelope"
               xmlns:wsa="http://schemas.xmlsoap.org/ws/2004/08/addressing"
               xmlns:wsd="http://schemas.xmlsoap.org/ws/2005/04/discovery"
               xmlns:simple2="http://schemas.sample.org/SimpleService2">
  <soap:Header>
    <wsa:To>urn:schemas-xmlsoap-org:ws:2005:04:discovery</wsa:To>
    <wsa:Action>http://schemas.xmlsoap.org/ws/2005/04/discovery/Probe</wsa:Action>
    <wsa:MessageID>urn:uuid:52f964b0-fdcf-c8c9-b9c7-0000006a39c7</wsa:MessageID>
  </soap:Header>
  <soap:Body>
    <wsd:Probe>
      <wsd:Types>simple2:SimpleServiceType2</wsd:Types>
    </wsd:Probe>
  </soap:Body>
</soap:Envelope>
```

Listing 6-11 demonstrates how the probe match of the device in Listing 6-7 might look. You can see that the probe match is a response to the probe message in Listing 6-10, because the RelatesTo tag points to the message ID of the probe message. The message body holds the details about the probe match, such as the host service and transport address of the device.

Listing 6-11. *A Probe Match in the SOAP Format*

```
<?xml version='1.0' encoding='UTF-8'?>
<soap:Envelope xmlns:soap="http://www.w3.org/2003/05/soap-envelope"
               xmlns:wsdp="http://schemas.xmlsoap.org/ws/2006/02/devprof"
               xmlns:wsa="http://schemas.xmlsoap.org/ws/2004/08/addressing"
               xmlns:wsd="http://schemas.xmlsoap.org/ws/2005/04/discovery"
               xmlns:simple2="http://schemas.sample.org/SimpleService2">
  <soap:Header>
    <wsa:To>
      http://schemas.xmlsoap.org/ws/2004/08/addressing/role/anonymous
    </wsa:To>
    <wsa:Action>
      http://schemas.xmlsoap.org/ws/2005/04/discovery/ProbeMatches
    </wsa:Action>
    <wsa:MessageID>urn:uuid:fe7d7b1b-fd58-c8c9-aadf-0000005f697a</wsa:MessageID>
    <wsa:RelatesTo>urn:uuid:52f964b0-fdcf-c8c9-b9c7-0000006a39c7</wsa:RelatesTo>
    <wsd:AppSequence InstanceId="1195981003"
                     SequenceId="urn:uuid:c883e4a8-9af4-4bf4-aaaf-06394151d6c0"
                     MessageNumber="4"
    />
  </soap:Header>
  <soap:Body>
    <wsd:ProbeMatches>
```

```
    <wsd:ProbeMatch>
      <wsa:EndpointReference>
        <wsa:Address>urn:uuid:c5201073-fa27-c8c9-9634-0000001dd159</wsa:Address>
      </wsa:EndpointReference>
      <wsd:Types>wsdp:Device simple1:SimpleDeviceType1</wsd:Types>
      <wsd:XAddrs>
        http://127.0.0.1:8084/c5201073-fa27-c8c9-9634-0000001dd159
      </wsd:XAddrs>
      <wsd:MetadataVersion>1</wsd:MetadataVersion>
    </wsd:ProbeMatch>
  </wsd:ProbeMatches>
</soap:Body>
</soap:Envelope>
```

Direct Probing

If you already know the transport address that includes the IP address of a device (e.g., `http://192.168.0.1:8084/c5201073-fa27-c8c9-9634-0000001dd159`), you can use the `DirectProbe` method to probe for the device. This method does not send a UDP multicast but will send a probe message directly to the device. The results returned with this method are similar those returned with the `Probe` method. We will apply direct probing later when catching the announcement message of a device that is newly available to the network.

Resolving Devices

You may know the unique ID (endpoint address or logical address) of a well known device but not its transport address, particularly if you have already discovered a device and stored the ID in your application settings. Resolving allows you to locate an already known device by providing you the ability to get information about a device, including its transport address, using its endpoint address. To resolve a client with its endpoint address, you need to call the `Resolve` method (see Listing 6-12). You will get either one resolve match or nothing (`null`) if the device could not be resolved. A resolve match contains information similar to a probe match. As already shown, a probe match is a `DpwsServiceDescriptions` object that is a collection of `DpwsServiceDescription` objects. A resolve match is a single `DpwsServiceDescription` object.

Listing 6-12. *Resolving a Known Device with its Endpoint Address*

```
using System;
using Microsoft.SPOT;
using Dpws.Client;
using Dpws.Client.Discovery;

namespace MFResolvingClientSample
{
    public class ResolvingClient : DpwsClient
    {
```

```
public void PrintResolveMatchInfo()
{
    Debug.Print("Resolving a device...");
    string endpointAddr = "urn:uuid:c5201073-fa27-c8c9-9634-0000001dd159";
    DpwsServiceDescription resolveMatch =
                            this.DiscoveryClient.Resolve(endpointAddr);
    if (resolveMatch != null)
    {
        // Print resolve match information
        Debug.Print("");
        Debug.Print("Resolve Match:");

        Debug.Print("Endpoint Address = " +
                    resolveMatch.Endpoint.Address.AbsoluteUri);

        Debug.Print("Types:");
        for (int t = 0; t < resolveMatch.ServiceTypes.Count; ++t)
        {
            DpwsServiceType matchType = resolveMatch.ServiceTypes[t];
            Debug.Print("\tName = " + matchType.TypeName);
            Debug.Print("\tNamespace = " + matchType.NamespaceUri);
            Debug.Print("");
        }

        Debug.Print("XAddrs:");
        foreach (string xaddr in resolveMatch.XAddrs)
            Debug.Print("\tTransport Address = " + xaddr);

        Debug.Print("Metadata Version = " +
                    resolveMatch.MetadataVersion);
    }
    else
        Debug.Print("Device cannot be resolved.");
    }
  }
}
```

■Note You can find the MFResolvingClientSample project in this chapter's directory in the Web
Services subdirectory.

Detecting Newly Available Devices with the "Hello" and "Bye" Messages

To avoid the need for polling, when a service device joins the network, it sends a multicast
announcement message. By listening to this message, clients can detect newly available
service devices without repeated probing.

When a device joins the network, it always sends a multicast Hello message, and when it leaves the network, it may send an optional Bye message. A device may not have the ability to send a Bye message, for example, when it is power cycled.

Listing 6-13 shows a client that catches Hello events of newly available devices. It also listens to Bye messages to get notified when a device leaves the network. You can listen to the Hello and Bye messages by subscribing to the event handlers of the DpwsClient class:

```
DpwsClient client = new DpwsClient();
client.HelloEvent += new HelloEventHandler(client_HelloEvent);
client.ByeEvent += new ByeEventHandler(client_ByeEvent);
```

To receive these Hello and Bye events, the client must be live. To keep a client from terminating, you need to pause the main thread for an infinite amount of time (see Listing 6-13). The DPWS stack (UDP and HTTP services) keeps running in a separate thread. To test this example, you need to first start the client and then start the device. If you're running both the client and device project on an emulator on your PC, you need to set the IgnoreRequestFromThisIP property of the client to false so that the client will get the Hello and Bye messages, just like you did for the device (using the IgnoreLocalClientRequest property) that listens for probing and resolving.

The Hello message of a new device provides information similar to a probe or resolve match. Also like the probe and resolve matches, the argument for the Hello event handler is a DpwsServiceDescription object that contains the Device service and optionally the host service of a device.

Unlike a probe or resolve match, the Hello event provides at most one transport address in the form of a string. For security reasons, the transport address is optional, because a Hello message is multicast with UDP. A probe or response match is unicast to the caller. DPWS stacks, other than those using the .NET Micro Framework, might never expose transport addresses that disclose the IP addresses of private networks. A DPWS stack implementation also should not send an IP version 6 address to an IP version 4 client. Therefore, you should not count on the transport address from a Hello message. Instead, use the endpoint address (helloEventArgs. Endpoint.Address) to resolve the transport address of a device.

A device needs to be started explicitly, as shown in Listing 6-7. Whenever a device is started with the Start method of the Device class, it sends an announcement (Hello) message. The Device class further has a Stop method that will shut down the DPWS stack and all its listening threads and broadcast a Bye event.

Listing 6-13. *Catching the Hello and Bye Events*

```
using System;
using System.Threading;
using Microsoft.SPOT;
using Dpws.Client;
using Dpws.Client.Discovery;
using Ws.Services.Utilities;

namespace MFHelloByeEventCatchingClient
{
    public class Program
    {
```

```
public static void Main()
{
    using (DpwsClient client = new DpwsClient()) // initializing
    {
        // Set this client property if you want to
        // ignore this devices request
        client.IgnoreRequestFromThisIP = false;
        client.HelloEvent += new HelloEventHandler(client_HelloEvent);
        client.ByeEvent += new ByeEventHandler(client_ByeEvent);

        // Keep the client alive
        Thread.Sleep(Timeout.Infinite);
    }
}

private static void client_HelloEvent(object obj,
                                      DpwsServiceDescription helloEventArgs)
{
    // Print Hello event information
    Debug.Print("");
    Debug.Print("Hello Event:");

    Debug.Print("Endpoint Address = " +
                helloEventArgs.Endpoint.Address.AbsoluteUri);

    Debug.Print("Types:");
    for (int t = 0; t < helloEventArgs.ServiceTypes.Count; ++t)
    {
        DpwsServiceType serviceType = helloEventArgs.ServiceTypes[t];
        Debug.Print("\tName = " + serviceType.TypeName);
        Debug.Print("\tNamespace = " + serviceType.NamespaceUri);
        Debug.Print("");
    }

    Debug.Print("XAddrs:");
    foreach (string xaddr in helloEventArgs.XAddrs)
        Debug.Print("\tTransport Address = " + xaddr);

    Debug.Print("Metadata Version = " +
                helloEventArgs.MetadataVersion);
}

private static void client_ByeEvent(object obj,
                                    DpwsServiceDescription byeEventArgs)
{
```

```
                // Print Bye event information
                Debug.Print("");
                Debug.Print("Bye Event:");

                Debug.Print("Endpoint Address = " +
                            byeEventArgs.Endpoint.Address.AbsoluteUri);

                Debug.Print("XAddrs:");
                foreach (string xaddr in byeEventArgs.XAddrs)
                    Debug.Print("\tTransport Address = " + xaddr);
            }
        }
}
```

■**Note** You can find the MFHelloByeEventCatchingClientSample project in this chapter's directory in the Web Services subdirectory.

Looking at SOAP Messages for the Hello and Bye Events

Listing 6-14 and 6-15 demonstrate hypothetical Hello and Bye messages sent from a device in the SOAP format. You can see a message ID that identifies the message and the Action tag that indicates a Hello or Bye message. The To tag does not indicate an individual device address, because a Hello or Bye message is sent as a multicast UDP message.

The message body contains an endpoint and optionally one transport address. With a Hello message, the body contains further details about the host service, if there is one, as well as the current metadata version.

Listing 6-14. *A Hello Message*

```xml
<?xml version='1.0' encoding='UTF-8'?>
<soap:Envelope xmlns:soap="http://www.w3.org/2003/05/soap-envelope"
               xmlns:wsdp="http://schemas.xmlsoap.org/ws/2006/02/devprof"
               xmlns:wsa="http://schemas.xmlsoap.org/ws/2004/08/addressing"
               xmlns:wsd="http://schemas.xmlsoap.org/ws/2005/04/discovery"
               xmlns:simple1="http://schemas.sample.org/SimpleService1"
>
  <soap:Header>
    <wsa:To>urn:schemas-xmlsoap-org:ws:2005:04:discovery</wsa:To>
    <wsa:Action>http://schemas.xmlsoap.org/ws/2005/04/discovery/Hello</wsa:Action>
    <wsa:MessageID>urn:uuid:e8a359d5-ff30-c8c9-adff-00000067adff</wsa:MessageID>
    <wsd:AppSequence InstanceId="1196184014"
                     SequenceId="urn:uuid:c883e4a8-9af4-4bf4-aaaf-06394151d6c0"
                     MessageNumber="1"
    />
  </soap:Header>
```

```
  <soap:Body>
    <wsd:Hello>
      <wsa:EndpointReference>
        <wsa:Address>urn:uuid:c5201073-fa27-c8c9-9634-0000001dd159</wsa:Address>
      </wsa:EndpointReference>
      <wsd:Types>wsdp:Device simple1:SimpleServiceType1</wsd:Types>
      <wsd:XAddrs>
        http://169.254.2.2:8084/c5201073-fa27-c8c9-9634-0000001dd159
      </wsd:XAddrs>
      <wsd:MetadataVersion>1</wsd:MetadataVersion>
    </wsd:Hello>
  </soap:Body>
</soap:Envelope>
```

Listing 6-15. *A Bye Message*

```
<?xml version='1.0' encoding='UTF-8'?>
<soap:Envelope xmlns:soap="http://www.w3.org/2003/05/soap-envelope"
               xmlns:wsdp="http://schemas.xmlsoap.org/ws/2006/02/devprof"
               xmlns:wsa="http://schemas.xmlsoap.org/ws/2004/08/addressing"
               xmlns:wsd="http://schemas.xmlsoap.org/ws/2005/04/discovery"
>
  <soap:Header>
    <wsa:To>urn:schemas-xmlsoap-org:ws:2005:04:discovery</wsa:To>
    <wsa:Action>http://schemas.xmlsoap.org/ws/2005/04/discovery/Bye</wsa:Action>
    <wsa:MessageID>urn:uuid:ea5861d2-ff30-c8c9-be73-000000ad338c</wsa:MessageID>
    <wsd:AppSequence InstanceId="1196184014"
                     SequenceId="urn:uuid:c883e4a8-9af4-4bf4-aaaf-06394151d6c0"
                     MessageNumber="2"/>
  </soap:Header>
  <soap:Body>
    <wsd:Bye>
      <wsa:EndpointReference>
        <wsa:Address>urn:uuid:c5201073-fa27-c8c9-9634-0000001dd159</wsa:Address>
      </wsa:EndpointReference>
      <wsd:XAddrs>
        http://169.254.2.2:8084/c5201073-fa27-c8c9-9634-0000001dd159
      </wsd:XAddrs>
    </wsd:Bye>
  </soap:Body>
</soap:Envelope>
```

This section about discovery illustrates how to use different discovery mechanisms to find and locate devices in a network. You now know how to use a device filter when probing, resolving, or listening for newly available devices. Each discovery technique will provide you with a little information about a device, like its host service type, metadata version, and endpoint and transport addresses. In the next section, we will explore how to find out more about a device and the services it hosts.

Description

In this section, you will learn how to get more information about a device, as you did with probe and resolve matches and announcement events. This section describes how to write self-describing devices that provide metadata to clients.

Metadata

Once you obtain the transport address of a device with resolving after probing or from a Hello message, you are able to find out more about the characteristics of that device and the services it hosts. For example, you need to request the description (metadata) of a device in order to get a service ID for your desired service to access that service on the device. A client may send a Get Metadata message directly to the device to get a detailed description of the device.

The Get Metadata request will return the following descriptions:

- The ThisModel metadata provides device type information, like the manufacturer name, model name, and model number.

- The ThisDevice metadata provides information about the device itself, such as the friendly name, serial number, and firmware version.

- The Relationship metadata is the list of services hosted by the device, which comprises the service ID (endpoint) and the types of each of the hosted services.

A Self-Describing Device that Provides Metadata

You can set the metadata for the ThisModel instance that describes the device model, which might include the manufacturer and model names, with the following static properties:

```
Device.ThisModel.Manufacturer = "Apress, Inc.";
Device.ThisModel.ManufacturerUrl = "http://www.apress.com";
Device.ThisModel.ModelName = "MetadataProvidingModel";
Device.ThisModel.ModelNumber = "12345";
Device.ThisModel.ModelUrl = "http://www.apress.com";
Device.ThisModel.PresentationUrl = "http://www.apress.com";
```

With the Any property of the ThisModel class you can include further arbitrary information in the form of XML data to provide it to clients.

You can provide a description of your device itself with the ThisDevice property that provides an instance of the ThisDevice class:

```
Device.ThisDevice.FriendlyName = "Describing device that provides metadata";
Device.ThisDevice.FirmwareVersion = "demo";
Device.ThisDevice.SerialNumber = "12345678";
```

All properties accept a string value. The ThisDevice class also provides an Any property for arbitrary data.

Whenever the ThisModel or ThisDevice data changes, you need to increase the metadata version number of a device. The version of a device's metadata is sent with a probe match, resolve match, or Hello message to indicate to clients that have cached the metadata of a device whether they have the latest metadata.

Listing 6-16 shows the complete code of a hypothetical self-describing device.

Listing 6-16. *A Self-Describing Device That Provides Metadata*

```
using System;
using System.Threading;
using Ws.Services.Xml;
using Ws.Services.Utilities;
using Dpws.Device;
using Dpws.Device.Services;

namespace MFMetadataProvidingDeviceSample
{
    public class Program
    {
        public static void Main()
        {
            // *** Relationship (Services) ***
            // Set a simple service without any
            // operations and event as host service
            DpwsHostedService service1 = new DpwsHostedService();
            service1.ServiceTypeName = "SimpleServiceType1";
            service1.ServiceNamespace =
                    new WsXmlNamespace("simple1",
                                        "http://schemas.sample.org/SimpleService1");
            service1.ServiceID = "urn:uuid:cf16db78-02c9-c8ca-b37b-0000004071f6";
            // set the service as host service
            Device.Host = service1;
            //
            // Add a second service as hosted service
            DpwsHostedService service2 = new DpwsHostedService();
            service2.ServiceTypeName = "SimpleServiceType2";
            service2.ServiceNamespace =
                    new WsXmlNamespace("simple2",
                                        "http://schemas.sample.org/SimpleService2");
            service2.ServiceID = "urn:uuid:ec499d62-02c9-c8ca-b7ee-0000000bf3dd";
            // Add the service as hosted service
            Device.HostedServices.Add(service2);

            // Let clients identify this device
            Device.EndpointAddress =
                            "urn:uuid:c5201073-fa27-c8c9-9634-0000001dd159";
            // Set this device property if you want to ignore this client's request
            Device.IgnoreLocalClientRequest = false;
```

```
                // Metadata
                // ThisModel
                Device.ThisModel.Manufacturer = "Apress, Inc.";
                Device.ThisModel.ManufacturerUrl = "http://www.apress.com";
                Device.ThisModel.ModelName = "MetadataProvidingModel";
                Device.ThisModel.ModelNumber = "12345";
                Device.ThisModel.ModelUrl = "http://www.apress.com";
                Device.ThisModel.PresentationUrl = "http://www.apress.com";
                // ThisDevice
                Device.ThisDevice.FriendlyName =
                                "Describing device that provides metadata";
                Device.ThisDevice.FirmwareVersion = "demo";
                Device.ThisDevice.SerialNumber = "12345678";

                // Start the device
                Device.Start();

                // Keep the device alive
                Thread.Sleep(Timeout.Infinite);
        }
    }
}
```

■**Note** You can find the MFMetadataProvidingDeviceSample project in this chapter's directory in the Web Services subdirectory.

In the next section, you will learn how a client can obtain the description (metadata) of a device.

Obtaining Device Metadata

To obtain a device's metadata, you need to know the device's transport address. The DpwsMexClient class is responsible for getting the metadata of a device. First, you need to create a DpwsMexClient object and invoke the Get method with the transport address of the desired device as shown in Listing 6-17. The Get method will return either a DpwsMetadata object that provides the description or null if no metadata could be obtained.

Listing 6-17. *Querying Metadata*

```
DpwsMexClient mexClient = new DpwsMexClient();
DpwsMetadata metadata = mexClient.Get(deviceTransportAddr);
if (metadata != null)
{
    // Metadata obtained
}
```

The DpwsMetdata class (see Listing 6-18) provides the Get method and contains the ThisModel and ThisDevice descriptions and information about the host service and the hosted services of a device via the Relationship property that is a DpwsRelationship instance.

Listing 6-18. *The Dpws.Client.Discovery.DpwsMetadata Class*

```
using System;
using System.Xml;

namespace Dpws.Client.Discovery
{
    public class DpwsMetadata
    {
        public readonly DpwsThisModel ThisModel;
        public readonly DpwsThisDevice ThisDevice;
        public readonly DpwsRelationship Relationship;

        public DpwsMetadata(XmlReader reader);
    }
}
```

The Host property of the DpwsRelationship class provides you a host service description. First, you need to check if the device has a host service by comparing the Host property value against null. Its ServiceID property provides the endpoint (logical) address of the service, and the transport address (the physical device address followed by the logical service address) of the service you can obtain with host.EndpointRefs[0].Address.AbsoluteUri.

Each service provides further a list of service type namespaces it relates to. The list contains only the value of the ServiceNamespace property of the DpwsHostedService object and the prefix of the service namespace. You will get all items with the ServiceTypes collection via the metadata description.

The following piece of code will print the metadata for a device's host service:

```
DpwsMexService host = metadata.Relationship.Host;
if (host != null)
{
    Debug.Print("Host:");
    Debug.Print("\tServiceID: " + host.ServiceID);
    Debug.Print("\tAddress: " + host.EndpointRefs[0].Address.AbsoluteUri);
    Debug.Print("\tTypes:");
    for (int t = 0; t < host.ServiceTypes.Count; ++t)
    {
        DpwsServiceType serviceType = host.ServiceTypes[t];
        Debug.Print("\t\tName = " + serviceType.TypeName);
        Debug.Print("\t\tNamespace = " + serviceType.NamespaceUri);
        Debug.Print("");
    }
}
```

> **Note** If you are using the `Address.AbsoluteUri` property to get the transport address of a host service or hosted service, as shown in the previous code, you need to add a reference to the `MFDpwsExtensions.dll` to your project.

The description of a hosted service looks similar to the host service's description. The `HostedServices` property provides a list of `DpwsMexService` objects. Each `DpwsMexService` provides a service ID, transport address, and a collection of service type namespaces.

```
DpwsMexServices hostedServices = metadata.Relationship.HostedServices;
if (hostedServices != null)
{
    Debug.Print("HostedServices:");
    for (int i = 0; i < hostedServices.Count; i++)
    {
        DpwsMexService hostedService = hostedServices[i];
        Debug.Print("\tService ID: " + hostedService.ServiceID);
        Debug.Print("\tAddress: " +
                                hostedService.EndpointRefs[0].Address.AbsoluteUri);
        Debug.Print("\tTypes:");
        for (int t = 0; t < hostedService.ServiceTypes.Count; ++t)
        {
            DpwsServiceType serviceType = hostedService.ServiceTypes[t];
            Debug.Print("\t\tName = " + serviceType.TypeName);
            Debug.Print("\t\tNamespace = " + serviceType.NamespaceUri);
            Debug.Print("");
        }
    }
}
```

> **Note** You can find the `MFMetadataGettingClientSample` project in this chapter's directory in the `Web Services` subdirectory.

Exchanging Metadata with SOAP Messages

Let's take a closer look at the SOAP messages used for metadata exchange. The message that the client sends to request a device's metadata looks quite simple. You can see an example in Listing 6-19. The message contains no parameters in the message body; the header indicates the endpoint address of the target device; and the `Action` tag indicates that it is a metadata request.

Listing 6-19. *A SOAP Message to Request the Metadata of a Device*

```
<?xml version='1.0' encoding='UTF-8'?>
<soap:Envelope xmlns:soap="http://www.w3.org/2003/05/soap-envelope"
               xmlns:wsa="http://schemas.xmlsoap.org/ws/2004/08/addressing"
>
  <soap:Header>
    <wsa:To> urn:uuid:bde0943a-0516-c8ca-80a6-000000b525ed</wsa:To>
    <wsa:Action>http://schemas.xmlsoap.org/ws/2004/09/transfer/Get</wsa:Action>
    <wsa:ReplyTo>
      <wsa:Address>
        http://schemas.xmlsoap.org/ws/2004/08/addressing/role/anonymous
      </wsa:Address>
    </wsa:ReplyTo>
    <wsa:MessageID>urn:uuid:864528bb-045a-c8ca-a007-0000001463b9</wsa:MessageID>
  </soap:Header>
  <soap:Body>
  </soap:Body>
</soap:Envelope>
```

The response containing the description that the device sends back to a client is much more complex (see Listing 6-20). The `RelatesTo` tag indicates that this is a response to the metadata request message. The message body contains a `Metadata` tag that embeds three `MetadataSection` tags. The `Dialect` parameter of `MetadataSection` specifies the purpose, such as `ThisModel`, `ThisDevice`, or `Relationship`. The relationship section consists of zero or one `Host` tags and zero or more `Hosted` sections that contain the information about the host service and hosted services.

Listing 6-20. *Metadata Response*

```
<?xml version='1.0' encoding='UTF-8'?>
<soap:Envelope xmlns:soap="http://www.w3.org/2003/05/soap-envelope"
               xmlns:wsdp="http://schemas.xmlsoap.org/ws/2006/02/devprof"
               xmlns:wsa="http://schemas.xmlsoap.org/ws/2004/08/addressing"
               xmlns:wsx="http://schemas.xmlsoap.org/ws/2004/09/mex"
               xmlns:wsd="http://schemas.xmlsoap.org/ws/2005/04/discovery"
               xmlns:simple2="http://schemas.sample.org/SimpleService2"
>
  <soap:Header>
    <wsa:To>http://schemas.xmlsoap.org/ws/2004/08/addressing/role/anonymous</wsa:To>
    <wsa:Action>
      http://schemas.xmlsoap.org/ws/2004/09/transfer/GetResponse
    </wsa:Action>
    <wsa:MessageID>urn:uuid:85fa1e49-045a-c8ca-b307-000000783a18</wsa:MessageID>
    <wsa:RelatesTo>urn:uuid:864528bb-045a-c8ca-a007-0000001463b9</wsa:RelatesTo>
    <wsd:AppSequence InstanceId="1196751381"
                     SequenceId="urn:uuid:c883e4a8-9af4-4bf4-aaaf-06394151d6c0"
                     MessageNumber="3"
    />
```

```
    </soap:Header>
    <soap:Body>
      <wsx:Metadata>
        <wsx:MetadataSection
          Dialect="http://schemas.xmlsoap.org/ws/2006/02/devprof/ThisModel"
        >
          <wsdp:ThisModel>
            <wsdp:Manufacturer>Apress, Inc.</wsdp:Manufacturer>
            <wsdp:ManufacturerUrl>http://www.apress.com/</wsdp:ManufacturerUrl>
            <wsdp:ModelName>MetadataProvidingModel</wsdp:ModelName>
            <wsdp:ModelNumber>12345</wsdp:ModelNumber>
            <wsdp:ModelUrl>http://www.apress.com/</wsdp:ModelUrl>
            <wsdp:PresentationUrl>http://www.apress.com/</wsdp:PresentationUrl>
            <wsdp:ModelName>MetadataProvidingModel</wsdp:ModelName>
          </wsdp:ThisModel>
        </wsx:MetadataSection>
        <wsx:MetadataSection
              Dialect="http://schemas.xmlsoap.org/ws/2006/02/devprof/ThisDevice"
        >
          <wsdp:ThisDevice>
            <wsdp:FriendlyName>
              Describing device that provides metadata
            </wsdp:FriendlyName>
            <wsdp:FirmwareVersion>demo</wsdp:FirmwareVersion>
            <wsdp:SerialNumber>12345678</wsdp:SerialNumber>
          </wsdp:ThisDevice>
        </wsx:MetadataSection>
        <wsx:MetadataSection
              Dialect="http://schemas.xmlsoap.org/ws/2006/02/devprof/Relationship"
        >
          <wsdp:Relationship
                      Type="http://schemas.xmlsoap.org/ws/2006/02/devprof/host"
          >
          <wsdp:Host>
            <wsa:EndpointReference>
              <wsa:Address>
                http://127.0.0.1:8084/cf16db78-02c9-c8ca-b37b-0000004071f6
              </wsa:Address>
            </wsa:EndpointReference>
            <wsdp:Types>simple1:SimpleServiceType1</wsdp:Types>
            <wsdp:ServiceId>
              urn:uuid:cf16db78-02c9-c8ca-b37b-0000004071f6
            </wsdp:ServiceId>
          </wsdp:Host>
```

```
      <wsdp:Hosted>
        <wsa:EndpointReference>
          <wsa:Address>
            http://127.0.0.1:8084/ec499d62-02c9-c8ca-b7ee-0000000bf3dd
          </wsa:Address>
        </wsa:EndpointReference>
        <wsdp:Types>simple2:SimpleServiceType2</wsdp:Types>
        <wsdp:ServiceId>
          urn:uuid:ec499d62-02c9-c8ca-b7ee-0000000bf3dd
        </wsdp:ServiceId>
      </wsdp:Hosted>
      </wsdp:Relationship>
    </wsx:MetadataSection>
  </wsx:Metadata>
  </soap:Body>
</soap:Envelope>
```

Control

Now that you are able to discover and locate devices with a particular service, you will learn how you can implement service operations on a device to take control over this device from a client. You will also learn the difference between one-way and two-way requests.

Service Operations

Once a client has located a suitable service-providing device, the client can act as a controlling device; it can exert control over a controlled device. To invoke an operation on a device's service, the controlling device (client) sends a control message directly to the service endpoint. Depending on the service operation, it may return a response message with command-specific information.

A service may provide zero or more service operations to be invoked by a client. A service operation can be seen as a kind of method call. Operations may or may not accept input parameters from the caller and may or may not return data to the caller. Operations that do not return a response message are one-way requests, and operations providing a result are two-way requests.

One-Way Requests

Whenever you do not need any feedback and results from a remote operation call, a one-way request might be the best choice.

Implementing the Service

To implement a device with a service that provides a one-way operation, you can use the devices from Listing 6-7 and Listing 6-16 as a base. This time, you must add a working service to the hosted service collection instead of the empty dummy service we used with the discovery samples. Therefore, you should derive a custom service from DpwsHostedService and add it to the device as shown here:

```
Device.HostedServices.Add(new OneWayOperationService());
```

You can do the initialization of the service's `ServiceTypeName`, `ServiceNamespace`, and `ServiceID` properties in the constructor of the custom service class. Until now, there has been nothing special on a device with a functional service.

Now, you will learn how to implement a service operation that accepts one integer argument and does not return anything to the caller.

In the constructor, you need to add a service operation to the device. A service can provide zero or more operations for the clients. A service operation is uniquely described with a qualified name that consists of a namespace and method name.

```
// Add the one-way service operation
WsServiceOperation operation =
                new ServiceOperation(this.ServiceNamespace.NamespaceURI, // namespace
                                    "MyOneWayOperation"); // method name
this.ServiceOperations.Add(operation);
```

Next, you need to implement the actual operation method. The method name must correspond to the operation name you want to provide. The operation method must be declared `public` due to a restriction of the present 2.5 release. Each service operation method has the following signature:

```
public byte[] MyOneWayOperation(WsWsaHeader header,
                                XmlReader reader)
{
    …
}
```

The method accepts the header of the SOAP request and an `XmlReader` object to access the message body, from which you can then extract the arguments for that method. The DPWS stack does not use the body element with a SOAP message that is sent to invoke an operation on a service. Therefore, you can put any additional input information for your service operation into the message body. Listing 6-21 shows how a hypothetical SOAP request to invoke our `MyOneWayOperation` operation on a service might look. The message is sent from the client directly to the service endpoint. You can see this in the target transport address in the `To` tag of the message header. This address consists of the device's IP address and the service ID as defined earlier. The `Action` tag indicates the qualified name of the service operation. Also, our custom integer argument is passed within the message body.

Listing 6-21. *SOAP Request to Invoke MyOneWayOperation*

```
<?xml version='1.0' encoding='UTF-8'?>
<soap:Envelope xmlns:soap="http://www.w3.org/2003/05/soap-envelope"
               xmlns:wsa="http://schemas.xmlsoap.org/ws/2004/08/addressing"
               xmlns:oneWay="http://schemas.sample.org/OneWayOperationService"
>
  <soap:Header>
    <wsa:To>http://169.254.2.2:8084/93252386-0724-c8ca-bd31-000000732d93</wsa:To>
    <wsa:Action>
      http://schemas.sample.org/OneWayOperationService/MyOneWayOperation
    </wsa:Action>
```

```
  <wsa:From>
    <wsa:Address>urn:uuid:431e8a55-0a6a-c8ca-bc42-000000879b6c</wsa:Address>
  </wsa:From>
  <wsa:MessageID>urn:uuid:4330f29f-0a6a-c8ca-b037-000000757037</wsa:MessageID>
 </soap:Header>
 <soap:Body>
   <oneWay:MyOneWayRequest>
     <oneWay:A>99</oneWay:A>
   </oneWay:MyOneWayRequest>
 </soap:Body>
</soap:Envelope>
```

The following code shows an implementation of a service operation that extracts the integer argument from the body of the SOAP request message in Listing 6-21. You can move to the XML node with the parameter value by passing the node name MyOneWayRequest and the namespace URI of the service to the ReadStartElement method. Then you can read the parameter value from node A with the ReadElementString method. The ReadElementString method returns the string representation of the node value. You can extract the integer value from the XML string with the Convert.ToInt32 method of the DpwsExtension.dll assembly.

```
public byte[] MyOneWayOperation(WsWsaHeader header, XmlReader reader)
{
    reader.ReadStartElement("MyOneWayRequest", this.ServiceNamespace.NamespaceURI);

    // Extract parameter A from SOAP message body
    string str = reader.ReadElementString("A", this.ServiceNamespace.NamespaceURI);
    int a = System.Ext.Convert.ToInt32(str);

    Debug.Print("MyOneWayOperation with A=" + a + " executed.");
    return null; // No response it is a one-way operation
}
```

You should return null as the response, since the operation is one-way.

Implementing the Client

Now that you have a device that provides a service with a one-way operation, we will explore how to implement a client that invokes this operation on the device. It is good practice to separate all the controlling code into a DpwsClient subclass. Then, you can use this controller class like a common local class within your application to hide all the remoting details. For example, calling a method on the controller class will generate a SOAP message, send it to the service endpoint, and invoke the method on the service device. You could even implement properties that internally call get and set methods of the service endpoint.

In order to use a service, you need to obtain the transport address of the service endpoint. Therefore, you need to define the search criteria and probe for devices with a particular service. The service that provides the one-way operation, for example, was of the custom type OneWayOperationServiceType. Since you are looking for a device with an OneWayOperationServiceType service, you probe for this service type to return all connected devices that have it. Next, you need to recall the transport address of the first device and request that device's metadata. Once you receive the metadata, you need to find the desired OneWayOperationServiceType service. At this point, you know the discovered device has a OneWayOperationServiceType service, but you need to find that service (the device could have more than one). Therefore, you need to check the metadata of the host service and hosted services. Once you have found the desired service, you need to remember the service transport address (device IP address followed by service ID) and pass it to the constructor of the custom service controller when creating a usable controller object. The static FindFirst method in Listing 6-22 uses this approach and presents a reusable class to obtain a service's transport address if a suitable service on a remote device was found. The FindFirst method accepts the type name and namespace URI of the service to look for.

Listing 6-22. *Obtaining the Transport Address for the First Available Device*

```
using System;
using Microsoft.SPOT;
using Dpws.Client;
using Dpws.Client.Discovery;

namespace MFOneWayOperationClientSample
{
    public class MyClient : DpwsClient
    {
        /// <summary>
        /// Looks for devices that host a service identified by its type and
        /// namespace.
        /// It returns the transport address of the first matching service.
        /// </summary>
        public string FindFirst(string serviceTypeName, string namespaceUri)
        {
            if (serviceTypeName == null)
                throw new ArgumentNullException();
            if (namespaceUri == null)
                throw new ArgumentNullException();

            Debug.Print("Discovering service devices...");
            // Define search criterias
            DpwsServiceType serviceType = new DpwsServiceType(serviceTypeName,
                                                              namespaceUri);
            DpwsServiceTypes filters = new DpwsServiceTypes();
            filters.Add(serviceType);
            // Probe for devices
            DpwsServiceDescriptions probeMatches =
                                          this.DiscoveryClient.Probe(filters);
            if (probeMatches != null && probeMatches.Count > 0)
            {
                // Remember transport address of the first device
                string deviceTransportAddress = probeMatches[0].XAddrs[0];
```

```
            // Request metadata to get the desired service and its ID
            DpwsMexClient mexClient = new DpwsMexClient();
            DpwsMetadata metadata = mexClient.Get(deviceTransportAddress);
            // Check host service
            DpwsMexService host = metadata.Relationship.Host;
            if (host != null) // has host service
            {
                if (host.ServiceTypes[serviceTypeName] != null)
                    return host.EndpointRefs[0].Address.AbsoluteUri;
            }
            // Check hosted services
            DpwsMexServices hostedServices =
                                    metadata.Relationship.HostedServices;
            if (hostedServices != null)
            {
                for(int i = 0; i < hostedServices.Count; ++i)
                {
                    DpwsMexService hostedService = hostedServices[i];
                    if (hostedService.ServiceTypes[serviceTypeName] != null)
                    {
                        return
                            hostedService.EndpointRefs[0].Address.AbsoluteUri;
                    }
                }
            }
        }
        Debug.Print("No service found.");
        return null;
    }
}
}
```

This static FindFirst method will return the transport address of the target service that you can use to create a OneWayOperationServiceController object by passing the transport address of the target service to the controller's constructor. You can invoke the actual operation on the service by calling the MyOneWayOperation method of the controller. This method (see Listing 6-23) will send a SOAP request to the service endpoint to invoke the operation on the client using the SendRequest method of the Dpws.Client.Transport.DpwsHttpClient class in the MFDpwsClient.dll assembly. This method accepts a byte buffer with the SOAP message and the transport address of the target service. In addition, it accepts a flag that indicates whether the method should wait for a result. Setting the isOneWay parameter to true will close the HTTP session immediately after the request is sent, without waiting for any response. You should set the isChunked parameter to false. The target service's transport address is the one that was obtained from the FindFirst method (see Listing 6-22) and passed to the controller's constructor when it was created.

Listing 6-23. *Invoking a Service Operation with a One-Way Request*

```
public void MyOneWayOperation(int a)
{
    // Create HttpClient and send request
    Debug.Print("Sending Request:");
    byte[] request = BuildMyOneWayRequest(a);
    Debug.Print(new string(Encoding.UTF8.GetChars(request)));
    DpwsHttpClient httpClient = new DpwsHttpClient();
    httpClient.SendRequest(request, // soap message
                           this.serviceTransportAddress,
                           true, // is one-way?
                           false // is chunked?
                           );
}
```

The SOAP request message is built in the BuildMyOneWayRequest method. To invoke the MyOneWayOperation method on the service, you need to build a request message similar to the one in Listing 6-21. Listing 6-24 demonstrates how to build a SOAP request message programmatically.

Listing 6-24. *Building a SOAP Message*

```
private byte[] BuildMyOneWayRequest(int a)
{
    MemoryStream soapStream = new MemoryStream();
    XmlWriter xmlWriter = XmlWriter.Create(soapStream);

    // Write processing instructions and root element
    xmlWriter.WriteProcessingInstruction("xml", "version='1.0' encoding='UTF-8'");
    xmlWriter.WriteStartElement("soap", "Envelope",
                                WsWellKnownUri.SoapNamespaceUri);

    // Write namespaces
    xmlWriter.WriteAttributeString("xmlns", "wsa", null,
                                     WsWellKnownUri.WsaNamespaceUri);
    // Write our namespace
    xmlWriter.WriteAttributeString("xmlns", c_namespacePrefix, null,
                                     c_namespaceUri);

    // Write header
    xmlWriter.WriteStartElement("soap", "Header", null);
    xmlWriter.WriteStartElement("wsa", "To", null);
    xmlWriter.WriteString(this.serviceTransportAddress);
    xmlWriter.WriteEndElement(); // End To
    // Action indicates the desired operation to execute
    xmlWriter.WriteStartElement("wsa", "Action", null);
```

```
xmlWriter.WriteString(c_namespaceUri + "/" + "MyOneWayOperation");
xmlWriter.WriteEndElement(); // End Action
xmlWriter.WriteStartElement("wsa", "From", null);
xmlWriter.WriteStartElement("wsa", "Address", null);
xmlWriter.WriteString(this.EndpointAddress); // client endpoint addr
xmlWriter.WriteEndElement(); // End Address
xmlWriter.WriteEndElement(); // End From
xmlWriter.WriteStartElement("wsa", "MessageID", null);
xmlWriter.WriteString("urn:uuid:" + Guid.NewGuid());
xmlWriter.WriteEndElement(); // End MessageID
xmlWriter.WriteEndElement(); // End Header

// write body
xmlWriter.WriteStartElement("soap", "Body", null);
// This is the container for our data
xmlWriter.WriteStartElement(c_namespacePrefix, "MyOneWayRequest", null);
// The actual parameter value
xmlWriter.WriteStartElement(c_namespacePrefix, "A", null);
xmlWriter.WriteString(a.ToString());
xmlWriter.WriteEndElement(); // End A
xmlWriter.WriteEndElement(); // End MyOneWayRequest
xmlWriter.WriteEndElement(); // End Body

xmlWriter.WriteEndElement();

// Create return buffer and close writer
xmlWriter.Flush();
byte[] soapBuffer = soapStream.ToArray();
xmlWriter.Close();

return soapBuffer;
}
```

Two-Way Requests

Two-way requests are similar to one-way requests, but the method for a two-way operation *must* return a valid SOAP message that contains the result information for the caller.

Listing 6-25 shows an operation that accepts two integer parameters and returns their quotient. Extracting both arguments is done in the same way as in the previous, one-way operation.

Listing 6-25. *A Two-Way Operation That Accepts Two Integers and Returns the Quotient*

```
public byte[] MyTwoWayOperation(WsWsaHeader header, XmlReader reader)
{
    reader.ReadStartElement("MyTwoWayRequest", this.ServiceNamespace.NamespaceURI);
```

```
    // Extract parameter A from SOAP message body
    string strA = reader.ReadElementString("A", this.ServiceNamespace.NamespaceURI);
    int a = System.Ext.Convert.ToInt32(strA);
    // Extract parameter B from SOAP message body
    string strB = reader.ReadElementString("B", this.ServiceNamespace.NamespaceURI);
    int b = System.Ext.Convert.ToInt32(strB);

    Debug.Print("MyTwoWayOperation with A=" + a + " / B=" + b + " executed.");
    int quotient = a / b;
    Debug.Print("Operation returns " + quotient + ".");
    return BuildMyTwoWayResponse(header, quotient);
}
```

The method returns a SOAP response message that is built with the BuildMyTwoWayReponse method (see Listing 6-26). The BuildMyTwoWayReponse method accepts the quotient value to return to the caller and the message header of the request message. You need to have the header of the request message, because it contains the message ID of the request to insert into the RelatesTo tag, so the caller knows that this is the response to its request. Further, the To tag will get the value of the request From tag to route the response back to the sender. You can set an arbitrary value to the Action tag for the operation response, because it is ignored by the DPWS stack, and the RelatesTo value already indicates the origin. In Listing 6-27, you can see an example for the response message.

Listing 6-26. *Building a SOAP Response*

```
public byte[] BuildMyTwoWayResponse(WsWsaHeader header, int quotient)
{
    MemoryStream soapStream = new MemoryStream();
    XmlWriter xmlWriter = XmlWriter.Create(soapStream);

    // Write processing instructions and root element
    xmlWriter.WriteProcessingInstruction("xml", "version='1.0' encoding='UTF-8'");
    xmlWriter.WriteStartElement("soap", "Envelope",
                                WsWellKnownUri.SoapNamespaceUri);

    // Write namespaces
    xmlWriter.WriteAttributeString("xmlns", "wsa", null,
                                    WsWellKnownUri.WsaNamespaceUri);
    xmlWriter.WriteAttributeString("xmlns", "twoWay", null, c_namespaceUri);

    // Write header
    xmlWriter.WriteStartElement("soap", "Header", null);
    xmlWriter.WriteStartElement("wsa", "To", null);
    xmlWriter.WriteString(header.From.Address.AbsoluteUri);
    xmlWriter.WriteEndElement();
    xmlWriter.WriteStartElement("wsa", "Action", null);
    xmlWriter.WriteString(c_namespaceUri + "/TwoWayOperationResponse");
    xmlWriter.WriteEndElement();
```

```
    xmlWriter.WriteStartElement("wsa", "RelatesTo", null);
    xmlWriter.WriteString(header.MessageID);
    xmlWriter.WriteEndElement(); // End RelatesTo
    xmlWriter.WriteStartElement("wsa", "MessageID", null);
    xmlWriter.WriteString("urn:uuid:" + Guid.NewGuid());
    xmlWriter.WriteEndElement(); // End MessageID
    xmlWriter.WriteEndElement(); // End Header

    // write body
    xmlWriter.WriteStartElement("soap", "Body", null);
    xmlWriter.WriteStartElement("twoWay", "MyTwoWayResponse", null);
    xmlWriter.WriteStartElement("twoWay", "Quotient", null);
    xmlWriter.WriteString(quotient.ToString());
    xmlWriter.WriteEndElement(); // End Quotient
    xmlWriter.WriteEndElement(); // End MyTwoWayResponse
    xmlWriter.WriteEndElement(); // End Body

    xmlWriter.WriteEndElement();

    // Create return buffer and close writer
    xmlWriter.Flush();
    byte[] soapBuffer = soapStream.ToArray();
    xmlWriter.Close();

    return soapBuffer;
}
```

Listing 6-27. *An Example SOAP Response*

```
<?xml version='1.0' encoding='UTF-8'?>
<soap:Envelope xmlns:soap="http://www.w3.org/2003/05/soap-envelope"
               xmlns:wsa="http://schemas.xmlsoap.org/ws/2004/08/addressing"
               xmlns:twoWay="http://schemas.sample.org/TwoWayOperationService"
>
  <soap:Header>
    <wsa:To>urn:uuid:f888d660-0c33-c8ca-b05b-000000270d0d</wsa:To>
    <wsa:Action>
      http://schemas.sample.org/TwoWayOperationService/TwoWayOperationResponse
    </wsa:Action>
    <wsa:RelatesTo>urn:uuid:f89a159f-0c33-c8ca-a738-000000d9e738</wsa:RelatesTo>
    <wsa:MessageID>urn:uuid:f875bf65-0c33-c8ca-b19b-00000046666e</wsa:MessageID>
  </soap:Header>
  <soap:Body>
    <twoWay:MyTwoWayResponse>
      <twoWay:Quotient>5</twoWay:Quotient>
    </twoWay:MyTwoWayResponse>
  </soap:Body>
</soap:Envelope>
```

On the client that invokes the two-way operation, you must indicate that it is a two-way operation when using the `SendRequest` method of `DpwsHttpClient`. You can do so by passing `false` for the `isOneWay` argument (see Listing 6-28), which lets the client wait for a response and keeps the HTTP session active until the response is transferred. Setting the `isOneWay` argument to `false` is very important; if you don't, `SendRequest` will return `null` each time.

Listing 6-28. *Invoking a Two-Way Operation and Parsing the Response*

```
public int MyTwoWayOperation(int a, int b)
{
    // Create HttpClient and send request
    Debug.Print("Sending Request:");
    byte[] request = BuildMyTwoWayRequest(a, b);
    Debug.Print(new string(Encoding.UTF8.GetChars(request)));
    DpwsHttpClient httpClient = new DpwsHttpClient();
    DpwsSoapResponse response =
                        httpClient.SendRequest(request, // soap message
                                               this.serviceTransportAddress,
                                               false, // is one way?
                                               false // is chunked?
                                               );
    if (response == null)
        throw new InvalidOperationException("Two-way response was null.");
    try
    {
        return ParseTwoWayResponse(response.Reader);
    }
    finally
    {
        response.Reader.Close();
    }
}
```

Handling Faults

Sometimes, you may need to inform the caller of an operation that an error occurred during method execution. For local methods, an exception is thrown once an error has occurred. The DPWS specification uses faults for error handling. A fault is described with the following four text attributes:

- Code

- Subcode

- Reason

- Detail

Faults are indicated to the sender of a two-way request by returning a SOAP response with the Action tag set to http://schemas.xmlsoap.org/ws/2004/08/addressing/fault in the header instead of an operation-specific response.

For example, if you try to invoke an operation that does not exist on a service, you will get back a fault message like the one shown in Listing 6-29.

Listing 6-29. *An Example Fault Response*

```xml
<?xml version='1.0' encoding='UTF-8'?>
<soap:Envelope xmlns:soap="http://www.w3.org/2003/05/soap-envelope"
               xmlns:wsa="http://schemas.xmlsoap.org/ws/2004/08/addressing"
               xmlns:Ws="http://schemas.xmlsoap.org/ws/2006/02/devprof"
>
  <soap:Header>
    <wsa:To>urn:schemas-xmlsoap-org:ws:2004:08:fault</wsa:To>
    <wsa:Action>http://schemas.xmlsoap.org/ws/2004/08/addressing/fault</wsa:Action>
    <wsa:RelatesTo>urn:uuid:27561cba-0c41-c8ca-8662-000000ddc662</wsa:RelatesTo>
    <wsa:MessageID>urn:uuid:27455d7e-0c41-c8ca-8a6d-0000003fc392</wsa:MessageID>
  </soap:Header>
  <soap:Body>
    <wsa:Fault>
      <wsa:Code>
        <wsa:Value>soap:Sender</wsa:Value>
        <wsa:Subcode>
          <wsa:Value>wsa:DestinationUnreachable</wsa:Value>
        </wsa:Subcode>
      </wsa:Code>
      <wsa:Reason>
        <wsa:Text lang="en">
          No route can be determined to reach the destination role defined by the
          WS=Addressing To.
        </wsa:Text>
      </wsa:Reason>
      <Ws:Detail>
      </Ws:Detail>
    </wsa:Fault>
  </soap:Body>
</soap:Envelope>
```

Indicating a Fault Condition

If errors occur during the execution of a service operation, you need to indicate the error situation to the caller by returning a fault response instead of the normal response. You can build the SOAP fault response message from scratch, but the .NET Micro Framework provides the WsFaultException class to do this for you.

The WsFaultException enables you to create and return a fault by specifying a fault type and fault message.

You can return a fault response with the following code:

```
throw new WsFaultException(header, WsFaultType.Exception, "Describe details here.");
```

The WsFaultException constructor accepts the message header of the preceding request so that it can build a response to exactly this request. In addition, you need to specify an exception type and a detailed description. The WsFaultType enumeration allows you to specify one of the following exception types:

- Exception

- ArgumentException

- ArgumentNullException

- InvalidOperationException

- XmlException

This enumeration contains some more fault types, not mentioned previously, that are used internally by the DPWS stack to indicate addressing and eventing faults.

Listing 6-30 shows the two-way operation method from Listing 6-25 with additional fault handling. The method detects if the input arguments are missing and returns a fault response if the caller tries to divide by zero.

Listing 6-30. *A Service Operation with Fault Handling*

```
public byte[] MyTwoWayOperation(WsWsaHeader header, XmlReader reader)
{
    try
    {
        reader.ReadStartElement("MyTwoWayRequest",
                                this.ServiceNamespace.NamespaceURI);

        // Extract parameter A from SOAP message body
        string strA = reader.ReadElementString("A",
                                                this.ServiceNamespace.NamespaceURI);

        int a = System.Ext.Convert.ToInt32(strA);
        // Extract parameter B from SOAP message body
        string strB = reader.ReadElementString("B",
                                                this.ServiceNamespace.NamespaceURI);
        int b = System.Ext.Convert.ToInt32(strB);
        if (b == 0)
            throw new WsFaultException(header, WsFaultType.ArgumentException,
                                "Division by zero. Argument B must not be zero.");

        Debug.Print("MyTwoWayOperation with A=" + a + " / B=" + b + " executed.");
        int quotient = a / b;
        Debug.Print("Operation returns " + quotient + ".");
        return BuildMyTwoWayResponse(header, quotient);
    }
```

```
catch (XmlException ex)
{
    throw new WsFaultException(header, WsFaultType.XmlException, ex.Message);
}
catch (WsFaultException)
{
    throw; // rethrow fault exception as it is
}
catch (Exception ex) // all other exception types
{
    throw new WsFaultException(header, WsFaultType.Exception, ex.Message);
}
}
```

All WsFaultException instances thrown in a two-way service operation will be returned to the remote caller of the method (client).

The first exception handler in the listing catches all XmlException instances and then returns an XML fault with the exception message to the caller. The second handler catches WsFaultException objects that were already thrown in the method, like if the b argument is zero. The last handler catches all other exception types and returns a fault including the exception's message. If you want to provide more information about a caught exception than just its message, use the ToString to obtain more information that can be passed to the WsFaultException constructor.

Detecting and Handling a Fault

Once the client receives a response message, it needs to check whether or not the message is a fault response. The Action tag in the SOAP message header has the value http://schemas. xmlsoap.org/ws/2004/08/addressing/fault for fault messages. The Subcode tag indicates the fault type. You can use it to get the exception type. The Reason tag gives a description based on the fault type, and the Detail tag contains the custom fault description that you can pass to the RaiseFault method.

For example, assuming a service operation returns a fault response built with the following code:

```
throw new WsFaultException(header, WsFaultType.ArgumentException,
                    "Division by zero. Argument B must not be zero.");
```

you will get the following information with the fault response:

- *Code*: soap:Receiver

- *Subcode*: Ws:ArgumentException

- *Reason*: One of the arguments provided to a method is not valid.

- *Detail*: Division by zero. Argument B must not be zero.

It is advisable to detect a fault and then throw an exception, as this is the common way to handle errors in the .NET platform. That means the client calls a remote operation on a service device. The service returns a fault response to the caller if an error occurred during execution of the service method. The client detects the fault in the response and throws an exception (on the client). This approach allows you to call remote methods just like local methods within your application.

The code in Listing 6-31 shows the reusable CheckFaultResponse method that allows you check if a response is a fault response. This method throws an exception if a fault occurred. The exception message contains the fault reason, detail, and the exception type indicated in the subcode. You need to call the CheckFaultResponse method and pass the response to it right after you receive the DpwsSoapResponse response from the SendRequest method of the DpwsHttpClient class.

Listing 6-31. *A Reusable Method to Check a Response for Faults*

```
private void CheckFaultResponse(DpwsSoapResponse response)
{
    if (response == null)
        throw new Exception("Response was null.");
    // Check for fault message
    if (response.Header.Action ==
                        "http://schemas.xmlsoap.org/ws/2004/08/addressing/fault")
    {
        // Parse fault message
        response.Reader.ReadStartElement("Fault", WsWellKnownUri.WsaNamespaceUri);

        response.Reader.ReadStartElement("Code", WsWellKnownUri.WsaNamespaceUri);
        string code = response.Reader.ReadElementString("Value",
                                                WsWellKnownUri.WsaNamespaceUri);
        response.Reader.ReadStartElement("Subcode", WsWellKnownUri.WsaNamespaceUri);
        string subcode = response.Reader.ReadElementString("Value",
                                                WsWellKnownUri.WsaNamespaceUri);
        response.Reader.ReadEndElement();
        response.Reader.ReadEndElement();

        response.Reader.ReadStartElement("Reason", WsWellKnownUri.WsaNamespaceUri);
        string reason = response.Reader.ReadElementString("Text",
                                                WsWellKnownUri.WsaNamespaceUri);
        response.Reader.ReadEndElement();

        string detail = response.Reader.ReadElementString("Detail",
                                                WsWellKnownUri.WsdpNamespaceUri);

        Debug.Print("Fault response received:");
        Debug.Print("Code: " + code);
        Debug.Print("Subcode: " + subcode);
        Debug.Print("Reason: " + reason);
        Debug.Print("Detail: " + detail);

        string exceptionMessage = reason + "\n" + detail +
                            "\nCode: " + code +
                            "\nSubcode: " + subcode;
```

```
        // Throw exception depending on sub code
        switch (subcode)
        {
            case "Ws:Exception":
                throw new Exception(exceptionMessage);
            case "Ws:ArgumentException":
                throw new ArgumentException(exceptionMessage);
            case "Ws:ArgumentNullException":
                throw new ArgumentNullException(exceptionMessage);
            case "Ws:InvalidOperationException":
                throw new InvalidOperationException(exceptionMessage);
            case "Ws:XmlException":
                throw new XmlException(exceptionMessage);
            default:
                throw new Exception(exceptionMessage);
        }
    }
}
```

Events

The DPWS standard defines an eventing mechanism that allows devices to send a notification to clients that have subscribed to a particular event. DPWS eventing can be compared to events with the .NET Framework in that one or more clients can subscribe to an event. DPWS eventing provides an asynchronous notification mechanism that, for example, allows a printer device to notify a client that it is out of paper or that a print job is done or enables a portable battery-driven device to notify a client that its battery is low.

Event notifications are, like control messages, simply SOAP messages. The client provides an endpoint event handler method that is similar to a service operation endpoint. Event notifications are sent as one-way messages, so an event handler does not return a response. With DPWS eventing, a client (called an event sink) needs to register interest in receiving (that is, subscribe to) messages about an event (notifications) from a service (event source). A subscription is provided from an event source to an event sink and may expire over time, though the event sink may renew the subscription. The DPWS standard provides three built-in operations to manage event subscriptions: Subscribe, Renew, and Unsubscribe. There is also the GetStatus operation to query the status of an event subscription. If the subscription is valid and has not expired, you will get a response message.

If the event source terminates a subscription unexpectedly, the event source should send a Subscription End SOAP message to the client. This message will not be sent if an event subscription expires.

Implementing the Event Source on the Device

To add an event source on a service, you need to create a DpwsWseEventSource object and describe it with a prefix, namespace, and event name. The event name is, like with operations, the name of the event handler method at the client side. You must add the DpwsWseEndpoint object to the EventSources collection of your service. A good place to do this is the constructor of your service (see Listing 6-32).

Listing 6-32. *Adding an Event Source*

```
DpwsWseEventSource eventSource =
                    new DpwsWseEventSource(this.ServiceNamespace.Prefix,
                                           this.ServiceNamespace.NamespaceURI,
                                           "SimpleEvent"); // event name
this.EventSources.Add(eventSource);
```

Next, you need to implement a method that fires your event. In order to fire an event for a particular event source, you need to have an event source instance. You can either remember the instance from the constructor when you added it to the event source collection, or you can obtain it from the event source collection by the event name. The subscription manager provides a method to fire an event. The method accepts an instance of the service that fires the event, an event source, and a SOAP message header and body for the event notification message. You are responsible for building the message body that may contain additional parameters yourself. The code in Listing 6-33 shows an example of a method that fires an event with an integer parameter.

Listing 6-33. *Firing an Event*

```
public void FireSimpleEvent(int a)
{
    DpwsWseEventSource eventSource = this.EventSources["SimpleEvent"];
    WsWsaHeader header = new WsWsaHeader(c_namespaceUri + "/SimpleEvent", null,
                                         null, null, null, null);
    Device.SubscriptionManager.FireEvent(this, // hosted service
                                         eventSource,
                                         header,
                                         BuildSimpleEventMessageBody(a)
                                         );
    Debug.Print("Simple event was fired with param a=" + a + ".");
}
```

An event notification SOAP message looks similar to a control message. It can provide arguments to the event handlers (event sinks) in the same way that you can invoke service operations (see Listing 6-34). The only difference is that an event notification may be sent to more than one event sink.

Listing 6-34. *Building a SOAP Event Message Body Including a Parameter*

```
private string BuildSimpleEventMessageBody(int a)
{
    return "<evnt:SimpleEvent xmlns:evnt='" + c_namespaceUri + "'>" +
           "<evnt:A>" + a + "</evnt:A>" +
           "</evnt:SimpleEvent>";
}
```

Implementing an Event Sink on the Client

In this section, you will learn how to implement an event handler on the client side and how to subscribe to an event.

To test the eventing scenario with a service and client on your development PC's emulator, you need to set the `IgnoreRequestFromThisIP` property of your client to `false` in your client's constructor. Otherwise, the client will ignore event notifications coming from a device on the same PC.

Next, you need to register your event handler method on the client in its constructor (see Listing 6-35), like you did with service operations on a device. An event sink is described by a prefix, namespace, and event name. The event name must be the same as the method name of your event handler method.

Listing 6-35. *Registering the Event Sink*

```
this.ServiceOperations.Add(
                    new WsServiceOperation(c_namespaceUri, // namespace
                                           "SimpleEvent")  // event (method) name
                    );
```

Next, you need to subscribe to an event (see Listing 6-36). The eventing client provides a `Subscribe` method to do that. The method accepts a subscription type that consists of the namespace prefix, namespace, and event name. Further, it accepts the transport address of the event source and the address of the event sink. You can also specify an expiration time and an event identifier, or you can specify `null` for the `expires` argument if the subscription should never expire. For the event identifier, you can pass `null` if you have only one event and do not need to distinguish among several events.

Listing 6-36. *Subscribing to an Event*

```
DpwsServiceType subscriptionType = new DpwsServiceType("SimpleEvent",
                                             c_namespaceUri);
DpwsSubscribeRequest request =
        new DpwsSubscribeRequest(subscriptionType,        // subscription type
                                 serviceTransportAddress, // event source address
                                 this.TransportAddress,   // notify to address
                                 null,                    // expires
                                 null                     // event identifier
                                 );
this.EventingClient.Subscribe(request);
```

The `expires` argument is accepted as a string in the form `PYMDTHMS`. It must start with a "P." For example, the value `PT1H` specifies that the subscription expires after one hour. For the DPWS specification, the .NET Micro Framework DPWS stack supports only relative durations, not absolute expiration times.

In addition to the `Subscribe` method, the eventing client provides the `Renew`, `Unsubscribe`, and `GetStatus` methods. The `Subscribe` method returns a `DpwsSubscribeResponse` object with a subscription ID. You need to use this information to identify your subscription when renewing or unsubscribing it.

The actual event handler method looks like a service operation method. It has the same type of signature, and you can extract the input arguments from the SOAP message body in the same way as with service operations. An event handler always should return an empty byte array (new byte[0]), since event handlers do not provide a response. You must not return null, because that would cause an error with the current 2.5 DPWS stack release.

```
private byte[] SimpleEvent(WsWsaHeader header, XmlReader reader)
{
    reader.ReadStartElement("SimpleEvent", c_namespaceUri);

    // Extract parameter Quotient from SOAP message body
    string str = reader.ReadElementString("A", c_namespaceUri);
    int a = System.Ext.Convert.ToInt32(str);
    Debug.Print("Simple event notification was received with A=" +
            a + ".");

    // Event handlers provide no response (but do not return null).
    return new byte[0];
}
```

The DpwsClient class provides an event handler for the subscription end event (SubscriptionEndEvent).

Learning More About DPWS

Use the following sources to learn more about DPWS:

- *DPWS*: http://specs.xmlsoap.org/ws/2006/02/devprof

- *WS-Discovery*: http://schemas.xmlsoap.org/ws/2005/04/discovery

- *WS-MetadataExchange*: http://schemas.xmlsoap.org/ws/2004/09/mex

- *WS-Addressing*: www.w3.org/Submission/ws-addressing

- *WS-Eventing*: www.w3.org/Submission/WS-Eventing

- *Web Services on devices*: http://msdn2.microsoft.com/en-us/library/aa826001.aspx

Summary

In this chapter, you learned a lot of things about networking.

The first half covered low-level socket programming and demonstrated how you can write a client and server and let them communicate with both connection-based TCP/IP and connectionless UDP. It also showed how you can obtain information about the network capabilities of your device and configure your device programmatically.

The second half explored Web Services on devices. You learned how the DPWS stack works, how you can use the .NET Micro Framework to build a device that provides services to clients, and how clients can consume services of a device. This chapter defined logical and physical addresses and the difference between host and hosted services. It also covered dynamic discovery of devices and detecting newly available devices. You now know how to probe for devices, resolve devices, and exchange metadata. You also learned how controlling and eventing work and how you can implement them with the .NET Micro Framework. Now, you are ready to use this promising technology to build complex communication scenarios.

The next chapter describes and compares various wireless communication technologies. You will learn about using Ethernet networking wirelessly and learn more about other wireless communication approaches.

CHAPTER 7

■■■

Wireless Communication

If a microcontroller needs to communicate wirelessly with other devices such as PCs, PDAs, other microcontrollers, or sensors, wireless LAN, Bluetooth, Z-Wave, and, more recently, ZigBee are the four main technologies you can use to facilitate that communication. The most suitable of these technologies to use depends on your application, as all technologies were conceived for a certain purpose and are optimized for that.

In the previous chapter, you learned how to program networking applications. You can use this know-how to also work with wireless LAN communications. This chapter will show you how you can add wireless functionality to your .NET Micro Framework hardware with original equipment manufacturer (OEM) modules. At the end of the chapter, I will compare these technologies to help you decide which technology best fits your application.

Wireless LAN

Wireless local area network (WLAN) is the wireless version of the Ethernet LAN technology; this technology is called also Wi-Fi (Wireless Fidelity). WLAN is defined by the industry standard of the IEEE 802.11 family, and the IEEE 802.11b subtype is most often used.

IEEE 802.11b transmits on the 2.4 GHz frequency and has a bandwidth of up to 11 mega-bits per second. Commercial equipment has a range of up to 100 meters in an open outdoor area and can be increased to 300 meters by external antennas. WLAN is a common standard and is supported currently on many PDAs, notebooks, and PCs. Due to the high transmission speed, WLAN is the best choice for PC networks, wireless Internet, and video streaming, for example.

To be able to use WLAN with a .NET Micro Framework device, WLAN must be integrated on the device. You can find more information about available devices and their capabilities in Chapter 2.

The programming of WLAN is accomplished in the same way as networking via Ethernet LAN—by using network sockets. Therefore, please refer to Chapter 6, which covered networking, for more information.

■**Note** The Digi Connect devices were, for a long time, the only network-enabled devices. The Digi Connect devices used a built-in TCP/IP stack implemented by Digi for the network support. Network programming was accomplished, then, with classes and methods from the .NET Micro Framework base class library, which, under the hood, take services from the Digi stack. However, Microsoft implemented its own TCP/IP stack for the .NET Micro Framework that is available since, and built into, the .NET Micro Framework 2.5 firmware. Since that's available, a larger spectrum of platforms with (wireless) network support will follow.

Bluetooth

Bluetooth technology came from a 1994 study by the Ericsson company, which sought to find a replacement for cable connections. Due to the results of the study, the companies Ericsson, Nokia, IBM, Toshiba, and Intel adopted the specification as industry standard IEEE 802.15.2. The name comes from the Danish Viking King Harald Blatand (in English, "Bluetooth"), who united nearly all of Scandinavia in the 10th century. The Bluetooth name honors the high level of Scandinavian participation in the development. In addition, it embodies the hope that one day all mobile devices will be united and able to communicate with one another.

The Bluetooth technology was developed as an inexpensive cable replacement for connecting mobile and stationary equipment. A large number of mobile phones, PDAs, and some notebooks already integrate Bluetooth. Additionally, this technology can be retooled simply and inexpensively by USB-Bluetooth modules for the PC or notebook.

IEEE 802.15.2 sends, like WLAN, on the 2.4 GHz frequency. The effective net transmission rate for Bluetooth version 1.0, 1.0B, 1.1, and 1.2 amounts to 730 kilobits per second, and for Bluetooth version 2.1 with enhanced data rate (EDR) transmission, it amounts to up to 2.1 megabits per second. Version 2.1 with EDR is backward compatible with the first versions.

The Bluetooth standard specifies how devices detect each other and establish connections among themselves, and how the data communication is performed and secured. For Bluetooth devices, there are three power classes, resulting in three different sending ranges and power consumption rates, as shown in Table 7-1.

Table 7-1. *Bluetooth Power Classes*

Type	Sending Range	Sending Power
Class 3 Devices	10 m	1 milliwatt (mW)
Class 2 Devices	20 m	2 mW
Class 1 Devices	100 m	100 mW

Several Bluetooth profiles are defined; each describes a different intended purpose or different characteristics of a device. Thus there is a profile for accessing printers, one for head sets, one for serial data exchange, and still many more.

The .NET Micro Framework does not support Bluetooth directly. There are, however, several Bluetooth-Serial adapters, which are available as OEM modules. These are then wired to the serial port of a device and redirect all serial data to and from the air.

Additionally, some modules for interfacing with the SPI or I^{2}C bus are available.

These modules are mostly passive modules (acceptors); in other words, they cannot detect other equipment and are not able to initiate connections. The modules can be detected only by other devices, which the connections initiate. Additionally, only the serial port profile (SPP) is supported with these adapters.

To configure such a Bluetooth adapter, you have two options for bringing it into configuration mode. First, you can drive a control pin. When an adapter is in configuration mode, it will listen to configuration commands. The other way to set up an adapter is to send special AT commands to it, thus data exchange and configuration do not disturb one another. Commands are text lines that start with AT (Attention), which tells the adapter that a configuration command follows. You can use configuration, for example, to set up the baud rate for interfacing with the microcontroller, or you can give the device a friendly name under which it can be seen by other devices. A microcontroller with a Bluetooth adapter can be detected and identified by a remote PDA or a PC, which might then establish a connection. On a PC or PDA, every remote Bluetooth device with SPP is assigned to a virtual COM port. Because of that, you can exchange data between two Bluetooth devices very easily. Both on the microcontroller with the .NET Micro Framework and on the remote side, you exchange data exactly the same as if both devices are connected with a serial cable.

Additionally, there are Bluetooth-Serial adapters, like the Promi SD, with which other Bluetooth devices can be detected. The Promi SD is able to connect to other modules (acts as initiator). To do this, you have to send special AT commands over the serial port to the device. In this way, two microcontrollers can talk to one another.

ZigBee

ZigBee is a very new technology for wireless communication. ZigBee was defined by the ZigBee Alliance (www.zigbee.org), which is comprised of the companies Phillips, Siemens, Samsung, Motorola, and Texas Instruments, among others. ZigBee is described by the industry standard IEEE 802.15.4. The name "ZigBee" comes from the zigzag dance honey bees use to communicate with other bees in the hive.

ZigBee focuses particularly on connecting and controlling home equipment. With ZigBee, you can access and control household appliances, sensors, and actors over short distances. Concrete applications would be, for example, monitoring a smoke detector or automatically controlling a light switch in your home.

The ZigBee technology sends in the frequency range of 2.4 GHz, like the two other wireless technologies. One of the primary goals of ZigBee was to work for very low-power devices. Therefore, the sensors' battery life can be several months or years. The data rate with ZigBee is relatively small and amounts to 20 to 25 kilobits per second. With this technology, the low-power requirement was placed before the bandwidth. Besides, to remotely control a light switch, you do not need high transmission rates. The range of IEEE 802.15.4 is 20 to 100 meters. A ZigBee network can consist of up to 250 devices (with Bluetooth, the network can consist of only 7).

ZigBee operates as WLAN on the 2.4 GHz bandwidth and can interfere with WLAN, which can be a problem in home automation control where WLAN (including Voice over IP telephony) is becoming more and more popular.

The following device types can be in a ZigBee network:

- The *network coordinator* knows and manages the whole network. The coordinator is the most complex device variant, and it has the greatest resource requirements. There is exactly one coordinator per network.

- A *full-function device (FFD)* implements the complete function range in accordance with the standard. An FFD device can communicate with other devices and can act as a network router or the coordinator.

- A *reduced-function device (RFD)* possesses a reduced function range, only the range necessary to communicate as a network node with the network coordinator. This is the simplest and least expensive type of device.

ZigBee is not supported directly by the .NET Micro Framework. However, there are already OEM modules to interface with the serial port or SPI bus. Most of these OEM modules are meant for network terminals and support from there only the RFD standard.

Z-Wave

Z-Wave is a wireless communication standard developed by the Danish company Zensys and the Z-Wave Alliance. The Z-Wave Alliance consists of over 160 members who create or plan to create home automation equipment. Key members are Leviton, Intermatic, and Honeywell.

Z-Wave is a proprietary wireless protocol oriented to the residential control and automation market. Zensys offers an integrated circuit (IC) coupled with the Z-Wave stack.

In comparison to the competing technology ZigBee, Z-Wave focuses also on home automation control but is designed for a low data rate, small stack size, low costs, and low power consumption. Z-Wave devices can operate in the industrial, scientific, and medical (ISM) band on a single frequency at 900 MHz, so they will not interfere with WLAN (including Voice over IP telephony) when in use for home automation control. The data rate with Z-Wave is around 10 kilobits per second. Each Z-Wave network may include up to 232 nodes and consists of two sets of nodes: controllers and slave devices. The sending range of Z-Wave ranges from 10 meters (indoors) to 75 meters (outdoors). Z-Wave use is widespread, and several devices already exist for residential control.

Z-Wave is not supported directly by the .NET Micro Framework. However, there are already OEM modules to interface with the serial port. The company ControlThink developed a library called ThinkRemote for accessing Z-Wave with the .NET Micro Framework. It is used with SideShow-enabled remote controls, since SideShow is implemented and based on the .NET Micro Framework.

Comparing Wireless Technologies

Table 7-2 shows all four wireless technologies that were presented in this chapter. It compares several features of the technologies. You can see that WLAN is the most powerful, but most resource requiring and expensive technology. The simplest and low-cost but low-power technology is Z-Wave. This table will help you to find the most suitable technology for your wireless application with lowest hardware costs and energy-consumption.

Table 7-2. *Comparison of WLAN, Bluetooth, ZigBee, and Z-Wave*

Feature	WLAN	Bluetooth	ZigBee	Z-Wave
Maximum bandwidth	11 megabits/second (Mb/s)	1 / 2.1 Mb/s	0.2 Mb/s	0.1 Mb/s
Power consumption (battery life)	High (1–3 hours)	Medium (4–8 hours)	Very low (2–3 years)	Ultra low (several years)
Maximum distance	100/300 m	10/20/100 m (Class 3/2/1)	20–100 m	10–75 m
Hardware costs	High	Medium	Low	Very low
Footprint of protocol stack	>100 kilobytes (KB)	approximately 100 KB	approximately 32 KB	32 KB
Industry standard	IEEE 802.11 a, b, and g	IEEE 802.15.2	IEEE 802.15.4	Zensys proprietary technology
Frequency	2.4 GHz	2.4 GHz	2.4 GHz	900 MHz
Maximum number of network nodes	Nearly unlimited	7 (generally, 2 are used)	250	232
Spreading	High (PC, Notebook, PDA)	High (notebooks, PCs, PDAs, smartphones, and mobile phones)	Low (sensors and actors)	High (sensors and actors)
Example applications	PC networking, wireless Internet, and video streaming	Replacing cables, serving as a kind of wireless USB, and driving head sets, wireless printing, and file transfers	Home automation, industrial control, remote controls, sensors, switches, and smoke detectors	Home automation

Links to Bluetooth, ZigBee, and Z-Wave OEM Modules

The following list shows you where you can find some OEM modules to connect to the serial port to use Bluetooth, ZigBee, or Z-Wave wireless communication with your .NET Micro Framework devices.

- Bluetooth-Serial OEM modules:

  - *LinTech's Bluetooth industry adapter*: www.lintech.de/index.php?index=19&pc=4

  - *Blue Serial's OEM module*: www.blueserial.com

  - *BTWin BM6001*: www.widecastint.com/english/PIB-OEM_serial_board.asp

  - *Amber Wireless's BlueNiceCom*: www.amber-wireless.de/en/produkte/bluetooth/index.php

  - *Socket's KwikBlue BC02*: www.socketmobile.com/products/oem-embedded-hardware/bluetooth-wireless-technology/?Subject=KwikBlueBC02Modules

  - *A7 Engineering's EmbeddedBlue module*: www.a7eng.com/products/embeddedblue/embeddedblue.htm

- ZigBee-Serial OEM Modules:

  - *Enustech's EZBee-001 and EZBee-100*: www.widecastint.com/download_main/EZBee_module_manual1.2.pdf

  - *Meshnetics's ZigBit OEM Module*: www.meshnetics.com/wsn-hardware/zigbee-module/

- Z-Wave-Serial OEM modules:

  - *Zensys's Z-Wave developer's kit version 4.x*: www.zen-sys.com/index.php?page=9

Summary

This chapter presented various wireless communication technologies—Wireless LAN, Bluetooth, ZigBee, and Z-Wave—that you can add to your .NET Micro Framework devices. The chapter also presented a comparison of these technologies, which you can use to help you decide which is best suited for your application. At the end, you learned where you can find more information about OEM modules on the Web.

In Chapter 5, which covered accessing hardware, you learned how to access the serial port. Use that information to help you in interfacing with Bluetooth, ZigBee, and Z-Wave OEM modules. For WLAN communication, refer to Chapter 6, where you learned how to program network connections with sockets.

In the next chapter, we move on to cryptography, to make your network and wireless communication secure.

CHAPTER 8

■ ■ ■

Cryptography

The .NET Micro Framework provides two encryption algorithms: the symmetrical encryption algorithm XTEA (eXtended Tiny Encryption Algorithm), which uses the same key for encoding and decoding, and the common asymmetrical method RSA, which operates with public and private keys.

Further, you can verify signed data with the .NET Micro Framework. Unfortunately, however, there are no methods to sign data with a .NET Micro Framework application.

Encryption is necessary whenever data is to be exchanged with other devices such as PCs, PDAs, smartphones, or other .NET Micro Framework devices over a network, WLAN, Bluetooth, ZigBee, or the serial interface.

Data signing is often used for license files or for validating the sender of a message: only users with the private key can create and sign a license file or message. But any user with the public key can validate data against it. Sender validation is used to check if the data comes from an expected sender.

In the previous chapters, you learned how to communicate over a network and how to communicate wirelessly with other devices. This chapter explores cryptography and demonstrates how you can use symmetric and asymmetric encryption and authentication with the .NET Micro Framework to keep those communications secure. It will also explain how to communicate securely with other devices like PCs, PDAs, or smartphones that run the full .NET or .NET Compact Framework.

XTEA: A Symmetric Algorithm

The XTEA (eXtended Tiny Encryption Algorithm) was developed in 1997 by David Wheeler and Roger Needham of the Cambridge Computer Laboratory. Like the name suggests, the XTEA, which is not patented, descends from the TEA and fixes some weak points of the TEA. XTEA is a block-based encryption method with a block size of 8 bytes and a key length of 16 bytes (128 bits). The algorithm uses a symmetrical key, which means data is encrypted and decrypted with the same key. This method is simple to implement and is relatively well performing.

The implementation of the algorithm in the .NET Micro Framework uses cipher block chaining (CBC) with cipher byte stealing (CBS). With the CBC, blocks are encrypted successively, and for each block an XOR operation is performed (that is, it's XORed) before encryption with the previous, already encrypted block. The first block is XORed with an initialization vector. Decoding is done the same way, in reverse order. If the length of the data to encrypt is not exactly divisible by the block length (8 bytes), then with the CBS, the last incomplete block is filled up with the bytes of the preceding complete block, so that it possesses a block that's exactly 8 bytes in length. After the incomplete block is filled, the two last blocks are exchanged, and the last block is trimmed so that the message again has its original length. The length of the cipher data is thus identical to the original data. Known text attacks can be prevented by CBC and CBS.

Using XTEA

XTEA is absent from the full .NET Framework but is represented in the .NET Micro Framework by the `Key_TinyEncryptionAlgorithm` class in the `Microsoft.SPOT.Cryptography` namespace in the `Microsoft.SPOT.Native.dll` assembly.

The following code snippet shows encryption and deciphering with XTEA:

```
byte[] key = new byte[] { 1, 2, 3, 4, 5, 6, 7, 8, 9, 10, 11, 12, 13, 14, 15, 16 };
byte[] iv = new byte[] { 1, 2, 3, 4, 5, 6, 7, 8 };

Key_TinyEncryptionAlgorithm xtea = new Key_TinyEncryptionAlgorithm(key);

string plainText = "Hello World!"; //original message, min length is 8 bytes
byte[] plainBytes = System.Text.Encoding.UTF8.GetBytes(plainText);

//Encryption
byte[] cipherBytes = xtea.Encrypt(plainBytes, 0, plainBytes.Length, iv);
//Decryption
byte[] restoredBytes = xtea.Decrypt(cipherBytes, 0, cipherBytes.Length, iv);
```

The key is passed to the constructor when creating an instance of the algorithm class. The key must not be `null`. If the used key is shorter than 16 bytes, it is filled up at the end with zero-bytes. If it is longer than 16 bytes, only the first 16 bytes are used.

The encryption is done with the `Encrypt` method and the decryption with `Decrypt`. You should consider that the minimum length of the data to encrypt or decipher must equal the length of one block, that is, 8 bytes. With less than 8 bytes, no exception is thrown, and the data will not be extended with zero-bytes, but an array with 8 zero-bytes will be returned.

For both encryption and deciphering, an initialization vector is specified, and you naturally need to use the same initialization vector with both operations. 8 bytes, the length of one block, are thus used by the initialization vector for the XOR operation of the first block. If either zero or less than 8 bytes are passed, then either 8 zero-bytes are used or the block is filled up at the end with zero-bytes. With more than 8 bytes, only the first 8 bytes are important. A zero-byte does not change the data in the XOR operation at all.

The `Key_TinyEncryptionAlgorithm` class possesses the following method:

```
public String GetActivationString (ushort region, ushort model)
```

with which passwords of 16 characters (digits and upper-case characters) can be created in a simple manner. If you convert these with `Encoding.UTF8.GetBytes` into a byte array, you can use that array as XTEA key. The characters of the passwords are generated on the basis of regional code and a hardware or system model ID.

XTEA for the Full .NET and .NET Compact Frameworks

Unfortunately, XTEA encryption and decryption are available only for the .NET Micro Framework. Thus only .NET Micro Framework devices are able to exchange encrypted data with one another, which seriously limits XTEA's use: you might need to communicate with a PC, a notebook, a PDA, or a smartphone. Therefore, I implemented the XTEA algorithm with CBC and CBS for the full .NET Framework as a class with an identical interface for the encryption and decryption. The class can be used additionally with the .NET Compact Framework. You can find the source code of this class in the source code directory for this chapter, so there is nothing to prevent you from communicating securely with the devices already mentioned.

RSA: An Asymmetric Algorithm

In addition to the XTEA for the .NET Micro Framework, RSA encryption is also available. RSA is an asymmetrical encryption algorithm that is capable of encrypting and digital signing data.

RSA was named after its inventors Ronald L. Rivest, Adi Shamir, and Leonard Adleman. It uses public and private keys: The private key is used for decryption and data signing. With the public key, data can be encrypted, or signatures can be validated.

If the private key is kept secret, the private key can be calculated from the public key only with much effort, if at all.

Common Key Pair Scenarios

This section demonstrates some common scenarios for asymmetric cryptography with public/private key pairs like RSA uses. You will need to learn how to use the key pairs and understand the cryptography flow before you learn how to use RSA encryption with the .NET Micro Framework.

Please keep the following rules in mind:

- The *public key* is used for *encrypting* and *verifying signatures.*

- The *private key* is used for *decrypting* and *signing data.*

Using Key Pairs for Secure Communication

If someone—let's say his name is Marek—wants to securely communicate with someone else—call her Leonie—they need to use their public/private key pair as explained in the following cryptography flow:

1. Marek needs to know Leonie's public key, and Leonie needs to get Marek's public key. They each need to possess their own private key and the public key of the other person.

2. Marek encrypts a message addressed to Leonie using Leonie's public key and sends it to her.

3. Leonie decrypts Marek's message using her private key.

4. Leonie replies. She encrypts the message using Marek's public key and sends it to him.

5. Marek decrypts Leonie's message using his private key.

6. Marek replies. He encrypts the message with Leonie's public key, and sends it to her. They can repeat this flow of encrypted messages indefinitely.

A Hybrid Approach to Encryption

RSA is very slow. To encrypt a large amount of data, using symmetrical algorithms like the XTEA in conjunction with RSA is recommended. First, one communication partner creates a random XTEA key, encrypts it with the public RSA key, and sends it to the other communication partner. The other side decrypts the received XTEA key with the private RSA key and is now able to use the XTEA key for fast data encryption and decryption.

Let's assume that Marek and Leonie have not seen one another in a long time, so they have a lot of things to discuss. The following cryptography flow demonstrates using the key pair with the hybrid approach:

1. Marek needs to know Leonie's public key, and Leonie needs to get Marek's public key. They each need to possess their own private key and the public key of the other person.

2. Marek generates a random symmetric XTEA key.

3. Marek encrypts the symmetric XTEA key with Leonie's public RSA key and sends it to her, usually in a message.

4. Leonie decrypts Marek's message using her private RSA key and now knows the symmetric XTEA key.

5. Leonie and Marek exchange encrypted data using the symmetric XTEA key.

Using Key Pairs for Authentication

Asymmetric keys allow you to digitally sign data. Because Leonie's public key can be used by many other people, how can Leonie be sure that Marek really wrote a message for her and encrypted it using her public key? Marek needs to sign the message with his private key, so Leonie can verify the signature. If the signature is valid, Leonie knows the message must have come from Marek, because only Marek can generate a signature with his private key. The following steps illustrate the cryptography flow for sender authentication. For simplification Marek and Leonie will use signed, but not encrypted, data in this example, though combining encryption and signing is surely possible.

1. Marek needs to know Leonie's public key and Leonie needs to get Marek's public key. They each need to possess their own private key and the public key of the other person.

2. Marek signs a message addressed to Leonie with his own private key and sends it to her.

3. Leonie verifies Marek's signed message using Marek's public key. Now, they know for sure if the message was from Marek.

4. Leonie replies, signs the message with her private key, and sends it to him.

5. Marek verifies Leonie's signed message using Leonie's public key.

6. Marek replies, signs the message with his private key, and sends it to her. They can continue sending signed messages in this way until they're all caught up after their time apart.

Creating Private and Public Keys

RSA encoding takes place in the .NET Micro Framework with the `Microsoft.SPOT.Key_RSA` class. Although the full .NET and .NET Compact Frameworks also contain a class for RSA encryption with an identical underlying algorithm, these classes are not compatible with each other. The keys are stored in different formats, and the cipher data uses different byte orders.

You cannot create private and public keys with a .NET Micro Framework application. You need to create your RSA keys for the .NET Micro Framework on a PC with the `MetaDataProcessor.exe` console application, and then to implement the keys into your .NET Micro Framework application code. You can find this tool in the `Tools` subdirectory of the .NET Micro Framework SDK. The `-?` command-line option will show you an overview of the available command-line parameters. Most are used in the build process by Visual Studio.

You need to enter the following commands at the command-line prompt to create a public and private key pair:

```
cd "C:\Program Files\Microsoft .NET Micro Framework\v2.0.3036\Tools"
metadataprocessor  -create_key_pair c:\private.bin c:\public.bin
metadataprocessor -dump_key c:\private.bin >> c:\private.txt
metadataprocessor -dump_key c:\public.bin >> c:\public.txt
```

Afterward, the `private.txt` file contains the modulus and private exponent, and the `public.txt` file contains the modulus and public exponent. Actually, you only need the `private.txt` file, because the modulus of the private and public keys in a pair is identical, and the public exponent is always the same constant. The modulus and exponent are always 128 bytes long for both the private and public keys. Listing 8-1 shows how the contents of the `private.txt` file might look. Since the keys are generated randomly and are unique, you will surely get different results.

Listing 8-1. *A Private Key in private.txt*

```
//typedef struct tagRSAKey
//{
//    DWORD exponent_len;
//    RSABuffer module;
//    RSABuffer exponent;
//} RSAKey, *PRSAKey;
RSAKey myKey =
{
   0x00000020,
{
    0x0d,  0x42,  0x27,  0x57,  0xed,  0xbb,  0xdf,  0xe1,  0x51,  0x27,
    0xe2,  0x62,  0xd5,  0x60,  0x75,  0x6c,  0x2b,  0x63,  0xd3,  0x45,
    0xe3,  0x63,  0x3d,  0x15,  0xf5,  0x4a,  0x38,  0xa7,  0xc9,  0x58,
    0x92,  0xac,  0x58,  0xf4,  0x77,  0xc6,  0x68,  0x1f,  0xa8,  0x0b,
    0xa6,  0x4a,  0x68,  0xe3,  0xeb,  0xed,  0x89,  0xf4,  0x26,  0x19,
    0x92,  0x42,  0x92,  0xd8,  0xec,  0x93,  0xfb,  0xc4,  0x6d,  0x56,
    0x16,  0x58,  0xba,  0xf7,  0xc9,  0x87,  0xcc,  0x07,  0x45,  0x57,
    0x25,  0xef,  0xb8,  0xeb,  0xbb,  0xa7,  0x2b,  0x83,  0xca,  0x9b,
    0xbc,  0xcf,  0x0b,  0x60,  0xd7,  0x8f,  0x7e,  0xdd,  0x28,  0xc5,
```

```
    0x08,   0x1a,   0xd2,   0x2c,   0x25,   0x70,   0xc8,   0x01,   0x20,   0xc8,
    0xc4,   0xaa,   0xf5,   0x65,   0x14,   0x1b,   0xf0,   0x22,   0x25,   0x9e,
    0x0e,   0x21,   0xd0,   0xa3,   0xac,   0xb7,   0xaf,   0x35,   0x31,   0x04,
    0xb0,   0xfb,   0xdd,   0x09,   0x86,   0xe7,   0x25,   0xcf,
},
{
    0x41,   0xcd,   0x1d,   0xd3,   0xa7,   0x96,   0xe8,   0xbe,   0xc6,   0x23,
    0x42,   0x48,   0x80,   0xc5,   0x62,   0x62,   0x77,   0xac,   0x5c,   0x7c,
    0xb9,   0x22,   0xd7,   0x9f,   0xfb,   0x40,   0x59,   0xf2,   0x04,   0xf4,
    0xab,   0xa1,   0xf2,   0xba,   0x19,   0xda,   0x51,   0x23,   0x5a,   0x49,
    0xf9,   0x22,   0x67,   0x8e,   0xc0,   0x6a,   0x9e,   0x45,   0xc7,   0x20,
    0xfa,   0xf3,   0x6d,   0xb9,   0x6e,   0x54,   0x60,   0xff,   0x17,   0xa0,
    0x66,   0x71,   0xfb,   0xfa,   0x1b,   0xe2,   0xb2,   0xf2,   0xf9,   0xce,
    0xd5,   0x15,   0xaf,   0xf1,   0xb8,   0xfb,   0x36,   0x72,   0x43,   0x07,
    0x00,   0xb1,   0xd8,   0xb2,   0x4d,   0x23,   0xc4,   0xc9,   0xac,   0xed,
    0xc8,   0xe0,   0xc6,   0x03,   0x7d,   0xc7,   0x1d,   0x1b,   0x73,   0xea,
    0xe7,   0x36,   0xc9,   0x4f,   0x7e,   0x28,   0xb8,   0xc4,   0x7c,   0x3f,
    0x4d,   0x1c,   0x2d,   0x4f,   0x42,   0xab,   0x8e,   0x4d,   0xac,   0xa3,
    0x56,   0x1f,   0xfd,   0x69,   0x13,   0x7e,   0x2f,   0x16,
},
};
```

Now, you can copy and paste the bytes in hexadecimal format via the clipboard into a C#
source code file, so that the whole file's code looks like Listing 8-2.

Listing 8-2. *A Private Key in a C# Code File*

```
byte[] modulus = new byte[] {
    0x0d, 0x42, 0x27, 0x57, 0xed, 0xbb, 0xdf, 0xe1,
    0x51, 0x27, 0xe2, 0x62, 0xd5, 0x60, 0x75, 0x6c,
    0x2b, 0x63, 0xd3, 0x45, 0xe3, 0x63, 0x3d, 0x15,
    0xf5, 0x4a, 0x38, 0xa7, 0xc9, 0x58, 0x92, 0xac,
    0x58, 0xf4, 0x77, 0xc6, 0x68, 0x1f, 0xa8, 0x0b,
    0xa6, 0x4a, 0x68, 0xe3, 0xeb, 0xed, 0x89, 0xf4,
    0x26, 0x19, 0x92, 0x42, 0x92, 0xd8, 0xec, 0x93,
    0xfb, 0xc4, 0x6d, 0x56, 0x16, 0x58, 0xba, 0xf7,
    0xc9, 0x87, 0xcc, 0x07, 0x45, 0x57, 0x25, 0xef,
    0xb8, 0xeb, 0xbb, 0xa7, 0x2b, 0x83, 0xca, 0x9b,
    0xbc, 0xcf, 0x0b, 0x60, 0xd7, 0x8f, 0x7e, 0xdd,
    0x28, 0xc5, 0x08, 0x1a, 0xd2, 0x2c, 0x25, 0x70,
    0xc8, 0x01, 0x20, 0xc8, 0xc4, 0xaa, 0xf5, 0x65,
    0x14, 0x1b, 0xf0, 0x22, 0x25, 0x9e, 0x0e, 0x21,
    0xd0, 0xa3, 0xac, 0xb7, 0xaf, 0x35, 0x31, 0x04,
    0xb0, 0xfb, 0xdd, 0x09, 0x86, 0xe7, 0x25, 0xcf };
```

```
byte[] privateExponent = new byte[] {
    0x41, 0xcd, 0x1d, 0xd3, 0xa7, 0x96, 0xe8, 0xbe,
    0xc6, 0x23, 0x42, 0x48, 0x80, 0xc5, 0x62, 0x62,
    0x77, 0xac, 0x5c, 0x7c, 0xb9, 0x22, 0xd7, 0x9f,
    0xfb, 0x40, 0x59, 0xf2, 0x04, 0xf4, 0xab, 0xa1,
    0xf2, 0xba, 0x19, 0xda, 0x51, 0x23, 0x5a, 0x49,
    0xf9, 0x22, 0x67, 0x8e, 0xc0, 0x6a, 0x9e, 0x45,
    0xc7, 0x20, 0xfa, 0xf3, 0x6d, 0xb9, 0x6e, 0x54,
    0x60, 0xff, 0x17, 0xa0, 0x66, 0x71, 0xfb, 0xfa,
    0x1b, 0xe2, 0xb2, 0xf2, 0xf9, 0xce, 0xd5, 0x15,
    0xaf, 0xf1, 0xb8, 0xfb, 0x36, 0x72, 0x43, 0x07,
    0x00, 0xb1, 0xd8, 0xb2, 0x4d, 0x23, 0xc4, 0xc9,
    0xac, 0xed, 0xc8, 0xe0, 0xc6, 0x03, 0x7d, 0xc7,
    0x1d, 0x1b, 0x73, 0xea, 0xe7, 0x36, 0xc9, 0x4f,
    0x7e, 0x28, 0xb8, 0xc4, 0x7c, 0x3f, 0x4d, 0x1c,
    0x2d, 0x4f, 0x42, 0xab, 0x8e, 0x4d, 0xac, 0xa3,
    0x56, 0x1f, 0xfd, 0x69, 0x13, 0x7e, 0x2f, 0x16 };
byte[] publicExponent = new byte[] {
    0x01, 0x00, 0x01, 0x00, 0x00, 0x00, 0x00, 0x00,
    0x00, 0x00, 0x00, 0x00, 0x00, 0x00, 0x00, 0x00,
    0x00, 0x00, 0x00, 0x00, 0x00, 0x00, 0x00, 0x00,
    0x00, 0x00, 0x00, 0x00, 0x00, 0x00, 0x00, 0x00,
    0x00, 0x00, 0x00, 0x00, 0x00, 0x00, 0x00, 0x00,
    0x00, 0x00, 0x00, 0x00, 0x00, 0x00, 0x00, 0x00,
    0x00, 0x00, 0x00, 0x00, 0x00, 0x00, 0x00, 0x00,
    0x00, 0x00, 0x00, 0x00, 0x00, 0x00, 0x00, 0x00,
    0x00, 0x00, 0x00, 0x00, 0x00, 0x00, 0x00, 0x00,
    0x00, 0x00, 0x00, 0x00, 0x00, 0x00, 0x00, 0x00,
    0x00, 0x00, 0x00, 0x00, 0x00, 0x00, 0x00, 0x00,
    0x00, 0x00, 0x00, 0x00, 0x00, 0x00, 0x00, 0x00,
    0x00, 0x00, 0x00, 0x00, 0x00, 0x00, 0x00, 0x00,
    0x00, 0x00, 0x00, 0x00, 0x00, 0x00, 0x00, 0x00,
    0x00, 0x00, 0x00, 0x00, 0x00, 0x00, 0x00, 0x00,
    0x00, 0x00, 0x00, 0x00, 0x00, 0x00, 0x00, 0x00 };
```

The public exponent is, as already mentioned, always the same. All 128 bytes are zeros except the first and the third bytes. In order to avoid unnecessarily inflating a .NET Micro Framework assembly by the initialization, the following lines of code perform exactly the same initialization as Listing 8-2 but without wasting storage capacity:

```
byte[] publicExponent = new byte[128];
publicExponent[0] = 0x01;
publicExponent[2] = 0x01;
```

Encryption and Decryption with RSA

Both the Key_RSA class and the Key_TinyEncryptionAlgorithm class are derived from the common base class Key, which exposes the two methods Encrypt and Decrypt. In the case of the RSA encryption, no CBC will be used; therefore, for the initialization vector, you should pass the value null to the Encrypt and Decrypt methods. Listing 8-3 demonstrates how you can encrypt and decrypt data with RSA.

Listing 8-3. *Encryption and Decryption with RSA*

```
byte[] modulus = new byte[] { ... };
byte[] privateExponent = new byte[] { ... };
byte[] publicExponent = new byte[128];
publicExponent[0] = 0x01;
publicExponent[2] = 0x01;

string plainText = "Hello World!";
byte[] plainBytes = Encoding.UTF8.GetBytes(plainText);

//Encryption
Key_RSA encryptor = new Key_RSA(modulus, publicExponent);
byte[] cipherBytes = encryptor.Encrypt(plainBytes, 0, plainBytes.Length, null);

//Decryption
Key_RSA decryptor = new Key_RSA(modulus, privateExponent);
byte[] restoredBytes = decryptor.Decrypt(cipherBytes, 0, cipherBytes.Length, null);
```

■**Caution** The RSA cipher data is longer than the original data. After decryption, the byte array with the restored data is not the length of the original data again but the length of the encrypted data. At the end, zero bytes are filled up. Here, the change in length most probably concerns an unwanted behavior.

Creating and Verifying Signatures

As I mentioned previously, with the .NET Micro Framework, you can only verify signatures—you cannot create them. You need to create signatures on a PC with the MetaDataProcessor.exe console program from the .NET Micro Framework SDK. With the -sign_file option, you can sign a file, and with -verify_signature, you can verify the signature of a signed file.

With the following commands on the command prompt, a signature for the HelloWorld.txt file will be created and written into the file RsaSignature.bin:

```
cd "C:\Program Files\Microsoft .NET Micro Framework\v2.0.3036\Tools"
metadataprocessor -sign_file c:\helloworld.txt c:\private.bin c:\RsaSignature.bin
```

The signature is stored in a binary format, and there is no easy way to convert the binary signature into a readable format, as there is for the keys. Therefore, the RsaSignature.bin file is embedded as a binary resource into a .NET Micro Framework application. Listing 8-4 shows how to verify a signature with the .NET Micro Framework.

Listing 8-4. *Verifying an RSA Signature*

```
byte[] modulus = new byte[] { … };
byte[] publicExponent = new byte[128];
publicExponent[0] = 0x01;
publicExponent[2] = 0x01;
byte[] signature = Resources.GetBytes(Resources.BinaryResources.RsaSignature);

string messageText = "Hello World!";
byte[] messageBytes = Encoding.UTF8.GetBytes(messageText);

//Verification of a signature
Key_RSA rsa = new Key_RSA(modulus, publicExponent);
bool valid = rsa.VerifySignature(messageBytes, 0, messageBytes.Length,
                                 signature, 0, signature.Length);
if (valid)
    Debug.Print("Signature is valid.")
else
    Debug.Print("Signature is NOT valid.");
```

Summary

You now understand how symmetric and asymmetric encryption can be used with the .NET Micro Framework. This chapter illustrated how to use key pairs for different scenarios and provided a solution for exchanging a large amount of data in a well-performing way. Because you may require a secure data exchange with networking and for wireless communications, this chapter also showed you how you can securely communicate with other devices like PCs, PDAs, and smart-phones using XTEA.

The next chapter moves on to advanced topics like multithreading and binary serialization.

CHAPTER 9

■ ■ ■

Advanced .NET Micro Framework Programming

This chapter covers advanced topics like multithreading and thread synchronization. You will also learn about weak delegates and execution constraints, including how and when to use them. This chapter also teaches you how to use binary serialization effectively and how to persist data permanently in flash memory using extended weak references.

Multithreading and Synchronization

In .NET, parallel program execution is possible using multiple threads. A thread is an independent code path that can run parallel to other threads. With threads, you can process several tasks simultaneously.

Threads are more lightweight than processes; that means the system can switch between threads faster. In the .NET Micro Framework, only one application (process) can run at a time, so for parallel program execution with the .NET Micro Framework, only threads are applicable.

A .NET application starts as an individual thread, the main thread. The main thread is created automatically by the runtime environment. An application can consist of several threads, and the different threads can access common data. Therefore, you need to synchronize access to shared resources from different threads.

Threads run on single-processor systems, and like all platforms for the .NET Micro Framework, are not actually parallel, but the runtime environment alternates among threads to provide each thread processor time. You can control the assignment of computing time more precisely by setting the thread priority of each thread. Thus important tasks can be processed faster than, for example, some monitoring in the background. The thread priority indicates how much processor time a thread gets compared to other threads.

■**Tip** You can find a very detailed description of multithreading and synchronization with the .NET Framework at www.albahari.com/threading/threading.pdf.

Using Threads

Threads are programmed in the .NET Micro Framework in a way that's similar to the full .NET Framework. Of course, the functionality has been reduced to a minimum. Nevertheless, the most necessary methods and properties are available. A thread is represented by the System. Threading.Thread class, as shown in Listing 9-1.

Listing 9-1. *The System.Threading.Thread Class*

```
using System;

namespace System.Threading
{
    public sealed class Thread
    {
        public Thread(ThreadStart start);

        public static Thread CurrentThread { get; }
        public bool IsAlive { get; }
        public ThreadPriority Priority { get; set; }
        public ThreadState ThreadState { get; }

        public void Abort();
        public static AppDomain GetDomain();
        public void Join();
        public bool Join(int millisecondsTimeout);
        public bool Join(TimeSpan timeout);
        public void Resume();
        public static void Sleep(int millisecondsTimeout);
        public void Start();
        public void Suspend();
    }
}
```

■Note The static Sleep method of the Thread class has already been used in several sample programs. You should consider that the thread from which the method is called is always paused. That means calling the Sleep method from the main thread will pause the main thread, and calling the method from code that is executed from a background thread will pause the background thread.

Now you will learn how to create and start a thread. Listing 9-2 shows how this is done. You need to pass a pointer to a parameterless method containing the task you want to process with the constructor. That method is called a callback, or thread, method and can be static or belong to an object instance. Afterward, you need to start the thread with its Start method. The thread is terminated as soon as the thread worker method is done.

Listing 9-2. *Creating and Starting a Thread*

```
public class Program
{
    public static void Main()
    {
        Thread myThread = new Thread(MyThreadMethod);
        myThread.Start();
        //main thread continues here

        ...
    }

    private static void MyThreadMethod()
    {
        //do some work here
    }
}
```

It is possible to wait for completion or termination of another thread before moving on with the application, which is done by calling the Join method of the thread you want to wait for. There are three overloads of this method (see Listing 9-1): the parameterless version blocks and waits infinitely for the termination. The other two variants expect a timeout parameter indicating the maximum waiting time. The methods return true if the thread was terminated in the specified time and false if the thread is still alive.

Synchronization

Conflicts can occur any time several threads access shared resources, so you need to synchronize access to shared data.

■**Caution** The interrupt method of an interrupt port and the timer method of a timer are each called in the context of a separate thread. Access to resources within these methods has to be synchronized as well.

The .NET Framework provides several possibilities for synchronization. A simple way to prevent a method from being executed by several threads at the same time is to mark the method as synchronized by adding the following attribute:

```
[MethodImpl(MethodImplOptions.Synchronized)]
private void MySynchronizedMethod()
{
    //...
}
```

The synchronized method will be locked for other threads as soon as it is entered by a thread. Other threads trying to execute this method are blocked until the locking thread returns from the method.

In the preceding example, the method will be locked during the entire time a thread is executing it, even if critical resources are accessed only in a small part of the entire method. A better approach is to lock a method only during the execution of critical parts. That type of access to objects can be synchronized with the `Monitor` class from the `System.Threading` namespace:

```
private static MyThreadMethod1()
{
        ...
        Monitor.Enter(myCriticalObject);
        //access shared data here
        Monitor.Exit(myCriticalObject);
        ...
}

private static MyThreadMethod2()
{
        ...
        Monitor.Enter(myCriticalObject);
        //access shared data here
        Monitor.Exit(myCriticalObject);
        ...
}
```

Both thread methods are executed at the same time, and both access the same data at the same time. After the `Enter` method is called, other threads reaching `Enter` will be blocked until the `Exit` method is called by the locking thread. You should place the `Exit` call within the `finally` block of an exception handler, so the lock is released in case of an exception so that other threads will not be blocked forever. To simplify this situation, you can use the C# keyword `lock`.

```
lock(myCriticalObject)
{
    //access data
}
```

The preceding construct is compiled by the C# compiler to the following code:

```
try
{
    Monitor.Enter(myCriticalObject);
    //access data
}
catch(Exception)
{
    Monitor.Exit(myCriticalObject);
}
```

The Interlocked class from the System.Threading namespace offers the possibility to increment or decrement by one an integer variable or swap the value of two variables as an atomic operation that cannot be interrupted. An atomic operation is always executed completely and, therefore, will not be interrupted by another thread during execution.

Events

In addition to using the Monitor class or the lock construct to synchronize access to shared resources, you can use events. Events allow you to signal other waiting threads that a certain action, like the completion of a task, has occurred. You can also wait for multiple events.

For synchronization with events, there are the two classes: ManualResetEvent and AutoResetEvent. These classes differ only in the fact that you must reset the status of a ManualResetEvent manually after signaling an event. Both classes are in the System.Threading namespace, and both inherit from the abstract WaitHandle class, which possesses the methods represented in Listing 9-3. The documentation of the .NET Micro Framework SDK is not correct and describes only two members of this class.

Listing 9-3. *The System.Threading.WaitHandle Base Class of ManualResetEvent and AutoResetEvent*

```
namespace System.Threading
{
    public abstract class WaitHandle : MarshalByRefObject
    {
        public const int WaitTimeout = 258;

        protected WaitHandle();

        public static bool WaitAll(WaitHandle[] waitHandles);
        public static bool WaitAll(WaitHandle[] waitHandles,
                               int millisecondsTimeout, bool exitContext);
        public static int WaitAny(WaitHandle[] waitHandles);
        public static int WaitAny(WaitHandle[] waitHandles,
                               int millisecondsTimeout, bool exitContext);
        public virtual bool WaitOne();
        public virtual bool WaitOne(int millisecondsTimeout, bool exitContext);
    }
}
```

The two event classes, ManualResetEvent and AutoResetEvent, possess the methods Set and Reset. When creating an instance of an event class, you can pass the initial state to the constructor. After an AutoResetEvent object is set, it remains signaled until another thread waits for this event (at which time, it resets automatically).

In Listing 9-4, you can see how to use the AutoResetEvent class. The main thread creates a new thread, starts it, and waits until the created thread signals this event.

Listing 9-4. *Using AutoResetEvent*

```
using System;
using System.Threading;
using Microsoft.SPOT;

namespace ThreadingEventSample
{
    public class Program
    {
        private static AutoResetEvent ev = new AutoResetEvent(false);

        static void Main()
        {
            Thread thr = new Thread(WaitForEvent);
            thr.Start();

            Debug.Print("Waiting...");
            ev.WaitOne(); //waiting for notification
            Debug.Print("Notified");
        }

        private static void WaitForEvent()
        {
            Thread.Sleep(1000); //sleep to simulate doing something
            ev.Set(); //wake up other thread
        }
    }
}
```

Weak Delegates

As long as an object in the .NET Framework is somehow referenced, it is not disposed of by the garbage collector. An object can be referenced not only by variables but also by delegates.

```
type1.MyEvent += type2.MyEventRaised;
```

Even if no variable refers to the `type2` object in the preceding example, because of the registered callback method, the `type2` object is still referenced by `type1`. The `type2` object can be disposed of only after `type1` is.

If you want to be able to dispose of `type2` as soon as no variable points to it, without having to remove the event handler manually with the minus operator (`-=`), use the `WeakDelegate` class. This class is only available in the .NET Micro Framework and, therefore, in the `Microsoft.SPOT` namespace. No changes are visible on the interface for the users of a class with weak delegates. You only need to change the implementation of the event in the `Type1` class. In order to use a weak delegate instead of a strong delegate, `Type1` must look as it does in Listing 9-5.

Listing 9-5. *A Class with a Weak Delegate*

```
internal sealed class Type1
{
    //the prototype of MyEvent's callback methods
    public delegate void MyEventHandler(Object sender, String s);

    //a private field for the (weak) delegates
    private MyEventHandler myEvent;

    //weak delegate
    public event MyEventHandler MyEvent
    {
        [MethodImpl(MethodImplOptions.Synchronized)]
        Add
        {
            //Combine turns the delegate referred to by value into a weak delegate
            this.myEvent = (MyEventHandler)WeakDelegate.Combine(this.myEvent,
                                                        value);
        }

        [MethodImpl(MethodImplOptions.Synchronized)]
        Remove
        {
            //Remove deletes the delegate referred to by value from the delegate chain
            this.myEvent = (MyEventHandler)WeakDelegate.Remove(this.myEvent,
                                                        value);
        }
    }
}
```

When registering and removing a callback method from the list with linked event handlers, you have to call the static methods Combine and Remove of the WeakDelegate class.

■**Tip** The WeakDelegates sample project included in the .NET Micro Framework SDK demonstrates the use of weak delegates.

Execution Constraints

Execution constraints give you the possibility to monitor whether a certain operation is completed within a determined amount of time. The execution time is monitored by a background thread. After an operation is completed, the monitoring is stopped by uninstalling the execution constraint.

Execution constraints are represented by the `Microsoft.SPOT.ExecutionConstraint` class. You can install and activate an execution constraint with the static method `Install`. The `Install` method expects the greatest acceptable amount of time in milliseconds. Additionally, the `priority` integer parameter specifies a thread priority. This parameter does not seem to be used, however, by the runtime environment, thus you can pass 0 here confidently.

After completion of the monitored operation, you need to uninstall the execution constraint by calling the method `Install` with –1 for the `timeout` parameter.

If the monitored operation lasts longer than was forced, `Microsoft.SPOT.ConstraintException` is thrown. The elapsed time is not analyzed when the execution constraints are uninstalled, but the background thread throws the exception immediately on expiration of the forced time.

The example in Listing 9-6 demonstrates the use of execution constraints. Two operations are checked. Both operations must be completed in a maximum of 100 milliseconds. Like the operations, `Thread.Sleep` is executed once within 50 milliseconds and once within 100 milliseconds.

The first operation is executed successfully within the permitted time, and the debug message is put out. For the second operation, a `ConstraintException` is thrown.

Listing 9-6. *Using Execution Contraints*

```
using System;
using Microsoft.SPOT;
using System.Threading;

namespace ExecutionConstraintSample
{
    public class Program
    {
        public static void Main()
        {
            const int timeout = 100; // 100 ms = max. accepted duration of operation

            ExecutionConstraint.Install(timeout, 0); //install to check constraint
            //do something which must take less than timeout
            Thread.Sleep(50); //operation is executed in less time
            //end of operation
            ExecutionConstraint.Install(-1, 0); //uninstall
            Debug.Print("First operation successfully executed.");

            ExecutionConstraint.Install(timeout, 0); //install to check constraint
            //do something which must take less than timeout
            //operation takes longer as forced,
            //so an exception will be thrown after timeout ms
            Thread.Sleep(150);
            //end of operation
            ExecutionConstraint.Install(-1, 0); //uninstall
            Debug.Print("Second operation successfully executed.");
        }
    }
}
```

> ■Execution constraints (and Listing 9-6) do not work as expected in version 2.5 of the .NET Micro Framework, though they work fine with version 2.0. This error is supposed to be fixed with a service pack for version 2.5.

Binary Serialization

The term "binary serialization" of objects refers to the process of bringing the status of classes and structures, or more exactly, the values of the fields (variables), into a defined order and formatting them into a sequence of bytes. Deserialization creates an instance of the class and recovers the status from the array of bytes. There are further types of serialization, like the transformation of objects to the XML format. In the .NET Micro Framework, however, only binary serialization is implemented.

The full .NET Framework provides a binary serialization that can be found in the System. Runtime.Serialization.Formatters.Binary class. Against this, the .NET Micro Framework provides a binary serialization that can be found in the Microsoft.SPOT.Reflection namespace in the Microsoft.SPOT.Native.dll assembly. These two binary serializations are not compatible with each other. That means you cannot deserialize an object with the full .NET Framework from a byte stream that was created with the .NET Micro Framework and vice versa. The serialization in the .NET Micro Framework offers a very exact configuration, and the data can be stored very compactly.

The serialization was generally implemented; that means any classes and structures can be serialized. You can configure the serialization by specifying attributes. By means of reflection, the metadata of a class or a structure will be determined and accessed, and with the information from the attributes and the data type of a field, the runtime knows how to store the value.

This section discusses, in detail, binary serialization with the .NET Micro Framework, because this approach offers a simple and efficient way to store data. If you know exactly how the binary serialization in the .NET Micro Framework works, the storage size of the serialized data can be reduced to a minimum by direct configuration.

With binary serialization, you can transform an object into a byte array to store data easily in a file, store it in RAM, or transfer it over the serial interface or sockets with just one line of code. In the .NET Micro Framework, the binary serialization is also important for using extended weak references. With extended weak references classes can be serialized persistent to the flash memory and can be recovered after power cycling the device.

Usage

With the Serialize method from the Reflection class, you can transform an object into a byte array, and the Deserialize method will restore it (see Listing 9-7).

Listing 9-7. *Binary Serialization and Deserialization*

```
SerializableClass1 o = new SerializableClass1(1, "2", 3, MyEnum.B, 3.1f);
byte[] buffer1 = Reflection.Serialize(o, typeof(SerializableClass1));
SerializableClass1 restored =
    (SerializableClass1)Reflection.Deserialize(buffer1, typeof(SerializableClass1));
```

For both methods, Serialize and Deserialize, you need to specify the type of the class or structure that you want to serialize or deserialize. The object that you want to serialize must be of exactly the specified type, and descendants of the specified type are not allowed. Naturally, the specified type must be the same for serialization and deserialization. With the Serialize method, theoretically, the runtime environment could also determine the type from the object to serialize. For example, the variable o in Listing 9-7 is of the type SerializableClass1, and passing the type of o with the second argument again to the Deserialize method with the value typeof(SerializableClass1) seems to be unnecessary. But probably, in future versions of the .NET Micro Framework, it will be possible to serialize an object that is a descendant of the specified type exactly the same as in the full .NET Framework. Then, only the fields of the base class would be stored and newly added fields would not be considered. With Deserialize, an instance of the base class would be created.

The Deserialize method returns an instance of the type object. Therefore, you must cast the return value into the desired data type. To serialize a class or a structure, you must provide it with the System.SerializableAttribute attribute. If you serialize a class that was not marked as serializable with this attribute, the Serialize method returns null instead of a byte array.

All fields—that is, public, private, protected, internal, or protected internal fields—are serialized. Also, fields defined as readonly are serialized. Fields declared as readonly are frequently used if they are initialized either directly with the declaration or in the constructor and will not be changed at a later time.

The serializable MySerializableClass class in Listing 9-8 possesses some public and protected fields of different data types. The fields are initialized in the constructor, and the ToString method displays the values of the fields.

Listing 9-8. *MySerializableClass, an Example of a Serializable Class*

```
using System;
using Microsoft.SPOT;

namespace BinarySerializationSample
{
    public enum MyEnum : short { A, B, C };

    [Serializable]
    public class MySerializableClass
    {
        public int a;
        public string b;
        private byte c;
        private MyEnum d;
        private float e;
        private DateTime dt;

        public MySerializableClass(int a, string b, byte c, MyEnum d, float e)
        {
            this.a = a;
            this.b = b;
            this.c = c;
```

```
            this.d = d;
            this.e = e;
            this.dt = this.dt = new DateTime(2007, 1, 22);
        }

        public override string ToString()
        {
            return "a=" + a.ToString() + ", b=" + b + ", c=" + c.ToString() +
                    ", d=" + d.ToString() + ", e=" + e.ToString();
        }
    }
}
```

The program in Listing 9-9 serializes an instance of the MySerializableClass class and re-creates a new instance with identical contents from the byte array.

Listing 9-9. *Serializing and Deserializing MySerializableClass*

```
using System;
using Microsoft.SPOT;

namespace BinarySerializationSample
{
    public class Program
    {
        public static void Main()
        {
            MySerializableClass original =
                        new MySerializableClass(1, "ABCD", 3, MyEnum.B, 0.1f);
            Debug.Print("original: " + original.ToString());
            byte[] buffer = Reflection.Serialize(original,
                                            typeof(MySerializableClass));
            MySerializableClass restored =
                (MySerializableClass)Reflection.Deserialize(buffer,
                                            typeof(MySerializableClass));
            Debug.Print("restored: " + restored.ToString());
            Debug.Print("Number of bytes: " + buffer.Length.ToString());
            Debug.Print(BufferToString(buffer));
        }

        #region diagnostics helpers
        private static string ByteToHex(byte b)
        {
            const string hex = "0123456789ABCDEF";
            int lowNibble = b & 0x0F;
            int highNibble = (b & 0xF0) >> 4;
            string s = new string(new char[] { hex[highNibble], hex[lowNibble] });
            return s;
        }
```

```
        private static string BufferToString(byte[] buffer)
        {
            if (buffer == null)
                throw new ArgumentNullException("buffer");
            string s = string.Empty;
            for(int i = 0; i < buffer.Length; i++)
            {
                s += ByteToHex(buffer[i]) + " ";
                if (i > 0 && i % 16 == 0)
                    s += "\n";
            }
            return s;
        }
        #endregion
    }
}
```

The application in Listing 9-9 produces the following output in the debug window:

```
original: a=1, b=ABCD, c=3, d=1, e=0.1
restored: a=1, b=ABCD, c=3, d=1, e=0.1
Number of bytes: 24
00 00 00 01 04 41 42 43 44 03 00 01 3D CC CC CD 08
C9 0B CF 64 D3 C0 00
```

If you do not want a field to be serialized, it can be excluded from serialization with the System.NonSerializedAttribute attribute.

If a field is not of a primitive type, the data type must have the System.SerializableAttribute attribute, so that the field can be serialized. Primitive types are all integer types and floating point types, as well as bool and enum. The attribute is not inheritable; that is, even if any class from which a class inherits is serializable, the derived class always needs to have the attribute also. That means if you want a subclass of a serializable class to be serializable as well, you need to mark the subclass with the Serializable attribute again.

Storage Format and Configuration

In this section, you will learn in which formats certain data types are serialized, and in the next section, you will learn how the standard behavior can be optimized to get still more compact storage. The individual fields of a type are serialized in the order of declaration. The binary serialization in the .NET Micro Framework always writes the most significant bytes first. The configuration has bit granularity and can take place down to the bit level. The first bit is the most significant.

Default Storage Formats

The following list outlines the storage formats of the individual data types:

- *Ordinal types:*

  - bool: A Boolean value is stored as 1 byte by default. The most significant bit of that byte indicates the logical state. Assigning 0 to the first (most significant bit) means false, and assigning 1, true. For example, the byte 0x80 corresponds to true.

  - byte and sbyte: These are written by default as exactly 1 byte (8 bits).

  - short and ushort: These are written by default as exactly 2 bytes (16 bits).

  - int and uint: These are written by default as exactly 4 bytes (32 bits).

  - long and ulong: These are written by default as exactly 8 bytes (64 bits).

  - char: This is written by default as exactly 2 bytes (16 bits).

  - enum: This is written by default as 1, 2 ,4, or 8 bytes (8 to 64 bits), depending on the underlying integer type of the enumeration.

■**Tip** For enumerations, you can specify the underlying integer type in C#. Possible types are byte, sbyte, short, ushort, int, uint, long, and ulong, for example, public enum MyEnum: byte {A, B, C};. Without the indication of a type, an enumeration is based on a 32-bit signed integer (int). Depending on underlying type, 1 to 8 bytes are serialized.

- *Types treated like ordinal types:*

  - DateTime: This type stores the number of ticks as an unsigned 64-bit value (ulong).

  - TimeSpan: This type stores the number of ticks as a signed 64-bit value (long).

- *Floating point numbers:*

  - float: This is written by default as exactly 4 bytes (32 bits).

  - double: This is written by default as exactly 8 bytes (64 bits).

  - decimal: This type is not available for the .NET Micro Framework.

- *Strings:* Strings are stored in the UTF8 format. The length of the UTF8 representation is placed in front of the string. The number of bytes is written as a compressed unsigned integer. Depending on the length of the string, the compressed integer takes either 1, 2, or 4 bytes. String fields with the value null are indicated by the byte 0xFF.

- *Arrays:* The number of elements in an array is placed in front of the actual item data in the form of a compressed unsigned integer.

- *Array lists:* An ArrayList is stored similarly to an array, with the number of items preceding the data.

Configuring Serialization with Attributes

With the `SerializationHintsAttribute` attribute from the `Microsoft.SPOT` namespace, you are able to configure and optimize the serialization. By indicating well known information, more compact storage becomes possible, since the information need not be stored together with the data in each serialization. For example, if you know that an array will always have exactly four elements, you can indicate the array length using the attribute. Then, it is not necessary to write the array length before the actual element data.

Properties of the SerializationHintsAttribute Class

The following sections cover how you can configure and optimize the serialization using the `SerializationHintsAttribute` class.

int BitPacked

`BitPacked` indicates the number of bits that are to be stored for an ordinal type. If `BitPacked` is 0, the default size of a data type is used (for example, 4 bytes for an `int` and 1 byte for the `byte` type). For instance, if you specify `BitPacked` for a Boolean field as 1, then for the Boolean value, only 1 bit is stored, which is completely sufficient for `true` and `false`. Or for example, if you know that your byte field can have only values between 0 and 32, you can reduce its storage size by specifying 5 bits for `BitPacked` (32 equals 2^5). With signed number types, the sign is represented by a bit, so you need to consider this in the calculation of the value range. Within a byte, the storage begins with the most significant bit.

Also, you can apply `BitPacked` to arrays and the `ArrayList` class. In this case, the number of items, written before the data, will not be written as a compressed unsigned integer. Instead, noncompressed integers with the indicated bit width will be written if the array or list contains integers. That means you can control the bit width of the items of an integer array or list with the `BitPacked` property.

For strings, `BitPacked` cannot be used; the length is always written as a compressed integer in front of the string data.

long RangeBias

`RangeBias` can be applied to all ordinal types with the exception of `bool`. It enables you to reduce a value to be written so that it needs fewer bits. The value indicated in `RangeBias` is subtracted from the ordinal value before storing it. If, for example, your field will only have values from 500 to 550, the data type of the field must be a 16-bit integer, since the 8 bits of a byte are not sufficient. Knowing this, the necessary bit width can be reduced to 6, instead of 16, with `BitPacked`. A value of 500 for `RangeBias` causes the value 500 to be subtracted from the actual value before the serialization. Afterward, the remaining range of values from 0 to 50 requires only 6 bits. By default, 16 bits were thus serialized, but with 500 for `RangeBias` and 6 for `BitPacked`, only 6 bits need to be serialized. Negative values are permitted also for the `RangeBias` value.

■**Tip** With a DateTime value, you can store absolute time point values. By subtracting the number of ticks for a certain time point in the past, you can reduce the number of bytes to be serialized. You can serialize, for example, time points up to the May 5, 2235 in 7 bytes (BitPacket=56), if you subtract the number of ticks for the January 1, 2007 (RangeBias=0x8C8FB4EEA270000). Thus, you can save exactly one byte (using 7 bytes instead of 8 bytes) in the comparison to default behavior without specification.

ulong Scale

Like RangeBias, Scale helps save bits when serializing a value. Before serialization, a field is divided by the value of Scale. If a field contains only odd or only even values, the range of values can be reduced by half by using a scale of 2 (Scale=2). A combination of RangeBias and Scale is also possible. Here, however, the order of operation must be considered. It is valid for serialization

y = (x - RangeBias) / Scale

and for deserialization, using this formula:

x = y * Scale + RangeBias

■**Note** The BitPacked option is applicable for only ordinal types, DateTime, and TimeSpan. RangeBias and Scale are likewise applicable for ordinal types, DateTime, and TimeSpan. However, RangeBias and Scale will not work for bool.

int ArraySize

If the size of an array is fixed and well known, the fixed size can be indicated with ArraySize, and the size does not need to be placed before the items each time the array is serialized. ArraySize cannot be specified for ArrayList instances and strings. If a class you want to serialize contains only one array of simple data types and no other fields, you can specify –1 for ArraySize. Then, the length of the array can be variable, and the array length must not be placed in front. At deserialization, the number of elements can be determined from the length of the buffer and the well known size of the simple data type.

SerializationFlags Flags

The SerializationFlags enumeration provides some more hints to configure the serialization and contains the following members:

- `DemandTrusted`: This flag refers to a class or structure that you may serialize and indicates that objects of this type contain safety-relevant data and a serialization might not be possible in certain cases. However, that this flag seems to be ignored by the CLR.

- `PointerNeverNull`: `PointerNeverNull` can be applied on fields that are of a reference type, including classes. This flag indicates to the system that a field will never be `null` and appropriate marking need not be saved with storage again and again. Arrays are also classes and can be `null`; therefore, this indication is valid for array fields also. With strings, `PointerNeverNull` does not have an effect, because the string length, which is placed in front it, makes evident whether the string is `null`.

- `FixedType`: `FixedType` is likewise applicable only for fields that point to classes, and it shows that the field always points to an instance of the field type and never to a derived class of it. This indication is not necessary with sealed classes, since with those, you are already certain that there cannot be a derived class. For arrays, this flag does not have a meaning. Without this flag, an internal identifier for the used class is stored before the actual data. This type identifier is a type number from the internal list of the available types of the .NET Micro Framework.

The following additional flags are members of `SerializationFlags` and can be applied but are not used with the 2.0 and 2.5 releases of the .NET Micro Framework:

- `Compressed`

- `ElementsNeverNull`

- `Encrypted`

- `Optional`

In Listing 9-10, you can see how the binary serialization process is optimized with attributes.

Listing 9-10. *Optimizing Binary Serialization with Attributes*

```
using System;
using Microsoft.SPOT;
using System.Collections;

namespace BinarySerializationSample2
{
    public enum MyEnum { A, B, C };

    public interface IMyInterface
    {
        void SomeMethod();
    }
```

```csharp
[Serializable]
public class MyClass : IMyInterface
{
    public byte b = 0xAA;

    #region IMyInterface Members
    public void SomeMethod()
    {
    }
    #endregion
}

[Serializable]
public sealed class MySealedClass
{
    public byte b = 0xAA;
}

[Serializable]
public struct MyStruct
{
    public int a;
}

[Serializable]
[SerializationHints(Flags = SerializationFlags.DemandTrusted)]
public class MySerializableClass2
{
    [SerializationHints(BitPacked = 1)]
    public readonly bool a;
    [SerializationHints(BitPacked = 3)]
    private byte b; //for values from 0 - 7
    [SerializationHints(BitPacked = 2)]
    private MyEnum c; //only 3 members, so 2 bits are enough
    [SerializationHints(BitPacked = 4, RangeBias = 10)]
    public uint d = 25; //for values 10 - 25
    [SerializationHints(BitPacked = 4, RangeBias = 10, Scale = 2)]
    public uint e = 40; //for even values from 10 - 40
    public string f;
    private float g;
    //from 1. Jan. 2007 to 5. May 2235 are 7 instead of 8 Bytes required
    [SerializationHints(BitPacked = 56, RangeBias = 0x8C8FB4EEA270000)]
    private DateTime h = DateTime.Now;
    [SerializationHints(Flags = SerializationFlags.PointerNeverNull |
                                SerializationFlags.FixedType)]
```

```
        private MyClass i = new MyClass();
        [SerializationHints(Flags = SerializationFlags.PointerNeverNull)]
        private MySealedClass j = new MySealedClass();
        private IMyInterface k; //a type id needs to be stored
        public MyStruct l;
        [SerializationHints(ArraySize = 10,
                            Flags = SerializationFlags.PointerNeverNull)]
        public byte[] m = new byte[10];
        //for a 4 bit array size, 0 - 15 elements are possible
        [SerializationHints(BitPacked = 4,
                            Flags = SerializationFlags.PointerNeverNull)]
        public byte[] n = new byte[5];
        [SerializationHints(Flags = SerializationFlags.PointerNeverNull)]
        public ArrayList o = new ArrayList();
    }
}
```

Notes, Hints, and Lessons Learned

If arrays with items that are classes are to be serialized, those classes should be defined as sealed, since, otherwise, a data type identifier must be stored for each item. A hint flag like ElementFixedType does not exist.

Elements with the value null are possible only for items of a sealed class type. In this case, zero-bytes are written for all fields and deserialization will return an uninitialized object. With null elements of classes that are not sealed, you will get an error when trying to serialize it.

If BitPacked is applied to an ArrayList field, the number of items, as previously described, is placed in front of the element data in the indicated bit width of BitPacked instead of storing the number of items as a compressed unsigned integer. For example, if an ArrayList contains integer items, these are written in the indicated bit width.

If fields of the Type type are written, an internal type identifier is written. This type identifier is, as already mentioned, a type number from an internal list of all available data types. This list contains only types that are used (referenced directly) in an application and varies from application to application.

Exchanging Data with Other Devices

Unfortunately, the binary serialization of the .NET Micro Framework is specific and thus not available in the full .NET Framework and .NET Compact Framework, so only .NET Micro Framework devices can exchange serialized data with each other. This limits the use strongly. Nevertheless, you might also need to exchange data in a simple manner with a PC, notebook, PDA, or smartphone.

Therefore, I implemented the binary serialization for the full .NET Framework as a class with identical interfaces for serialization and deserialization. The class can also be used with the .NET Compact Framework and can be found in the BinarySerializationdesktopSample project located in this chapter's directory. Thus, nothing prevents you from easily exchanging serialized data with the devices mentioned previously.

The complete feature set of the original was, however, not implemented, so you need to consider some limitations:

- The internal type list with the type IDs is the other communication partner's, for example, a PC that's not well known. Therefore, fields of the Type data type are not possible.

- Fields that are of an interface type are not possible because of unknown internal type IDs.

- Additionally, you can only serialize class fields that are sealed classes or classes with the FixedType hint flag.

- The serialization of arrays and ArrayList classes was not implemented.

- For BitPacked, you must specify complete bytes, thus possible values are 8, 16, 24, 32, 40, 48, 56, and 64 bits.

- RangeBias and Scale were not implemented.

Storing Data Permanently in Flash Memory

With extended weak references in the .NET Micro Framework, you can store objects of serializable types compactly and permanently in the flash memory, so that the data is available after a power cycle of your device.

In order to use this feature, your device must support permanent storage in the flash memory. For execution on an emulator, you need to first create the stand-alone sample emulator project, EWRSampleEmulator, provided with the .NET Micro Framework SDK. When the emulator is compiled, it is registered automatically, and after that, you can select it in the project properties of a .NET Micro Framework application, as Emulator on the Micro Framework tab page (see Figure 9-1). This emulator stores the contents of its flash memory into a file on termination and loads that file on startup.

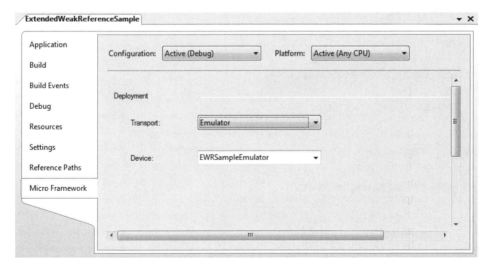

Figure 9-1. *Selecting the EWRSampleEmulator*

Normally in .NET, objects will be disposed of by the garbage collector as soon as they are no longer referenced. Objects that are referenced by static fields will never be collected and disposed of by the garbage collector and remain up in the memory until your application terminates. With weak references, on the one hand, it is possible to reference objects (e.g., with static fields) and, on the other hand, to let the garbage collector dispose of them if memory is low.

The `ExtendedWeakReference` class inherits from the `System.WeakReference` class, which is also available in the full .NET Framework, and is in the `Microsoft.SPOT` namespace. The `ExtendedWeakReference` class is specific for the .NET Micro Framework and extends the `System.WeakReference` class by adding the ability to persist objects in the flash memory. When assigning a data object to the `ExtendedWeakReference`, the data will be binary serialized compactly to the flash memory but will still be present in the RAM memory. When the system runs out of memory, the garbage collector will dispose of the data in the RAM memory. If the data is needed again later (after a power cycle), it can be recovered at any time from the flash memory. By means of specifying a priority, you can tell the garbage collector how important an object is and help the garbage collector to decide which objects to dispose of first.

Now, you will learn how you can log the number of boot starts of a device or an emulator and how to persist the current number permanently in the flash memory with an `ExtendedWeakReference`. First, you need to declare a static field of the type `ExtendedWeakReference`:

```
private static ExtendedWeakReference bootInfoExtendedWeakReference;
```

The field must be static, so that the extended weak reference is not released prematurely by the garbage collector. Otherwise, the whole approach would not work.

Additionally, you need a serializable class as shown in Listing 9-11, which contains the data to be stored.

Listing 9-11. *The Serializable Class Holding the Data to Be Stored*

```
//the class to be stored into flash memory, the class must be serializable
[Serializable]
internal sealed class MyBootInfo
{
    private int bootCount;

    public MyBootInfo(int bootCount)
    {
        this.bootCount = bootCount;
    }

    public int BootCount
    {
        get { return this.bootCount; }
    }
}
```

Further, you need to have a unique selector class to identify your data:

```
private static class MyUniqueSelectorType { }
```

After you have seen all the declarations, you will get the actual complete program code as shown in Listing 9-12.

Listing 9-12. *Persisting Objects in the Flash Memory with the Microsoft.SPOT. ExtendedWeakReference Class*

```csharp
using System;
using Microsoft.SPOT;

namespace ExtendedWeakReferenceSample
{
    public class Program
    {
        //the weak reference, must be a static reference to work properly
        private static ExtendedWeakReference bootInfoExtendedWeakReference;

        //this the selector class to identify the data
        private static class MyUniqueSelectorType { }

        public static void Main()
        {
            //try to recover the data or create the weak reference
            bootInfoExtendedWeakReference =
                ExtendedWeakReference.RecoverOrCreate(
                    //unique type to prevent other code from accessing our data
                    typeof(MyUniqueSelectorType),
                    0, //id that refers to the data we care about
                    ExtendedWeakReference.c_SurvivePowerdown |
                    ExtendedWeakReference.c_SurviveBoot);

            //set how important the data is
            bootInfoExtendedWeakReference.Priority =
                            (int)ExtendedWeakReference.PriorityLevel.Important;

            //try to get the persisted data
            //if we get the data, then putting it in the field myBootInfo creates a
            //strong reference to it, preventing the GC from collecting it
            MyBootInfo myBootInfo =
                            (MyBootInfo)bootInfoExtendedWeakReference.Target;

            if (myBootInfo == null)
            {
                //the data could not be obtained
                Debug.Print("This is the first time the device booted " +
                        "or the data was lost.");
                myBootInfo = new MyBootInfo(1); //first initialization
            }
```

```
        else
        {
            //the data could be obtained, display info
            Debug.Print("Number of boots = " + myBootInfo.BootCount);
            //increment number of boots
            myBootInfo = new MyBootInfo(myBootInfo.BootCount + 1);
        }

        //setting the Target property causes to write the data to flash memory
        bootInfoExtendedWeakReference.Target = myBootInfo;

        //give the system time to save it to flash
        System.Threading.Thread.Sleep(2000);
    }
  }
}
```

First, with the static RecoverOrCreate method of ExtendedWeakReference, either an already stored extended weak reference is read and recovered from the flash memory or a new one is created.

The first parameter for RecoverOrCreate is the selector, which is of the System.Type data type. In this example, the already declared private embedded class MyUniqueSelectorType will be provided as the selector; this embedded class is only accessible and known in the class within which it was defined. The second parameter is an integer identifier. The combination of selector and ID describes the ExtendedWeakReference uniquely. If you use extended weak references in several parts of your application or in other referenced assemblies, then it is guaranteed that those different references will not be mixed, because the used selector classes have only a limited visibility. The selector, then, has nothing to do with the class or structure that will be serialized. You might also use the MyBootInfo type as the selector. If the MyBootInfo class will be accessed from other places and is visible from there, your data will not be unique anymore.

Finally, the RecoverOrCreate method accepts the flags parameter, which describes the persistence of an ExtendedWeakReference data. If the data will survive after a device shuts down, the ExtendedWeakReference.c_SurvivePowerdown constant must be indicated. If the data should be still recoverable after new boots, you must specify ExtendedWeakReference.c_SurviveBoot. You can combine both flags. The data will then survive shutting down and rebooting the device.

■**Note** I do not know why constants need to be used to describe the flags parameter and no enumeration with enum is possible. According to Microsoft, the serialization originated from SPOT (Smart Personal Object Technology), the predecessor of today's .NET Micro Frameworks.

ExtendedWeakReference exposes a Priority property, which is used to indicate the importance of the data. Priority is an integer property. However, the ExtendedWeakReference class contains an embedded PriorityLevel enumeration (see Listing 9-13) with already predefined values for the priority. The garbage collector thus first will dispose data with the priority level OkayToThrowAway, then NiceToHave data, and so on.

Listing 9-13. *Priorities*

```
public enum PriorityLevel
{
    OkayToThrowAway =     1000,
    NiceToHave      =   500000,
    Important       =   750000,
    Critical        =  1000000,
    System          = 10000000,
}
```

When using the enumeration, this enumeration value must be cast to an integer before assigning it to the `Priority` property.

The serialized data of a reference is accessible with the `Target` property, which exposes an instance of the data as `object`. To access the data, you need a strong reference of the same type, `MyBootInfo`, as your data. The data is received and assigned to the strong reference with the `Target` property. If no data has been stored in the flash memory yet (i.e., with the first start), and no data could be recovered, then `Target` returns the value `null`.

If the value of the `myBootInfo` field is `null`, then no data was available. This is the case either with the first boot or if the data was lost, and the counter is initialized with the value 1 for the first boot. If `myBootInfo` is not `null`, the stored data could be successfully recovered. In this case, the counter is increased and printed out.

Afterward, `myBootInfo` contains the current counter value, which will be persisted to flash memory by assigning the updated data to the `Target` property. Assigning data to the `Target` property triggers the serialization to the flash memory.

Since the sample program will terminate directly after the serialization, you need to pause the application, so the runtime environment (CLR) gets enough time to write the data to the flash memory.

The approach with the strong reference on the basis of the `myBootInfo` local variable is necessary, since without assignment to `Target`, the data would not be written to the flash memory.

Summary

In this chapter, you learned how to program multithreaded applications to execute parallel tasks. The chapter also presented various ways to synchronize threads if they need to access shared resources. You now know how to use weak delegates to improve memory usage and avoid memory leaks. The chapter discussed execution constraints and how you can use them to monitor the execution time of a certain task. You also now know a lot of about binary serialization with the .NET Micro Framework and how to reduce the storage size using attributes. The source code for this chapter provides an implementation of the .NET Micro Framework's binary serialization for the full .NET Framework and .NET Compact Framework for a simple data exchange between these platforms. This chapter further described how to use binary serialization and extended weak references to store data permanently in flash memory.

The next chapter provides you information about how to write globalized and localized applications that are ready for the international market.

CHAPTER 10

Globalization and Localization

This chapter concerns, first of all, what kinds of resources you can use with the .NET Micro Framework and how you can use them. After that, you will learn how to write multilingual .NET Micro Framework applications on small devices for an international market. The chapter will introduce cultures and how you can add further cultures to a .NET Micro Framework application. You will learn how to print dates, times, and numbers appropriate for particular cultures (called globalization) and how you can use satellite assemblies to isolate and embed translated resources (called localization).

Resources

Resources are used in the .NET Framework to embed and deploy supplemental data with an application and to isolate and embed translations for an application. For example, you can embed images, texts, or whole files into an assembly. You can create resources for special languages or cultures, and depending on the selected current culture, an application can load the appropriate text or images. Since a file system does not exist on small devices with the .NET Micro Framework, additional resources provide an elegant way to deploy supplemental data for an application. Visual Studio offers outstanding support for handling resources.

The following kinds of resources are available for the .NET Micro Framework:

- Strings

- Images

- Fonts

- Binary data

The following image formats are supported by the .NET Micro Framework:

- Bitmap

- JPEG

- GIF

Images with indexed color palettes, as used for 16- and 256-color images, are not supported. Also not supported are images in the PNG and TIFF formats, as well as icons.

Fonts must be present in a special format (the .tinyfnt file format) for the .NET Micro Framework. This special format uses fixed size bitmaps as a simpler way to render fonts. Two sample .tinyfnt fonts are included in the Fonts subdirectory of your .NET Micro Framework installation. To create other fonts in the size, style, and language tailored to your application, you can use the TFConvert tool from the .NET Micro Framework SDK to create a .tinyfnt font from TrueType or OpenType font files. To use .tinyfnt fonts with your application, you need to embed such a font file in your assembly as a resource. Once a .tinyfnt font file is created, you cannot change its size and style anymore; it is fixed. To use different sizes and styles, you need to create and use different fonts.

Anything that is not recognized as text, images, or fonts is stored as a binary resource.

Creating and Editing Resources

A new .NET Micro Framework project created with the project template already contains a resource file. You can add a new resource file with Visual Studio using the menu command Project ➤ Add New Item ➤ Resource File (see Figure 10-1).

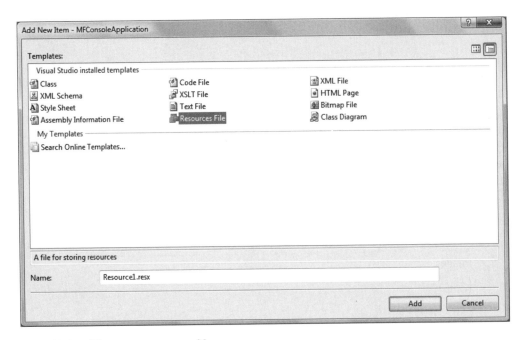

Figure 10-1. *Adding a new resource file*

You can double-click an entry ending with .resx in the Solution Explorer to open a designer for adding and editing resources (see Figure 10-2).

In the resource designer, you can display the different types of resources by clicking the left header column (see Figure 10-3).

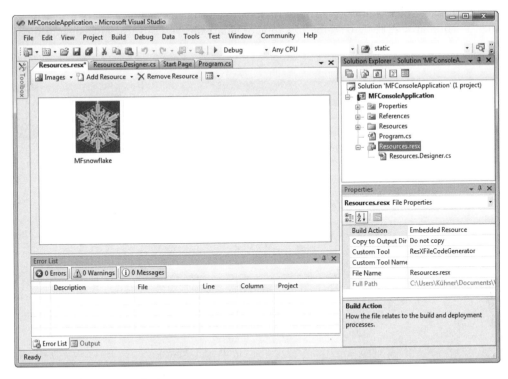

Figure 10-2. *The resource designer*

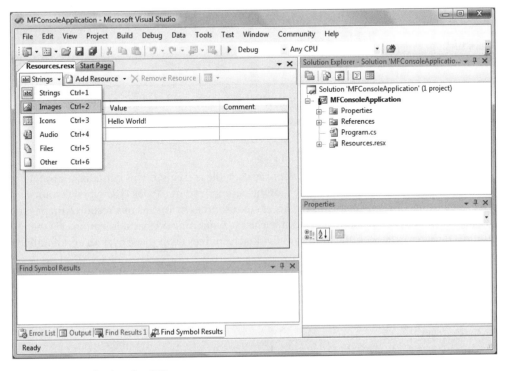

Figure 10-3. *Displaying the different resource types*

By clicking Add Resource (see Figure 10-4), you can add an existing resource from a file such as a bitmap, .NET Micro Framework font, or binary file. You can also add a new string or bitmap here.

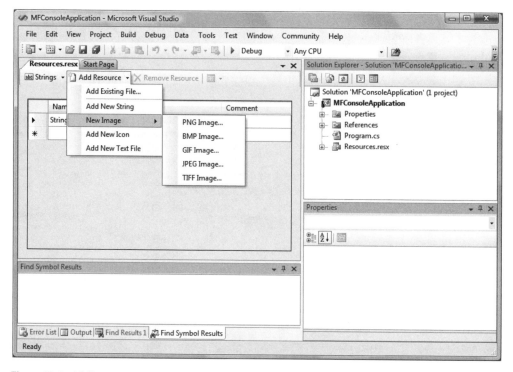

Figure 10-4. *Adding resources*

■**Caution** After you have created a new image resource directly in Visual Studio, you have to change the number of colors from the unsupported 256 colors to True Color.

For each resource file in a project, a source code file is created. This contains a strongly typed resource class for the simple access of the certain resource types. The typed resource class (see Listing 10-1) encapsulates the access to resources by means of a resource manager and the ResourceUtility class. The resource class is synchronized to modifications via the resource designer. The identification of individual resources takes place over an enumeration, which is likewise generated automatically.

Listing 10-1. *An Automatically Generated, Strongly Typed Resource Class*

```
//------------------------------------------------------------------------------
// <auto-generated>
//     This code was generated by a tool.
```

```
//      Runtime Version:2.0.50727.312
//
//      Changes to this file may cause incorrect behavior and will be lost if
//      the code is regenerated.
// </auto-generated>
//-----------------------------------------------------------------------------

namespace ResourceSample
{

    internal class Resources
    {
        private static System.Resources.ResourceManager manager;
        // Creates and returns a resource manager object.
        // It is created only once.
        internal static System.Resources.ResourceManager ResourceManager
        {
            get
            {
                if ((Resources.manager == null))
                {
                    Resources.manager =
                     new System.Resources.ResourceManager(
                                                // Qualified resource name
                                                "ResourceSample.Resources",
                                                // Assembly with the res.
                                                typeof(Resources).Assembly
                                                    );
                }
                return Resources.manager;
            }
        }
        // Access method for bitmap resources from a given bitmap resource ID
        // using the resource manager.
        internal static Microsoft.SPOT.Bitmap GetBitmap(
                                                    Resources.BitmapResources id
                                                    )
        {
            return
              ((Microsoft.SPOT.Bitmap)
              (Microsoft.SPOT.ResourceUtility.GetObject(ResourceManager, id)));
        }
        // Getting font resources
        internal static Microsoft.SPOT.Font GetFont(Resources.FontResources id)
        {
```

```
            return
              ((Microsoft.SPOT.Font)
              (Microsoft.SPOT.ResourceUtility.GetObject(ResourceManager, id)));
        }
        // Getting string resources
        internal static string GetString(Resources.StringResources id)
        {
            return
              ((string)
              (Microsoft.SPOT.ResourceUtility.GetObject(ResourceManager, id)));
        }
        // Getting binary resources
        internal static byte[] GetBytes(Resources.BinaryResources id)
        {
            return
              ((byte[])
              (Microsoft.SPOT.ResourceUtility.GetObject(ResourceManager, id)));
        }
        // Autogenerated string resource IDs
        // The numbers are not in a defined order
        [System.SerializableAttribute()]
        internal enum StringResources : short
        {
            HelloWorld = 3229,
            Copyright = 14498,
        }
        // Autogenerated binary resource IDs
        [System.SerializableAttribute()]
        internal enum BinaryResources : short
        {
            MyPDF = 7905,
        }
        // Autogenerated font resource IDs
        [System.SerializableAttribute()]
        internal enum FontResources : short
        {
            small = 13070,
        }
        // Autogenerated bitmap resource IDs
        [System.SerializableAttribute()]
        internal enum BitmapResources : short
        {
            MFsnowflake = 25406,
        }
    }
}
```

Working with Resources

In order to retrieve resource data, you must use the typed resource class in your application as demonstrated in Listing 10-2.

The resource class exposes the following methods for typed access of the resources:

- `string GetString()`

- `Microsoft.SPOT.Bitmap GetBitmap()`

- `Microsoft.SPOT.Font GetFont()`

- `byte[] GetBytes()`

Listing 10-2. *Using Resources*

```
using System;
using Microsoft.SPOT;

namespace ResourceSample
{
    public class Program
    {
        public static void Main()
        {
            Debug.Print(
                    Resources.GetString(Resources.StringResources.HelloWorld));
            Debug.Print(
                    Resources.GetString(Resources.StringResources.Copyright));

            Bitmap bmp =
                    Resources.GetBitmap(Resources.BitmapResources.MFsnowflake);
            Font font = Resources.GetFont(Resources.FontResources.small);
            byte[] buffer =
                    Resources.GetBytes(Resources.BinaryResources.MyPDF);
        }
    }
}
```

Cultures

Globalization of an application in the context of programming means making an application prepared for the international market. To accomplish that, several kinds of preparations are necessary; for example, dates, times, numbers, and currencies must be parsed and printed correctly.

A globalized application must thus handle and work with different cultures. A culture is defined by the language and optionally by a region. A culture defined only for a certain language without a region is a neutral culture.

The neutral culture for the German language is de. The German language in Germany is de-DE and in Austria, de-AT. If your application supports those two cultures and you tried to use de-CH (German for Switzerland) as the current culture, this culture would not be available, so the neutral culture de is taken instead, if it's available. If you request an unavailable culture and there is also no neutral culture for the language, the invariant culture that has an empty name ("") is used. This approach is called a resource fallback mechanism.

A culture is represented in the .NET Micro Framework, as in the full .NET Framework, by the System.CultureInfo class. Under Windows, nearly all cultures you can think of are already defined and can be determined and used by a .NET application. In the .NET Micro Framework, only two cultures are already defined and available. That is the invariant culture ("") and the neutral culture for the English language (en). You can create and install further custom cultures, however.

Creating and Installing Custom Cultures

A culture in the .NET Micro Framework defines information about the formatted output of dates and times, as well as number formatting. The format information is specified as string parameters. In Tables 10-1, 10-2, and 10-3, you can see all available parameters showing the number, date, and time values of the invariant culture.

Table 10-1. *Number Values of the Invariant Culture*

Name	Value
NumberDecimalSeparator	.
NumberGroupSeparator	,
NumberGroupSizes	3
NegativeSign	-
PositiveSign	+

Table 10-2. *Date Values of the Invariant Culture*

Name	Value
DateSeparator	/
LongDatePattern	dddd, dd MMMM yyyy
ShortDatePattern	MM/dd/yyyy
YearMonthPattern	yyyy MMMM
MonthDayPattern	MMMM dd
MonthNames	January|February|March|April|May|June|July|August|September|October|November|December
AbbreviatedMonthNames	Jan|Feb|Mar|Apr|May|Jun|Jul|Aug|Sep|Oct|Nov|Dec
DayNames	Sunday|Monday|Tuesday|Wednesday|Thursday|Friday|Saturday
AbbreviatedDayNames	Sun|Mon|Tue|Wed|Thu|Fri|Sat

Table 10-3. *Time Values of the Invariant Culture*

Name	Value
TimeSeparator	:
LongTimePattern	HH:mm:ss
ShortTimePattern	HH:mm
AMDesignator	AM
PMDesignator	PM

The parameter data of a culture is embedded as a resource string in one or more separate assemblies. The name of an assembly containing resources for cultures must begin with mscorlib, and that assembly must be referenced by the main assembly. A culture assembly is deployed only if it is referenced by an application.

If you decide to embed exactly one culture per assembly, the name of the culture must be appended to mscorlib, separated by a dot. Therefore, you need to store the culture de-DE in the mscorlib.de-DE resource assembly. You can place one neutral and further, regional subcultures for the German language into an assembly with the name mscorlib.de. You can store several different cultures in the mscorlib.resources assembly. The search order is always the same. To look for culture definitions, all referenced assemblies of an application are examined. First, mscorlib.<language>-<region> is searched inside the assemblies, followed by mscorlib.<language>, mscorlib.resources, and at last, mscorlib itself.

You do not need to specify all parameters for every culture because the resources use a fallback mechanism. If a parameter is not specified for a culture, it is looked up, if available, under the neutral parent culture with the appropriate language and then under the invariant culture.

You need to name a resource file for a culture exactly the same as the culture to be stored in it, and you need to place the resource file in the System.Globalization.Resources.CultureInfo namespace.

To add cultures, follow these steps:

1. First of all, you need to create a new project for a .NET Micro Framework class library assembly. You have to name the project for the class library, as mentioned before. You do not need the automatically created Class1.cs file, which is in the new project, so you should delete it.

2. Further, you have to change the standard namespace of a project on the Application tab page in the project properties to System.Globalization.Resources.CultureInfo (see Figure 10-5).

3. Now, add a new resource file with the name of the desired culture (for example, de or de-DE). You accomplish this by clicking the menu item and Project ➤ New Item ➤ Resource File. In the Solution Explorer, you can see the new resource file indicated by the extension .resx. Figure 10-6 shows a solution with several mixed cultures.

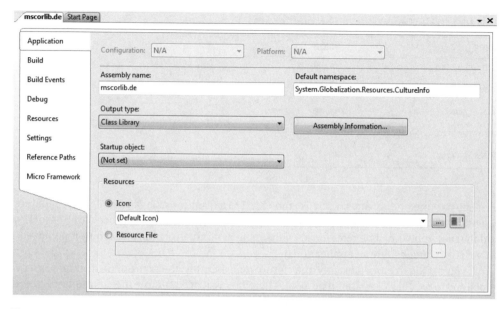

Figure 10-5. *Changing the standard namespace of a project*

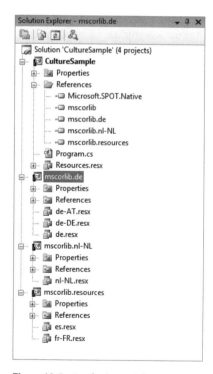

Figure 10-6. *A solution with several mixed cultures*

4. For the new resource file, a typed resource class is created and automatically added under it as a subitem. This class is not needed and should be deleted. So that this class is not re-created after each change in the resources, you need to clear the value of the parameter Custom Tool, which has the value ResXFileCodeGenerator, in the Properties window (see Figure 10-7).

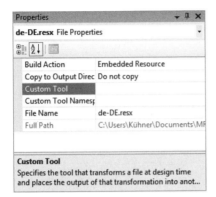

Figure 10-7. Deactivating the automatic generation of a typed resource class

5. Double-clicking that newly created resource in the Solution Explorer opens the resource designer, as shown in Figure 10-8. Here, the already described parameters can be created and edited as resource strings.

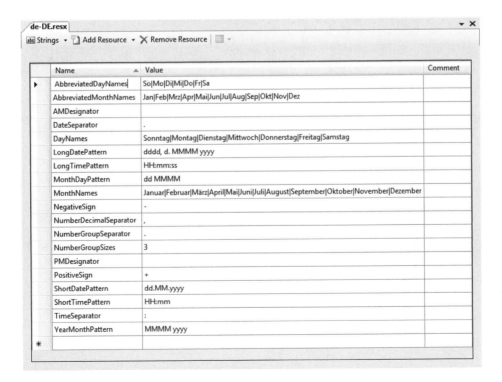

Figure 10-8. Editing culture parameters in the resource designer

However, it is very laborious to collect information about a culture, create a resource file, and add all the resource strings each time for every new culture. Therefore, I wrote a tool named CultureViewer (see Figure 10-9) that automates this process. This application lists all available cultures under Windows and displays all parameters and their values. In case that isn't enough, it further allows you to export a selected culture, including all parameter values, as a resource file with string resources. The only thing you have to do is add the exported .resx file to a project so that the new culture can be used.

You can find the CultureViewer tool in this chapter's directory, in the CultureViewer project.

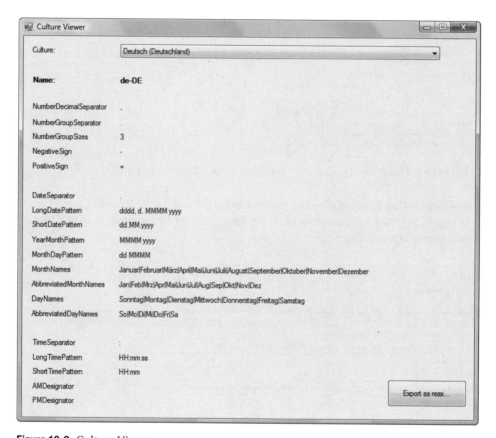

Figure 10-9. *Culture Viewer*

■**Tip** The CultureViewer tool always exports the complete parameter set. Parameter values, which are equal to those of their parent culture (if available) or to those in the built-in invariant culture, can be deleted manually, since they can be determined with the resource fallback mechanism from a superordinate culture.

Formatting Dates, Times, and Numbers

Now that you know how to create cultures, you will learn how to use them. Listing 10-3 demonstrates the usage of cultures. Date, time, and numbers are formatted and printed for several cultures in the respective culture's typical format.

Listing 10-3. *Using Cultures*

```
using System;
using Microsoft.SPOT;
using System.Threading;
using System.Globalization;

namespace CultureSample
{
    public class Class1
    {
        public static void Main()
        {
            Debug.Print(string.Empty);
            ListAvailableCultures();
            PrintSamples(CultureInfo.CurrentUICulture);
            PrintSamples(new CultureInfo("en"));
            PrintSamples(new CultureInfo("de-DE"));
            PrintSamples(new CultureInfo("de-AT"));
            PrintSamples(new CultureInfo("fr-FR"));

            CultureInfo culture;
            culture = new CultureInfo("de-CH");
            Debug.Print("Culture de-CH will fallback to '" + culture.Name +
                    "'");
            culture = new CultureInfo("fr-BE");
            Debug.Print("Culture fr-BE will fallback to '" + culture.Name +
                    "'");
            Debug.Print(string.Empty);
        }

        private static void ListAvailableCultures()
        {
            CultureInfo[] cultures =
                        CultureInfo.GetCultures(CultureTypes.AllCultures);
            Debug.Print("Available cultures:");
            foreach (CultureInfo culture in cultures)
                Debug.Print("Culture='" + culture.Name + "'");
            Debug.Print(string.Empty);
        }
```

```
        private static void PrintSamples(CultureInfo culture)
        {
            ResourceUtility.SetCurrentUICulture(culture);
            DateTime dt = DateTime.Now;
            Debug.Print("Requested Culture '" + culture.Name + "'");
            Debug.Print("Current Culture '" +
                        CultureInfo.CurrentUICulture.Name +
                        "'");
            Debug.Print("FullDateTime=LongDate+LongTime: " + dt.ToString("F"));
            Debug.Print("GeneralLongTime=ShortDate+LongTime: " +
                        dt.ToString("F"));
            Debug.Print("LongDate: " + dt.ToString("D"));
            Debug.Print("ShortDate: " + dt.ToString("d"));
            Debug.Print("LongTime: " + dt.ToString("T"));
            Debug.Print("ShortTime: " + dt.ToString("t"));
            Debug.Print("YearMonth: " + dt.ToString("y")); //or Y
            Debug.Print("MonthDay: " + dt.ToString("m")); // or M
            Debug.Print((-1234567.89).ToString());
            Debug.Print(string.Empty);
        }
    }
}
```

At the beginning, all available cultures are listed. They are collected with the following method:

```
CultureInfo[] cultures = CultureInfo.GetCultures(CultureTypes.AllCultures);
```

Before doing any output, you have to programmatically select the desired culture as the current culture. The current culture is used globally, and all formatting methods refer to it. You can set the current culture with the SetCurrentUICulture method of the ResourceUtility class. The current culture is then considered with all output.

You cannot pass an individual culture or IFormatProvider to the ToString methods as in the full .NET Framework.

At the end of the code, the function of the fallback mechanism will be demonstrated. If you try to create an instance of a culture that does not exist, an object of the next possible more general culture is created. The application from Listing 10-3 produces the following output:

```
Available cultures:
Culture='en'
Culture=''
Culture='nl-NL'
Culture='es'
Culture='fr-FR'
Culture='de-AT'
Culture='de-DE'
Culture='de'
```

```
Requested Culture ''
Current Culture ''
FullDateTime=LongDate+LongTime: Wednesday, 07 February 2007 00:10:53
GeneralLongTime=ShortDate+LongTime: Wednesday, 07 February 2007 00:10:53
LongDate: Wednesday, 07 February 2007
ShortDate: 02/07/2007
LongTime: 00:10:53
ShortTime: 00:10
YearMonth: 2007 February
MonthDay: February 07
-1234567.89

Requested Culture 'en'
Current Culture 'en'
FullDateTime=LongDate+LongTime: Wednesday, February 07, 2007 12:10:53 AM
GeneralLongTime=ShortDate+LongTime: Wednesday, February 07, 2007 12:10:53 AM
LongDate: Wednesday, February 07, 2007
ShortDate: 2/7/2007
LongTime: 12:10:53 AM
ShortTime: 12:10 AM
YearMonth: February, 2007
MonthDay: February 07
-1234567.89

Requested Culture 'de-DE'
Current Culture 'de-DE'
FullDateTime=LongDate+LongTime: Mittwoch, 7. Februar 2007 00:10:53
GeneralLongTime=ShortDate+LongTime: Mittwoch, 7. Februar 2007 00:10:53
LongDate: Mittwoch, 7. Februar 2007
ShortDate: 07.02.2007
LongTime: 00:10:53
ShortTime: 00:10
YearMonth: Februar 2007
MonthDay: 07 Februar
-1234567,89

Requested Culture 'de-AT'
Current Culture 'de-AT'
FullDateTime=LongDate+LongTime: Mittwoch, 07. Februar 2007 00:10:53
GeneralLongTime=ShortDate+LongTime: Mittwoch, 07. Februar 2007 00:10:53
LongDate: Mittwoch, 07. Februar 2007
ShortDate: 07.02.2007
LongTime: 00:10:53
ShortTime: 00:10
YearMonth: Februar 2007
MonthDay: 07 Februar
-1234567,89
```

```
Requested Culture 'fr-FR'
Current Culture 'fr-FR'
FullDateTime=LongDate+LongTime: mercredi 7 février 2007 00:10:53
GeneralLongTime=ShortDate+LongTime: mercredi 7 février 2007 00:10:53
LongDate: mercredi 7 février 2007
ShortDate: 07/02/2007
LongTime: 00:10:53
ShortTime: 00:10
YearMonth: février 2007
MonthDay: 7 février
-1234567,89

Culture de-CH will fallback to 'de'
Culture fr-BE will fallback to ''
```

■**Caution** In the .NET Micro Framework, there is still a bug in the output of floating point numbers in the format "N". If the decimal separator is a comma, and the thousands separator is a period, as is common in Germany, then, for example, 1234567.89 outputs as 1,234.567.89 instead of 1.234.567, 89.

The NumberGroupSizes parameter describes the size of the number groupings. Number groups are, in most cases, formed as thousands groups. It is also intended that the groups can have different sizes with some cultures, as is common, for example, in India. With this culture, NumberGroupSizes has the value "3|2". Groups of different sizes, though possible in the full .NET Framework, will cause an error in the .NET Micro Framework.

Persisting the Current Culture

When you have changed the current culture for an embedded application, you may want to persist these changes after power cycling a device. With the ResourceUtility. SetCurentUICulture method, you can set the current culture permanently. The ResourceUtility class retains the current culture by using an ExtendedWeakReference to store it permanently in the flash memory, as was described in the discussion about extended weak references in Chapter 9, supposing your device supports this.

Multilingual Applications

In the following sections, you will learn how to create and use satellite assemblies to isolate and embed your translated resources, and you will see how you can change the language at runtime.

Satellite Assemblies

Applications are developed with texts and messages in an initial language. The texts, pictures, and other resources that are to be translated later must be stored as resources. Translations for an application are stored in satellite assemblies. You can create satellite assemblies for execut-able files (.exe) and for library assemblies (.dll), and a satellite assembly contains the translation for exactly one culture. You can add satellite assemblies for further languages without having to change the application code, but only the appropriate satellite assembly containing the neces-sary translation for the selected language or culture is loaded into the memory.

Satellite assemblies always have the file extension .dll and usually contain no program code. In the full .NET Framework, satellite assemblies are placed in a separate subdirectory named as the respective culture; the names of the assemblies and resource files are identical to the originals. But there is no file system for the .NET Micro Framework, so the culture name is appended to the assembly name.

Translations are looked up with the resource fallback mechanism approach. For example, the resources for the culture de-DE of an assembly with the name MyAssembly.exe are successively searched in the assemblies MyAssembly.de-DE.dll, MyAssembly.de.dll, MyAssembly.resources.dll, and finally MyAssembly.exe itself.

Creating Satellite Assemblies

Now, you will learn by a concrete example how satellite assemblies are created. You can find the source code of the LocalizationSample sample project in this chapter's directory. The main or default language of this application is English. That means all text displayed by the application is in English and stored as string resources in the executable file, and without satellite assemblies, only English text is visible. The example demonstrates how to add a German translation, so that the text appears in the German language or culture after selecting this language. The satellite assembly contains text for the neutral culture de, and thus this satellite assembly will be loaded for the cultures de-DE, de-AT, de-CH, and so on with the resource fallback mechanism approach.

The procedure of creating satellite assemblies resembles adding new cultures. As you have already learned, the definition of a culture is likewise added as a string resource in a satellite assembly.

To create a new satellite assembly, you need to complete the following steps:

1. Add a new .NET Micro Framework class library project for the satellite assembly to the solution of your application by selecting File ➤ New Project. You have to name the new assembly like this: <name of the assembly to translate>.<culture name>. For this example, you need to name it LocalizationSample.de.

2. The automatically added Class1.cs source file is not needed, and you can safely remove it.

3. You have to set the default namespace of the satellite assembly to the same value as in the original assembly. For our example, it is LocalizationSample. To accomplish this, please change the default namespace to LocalizationSample in the project properties on the Application tab page.

4. Now, you need to add a new resource file for every resource file of the original assembly with the same name as in the original assembly. You can do this via the menu command Project ➤ New Item ➤ Resource File. Please be aware that an assembly may contain more than one resource file. Applications created with the .NET Micro Framework application project template will have a resource file with the name Resources.resx by default. You can see the newly created resource files in the Solution Explorer; they'll be indicated by the .resx file extension.

5. A corresponding strongly typed resource class will be created automatically for every new resource file. You do not need it, and you should delete it manually. To avoid automatic re-creation of such a class after changing a resource file, you need to clear the Custom Tool parameter of the resource, which has the value ResXFileCodeGenerator in the Properties window.

6. Double-click one of those newly created resource files in the Solution Explorer to open the resource designer. In this designer, you can add and edit the translated text as resource strings. The resource strings must have the same names as in the original application. Translating resources is not limited to text; it is possible to localize every possible kind of resources. If you do not add a resource to a satellite assembly, it will be loaded because of the resource fallback mechanism approach of the original application.

7. Finally, to be deployed, a satellite assembly must be referenced by the main application. If an application and satellite assembly are in the same solution, you can add a project reference; see Figure 10-10.

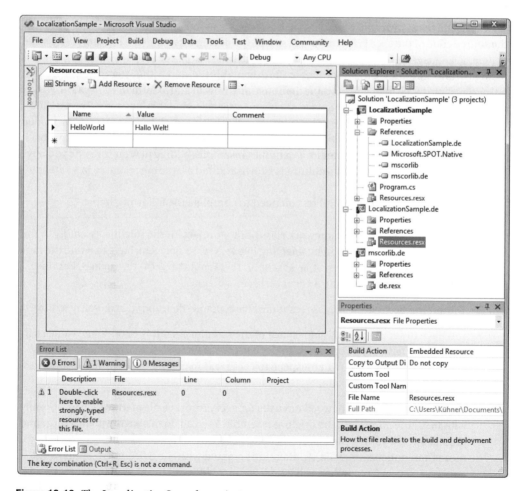

Figure 10-10. *The LocalizationSample project*

If you deploy and start the new application, the text will be still displayed in the English language; by default, the invariant culture is selected. Before the first access to resources, the current culture must be changed. The current culture is changed in our example with the following method call:

```
ResourceUtility.SetCurrentUICulture(new CultureInfo("de-DE"));
```

If the de-DE culture is missing and only the neutral culture de is available, the current culture is set by the runtime environment to de. Of course, the neutral culture for the German language can be selected directly with the following method call:

```
ResourceUtility.SetCurrentUICulture(new CultureInfo("de"));
```

After switching the language, you will see the localized text in the German language.

Changing the Language at Runtime

With the first access to resources via the automatically created typed resource class, a new resource manager for the current culture is created and assigned (see Listing 10-4). A subsequent change of the culture is ignored by the resource class, since the resource manager still exists for the old culture.

Listing 10-4. *The ResourceManager Property of the Resource Class*

```
internal class Resources
{
    private static System.Resources.ResourceManager manager;
    internal static System.Resources.ResourceManager ResourceManager
    {
        get
        {
            if ((Resources.manager == null))
            {
                Resources.manager = new System.Resources.ResourceManager(
                                        "LocalizationSample.Resources",
                                        typeof(Resources).Assembly);
            }
            return Resources.manager;
        }
    }
    ...
}
```

A solution for this issue is to create your own new resource manager manually. But you have to make do without the comfort of the typed resource class. Another way would be to reset the resource manager by assigning null to the field manager, so that, with the next access to resources, a new resource manager object will again be instantiated. Unfortunately, the manager field is private, and the property for it is read only. Therefore, the field cannot be modified from outside of the resource class. Adding a method to the resource class that resets the member is also the wrong approach, since the resource class is regenerated automatically after each modification to resources by Visual Studio and then the resource's own code extensions will get lost.

The key to this is reflection. With reflection, you can access members like private fields dynamically (see Listing 10-5).

Listing 10-5. *Accessing Private Fields with Reflection*

```
FieldInfo fieldInfo =
    typeof(Resources).GetField("manager",
                          BindingFlags.NonPublic | BindingFlags.Static);
fieldInfo.SetValue(null, null);
```

When accessing resources again, a new resource manager for the culture, which was changed in the meantime, is initialized, and all texts and other resources are available again from the new culture (see Listing 10-6).

Listing 10-6. *A Multilingual Application with Language Switching at Runtime*

```
using System;
using System.Globalization;
using System.Reflection;
using Microsoft.SPOT;

namespace LocalizationSample
{
    public class Program
    {
        public static void Main()
        {
            ResourceUtility.SetCurrentUICulture(new CultureInfo("de-DE"));
            Debug.Print("Current UI Culture='" +
                    CultureInfo.CurrentUICulture.Name +
                    "'");
            Debug.Print(
                Resources.GetString(Resources.StringResources.HelloWorld));

            ResourceUtility.SetCurrentUICulture(new CultureInfo("en"));
            Debug.Print("Current UI Culture='" +
                    CultureInfo.CurrentUICulture.Name +
                    "'");
            //we need to reset the resource manager
            //because language was changed during runtime
            ResetResourceManager();
            Debug.Print(
                Resources.GetString(Resources.StringResources.HelloWorld));
        }
```

```
    private static void ResetResourceManager()
    {
        FieldInfo fieldInfo =
                    typeof(Resources).GetField("manager",
                                            BindingFlags.NonPublic |
                                            BindingFlags.Static);
        fieldInfo.SetValue(null, null);
    }
  }
}
```

Summary

In this chapter, you learned a lot about resources. You now know what kinds of resources are possible with the .NET Micro Framework and how to embed and use them in your application. This chapter introduced cultures and how you can add further cultures to a .NET Micro Framework application. It also presented a tool to automatically generate culture definitions and demonstrated how to use those definitions to add custom cultures. You learned how to print dates, times, and numbers appropriate for particular cultures. You now know what satellite assemblies are, how the resource fallback mechanism works, and how you can use resources and cultures to create multilingual applications for the international market. This chapter also described how the current culture is persisted to survive a power cycle, and how you can change the culture (language) at runtime.

The know-how in this chapter is useful for the next chapter, which covers graphics and graphical user interfaces.

■ ■ ■

CHAPTER 11

Graphics and Graphical User Interfaces

Many resource-constrained devices do not need a complex graphical display. They provide an intuitive user interface with buttons and LEDs or a simple text display. However, there is a growing demand for devices that provide a complex user interface with a detailed graphical display. The .NET Micro Framework provides built-in support for color LCD displays, if your device has one.

In this chapter, we will explore how to create graphics and graphical user interfaces with the .NET Micro Framework for presentation on an LCD display. You will first learn how to draw directly onto the display with the Bitmap class, and later in this chapter, you will learn how to create complex graphical user interfaces and interaction using a kind of trimmed Windows Presentation Foundation (WPF) for the .NET Micro Framework. This part of the chapter presents the various built-in components and describes when and how to use them. For example, you will learn how to build rich list box menus, build text and image displays, respond to user input, and implement custom user interface elements.

Since images are embedded as resources into an assembly, you should have read the section about resources in Chapter 10.

Even if you do not write directly to bitmaps, and program graphical applications using the richer presentation classes, you should be familiar with the bitmap information presented in the first part of this chapter because the presentation classes internally use bitmaps for drawing; they are also helpful in deriving custom controls.

Drawing on the Display Using the Bitmap class

The Bitmap class provides support for setting particular pixels and drawing graphical elements such as lines, rectangles, and ellipses. You can also use it to draw other images and texts with different fonts. We will explore most of these features in detail later in this chapter.

You can find the Bitmap class in the Microsoft.SPOT namespace, in the Microsoft.SPOT. Graphics.dll assembly. To give you an overview of the possibilities, the Bitmap class is presented in Listing 11-1.

■**Note** The `Bitmap` class possesses further members that are not presented in Listing 11-1, because they are marked as obsolete. You do not need them, because they just provide other inflexible overloads. It seems that they were intended for the black and white displays of Microsoft's Smart Personal Object Technology (SPOT) watches, since most of the obsolete methods lack a color parameter.

Listing 11-1. *The Microsoft.SPOT.Bitmap Class*

```
using Microsoft.SPOT.Presentation.Media;
using System;

namespace Microsoft.SPOT
{
    public sealed class Bitmap : MarshalByRefObject
    {
        // constants
        public const ushort OpacityOpaque = 256;
        public const ushort OpacityTransparent = 0;

        // static properties
        public static readonly int CenterX;
        public static readonly int CenterY;
        public static readonly int MaxHeight;
        public static readonly int MaxWidth;

        // constructors
        public Bitmap(byte[] imageData, Bitmap.BitmapImageType type);
        public Bitmap(int width, int height);

        // determining dimensions
        public int Height { get; }
        public int Width { get; }

        // erasing the bitmap
        public void Clear();

        // drawing pixels
        public Color GetPixel(int xPos, int yPos);
        public void SetPixel(int xPos, int yPos, Color color);

        // drawing lines
        public void DrawLine(Color color, int thickness,
                             int x0, int y0, int x1, int y1);
```

```
// drawing rectangles
public void DrawRectangle(Color colorOutline, int thicknessOutline,
                          int x, int y, int width, int height,
                          int xCornerRadius, int yCornerRadius,
                          Color colorGradientStart,
                          int xGradientStart, int yGradientStart,
                          Color colorGradientEnd,
                          int xGradientEnd, int yGradientEnd,
                          ushort opacity);

// drawing ellipses
public void DrawEllipse(Color colorOutline,
                        int x, int y,
                        int xRadius, int yRadius);
public void DrawEllipse(Color colorOutline,
                        int thicknessOutline,
                        int x, int y,
                        int xRadius, int yRadius,
                        Color colorGradientStart,
                        int xGradientStart, int yGradientStart,
                        Color colorGradientEnd,
                        int xGradientEnd, int yGradientEnd,
                        double opacity);

// drawing other images
public void DrawImage(int xDst, int yDst,
                      Bitmap bitmap,
                      int xSrc, int ySrc, int width, int height);
public void DrawImage(int xDst, int yDst,
                      Bitmap bitmap,
                      int xSrc, int ySrc, int width, int height,
                      ushort opacity);
public void StretchImage(int xDst, int yDst, Bitmap bitmap,
                         int width, int height, ushort opacity);

// drawing text
public void DrawText(string text, Font font, Color color, int x, int y);
public void DrawTextInRect(string text, int x, int y, int width, int height,
                           uint dtFlags, Color color, Font font);
public bool DrawTextInRect(ref string text,
                           ref int xRelStart, ref int yRelStart,
                           int x, int y, int width, int height,
                           uint dtFlags, Color color, Font font);

// flushing content to display
public void Flush();
public void Flush(int x, int y, int width, int height);
```

```
        // setting transparency
        public void MakeTransparent(Color color);

        // clipping
        public void SetClippingRectangle(int x, int y, int width, int height);

        public enum BitmapImageType
        {
            TinyCLRBitmap = 0,
            Gif = 1,
            Jpeg = 2,
            Bmp = 3,
        }
    }
}
```

Using Bitmaps

You do not need to create a .NET Micro Framework window application to use bitmaps with a .NET Micro Framework project. This kind of application is intended for use with the more complex but richer presentation classes. To use bitmaps, you can just create a simple console application, but you need to add a reference to the `Microsoft.SPOT.Graphics.dll` library to your project.

You can easily test your applications on the sample emulator provided with the .NET Micro Framework. It has a color QVGA (320×240) display with a color depth of 16 bits per pixel. You will learn how you can configure the emulator display in the next chapter, which covers hardware emulation.

The `Bitmap` class provides two constructors. One creates a bitmap on the basis of specified binary image data. The other one creates an empty bitmap of a particular size. The following code creates an empty bitmap that's the size of the display:

```
ScreenMetrics metrics = ScreenMetrics.GetMetrics();
Bitmap bmp = new Bitmap(metrics.Width, metrics.Height);
```

The resolution of the display is determined at runtime with the `ScreenMetrics` class that resides in the `Microsoft.SPOT.Hardware` namespace in `Microsoft.SPOT.Graphics.dll`.

The color of the new bitmap is black, and you will not see it displayed yet: the bitmap is kept in memory, so you can draw on it and then display it. Graphic coordinates are specified in pixels, and the origin, with the coordinates (0, 0), is in the top-left corner. The following code will draw a white line from the top-left corner to the bottom-right corner on the bitmap:

```
bmp.DrawLine(Microsoft.SPOT.Presentation.Media.Color.White, // color
            1,                                               // line thickness
            0, 0,                                            // start point
            bmp.Width, bmp.Height);                          // end point
```

> ■**Caution** The present release of the .NET Micro Framework does not use the thickness parameter. That means drawing lines with a thickness greater than 1 pixel is not supported.

Flushing Bitmaps onto the Display

The preceding drawing operation will not display the line automatically onto your display. Drawing is performed to the bitmap buffer in memory. You need to call the Flush method of the bitmap to show it on your display.

Calling the bmp.Flush()method will copy your entire bitmap onto the display, as shown in Figure 11-1.

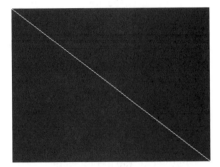

Figure 11-1. *Flushing the entire bitmap*

There is another Flush method that allows you to copy only a part of your bitmap onto the display. Using the following code snippet instead of the previous one will copy only a rectangular part to the display, as shown in Figure 11-2:

```
bmp.Flush(bmp.Width / 2 - 50,   //left
          bmp.Height / 2 - 50,  //top
          100,                  //width
          100);                 //height
```

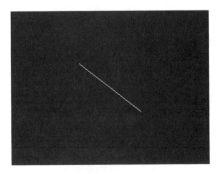

Figure 11-2. *Flushing part of a bitmap*

It is also possible to flush from a different source bitmap to your screen.

■**Caution** In order to flush bitmaps onto your display, you need to create the source bitmap with exactly the same dimensions as your display, even if you will flush only a part to your display.

Using Colors

In the previous example, you saw how to draw a white line. Colors are represented in the .NET Micro Framework with the `Microsoft.SPOT.Presentation.Media.Color` enumerated type in the `Microsoft.SPOT.Graphics.dll` library. This enumeration has only the members `Black` and `White`. But you can create your own color from red, green, and blue (RGB) intensity values with the `Microsoft.SPOT.Presentation.Media.ColorUtility` class. This class has a static `ColorFromRGB` method to create a custom color from the specified RGB intensity components. Table 11-1 lists the known colors from the full .NET Framework and their RGB intensities. You can use the RGB values from that table with the `ColorUtility.ColorFromRGB` method. For example, to create a yellow color, you need to use the following code:

```
Color yellowColor = ColorUtility.ColorFromRGB(0xFF, 0xFF, 0x00);
```

Yellow is a mix of red and green. The red, green, and blue intensities are accepted as byte values ranging from 0 to 255 (0xFF in hexadecimal). A color value is actually a 32-bit integer that uses 24 bits to store the RGB value. It is possible to cast an integer directly into a color value:

```
Color pinkColor = (Color)0xCBC0FF; // BBGGRR (R=0xFF, G=0xC0, B=0xCB)
```

The `ColorUtility` class has three helper methods—`GetRValue`, `GetGValue`, and `GetBValue`—to split a color into its red, green, and blue components.

The `ScreenMetrics` class provides the `BitsPerPixel` property to determine the supported color depth of your hardware configuration.

To set the color for an individual pixel, you can use the `SetPixel` method of the `Bitmap` class. The method accepts the x and y coordinates as well as the new color value. The method `GetPixel` will return the color value from a particular pixel on the bitmap.

Table 11-1. *Known Colors and Their RGB Values*

Name	Red	Green	Blue
AliceBlue	0xF0	0xF8	0xFF
AntiqueWhite	0xFA	0xEB	0xD7
Aqua	0x00	0xFF	0xFF
Aquamarine	0x7F	0xFF	0xD4
Azure	0xF0	0xFF	0xFF
Beige	0xF5	0xF5	0xDC
Bisque	0xFF	0xE4	0xC4

Table 11-1. *Known Colors and Their RGB Values (Continued)*

Name	Red	Green	Blue
Black	0x00	0x00	0x00
BlanchedAlmond	0xFF	0xEB	0xCD
Blue	0x00	0x00	0xFF
BlueViolet	0x8A	0x2B	0xE2
Brown	0xA5	0x2A	0x2A
BurlyWood	0xDE	0xB8	0x87
CadetBlue	0x5F	0x9E	0xA0
Chartreuse	0x7F	0xFF	0x00
Chocolate	0xD2	0x69	0x1E
Coral	0xFF	0x7F	0x50
CornflowerBlue	0x64	0x95	0xED
Cornsilk	0xFF	0xF8	0xDC
Crimson	0xDC	0x14	0x3C
Cyan	0x00	0xFF	0xFF
DarkBlue	0x00	0x00	0x8B
DarkCyan	0x00	0x8B	0x8B
DarkGoldenrod	0xB8	0x86	0x0B
DarkGray	0xA9	0xA9	0xA9
DarkGreen	0x00	0x64	0x00
DarkKhaki	0xBD	0xB7	0x6B
DarkMagenta	0x8B	0x00	0x8B
DarkOliveGreen	0x55	0x6B	0x2F
DarkOrange	0xFF	0x8C	0x00
DarkOrchid	0x99	0x32	0xCC
DarkRed	0x8B	0x00	0x00
DarkSalmon	0xE9	0x96	0x7A
DarkSeaGreen	0x8F	0xBC	0x8B
DarkSlateBlue	0x48	0x3D	0x8B
DarkSlateGray	0x2F	0x4F	0x4F
DarkTurquoise	0x00	0xCE	0xD1
DarkViolet	0x94	0x00	0xD3
DeepPink	0xFF	0x14	0x93

Table 11-1. *Known Colors and Their RGB Values (Continued)*

Name	Red	Green	Blue
DeepSkyBlue	0x00	0xBF	0xFF
DimGray	0x69	0x69	0x69
DodgerBlue	0x1E	0x90	0xFF
Firebrick	0xB2	0x22	0x22
FloralWhite	0xFF	0xFA	0xF0
ForestGreen	0x22	0x8B	0x22
Fuchsia	0xFF	0x00	0xFF
Gainsboro	0xDC	0xDC	0xDC
GhostWhite	0xF8	0xF8	0xFF
Gold	0xFF	0xD7	0x00
Goldenrod	0xDA	0xA5	0x20
Gray	0x80	0x80	0x80
Green	0x00	0x80	0x00
GreenYellow	0xAD	0xFF	0x2F
Honeydew	0xF0	0xFF	0xF0
HotPink	0xFF	0x69	0xB4
IndianRed	0xCD	0x5C	0x5C
Indigo	0x4B	0x00	0x82
Ivory	0xFF	0xFF	0xF0
Khaki	0xF0	0xE6	0x8C
Lavender	0xE6	0xE6	0xFA
LavenderBlush	0xFF	0xF0	0xF5
LawnGreen	0x7C	0xFC	0x00
LemonChiffon	0xFF	0xFA	0xCD
LightBlue	0xAD	0xD8	0xE6
LightCoral	0xF0	0x80	0x80
LightCyan	0xE0	0xFF	0xFF
LightGoldenrodYellow	0xFA	0xFA	0xD2
LightGreen	0x90	0xEE	0x90
LightGray	0xD3	0xD3	0xD3
LightPink	0xFF	0xB6	0xC1
LightSalmon	0xFF	0xA0	0x7A

Table 11-1. *Known Colors and Their RGB Values (Continued)*

Name	Red	Green	Blue
LightSeaGreen	0x20	0xB2	0xAA
LightSkyBlue	0x87	0xCE	0xFA
LightSlateGray	0x77	0x88	0x99
LightSteelBlue	0xB0	0xC4	0xDE
LightYellow	0xFF	0xFF	0xE0
Lime	0x00	0xFF	0x00
LimeGreen	0x32	0xCD	0x32
Linen	0xFA	0xF0	0xE6
Magenta	0xFF	0x00	0xFF
Maroon	0x80	0x00	0x00
MediumAquamarine	0x66	0xCD	0xAA
MediumBlue	0x00	0x00	0xCD
MediumOrchid	0xBA	0x55	0xD3
MediumPurple	0x93	0x70	0xDB
MediumSeaGreen	0x3C	0xB3	0x71
MediumSlateBlue	0x7B	0x68	0xEE
MediumSpringGreen	0x00	0xFA	0x9A
MediumTurquoise	0x48	0xD1	0xCC
MediumVioletRed	0xC7	0x15	0x85
MidnightBlue	0x19	0x19	0x70
MintCream	0xF5	0xFF	0xFA
MistyRose	0xFF	0xE4	0xE1
Moccasin	0xFF	0xE4	0xB5
NavajoWhite	0xFF	0xDE	0xAD
Navy	0x00	0x00	0x80
OldLace	0xFD	0xF5	0xE6
Olive	0x80	0x80	0x00
OliveDrab	0x6B	0x8E	0x23
Orange	0xFF	0xA5	0x00
OrangeRed	0xFF	0x45	0x00
Orchid	0xDA	0x70	0xD6
PaleGoldenrod	0xEE	0xE8	0xAA

Table 11-1. *Known Colors and Their RGB Values (Continued)*

Name	Red	Green	Blue
PaleGreen	0x98	0xFB	0x98
PaleTurquoise	0xAF	0xEE	0xEE
PaleVioletRed	0xDB	0x70	0x93
PapayaWhip	0xFF	0xEF	0xD5
PeachPuff	0xFF	0xDA	0xB9
Peru	0xCD	0x85	0x3F
Pink	0xFF	0xC0	0xCB
Plum	0xDD	0xA0	0xDD
PowderBlue	0xB0	0xE0	0xE6
Purple	0x80	0x00	0x80
Red	0xFF	0x00	0x00
RosyBrown	0xBC	0x8F	0x8F
RoyalBlue	0x41	0x69	0xE1
SaddleBrown	0x8B	0x45	0x13
Salmon	0xFA	0x80	0x72
SandyBrown	0xF4	0xA4	0x60
SeaGreen	0x2E	0x8B	0x57
SeaShell	0xFF	0xF5	0xEE
Sienna	0xA0	0x52	0x2D
Silver	0xC0	0xC0	0xC0
SkyBlue	0x87	0xCE	0xEB
SlateBlue	0x6A	0x5A	0xCD
SlateGray	0x70	0x80	0x90
Snow	0xFF	0xFA	0xFA
SpringGreen	0x00	0xFF	0x7F
SteelBlue	0x46	0x82	0xB4
Tan	0xD2	0xB4	0x8C
Teal	0x00	0x80	0x80
Thistle	0xD8	0xBF	0xD8
Tomato	0xFF	0x63	0x47

Table 11-1. *Known Colors and Their RGB Values (Continued)*

Name	Red	Green	Blue
Turquoise	0x40	0xE0	0xD0
Violet	0xEE	0x82	0xEE
Wheat	0xF5	0xDE	0xB3
White	0xFF	0xFF	0xFF
WhiteSmoke	0xF5	0xF5	0xF5
Yellow	0xFF	0xFF	0x00

Drawing Rectangles

The Bitmap class allows you to draw rectangles. Therefore, it provides a DrawRectangle method that accepts quite a lot of parameters to achieve some impressive graphical effects.

Drawing Solid-Filled Rectangles

The DrawRectangle method class in Listing 11-2 will draw a simple solid-filled white rectangle. In this example, no outline will be drawn, so the code uses an outline thickness of 0 pixels. The start color and end color are both set to white, which causes the rectangle to be filled entirely with the same color.

Listing 11-2. *Drawing a White, Solid-Filled Rectangle*

```
bmp.DrawRectangle(Color.White,          // outline color
                  0,                    // outline thickness
                  100, 100,             // x and y of top left corner
                  200, 100,             // width and height
                  0, 0,                 // x and y corner radius
                  Color.White,          // gradient start color
                  0, 0,                 // gradient start coordinates
                  Color.White,          // gradient end color
                  0, 0,                 // gradient end coordinates
                  Bitmap.OpacityOpaque); // opacity
```

Drawing a Rectangular Frame

To draw a rectangular frame, you need to set the opacity to Bitmap.OpacityTransparent (see Listing 11-3), which draws an unfilled rectangle with only a border with the selected border color and thickness. The border frame is always drawn fully opaque with the border color regardless of the opacity value; the opacity value only affects filling.

Listing 11-3. *Drawing a Rectangular Frame*

```
bmp.DrawRectangle(
                Color.White,                    // outline color
                1,                              // outline thickness
                100, 100,                       // x and y of top left corner
                200, 100,                       // width and height
                0, 0,                           // x and y corner radius
                Color.White,                    // gradient start color
                0, 0,                           // gradient start coordinates
                Color.White,                    // gradient end color
                0, 0,                           // gradient end coordinates
                Bitmap.OpacityTransparent);     // opacity
```

Drawing Rectangles with Opacity

You can get quite interesting effects when using the opacity parameter. Opacity values range from 0 to 256, where 0 (or the constant Bitmap.OpacityTransparent) does not draw a pixel and the value 256 (or Bitmap.OpacityOpaque) completely replaces what is underneath (the documentation for the SDK indicates that 0xFF, or 255, is opaque, which is not true). Figure 11-3 illustrates what effects are possible with reduced opacity values; the sample cascades three filled rectangles of different colors and draws the overlapping boxes in a for loop. Listing 11-4 shows the code to draw this art.

Figure 11-3. *Filled overlapping boxes using reduced opacity values*

Listing 11-4. *Drawing Filled Overlapping Boxes with Reduced Opacity*

```
using System;
using System.Threading;
using Microsoft.SPOT;
using Microsoft.SPOT.Hardware;
using Microsoft.SPOT.Presentation.Media;

namespace OpacityWithRectanglesSample
{
```

```
class Program
{
    static void Main(string[] args)
    {
        ScreenMetrics metrics = ScreenMetrics.GetMetrics();
        Bitmap bmp = new Bitmap(metrics.Width, metrics.Height);
        //drawing a white background
        bmp.DrawRectangle(Color.White,            // outline color
                          0,                      // outline thickness
                          0, 0,                   // x and y coordinates
                          bmp.Width, bmp.Height,  // width and height
                          0, 0,                   // x and y corner radius
                          Color.White,            // gradient start color
                          0, 0,                   // gradient start coordinates
                          Color.White,            // gradient end color
                          0, 0,                   // gradient end coordinates
                          Bitmap.OpacityOpaque);  // reduced opacity

        Color[] colors = new Color[] {
                          ColorUtility.ColorFromRGB(0xFF, 0, 0), // red
                          ColorUtility.ColorFromRGB(0, 0xFF, 0), // green
                          ColorUtility.ColorFromRGB(0, 0, 0xFF)  // blue
        };

        for (int i = 0; i < colors.Length; ++i)
        {
            Color color = colors[i];
            bmp.DrawRectangle(color,         // outline color
                              0,             // outline thickness
                              50 + i * 20,   // x
                              50 + i * 20,   // y
                              200, 100,      // width and height
                              0, 0,          // x and y corner radius
                              color,         // gradient start color
                              0, 0,          // gradient start coordinates
                              color,         // gradient end color
                              0, 0,          // gradient end coordinates
                              64);           // reduced opacity
        }

        bmp.Flush();
        Thread.Sleep(-1); //do not terminate app to see result
    }
}
}
```

Drawing Rectangles with Rounded Corners

In the previous examples, every rectangle was drawn with the corner radius values set to 0, so the rectangles were not drawn with rounded corners. Figure 11-4 shows a rectangle with rounded corners using the same corner radius of 30 pixels for x and y. The rectangle shown in Figure 11-5 was produced using different corner radius values for x and y.

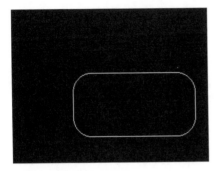

Figure 11-4. *Rectangle with a corner radius of 30 pixels for x and y*

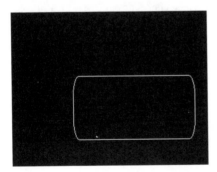

Figure 11-5. *Rectangle with a 10-pixel x radius and 30-pixel y radius*

■**Caution** The current release of the .NET Micro Framework does not allow you to use rounded corners and filling with rectangles at the same time. If you indicate a corner radius greater than zero, your rectangle will be drawn as a frame.

Drawing Rectangles with Color Gradients

In the preceding examples, all filled rectangles were drawn entirely filled with one color. By specifying different values for the start and end colors, you can achieve interesting color gradient effects. The code in Listing 11-5 produces a rectangle filled with a diagonal color gradient that starts in the top-left corner of the rectangle with white and ends in the bottom-right corner with black, as shown in Figure 11-6.

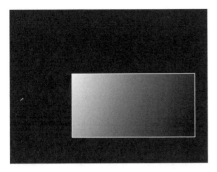

Figure 11-6. *Diagonal color gradient*

Listing 11-5. *Drawing a Diagonal Color Gradient*

```
bmp.DrawRectangle(Color.White,          // outline color
                  1,                    // outline thickness
                  100, 100,             // x and y of top left corner
                  200, 100,             // width and height
                  0, 0,                 // x and y corner radius
                  Color.White,          // gradient start color
                  100, 100,             // gradient start coordinates
                  Color.Black,          // gradient end color
                  100 + 200, 100 + 100, // gradient end coordinates
                  Bitmap.OpacityOpaque); // opacity
```

By specifying the same x coordinate for the gradient start and end colors, you achieve a vertical color gradient, as illustrated in Figure 11-7. Using the same y coordinate for start and end colors, you will produce a horizontal color gradient.

The gradient start and end coordinates are specified as screen coordinates, and they can lie outside of the rectangle. This causes the system to produce a color gradient starting at the start point with the start color and ending at the end point with the end color but showing only the part within your rectangle.

Figure 11-7. *Vertical color gradient*

Drawing Ellipses

The `Bitmap` class exposes the `DrawEllipse` method, which allows you to draw an ellipse. The method accepts a center point and x and y radii:

```
public void DrawEllipse(Color colorOutline,
                        int x, int y,
                        int xRadius,
                        int yRadius);
```

■**Caution** There is a second overload of the `DrawEllipse` method that accepts a thickness for the outline, color gradient settings, and an opacity value. With the present release of the .NET Micro Framework, none of these additional parameters work. You should not use this method. That means that, currently, you cannot draw filled circles or ellipses. If you need to render filled ellipses, a good but less flexible idea is to create a bitmap, add it to your application as a resource, and render it to the screen as we will discuss in the next section.

Drawing Images

In the following sections, you will learn how to draw one bitmap on another using different methods and techniques.

Drawing Full-Size Images

The `Bitmap` class provides a `DrawImage` method, which allows one bitmap to draw a part or all of another bitmap on itself.

The code in Listing 11-6 gets a bitmap from a resource, as explained in Chapter 10's discussion about globalization and localization. Then, the entire ball bitmap is rendered in its original size using the `DrawImage` method (see Figure 11-8). This method allows you to draw either the entire source image or only a part of it by varying the source coordinates and size. This kind of drawing does not perform any scaling; scaling an image is discussed in the next section. Using the `opacity` parameter, the entire source image can be blended with the destination image. Later in this chapter, we'll discuss how you can render an image with a transparent background.

Listing 11-6. *Rendering the Full-Size Ball Image*

```
ScreenMetrics metrics = ScreenMetrics.GetMetrics();
Bitmap bmp = new Bitmap(metrics.Width, metrics.Height);
Bitmap soccerBall = Resources.GetBitmap(Resources.BitmapResources.SoccerBall);
bmp.DrawImage(100, 50,                // destination coordinates
            soccerBall,               // source image
            0, 0,                     // source coordinates
            soccerBall.Width,         // source width
            soccerBall.Height,        // source height
            Bitmap.OpacityOpaque);    // opacity
bmp.Flush();
```

Figure 11-8. *The full-size ball image*

Drawing Scaled Images

The Bitmap class also provides a StretchImage method that allows one bitmap to draw all of another bitmap on itself by scaling the image to fit into a specified destination rectangle. You cannot draw a part of the source image; this drawing method will always render the entire source image but in a new size. The code in Listing 11-7 will render the entire ball image and perform a horizontal shrink and vertical stretch operation to fit the image into a destination rectangle that has half the width and double the height of the source image size (see Figure 11-9).

Listing 11-7. *Image Scaling*

```
ScreenMetrics metrics = ScreenMetrics.GetMetrics();
Bitmap bmp = new Bitmap(metrics.Width, metrics.Height);
Bitmap soccerBall = Resources.GetBitmap(Resources.BitmapResources.SoccerBall);
bmp.StretchImage(100, 50,              // destination coordinates
              soccerBall,              // source image
              soccerBall.Width / 2,  // half width
              soccerBall.Height * 2, // double height
              Bitmap.OpacityOpaque); // opacity
bmp.Flush();
```

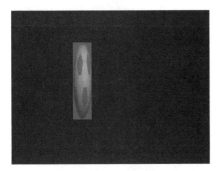

Figure 11-9. *Scaling the ball image to half its width and double its height*

Drawing Images with Transparent Backgrounds

With the opacity parameter, you select whether an entire bitmap will be rendered transparent, opaque, or something between. In contrast, the MakeTransparent method enables you to select a transparent color to draw, for example, the ball image with a transparent background. The MakeTransparent method accepts a color value. When rendering such a bitmap, each pixel of that color will not cover the underlaying pixels of the destination image that it's drawing on. For the ball image, we will obtain the color of the top-left corner pixel and choose it as the transparent color (see Listing 11-8).

Listing 11-8. *Selecting a Transparent Color*

```
ScreenMetrics metrics = ScreenMetrics.GetMetrics();
Bitmap bmp = new Bitmap(metrics.Width, metrics.Height);
Bitmap soccerBall = Resources.GetBitmap(Resources.BitmapResources.SoccerBall);
//make background of the ball transparent
//using the color of top left corner pixel
soccerBall.MakeTransparent(soccerBall.GetPixel(0, 0));
bmp.DrawImage(100, 50,              // destination coordinates
            soccerBall,             // source image
            0, 0,                   // source coordinates
            soccerBall.Width,       // source width
            soccerBall.Height,      // source height
            Bitmap.OpacityOpaque);  // opacity
bmp.Flush();
```

The .NET Micro Framework does not support modifying images of the Bitmap type after you create them. If you embed an image resource in your application from a bitmap file, calling the MakeTransparent method for such an image will cause an error. With JPEG images, you will not get an exception, but the image will not be rendered transparently. With GIF images, the system behaves as expected. Therefore, if using a bitmap or JPEG resource, you need to create a copy of the image and then make it transparent (see Listing 11-9). The best option is to use GIF images and then make them transparent by selecting one transparent color.

Listing 11-9. *Using a Transparent Background with Bitmap or JPEG Files*

```
Bitmap soccerBall = Resources.GetBitmap(Resources.BitmapResources.SoccerBall);
// create a copy
Bitmap soccerBallTransparent = new Bitmap(soccerBall.Width, soccerBall.Height);
soccerBallTransparent.DrawImage(0, 0,                   // destination coordinates
                        soccerBall,             // source image
                        0, 0,                   // source coordinates
                        soccerBall.Width,       // source width
                        soccerBall.Height,      // source height
                        Bitmap.OpacityOpaque);  // opacity
//make background of the ball transparent
//using the color of top left corner pixel
soccerBallTransparent.MakeTransparent(soccerBallTransparent.GetPixel(0, 0));
```

Listing 11-10 demonstrates how to program a moving ball that bounces back when it reaches the screen borders. The ball is rendered with a transparent background onto a color gradient background, as shown in Figure 11-10. In this example, the moving sprite is drawn flicker free using double buffering. That means each frame is prepared completely in a memory image buffer before flushing it to the display.

Before flushing, the code first loads the embedded sprite bitmap from the resources and initializes the background and the buffer bitmap that holds the current screen. In an endless loop, the application moves the sprite. The current screen position of the sprite (defined by the top-left corner of the sprite) is stored in the x and y variables. The variables xOfs and yOfs describe the moving direction and speed of the sprite. Every time the ball hits a border, both directions are inverted. The application changes the horizontal and vertical position with an equal absolute value, which causes the ball to move and bounce at a 45-degree angle.

Figure 11-10. *A moving ball on a color gradient background*

Listing 11-10. *Programming Sprites*

```
using System;
using System.Threading;
using Microsoft.SPOT;
using Microsoft.SPOT.Hardware;
using Microsoft.SPOT.Presentation.Media;

namespace BouncingBallSample
{
    public class Program
    {
        public static void Main()
        {
            ScreenMetrics metrics = ScreenMetrics.GetMetrics();
            //prepare background with a color gradient
            Bitmap backgroundImg = new Bitmap(metrics.Width, metrics.Height);
            backgroundImg.DrawRectangle(
                        Color.White,            // outline color
                        0,                      // outline thickness
                        0, 0,                   // x and y of top left corner
                        backgroundImg.Width,    // width
```

```
                        backgroundImg.Height,  // height
                        0, 0,                  // x and y corner radius
                        Color.White,           // gradient start color
                        0, 0,                  // gradient start coordinates
                        Color.Black,           // gradient end color
                        backgroundImg.Width,   // gradient end x coordinate
                        backgroundImg.Height,  // gradient end y coordinate
                        Bitmap.OpacityOpaque); // opacity
    //prepare a working buffer to hold graphics before flushing to display
    Bitmap bufferImg = new Bitmap(metrics.Width, metrics.Height);
    //our ball
    Bitmap soccerBallImg =
                Resources.GetBitmap(Resources.BitmapResources.SoccerBall);
    //make background of the ball transparent
    //using the color of top left corner pixel
    soccerBallImg.MakeTransparent(soccerBallImg.GetPixel(0, 0));

    int x = 100;
    int y = 50;
    int xOfs = 1;
    int yOfs = 1;
    while (true)
    {
        //copy background to buffer
        bufferImg.DrawImage(0, 0, backgroundImg, 0, 0,
                        backgroundImg.Width, backgroundImg.Height);
        //paint moving sprite object
        bufferImg.DrawImage(x, y,     // destination coordinates
                        soccerBallImg, // source image
                        0, 0,         // source coordinates
                        soccerBallImg.Width, soccerBallImg.Height,
                        Bitmap.OpacityOpaque);
        bufferImg.Flush(); //flush buffer to display
        Thread.Sleep(10);
        //invert direction if ball bounces at a wall
        if (x <= 0 || x >= metrics.Width - soccerBallImg.Width)
            xOfs = -xOfs;
        if (y <= 0 || y >= metrics.Height - soccerBallImg.Height)
            yOfs = -yOfs;
        //calculate new coordinates
        x += xOfs;
        y += yOfs;
    }
}
}
}
```

Drawing Text

This section presents various methods to render text using fonts.

Using Fonts

The .NET Micro Framework uses the `.tinyfnt` file format to work with fonts. This special format uses fixed size bitmaps for a simpler way to render fonts. Two sample `.tinyfnt` fonts are included in the `Fonts` subdirectory of your .NET Micro Framework installation. To create other fonts, in the size, style, and language tailored to your application, you can use the TFConvert tool to create a `.tinyfnt` font from TrueType or OpenType font files. That enables you to select the character sets and to even create fonts for displaying Cyrillic and Chinese characters. To get more information about creating `.tinyfnt` fonts with the TFConvert tool, please refer to the the TFConvert section (which includes useful web links) in Chapter 3 and the .NET Micro Framework SDK documentation where this is described in detail.

The .NET Micro Framework SDK provides a set of sample OpenType fonts that you can use to create `.tinyfnt` fonts to use with your applications. The fonts are located in the `\Tools\Fonts\TrueType` subdirectory of your .NET Micro Framework installation. The sample fonts are supplied under license from the Ascender Corporation. These fonts support a small character set that is a subset of the full font available from Ascender.

To use `.tinyfnt` fonts with your application, you need to embed such a font file into your assembly as a resource as described earlier. Once a `.tinyfnt` font file is created, you cannot change its size and style anymore; it is fixed. To use different sizes and styles, you need to create and use different fonts. The methods for rendering text accept a font value and a color value.

Drawing Text

The `Bitmap` class provides the `DrawText` method, which you can use to put text onto your display. The method accepts the text to be drawn, as well as the font and color to use and the position in which to place the text. The coordinates specify the top-left corner of the text to be drawn. Listing 11-11 demonstrates how you can create a bitmap that's the size of the display, get an embedded font resource, and draw white text using the font (see Figure 11-11).

Listing 11-11. *Drawing Text*

```
ScreenMetrics metrics = ScreenMetrics.GetMetrics();
Bitmap bmp = new Bitmap(metrics.Width, metrics.Height);
Font font = Resources.GetFont(Resources.FontResources.NinaB);
bmp.DrawText("Hello world.", // text
            font,           // font
            Color.White,    // color
            20, 20);        // x and y of top left corner
bmp.Flush();
```

Figure 11-11. *Drawing text*

Computing the Text Extent

You may want to calculate the size of a particular bit of text before drawing to make sure the text will fit correctly or to align the text. The Font class possesses a ComputeExtent method that enables you to do this.

The following code snippet will compute the size of a rectangle that is needed to show the text using the specified font. The method returns the two calculated width and height parameters. Because the method returns two parameters, it needs to use the out parameter construct to deliver the results instead of a single function return value.

```
Font myFont = Resources.GetFont(Resources.FontResources.NinaB);
int width, height;
myFont.ComputeExtent("Hello world.", out width, out height);
```

Drawing Text in a Rectangle

The DrawText method allows you to place a text at a particular position in your display. If you want to draw a text block and align and fit it within a box, DrawTextInRect will do this for you.

```
ScreenMetrics metrics = ScreenMetrics.GetMetrics();
Bitmap bmp = new Bitmap(metrics.Width, metrics.Height);
Font font = Resources.GetFont(Resources.FontResources.NinaB);
bmp.DrawTextInRect("Using the DrawTextInRect method allows you " +
                   "to draw a text block and align and fit it " +
                   "within a box.",
                   20, 20,      // x and y (rectangle top left)
                   200, 300,    // width and height of rectangle
                   Bitmap.DT_AlignmentLeft | Bitmap.DT_WordWrap, // flags
                   Color.White, // color
                   font);       // font
bmp.Flush();
```

The DrawTextInRect method accepts different alignment and trimming flags that can be combined to achieve different effects. In this case, the flags are not, as you might expect, enumeration types. They are constant members of the Bitmap class. Figures 11-12 to 11-15 show text that was drawn using different flag combinations.

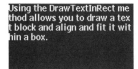

Figure 11-12. *Left alignment (DT_AlignmentLeft)*

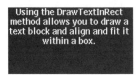

Figure 11-13. *Left alignment with word wrapping (DT_AlignmentLeft | DT_WordWrap)*

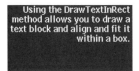

Figure 11-14. *Center alignment with word wrapping (DT_AlignmentCenter | DT_WordWrap)*

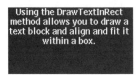

Figure 11-15. *Right alignment with word wrapping (DT_AlignmentRight | DT_WordWrap)*

The possible alignment and trimming flags that you can combine follow:

- `DT_AlignmentCenter`
- `DT_AlignmentLeft`
- `DT_AlignmentMask`
- `DT_AlignmentRight`
- `DT_IgnoreHeight`
- `DT_None`
- `DT_TrimmingCharacterEllipsis`
- `DT_TrimmingMask`
- `DT_TrimmingNone`
- `DT_TrimmingWordEllipsis`
- `DT_TruncateAtBottom`
- `DT_WordWrap`

There is another overload of the `DrawTextInRect` method. That method comes along with reference parameters for the input string and the x and y drawing positions. After drawing text, the method updates the x and y coordinates to tell you where on the display the drawing of the text finished. This allows you to draw parts of the text with a different color or font. Also, if the method cannot display the complete text within the specified rectangle, it returns the remaining text. In this case, the method returns `false` to indicate that there is some text left that could not displayed. The updated x and y coordinates and the remaining text are returned to the caller via out parameters. This enables you to build up a display to show text over multiple pages.

Listing 11-12 will display the word "Hello" in white and "world" in blue (see Figure 11-16). The updated text position is expressed relative to the rectangle but not in screen coordinates.

Figure 11-16. *Text displayed in different colors*

Listing 11-12. *Displaying Text in Different Colors*

```
ScreenMetrics metrics = ScreenMetrics.GetMetrics();
Bitmap bmp = new Bitmap(metrics.Width, metrics.Height);
Font font = Resources.GetFont(Resources.FontResources.NinaB);
int x = 0;
int y = 0;
string text = "Hello ";
bmp.DrawTextInRect(ref text,
                   ref x, ref y, // relative x and y text position in rectangle
                   20, 20,       // x and y (rectangle top left)
                   200, 300,     // width and height of rectangle
                   Bitmap.DT_AlignmentLeft | Bitmap.DT_WordWrap,
                   Color.White,  // color
                   font);        // font
Color blueColor = ColorUtility.ColorFromRGB(0x0, 0x0, 0xFF);
text = "world";
bmp.DrawTextInRect(ref text,
                   ref x, ref y, // relative x and y text position in rectangle
                   20, 20,       // x and y (rectangle top left)
                   200, 300,     // width and height of rectangle
                   Bitmap.DT_AlignmentLeft | Bitmap.DT_WordWrap,
                   blueColor,    // color
                   font);        // font
bmp.Flush();
```

■**Caution** Leading spaces will be trimmed from the beginning of text; they will not be printed. Trailing spaces at the end of text will remain. Therefore, you need to append the space separating the two words to "Hello" (don't add it before "world").

You might need to present so much text to the user that it won't actually fit into one page. In that case, you can display the information page by page and let the user scroll though the pages. The DrawTextInRect method helps you to build a paged text display (see Listing 11-13). Figure 11-17 shows the first page of the paged text display and Figure 11-18 the second page.

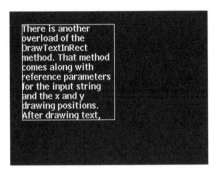

Figure 11-17. *First page of a paged text display*

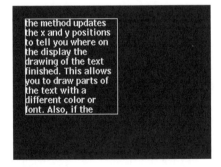

Figure 11-18. *Second page of a paged text display*

Listing 11-13. *Paged Text Display*

```
using System;
using System.Threading;
using Microsoft.SPOT;
using Microsoft.SPOT.Hardware;
using Microsoft.SPOT.Presentation.Media;

namespace PagedTextDisplaySample
{
```

```
public class Program
{
    public static void Main()
    {
        ScreenMetrics metrics = ScreenMetrics.GetMetrics();
        Bitmap bmp = new Bitmap(metrics.Width, metrics.Height);
        Font font = Resources.GetFont(Resources.FontResources.NinaB);
        string text = "There is another overload of the DrawTextInRect " +
                      "method. That method comes along with reference " +
                      "parameters for the input string and the x and y " +
                      "drawing positions. After drawing text, the " +
                      "method updates the x and y positions to tell you " +
                      "where on the display the drawing of the text " +
                      "finished. This allows you to draw parts of the text " +
                      "with a different color or font. Also, if the method " +
                      "cannot display the complete text within the specified " +
                      "rectangle, it returns the remaining text. " +
                      "In this case, the method returns false to indicate " +
                      "that there is some text left that could not be" +
                      "displayed. This enables you to build up a display " +
                      "to show text over multiple pages.";
        bool completed;
        do
        {
            int x = 0;
            int y = 0;
            //draw frame around text and clear old contents
            bmp.DrawRectangle(Color.White, 1, 20, 20, 150, 150,
                              0, 0, Color.Black, 0, 0, Color.Black, 0, 0,
                              Bitmap.OpacityOpaque);
            completed = bmp.DrawTextInRect(
                              ref text,
                              ref x, ref y, // x and y text position
                              20, 20,       // x and y (rectangle top left)
                              150, 150,     // width and height of rectangle
                              Bitmap.DT_AlignmentLeft | Bitmap.DT_WordWrap,
                              Color.White,  // color
                              font);        // font
            bmp.Flush();
            Thread.Sleep(3000); //display each page for three seconds
        } while (!completed);
        Thread.Sleep(-1);
    }
}
}
```

In the first part of this chapter, we explored how to draw graphical elements such as pixels, lines, rectangles, circles, and text onto bitmaps and flush them to your LCD display. You also learned how to program color gradients, sprites, and paged text displays. Now, you are prepared to go on with the second part of this chapter, where you will learn to build rich user interfaces and respond to user input and events using the Windows Presentation Foundation (WPF) classes of the .NET Micro Framework.

Creating Complex User Interfaces with Interaction

Now, we will explore the presentation classes of the .NET Micro Framework, and you will learn how to create complex user interfaces that respond to user input.

WPF

The Windows Presentation Foundation (WPF) is the latest way to create user interfaces for the PC. The WPF components have shipped since the .NET Framework 3.0. On the PC platform, the Extensible Application Markup Language (XAML), which is based on XML, enables you to describe WPF user interfaces separately from the program code. However, XAML provides only an additional way to describe a user interface; you can also build up your user interface with program code.

The presentation components for the .NET Micro Framework are a subset of the desktop WPF where the architecture is similar and the classes, methods, and properties of the components are in line with the desktop version. Despite their many likenesses, these two implementations are not the same. Although they have similar behaviors and names, the internal implementation details differ. The display components of the full .NET Framework and .NET Micro Framework reside in different namespaces: You can find the desktop classes in `System.Windows`, and for embedded devices, the presentation resources reside in the `Microsoft.SPOT.Presentation` namespace within the `Microsoft.SPOT.TinyCore.dll` assembly. The .NET Micro Framework does not support XAML; you need to create and configure your components with program code. This is actually not a big limitation, because a user interface for small, resource-constrained, embedded devices will not become as complex as those on larger systems.

Your First WPF Application

The .NET Micro Framework SDK installs a project template for .NET Micro Framework window applications for Visual Studio. To create a new WPF application for the .NET Micro Framework, select File ➤ New Project and then Micro Framework ➤ Window Application (see Figure 11-19).

Listing 11-14 shows a code file for an application created with the WPF project template. This project is just a simple "hello world" application, as shown in Figure 11-20. It has a main window with a label showing the text on it. The WPF does not use a bitmap for painting. Instead, the WPF uses the WPF text element to print text onto the screen (see Listing 11-14). The new project already contains a reference to the `Microsoft.SPOT.TinyCore.dll` assembly to use all the GUI classes.

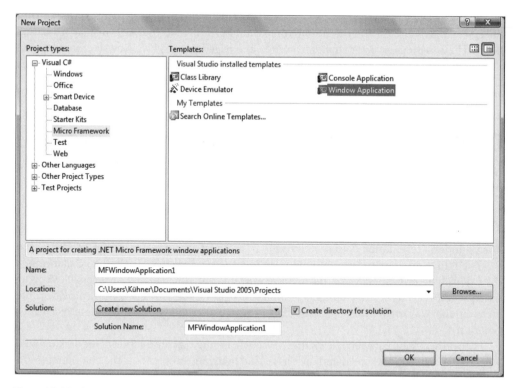

Figure 11-19. *Creating a new WPF project for the .NET Micro Framework*

Hello World!

Figure 11-20. *A new WPF project for the .NET Micro Framework*

Listing 11-14. *A Simple "Hello World" WPF Application Created with the Window Application Project Template*

```
using System;

using Microsoft.SPOT;
using Microsoft.SPOT.Input;
using Microsoft.SPOT.Presentation;
using Microsoft.SPOT.Presentation.Controls;

namespace MFWindowApplication1
{
    public class Program : Microsoft.SPOT.Application
    {
```

```
public static void Main()
{
    Program myApplication = new Program();

    Window mainWindow = myApplication.CreateWindow();

    // Create the object that configures the GPIO pins to buttons.
    GPIOButtonInputProvider inputProvider =
                                        new GPIOButtonInputProvider(null);

    // Start the application
    myApplication.Run(mainWindow);
}

private Window mainWindow;

public Window CreateWindow()
{
    // Create a window object and set its size to the
    // size of the display.
    mainWindow = new Window();
    mainWindow.Height = SystemMetrics.ScreenHeight;
    mainWindow.Width = SystemMetrics.ScreenWidth;

    // Create a single text control.
    Text text = new Text();

    text.Font = Resources.GetFont(Resources.FontResources.small);
    text.TextContent =
                    Resources.GetString(Resources.StringResources.String1);
    text.HorizontalAlignment =
                    Microsoft.SPOT.Presentation.HorizontalAlignment.Center;
    text.VerticalAlignment =
                    Microsoft.SPOT.Presentation.VerticalAlignment.Center;

    // Add the text control to the window.
    mainWindow.Child = text;

    // Connect the button handler to all of the buttons.
    mainWindow.AddHandler(Buttons.ButtonUpEvent,
                            new ButtonEventHandler(OnButtonUp), false);
```

```
                // Set the window visibility to visible.
                mainWindow.Visibility = Visibility.Visible;

                // Attach the button focus to the window.
                Buttons.Focus(mainWindow);

                return mainWindow;
            }

            private void OnButtonUp(object sender, ButtonEventArgs e)
            {
                // Print the button code to the Visual Studio output window.
                Debug.Print(e.Button.ToString());
            }
        }
    }
```

The Application Class

Each WPF application needs an Application object that owns the main window and other windows of the program. The Application class can be found in the Microsoft.SPOT namespace in the Microsoft.SPOT.TinyCore.dll assembly. First of all, it shows the main window and enters the message loop. Once the message loop is entered with the Run method, the method does not return until the last window is closed. You might know this behavior from WinForms applications. Listing 11-15 shows a minimal WPF application with an empty window. The members of the Application class are shown in Listing 11-16.

Listing 11-15. *A Minimal WPF Application*

```
using System;
using Microsoft.SPOT;
using Microsoft.SPOT.Presentation;

namespace MFWindowApplication7
{
    public class Program
    {
        public static void Main()
        {
            Application app = new Application();
            Window mainWindow = new Window();
            app.Run(mainWindow);
        }
    }
}
```

Listing 11-16. *The Microsoft.SPOT.Application Class*

```
using Microsoft.SPOT.Presentation;
using System;

namespace Microsoft.SPOT
{
    public class Application : DispatcherObject
    {
        public Application();

        public static Application Current { get; }
        public Window MainWindow { get; set; }
        public ShutdownMode ShutdownMode { get; set; }
        public WindowCollection Windows { get; }

        public event EventHandler Exit;
        public event EventHandler Startup;

        protected virtual void OnExit(EventArgs e);
        protected virtual void OnStartup(EventArgs e);
        public void Run();
        public void Run(Window window);
        public void Shutdown();
    }
}
```

Display Element Hierarchy

All display components descend from the UIElement class (see Listing 11-17) in the Microsoft.
SPOT.Presentation namespace. This class has properties common for all elements, for example,
those to manage the visibility and size of an element, and provides methods for rendering and
arrangement. Then there are the shapes and controls. Shapes are simple shapes like a line,
polygon, rectangle, and ellipse, and they inherit from the abstract Microsoft.Presentation.
Shapes.Shape class. Controls are elements that allow you to configure their appearance with background and foreground brushes as well as fonts. Controls can be divided into into the following
three categories:

- *Static controls*: Static controls, like the Text and Bitmap controls, do not contain
  child elements.

- *Content controls*: Content controls such as the Border and ListBoxItem can contain
  exactly one child that fills the controls area.

- *Panels*: Finally, the panel controls, such as the Canvas and Panel components, can
  contain several child elements. Panels are responsible for positioning and laying out
  their child elements.

Figure 11-21 shows the class hierarchy of the WPF display elements.

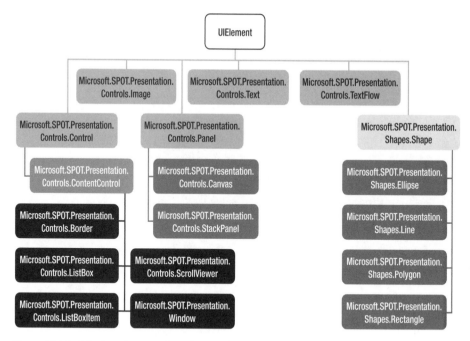

Figure 11-21. *Display element class hierarchy*

Listing 11-17. *The Microsoft.SPOT.Presentation.UIElement Class*

```
using Microsoft.SPOT;
using Microsoft.SPOT.Input;
using Microsoft.SPOT.Presentation.Media;
using System;

namespace Microsoft.SPOT.Presentation
{
    public abstract class UIElement : DispatcherObject
    {
        protected HorizontalAlignment _horizontalAlignment;
        protected VerticalAlignment _verticalAlignment;

        public UIElement();

        public int ActualHeight { get; }
        public int ActualWidth { get; }
        public int Height { get; set; }
        public HorizontalAlignment HorizontalAlignment { get; set; }
        protected EventHandlersStore InstanceEventHandlersStore { get; }
        public bool IsArrangeValid { get; }
        public bool IsEnabled { get; set; }
        public bool IsFocused { get; }
        public bool IsMeasureValid { get; }
```

```csharp
        public bool IsVisible { get; }
        protected UIElementCollection LogicalChildren { get; }
        public UIElement Parent { get; }
        public UIElement RootUIElement { get; }
        public VerticalAlignment VerticalAlignment { get; set; }
        public Visibility Visibility { get; set; }
        public int Width { get; set; }


        public event PropertyChangedEventHandler IsEnabledChanged;
        public event PropertyChangedEventHandler IsVisibleChanged;


        public void AddHandler(RoutedEvent routedEvent, Delegate handler,
                            bool handledEventsToo);
        public void AddToEventRoute(EventRoute route, RoutedEventArgs args);
        public void Arrange(int finalRectX, int finalRectY,
                        int finalRectWidth, int finalRectHeight);
        protected virtual void ArrangeOverride(int arrangeWidth, int arrangeHeight);
        public void GetDesiredSize(out int width, out int height);
        public void GetLayoutOffset(out int x, out int y);
        public void GetMargin(out int left, out int top,
                            out int right, out int bottom);
        public void GetRenderSize(out int width, out int height);
        public void Invalidate();
        public void InvalidateArrange();
        public void InvalidateMeasure();
        public void Measure(int availableWidth, int availableHeight);
        protected virtual void MeasureOverride(int availableWidth,
                                                int availableHeight,
                                                out int desiredWidth,
                                                out int desiredHeight);
        protected virtual void OnButtonDown(ButtonEventArgs e);
        protected virtual void OnButtonUp(ButtonEventArgs e);
        protected virtual void OnChildDesiredSizeChanged(UIElement child);
        protected internal virtual void OnChildrenChanged(UIElement added,
                                                UIElement removed,
                                                int indexAffected);
        protected virtual void OnGotFocus(FocusChangedEventArgs e);
        protected virtual void OnLostFocus(FocusChangedEventArgs e);
        protected virtual void OnPreviewButtonDown(ButtonEventArgs e);
        protected virtual void OnPreviewButtonUp(ButtonEventArgs e);
        public virtual void OnRender(DrawingContext dc);
        public void RaiseEvent(RoutedEventArgs args);
        public void SetMargin(int length);
        public void SetMargin(int left, int top, int right, int bottom);
        public void UpdateLayout();
    }
}
```

Laying Out Elements with a Panel Container

Now, you will learn how to arrange elements on the display using panel containers. Panels can hold several child elements (that are derived from UIElement) and are responsible for arranging them. The Panel class provides a base panel for the more complex panel subclasses StackPanel and Canvas.

The Panel Class

The simple Panel class does not position its child elements, similar to a ContentControl. But a panel can hold more than one child. The size of a Panel is determined by the maximum extent of its children. You can use a Panel element to overlay several elements, for example to draw a text over an underlying image (see Figure 11-22). The first child will be rendered first. Therefore, you need to add the image before the text to the panel, as shown in Listing 11-18.

Listing 11-18. *Overlaying Elements Using the Panel Class*

```
using System;

using Microsoft.SPOT;
using Microsoft.SPOT.Input;
using Microsoft.SPOT.Presentation;
using Microsoft.SPOT.Presentation.Controls;
using Microsoft.SPOT.Presentation.Media;

namespace PanelSample
{
    public class Program : Microsoft.SPOT.Application
    {
        public static void Main()
        {
            Program myApplication = new Program();

            Window mainWindow = myApplication.CreateWindow();

            // Start the application
            myApplication.Run(mainWindow);
        }

        private Window mainWindow;

        public Window CreateWindow()
        {
            // Create a window object and set its size to the
            // size of the display.
            mainWindow = new Window();
            mainWindow.Height = SystemMetrics.ScreenHeight;
            mainWindow.Width = SystemMetrics.ScreenWidth;
```

```
        // Create a single panel control.
        Panel panel = new Panel();

        Image image =
                new Image(Resources.GetBitmap(Resources.BitmapResources.Racer));
        image.HorizontalAlignment = HorizontalAlignment.Center;
        image.VerticalAlignment = VerticalAlignment.Center;
        panel.Children.Add(image);

        Font font = Resources.GetFont(Resources.FontResources.small);
        Text text = new Text(font, "I am a racer.");
        text.ForeColor = Colors.Red;
        text.HorizontalAlignment = HorizontalAlignment.Center;
        text.VerticalAlignment = VerticalAlignment.Center;
        panel.Children.Add(text);

        // Add the text control to the window.
        mainWindow.Child = panel;

        // Set the window visibility to visible.
        mainWindow.Visibility = Visibility.Visible;

        return mainWindow;
      }
    }
}
```

Figure 11-22. *Overlaying elements using the Panel class*

The Stack Panel

Now, we will explore the StackPanel class that descends from the Panel base class. A stack panel holds several elements (which are derived from UIElement) and arranges them on top of or beside each other depending of the Orientation property (horizontal or vertical).

The code sample in Listing 11-19 will create a window that has a child that is a vertical stack panel. The stack panel will hold text, an image, and a rectangle shape. The first item in the stack panel will be displayed at the top. You can see the display result of Listing 11-19 in Figure 11-23.

Figure 11-23. *Elements arranged using a vertical stack panel*

Listing 11-19. *Using a Vertical Stack Panel to Arrange Elements*

```
using System;

using Microsoft.SPOT;
using Microsoft.SPOT.Presentation;
using Microsoft.SPOT.Presentation.Controls;
using Microsoft.SPOT.Presentation.Shapes;
using Microsoft.SPOT.Presentation.Media;

namespace StackPanelSample
{
    public class Program : Microsoft.SPOT.Application
    {
        public static void Main()
        {
            Program myApplication = new Program();

            Window mainWindow = myApplication.CreateWindow();

            // Start the application
            myApplication.Run(mainWindow);
        }

        private Window mainWindow;

        public Window CreateWindow()
        {
            // Create a window object and set its size to the
            // size of the display.
            mainWindow = new Window();
            mainWindow.Height = SystemMetrics.ScreenHeight;
            mainWindow.Width = SystemMetrics.ScreenWidth;
```

```
        StackPanel panel = new StackPanel(Orientation.Vertical);

        // Create a single text control and add it to the panel
        Font font = Resources.GetFont(Resources.FontResources.small);
        Text text = new Text(font, "I am a racer.");
        text.HorizontalAlignment = HorizontalAlignment.Left;
        panel.Children.Add(text);

        // Create an image and add it to the panel
        Bitmap racer = Resources.GetBitmap(Resources.BitmapResources.Racer);
        Image image = new Image(racer);
        image.HorizontalAlignment = HorizontalAlignment.Left;
        panel.Children.Add(image);

        // Create a rectangle shape and add it to the panel
        Rectangle rect = new Rectangle();
        rect.HorizontalAlignment = HorizontalAlignment.Left;
        rect.Fill = new SolidColorBrush(Colors.Blue);
        rect.Width = 100;
        rect.Height = 50;
        panel.Children.Add(rect);

        // Add the panel to the window.
        mainWindow.Child = panel;

        // Set the window visibility to visible.
        mainWindow.Visibility = Visibility.Visible;

        return mainWindow;
    }
  }
}
```

For the text and image elements, we did not specify a particular width and height explicitly. Therefore, these controls will cover the whole width of its vertical parent stack panel. The height of an element in a vertical stack panel depends on the content (here, text and a bitmap file) and is calculated as the minimum height that is needed to display the text or bitmap. In these cases, the element's height is equal to the height of the text or bitmap.

In the "hello world" example in Listing 11-14, one Text element was added directly to the main window as a child. The Window class inherits from ContentControl that can have one discrete child that will be extended and will cover the whole client area of the window. In Listing 11-19, the vertical stack panel is the child of the window and covers the whole client area of the window.

All elements are aligned to the left side of the vertical stack panel, because the HorizontalAlignment properties of the three elements were set to HorizontalAlignment.Left. The HorizontalAlignment property is provided from the UIElement class and describes how the element content should be aligned if the element is wider than its content. Possible values for the HorizontalAlignment enumeration are Left, Right, Center, and Stretch. Stretch is very similar to Center and will not stretch the content of the text, image, or shape element. If the vertical stack panel is smaller than, for example, the image, Stretch behaves like Left and will align the image to the left side rather than in the center.

When you display a horizontal stack panel, you need to use the VerticalAlignment property. Possible values for the VerticalAlignment enumeration are Top, Bottom, Center, and Stretch. Figure 11-24 show a horizontal stack panel with top-aligned text, a centered image, and a bottom-aligned shape.

I am a racer.

Figure 11-24. *Using a horizontal stack panel to arrange elements with different vertical alignments*

You can further control the alignment by setting margins for each individual element. An element can have left, right, top, and bottom margins. This will add spacing between the elements or to the stack panel borders. You can either set all four margins to the same value with the SetMargin(int length) method inherited from UIElement or set each margin individually with the SetMargin(int left, int right, int top, int bottom) overload. Let's go back to our sample where all elements were left aligned in the vertical stack panel. If you set the left, right, top, and bottom margins of the image to 20 pixels, you will get a display as shown in Figure 11-25.

I am a racer.

Figure 11-25. *Using a horizontal stack panel to arrange elements where the image has left, right, top, and bottom margins of 20 pixels*

In the earlier examples, there were no explicit specifications of an element's width and height. For elements in a vertical stack panel, the element's width is set to the width of the stack panel, and the height is calculated by the dimension of the content. You can explicitly specify a height for an element in a vertical stack panel, but the width will be equal to the panel's client width. With a horizontal stack panel, you will be able to set the width of a child element. Figure 11-26 demonstrates how an explicit height of 200 pixels for the image will look with a vertical stack panel. Figure 11-27 shows the image with a 50-pixel height.

Figure 11-26. *The image with an explicit height of 200 pixels*

Figure 11-27. *The image with an explicit height of 50 pixels*

Exact Positioning of Components Using a Canvas

The stack panel uses the screen resolution to lay out the elements. But you do not have precise control on a pixel level where to place the elements. If you need to specify the exact pixel position of child elements, you should use the Canvas panel. Canvas derives from Panel and can be used like StackPanel, but it allows you to set the exact pixel position for the individual child elements with the methods SetTop and SetLeft. Listing 11-20 demonstrates how to use a canvas to place elements precisely, as illustrated in Figure 11-28.

Listing 11-20. *Exact Positioning of Elements with a Canvas*

```
using System;

using Microsoft.SPOT;
using Microsoft.SPOT.Presentation;
using Microsoft.SPOT.Presentation.Controls;
```

```csharp
using Microsoft.SPOT.Presentation.Shapes;
using Microsoft.SPOT.Presentation.Media;

namespace CanvasSample
{
    public class Program : Microsoft.SPOT.Application
    {
        public static void Main()
        {
            Program myApplication = new Program();

            Window mainWindow = myApplication.CreateWindow();

            // Start the application
            myApplication.Run(mainWindow);
        }

        private Window mainWindow;

        public Window CreateWindow()
        {
            // Create a window object and set its size to the
            // size of the display.
            mainWindow = new Window();
            mainWindow.Height = SystemMetrics.ScreenHeight;
            mainWindow.Width = SystemMetrics.ScreenWidth;

            Canvas canvas = new Canvas();

            // Create a single text control and add it to the canvas
            Font font = Resources.GetFont(Resources.FontResources.small);
            Text text = new Text(font, "I am a racer.");
            Canvas.SetLeft(text, 50);
            Canvas.SetTop(text, 200);
            canvas.Children.Add(text);

            // Create an image and add it to the canvas
            Bitmap racer = Resources.GetBitmap(Resources.BitmapResources.Racer);
            Image image = new Image(racer);
            Canvas.SetLeft(image, 10);
            Canvas.SetTop(image, 10);
            canvas.Children.Add(image);

            // Create a rectangle shape and add it to the canvas
            Rectangle rect = new Rectangle();
            rect.Fill = new SolidColorBrush(Colors.Blue);
            rect.Width = 100;
```

```
        rect.Height = 50;
        Canvas.SetLeft(rect, 200);
        Canvas.SetTop(rect, 50);
        canvas.Children.Add(rect);

        // Add the canvas to the window.
        mainWindow.Child = canvas;

        // Set the window visibility to visible.
        mainWindow.Visibility = Visibility.Visible;

        return mainWindow;
    }
  }
}
```

I am a racer.

Figure 11-28. *Exact positioning with a canvas*

The left and top positions for an element are set via the static SetLeft and SetTop methods of Canvas and not, as you might think, from the System.Windows.Forms framework with properties that belong to the elements itself. The SetLeft and SetTop methods accept the UI element to place and the left or top position in pixels relative to the top-left corner of the canvas. It assigns hidden position information with the element that allows the canvas to place an element within the canvas client area.

You do not need to specify a horizontal or vertical alignment here, because all elements are automatically resized to their content with a canvas (if no explicit width and height was set).

You should use the canvas to arrange your elements only if you really need pixel level control. Therefore, you need to know the display resolution of your final hardware to optimize the screen layout to exactly this resolution. For other resolutions, your layout might not look ideal. The stack panel does a great job when laying out your UI elements to best fit to your display.

Backgrounds for Controls Using Brushes

A control element can have its own individual background. This section demonstrates how to paint backgrounds using brushes and presents the different types of brushes supported by the .NET Micro Framework.

The Control class provides the Background, Foreground, and Font properties. The Background and Foreground properties are of the type Brush. Specifying a background brush allows a control to fill its background. The Foreground property cannot be used with any built-in controls, though you can use it with your custom controls.

Every control can have its own individual background that is filled entirely white by default. If you set a background to null, there will be no background drawn for the control (it is transparent), and you will see the background of its parent control.

The .NET Micro Framework provides the following classes that descend from Control: Window, Border, ListBox, ListBoxItem, ScrollViewer, and ContentControl (see the class hierarchy in Figure 11-21).

Brushes

Brushes can be used to fill a rectangular area, such as the background of a control, or to fill a shape element, such as a rectangle. There are three kinds of brushes that descend from the abstract Brush class in the Microsoft.Presentation.Media namespace: SolidColorBrush, LinearGradientBrush, and ImageBrush. The Brush class provides an Opacity property that allows you to control how the underlying pixels are blended with the new ones.

SolidColorBrush

The simplest brush is the SolidColorBrush, which only accepts a color value and inherits the Opacity property from the Brush class. This brush will fill the entire background of a control with the selected color.

If we take the code from Listing 11-20, where some elements were placed on a canvas, and add the instruction mainWindow.Background = new SolidColorBrush(Colors.Gray); , then we will get the main window with a background entirely filled with gray, as shown in Figure 11-29. The child elements of the canvas—Text, Image, and Rectangle—are not controls, so they cannot have individual backgrounds. The Colors class resides in the Microsoft.SPOT.Presentation. Media namespace in the Microsoft.SPOT.TinyCore.dll assembly, and provides the predefined colors Black, White, Gray, Red, Green, and Blue.

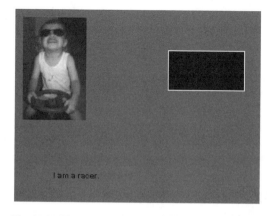

Figure 11-29. *Main window with a gray background*

LinearGradientBrush

It is also possible to render the background of a control or window with a color gradient; color gradients were discussed earlier in this chapter. The LinearGradientBrush accepts a start and end color and also the gradient start and end positions.

Now, the following instruction is added to the code in Listing 11-20:

```
mainWindow.Background =
    new LinearGradientBrush(Colors.White,              // start color
                            Colors.Red,                // end color
                            0,                         // start x
                            0,                         // start y
                            SystemMetrics.ScreenWidth, // end x
                            SystemMetrics.ScreenHeight // end y
                            );
```

The display is shown in Figure 11-30.

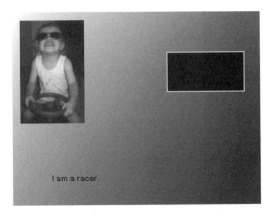

Figure 11-30. *Main window with a color gradient background*

ImageBrush

The ImageBrush allows you to fill a rectangular area with a bitmap. The bitmap can either be stretched to fit the rectangle's entire area or drawn unscaled and aligned with the top-left corner of the rectangle. The Stretch property allows you to control whether or not the bitmap should be stretched. By default, the bitmap will be stretched.

Now, we add the following code to Listing 11-20:

```
ImageBrush imageBrush =
            new  ImageBrush(Resources.GetBitmap(Resources.BitmapResources.Racer));
imageBrush.Stretch = Stretch.Fill;
mainWindow.Background = imageBrush;
```

You can see the stretched background image in Figure 11-31, and in Figure 11-32, the unscaled image using imageBrush.Stretch = Stretch.None;.

Figure 11-31. *A stretched background image*

Figure 11-32. *An unscaled background image*

Drawing Borders Around Elements

No element comes with direct support for drawing a border around it. However, the Border class, which is derived from ContentControl, displays a border around specific content. You can embed an element in a border control, and the Border control will then draw the border around the child element for you. The Border content control can contain only one discrete child element. To draw a border around more than one element, you need to add a panel element (Panel, StackPanel, or Canvas) to the border element as a child and then place multiple child elements within that panel element.

Listing 11-21 demonstrates how to draw a border around your window. The code in Listing 11-21 adds a Border control to a window as a child and then embeds a text element into the border; Figure 11-33 shows a border for the window. You can use any brush to draw the border. In this example, a linear gradient brush (LinearGradientBrush) from white to blue was used. The border thickness can be set with the SetBorderThickness method; you can set either equal values for the left, right, top, and bottom borders or each border thickness individually with the four-parameter overload of the method.

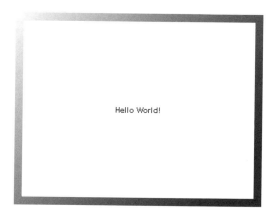

Figure 11-33. *A color gradient border around a window*

Listing 11-21. *Drawing a Color Gradient Border Around a Window*

```
using System;

using Microsoft.SPOT;
using Microsoft.SPOT.Presentation;
using Microsoft.SPOT.Presentation.Controls;
using Microsoft.SPOT.Presentation.Media;

namespace WindowBorderSample
{
    public class Program : Microsoft.SPOT.Application
    {
        public static void Main()
        {
            Program myApplication = new Program();

            Window mainWindow = myApplication.CreateWindow();

            // Start the application
            myApplication.Run(mainWindow);
        }

        private Window mainWindow;

        public Window CreateWindow()
        {
            // Create a window object and set its size to the
            // size of the display.
            mainWindow = new Window();
            mainWindow.Height = SystemMetrics.ScreenHeight;
            mainWindow.Width = SystemMetrics.ScreenWidth;
```

```
                    // Create a single text control.
                    Text text = new Text();

                    text.Font = Resources.GetFont(Resources.FontResources.small);
                    text.TextContent =
                                Resources.GetString(Resources.StringResources.String1);
                    text.HorizontalAlignment =
                                Microsoft.SPOT.Presentation.HorizontalAlignment.Center;
                    text.VerticalAlignment =
                                Microsoft.SPOT.Presentation.VerticalAlignment.Center;

                    Border border = new Border();
                    border.SetBorderThickness(10); // set a 10 pixel border for r,l,t,b
                    border.BorderBrush = new LinearGradientBrush(Colors.White,
                                                     Colors.Blue,
                                                     0, 0,
                                                     SystemMetrics.ScreenWidth,
                                                     SystemMetrics.ScreenHeight
                                                     );
                    border.Child = text; // Add the text element to the border control

                    // Add the border control to the window.
                    mainWindow.Child = border;

                    // Set the window visibility to visible.
                    mainWindow.Visibility = Visibility.Visible;

                    return mainWindow;
                }
        }
}
```

You can even draw borders for particular elements (see Figure 11-34). Listing 11-22 shows the code to add text with a border to a canvas; the Border control that encloses a text element is added to the canvas at the desired position. The Border control uses SolidColorBrush to draw the entire border in the color blue. The sample uses different border thicknesses.

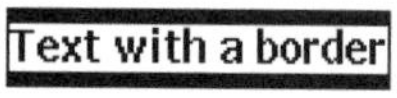

Text with a border

Figure 11-34. *A text element with a blue border*

Listing 11-22. *Displaying a Text Element with a Blue Border*

```
using System;

using Microsoft.SPOT;
using Microsoft.SPOT.Presentation;
```

```csharp
using Microsoft.SPOT.Presentation.Controls;
using Microsoft.SPOT.Presentation.Shapes;
using Microsoft.SPOT.Presentation.Media;

namespace ElementBorderSample
{
    public class Program : Microsoft.SPOT.Application
    {
        public static void Main()
        {
            Program myApplication = new Program();

            Window mainWindow = myApplication.CreateWindow();

            // Start the application
            myApplication.Run(mainWindow);
        }

        private Window mainWindow;

        public Window CreateWindow()
        {
            // Create a window object and set its size to the
            // size of the display.
            mainWindow = new Window();
            mainWindow.Height = SystemMetrics.ScreenHeight;
            mainWindow.Width = SystemMetrics.ScreenWidth;

            Canvas canvas = new Canvas();

            // Create a border for the text
            Border textBorder = new Border();
            textBorder.SetBorderThickness(1, 5, 1, 5);
            textBorder.BorderBrush = new SolidColorBrush(Colors.Blue);
            Canvas.SetLeft(textBorder, 20);
            Canvas.SetTop(textBorder, 150);

            // Create a single text control and add it to the canvas
            Font font = Resources.GetFont(Resources.FontResources.NinaB);
            Text text = new Text(font, "Text with a border");
            textBorder.Child = text; // Add the text to the border

            // Add the border to the canvas
            canvas.Children.Add(textBorder);

            // Add the canvas to the window.
            mainWindow.Child = canvas;
```

```
            // Set the window visibility to visible.
            mainWindow.Visibility = Visibility.Visible;

            return mainWindow;
        }
    }
}
```

You should be careful when using a color gradient brush to render a border, because when creating a `LinearGradientBrush` instance, you need to pass the start and end position of the gradient in screen coordinates to see the complete gradient. But that can be a challenge: you do not always know exactly where on your display and at what size the graphic engine will draw the border. In the previous example, we know the position and dimension of the main window, and that enables us to draw a gradient border there.

The `Border` element derives from `Control`, and therefore, it also provides a `Background` property. Setting a background brush will render your text element with a border and with a custom background. By default, the background is white. Specify `null` to render the border control with a transparent background. If you do not need a border but only a background, you should use the more lightweight `ContentControl` class to embed your element (`Border` is a direct subclass of `ContentControl`).

Displaying Shapes

You already saw the `Rectangle` shape in action in earlier samples. The .NET Micro Framework provides the following shape elements: `Line`, `Rectangle`, `Polygon`, and `Ellipse`. You can find these built-in shapes in the `Microsoft.SPOT.Presentation` namespace. You can derive custom shapes from the common abstract base class `Shape`. The `Shape` class provides a stroke pen and a fill brush but *no* background brush property like the `Control` class does.

The `Line` lement renders a diagonal line either from the top left to the bottom right or from the bottom left to the top right corner of its client area depending on the `Direction` property. The class accepts the bottom-right position with the constructor. Although the `Line` element inherits the `Fill` brush property, it does not support any kind of filling. The `Stroke` pen property describes the color of the line. The thickness will be ignored, as lines will always have a thickness of 1 pixel.

The `Rectangle` element renders a rectangle to your display. You need to specify the width and height. The `Fill` property is used to set a fill brush and the `Stroke` property is used for drawing the outer line. If you do not want the rectangle to be drawn filled, specify `null` for `Fill`, and if you do not want a frame around it, specify `null` for the `Stroke` property. The pen also indicates the thickness and color of the outer line.

The `Polygon` shape renders a closed polygon in the color described with the stroke pen. The lines will always have a thickness of 1 pixel, regardless of the specified pen, and will not be drawn filled. The coordinates of the polygon points are described with a one-dimensional integer array. The x coordinates have even indexes, and y coordinates have odd indexes.

The `Ellipse` shape draws an ellipse with particular x and y radii. The `Ellipse` element does not support filling, and the outer line thickness is always 1 pixel.

These shapes internally use the `Bitmap` class for rendering, and that class's limitations were pointed out in the first part of this chapter.

The Text Element

Displaying simple text is one of the most common tasks you need to do with your display. Let's look at the Text class (see Listing 11-23).

The Text element allows you to display simple text on the display, and it supports multi-line text. The TextContent property holds the text to display. The Font and ForeColor properties describe the appearance of the text. To print more than one line of text, you need to set the TextWrap property to true.

Listing 11-23. *The Microsoft.Presentation.Controls.Text Class*

```
using Microsoft.SPOT;
using Microsoft.SPOT.Presentation;
using Microsoft.SPOT.Presentation.Media;
using System;

namespace Microsoft.SPOT.Presentation.Controls
{
    public class Text : UIElement
    {
        protected Font _font;
        protected string _text;

        public Text();
        public Text(string content);
        public Text(Font font, string content);

        public Font Font { get; set; }
        public Color ForeColor { get; set; }
        public int LineHeight { get; }
        public TextAlignment TextAlignment { get; set; }
        public string TextContent { get; set; }
        public bool TextWrap { get; set; }
        public TextTrimming Trimming { get; set; }

        protected override void MeasureOverride(int availableWidth,
                                                int availableHeight,
                                                out int desiredWidth,
                                                out int desiredHeight);
        public override void OnRender(DrawingContext dc);
    }
}
```

If the element is larger than the text content, you can use the HorizontalAlignment and VerticalAlignment properties to align the text content using the same methods for laying out elements described earlier in the chapter. Furthermore, multiline text can be formatted with the TextAlignment property. Do not get this property mixed up with the HorizontalAlignment and VerticalAlignment properties inherited from UIElement. Valid values for the TextAlignment property are Center, Left, and Right. The text element uses the entire available width of the element for multiline text. Shorter lines will be aligned within the surrounding rectangle according to the text alignment settings.

The TextFlow Element

Sometimes, you might need to print multiline text with different fonts and colors, or you might want to display a large amount of text page by page or to make it scrollable. For purposes like these, the .NET Micro Framework provides the TextFlow element.

The TextFlow element holds a list of TextRun definitions, which describe text with a particular font and color.

You can add a text run to the list with the Add method of the TextRuns property. Repeating the command will add another text run after the existing text in the same line, and you can vary the font and color. To proceed on a new line, you need to pass the predefined, static, end-of-line text run, TextRun.EndOfLine, to the second overload of the Add method.

Listing 11-24 shows how to build a multiline text display, and Figure 11-35 illustrates the output.

Listing 11-24. *Building a Multiline Text Display with Different Fonts and Colors*

```
using System;

using Microsoft.SPOT;
using Microsoft.SPOT.Input;
using Microsoft.SPOT.Presentation;
using Microsoft.SPOT.Presentation.Controls;
using Microsoft.SPOT.Presentation.Media;

namespace TextFlowSample
{
    public class Program : Microsoft.SPOT.Application
    {
        public static void Main()
        {
            Program myApplication = new Program();

            Window mainWindow = myApplication.CreateWindow();

            // Start the application
            myApplication.Run(mainWindow);
        }

        private Window mainWindow;
```

```
public Window CreateWindow()
{
    // Create a window object and set its size to the
    // size of the display.
    mainWindow = new Window();
    mainWindow.Height = SystemMetrics.ScreenHeight;
    mainWindow.Width = SystemMetrics.ScreenWidth;

    Font font = Resources.GetFont(Resources.FontResources.NinaB);
    Font smallFont = Resources.GetFont(Resources.FontResources.small);

    TextFlow textFlow = new TextFlow();
    textFlow.TextRuns.Add("Hello world.", font, Colors.Black);
    textFlow.TextRuns.Add(" Hello world.", smallFont, Colors.Red);
    textFlow.TextRuns.Add(TextRun.EndOfLine);
    textFlow.TextRuns.Add("Hello world.", font, Colors.Green);

    // Add the text flow to the window.
    mainWindow.Child = textFlow;

    // Set the window visibility to visible.
    mainWindow.Visibility = Visibility.Visible;

    return mainWindow;
}
```

Hello world. Hello world.
Hello world.

Figure 11-35. *Text output with the TextFlow element*

Paged and Scrollable Text

The TextFlow element also allows you to scroll the text if there is not enough space to show all of it. There are two scroll modes: line by line and page by page.

The TextFlow element will handle scrolling for you. Therefore, you just need to set the input focus to your TextFlow element with Buttons.Focus(textFlow);, so the element can receive and handle the user's input. The TextFlow element will *not* render a scrollbar or arrows to indicate that it can scroll further, and the .NET Micro Framework provides no stand-alone scrollbar control.

The TextFlow is the first interactive component presented here (we will discuss other interactive components and handling user interaction and events later). For the sample in Listing 11-25, which produces a display like the one shown in Figure 11-36, you just need to know how to set the focus to your text flow element, so that you can scroll the text using the up and down buttons of your device or emulator. The code also creates an input provider instance to map the GPIO pins of the hardware buttons to button events for the user interface elements.

Listing 11-25. *Building a Scrollable Text Display That Lets the User Scroll Using GPIO Buttons*

```
using System;

using Microsoft.SPOT;
using Microsoft.SPOT.Input;
using Microsoft.SPOT.Presentation;
using Microsoft.SPOT.Presentation.Controls;
using Microsoft.SPOT.Presentation.Media;

namespace TextFlowScrollingSample
{
    public class Program : Microsoft.SPOT.Application
    {
        public static void Main()
        {
            Program myApplication = new Program();

            Window mainWindow = myApplication.CreateWindow();

            // Create the object that configures the GPIO pins to buttons.
            GPIOButtonInputProvider inputProvider =
                                            new GPIOButtonInputProvider(null);

            // Start the application
            myApplication.Run(mainWindow);
        }

        private Window mainWindow;

        public Window CreateWindow()
        {
            // Create a window object and set its size to the
            // size of the display.
            mainWindow = new Window();
            mainWindow.Height = SystemMetrics.ScreenHeight;
            mainWindow.Width = SystemMetrics.ScreenWidth;

            Font normalFont = Resources.GetFont(Resources.FontResources.NinaB);
            Font smallFont = Resources.GetFont(Resources.FontResources.small);

            TextFlow textFlow = new TextFlow();
            textFlow.ScrollingStyle = ScrollingStyle.LineByLine;
            // Add text
            Color[] colors = new Color[] { Colors.Black, Colors.Gray,
                                    Colors.Red, Colors.Green, Colors.Blue};
```

```
        for (int i = 0; i < 100; ++i)
        {
            Font font = (i % 2 == 0) ? normalFont : smallFont;
            Color color = colors[i % colors.Length];
            textFlow.TextRuns.Add("Hello world. ", font, color);
            if (i % 2 == 0)
                textFlow.TextRuns.Add(TextRun.EndOfLine);
        }

        // Add the text flow to the window.
        mainWindow.Child = textFlow;

        // Set the window visibility to visible.
        mainWindow.Visibility = Visibility.Visible;

        // Let the user scroll the text with buttons
        Buttons.Focus(textFlow);

        return mainWindow;
    }
    }
}
```

Hello world.
Hello world. **Hello world.**
Hello world. **Hello world.**
Hello world. **Hello world.**
Hello world. Hello world.
Hello world. **Hello world.**
Hello world. **Hello world.**
Hello world. **Hello world.**
Hello world. **Hello world.**
Hello world. Hello world.
Hello world. **Hello world.**
Hello world. **Hello world.**
Hello world. **Hello world.**
Hello world. **Hello world.**
Hello world. Hello world.
Hello world. **Hello world.**

Figure 11-36. *A scrollable text display*

The ScrollViewer Element

In the previous section, you learned how to create a scrollable text display. For other scenarios, you might need to present content to the user that does not fit entirely on your screen. Therefore, the .NET Micro Framework provides the ScrollViewer class (see Listing 11-26). ScrollViewer is a subclass of ContentControl that allows you to add one discrete child element and let the user scroll the content using the up, down, left, and right hardware buttons, similar to the TextFlow element. Like the TextFlow element, ScrollViewer does not show a scrollbar or arrows.

Listing 11-26. *The Microsoft.SPOT.Presentation.Controls.ScrollViewer Class*

```
using Microsoft.SPOT.Input;
using System;

namespace Microsoft.SPOT.Presentation.Controls
{
    public class ScrollViewer : ContentControl
    {
        public ScrollViewer();

        public int ExtentHeight { get; }
        public int ExtentWidth { get; }
        public int HorizontalOffset { get; set; }
        public int VerticalOffset { get; set; }
        public ScrollingStyle ScrollingStyle { get; set; }
        public int LineHeight { get; set; }
        public int LineWidth { get; set; }

        public event ScrollChangedEventHandler ScrollChanged;

        protected override void ArrangeOverride(int arrangeWidth,
                                                int arrangeHeight);
        protected override void MeasureOverride(int availableWidth,
                                                int availableHeight,
                                                out int desiredWidth,
                                                out int desiredHeight);
        protected override void OnButtonDown(ButtonEventArgs e);

        public void LineDown();
        public void LineLeft();
        public void LineRight();
        public void LineUp();
        public void PageDown();
        public void PageLeft();
        public void PageRight();
        public void PageUp();
    }
}
```

The sample in Listing 11-27 creates a scroll viewer and adds a canvas to it as a child element. The canvas holds several circle shapes that exceed the screen dimensions (see Figure 11-37). The scroll viewer is configured so that it will scroll line by line. The ScrollViewer control supports vertical and horizontal scrolling and responds to the left, right, up, and down hardware buttons if it has the input focus. You can configure how many pixels the content will scroll horizontally and vertically per key press using the LineWidth and LineHeight properties (assuming you are in line-by-line scroll mode and not in page-by-page mode).

The ScrollViewer automatically determines the maximum number of lines or pages to which it extends based on its child content. The ScrollViewer element in Listing 11-27 contains a Canvas element. The embedded Canvas panel does not calculate and provide its desired size; its provided desired size is always zero. Therefore, you need to set the canvas width and height explicitly.

The ScrollChange event handler notifies you if the content was scrolled. You can let the control react to user input or allow manual scrolling using the LineXXX or PageXXX methods. Further, you can directly set the horizontal and vertical scroll offsets programmatically. The scroll offset is accepted in pixels.

Listing 11-27. *Scrolling Arbitrary Content, Like a Canvas with Shapes*

```
using System;

using Microsoft.SPOT;
using Microsoft.SPOT.Input;
using Microsoft.SPOT.Presentation;
using Microsoft.SPOT.Presentation.Controls;
using Microsoft.SPOT.Presentation.Shapes;
using Microsoft.SPOT.Presentation.Media;

namespace ScrollViewerSample
{
    public class Program : Microsoft.SPOT.Application
    {
        public static void Main()
        {
            Program myApplication = new Program();

            Window mainWindow = myApplication.CreateWindow();

            // Create the object that configures the GPIO pins to buttons.
            GPIOButtonInputProvider inputProvider =
                                            new GPIOButtonInputProvider(null);

            // Start the application
            myApplication.Run(mainWindow);
        }

        private Window mainWindow;

        public Window CreateWindow()
        {
            // Create a window object and set its size to the
            // size of the display.
            mainWindow = new Window();
            mainWindow.Height = SystemMetrics.ScreenHeight;
            mainWindow.Width = SystemMetrics.ScreenWidth;
```

```
// Create a scrollviewer
ScrollViewer scrollViewer = new ScrollViewer();
scrollViewer.Background = new SolidColorBrush(Colors.Gray);
// scroll line by line with 10 pixels per line
scrollViewer.ScrollingStyle = ScrollingStyle.LineByLine;
scrollViewer.LineWidth = 10;
scrollViewer.LineHeight = 10;

// Create a canvas and add ellipse shapes
Canvas canvas = new Canvas();
for (int x = 0; x <= 20; ++x)
{
    for (int y = 0; y <= 20; ++y)
    {
        Ellipse ellipse = new Ellipse(10, 10);
        ellipse.Stroke = new Pen(Colors.White);
        canvas.Children.Add(ellipse);
        Canvas.SetLeft(ellipse, x * 30);
        Canvas.SetTop(ellipse, y * 30);
    }
}
//we need to set the size of a canvas explicitly
//because it doesn't calculate the desired size from its content
canvas.Width = 20 * 30 + 10 * 2;
canvas.Height = 20 * 30 + 10 * 2;
scrollViewer.Child = canvas;

// Add the scroll viewer to the window.
mainWindow.Child = scrollViewer;

// Set the window visibility to visible.
mainWindow.Visibility = Visibility.Visible;

// Attach the button focus to the scroll viewer
// to be able to scroll with the up down right and left buttons
Buttons.Focus(scrollViewer);

        return mainWindow;
    }
  }
}
```

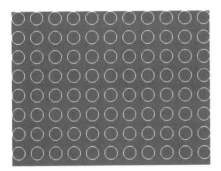

Figure 11-37. *Shapes on a canvas that can be scrolled using a scroll viewer*

List Box Menus

In this section, you will learn how to create menus using the `ListBox` class of the .NET Micro Framework. A list box holds a collection of selectable items and stacks them vertically. Exactly one item can be selected at a time, and the list box control handles scrolling the items vertically if necessary.

Adding Simple Text Items

Items of a list box are represented by the `ListBoxItem` class or its subclasses. The `ListBoxItem` class is another `ContentControl` subclass and can have one discrete child element, which enables you to place and present any content in a list box item.

First, we will create a list with simple text entries. To add a text item, you need to use the following statement:

```
listBox.Items.Add(new Text("Hello world."));
```

This overload of the `Add` method accepts a `UIElement` object and creates and adds a `ListBoxItem` instance containing that UI element. The previous statement does exactly the same as the following statement using the second overload of the `Add` method, which accepts a `ListBoxItem` object:

```
ListBoxItem item = new ListBoxItem();
item.Child = new Text("Hello world.");
listBox.Items.Add(item);
```

Getting Notified When a Selected Item Changes or Is Pressed

Listing 11-28 shows the complete code necessary to create a list box with text items. In order to let the user change the selected item with the up and down keys, you need to set the focus to your list box. If you want to be notified when the selected item is changed, you need the following code:

```
listBox.SelectionChanged +=
                    new SelectionChangedEventHandler(listBox_SelectionChanged);
```

You might want to use your list box as a kind of menu where the user can click a selected menu item using the Select key. Therefore, you need to subscribe to the following event handler in order to be notified and able to execute some commands:

```
listBox.AddHandler(Buttons.ButtonDownEvent,
                   new ButtonEventHandler(listBox_ButtonDown),
                   false);
```

Listing 11-28. *Creating a List Box with Text Items*

```
using System;

using Microsoft.SPOT;
using Microsoft.SPOT.Input;
using Microsoft.SPOT.Presentation;
using Microsoft.SPOT.Presentation.Controls;

namespace ListBoxWithTextItemsSample
{
    public class Program : Microsoft.SPOT.Application
    {
        public static void Main()
        {
            Program myApplication = new Program();

            Window mainWindow = myApplication.CreateWindow();

            // Create the object that configures the GPIO pins to buttons.
            GPIOButtonInputProvider inputProvider =
                                            new GPIOButtonInputProvider(null);

            // Start the application
            myApplication.Run(mainWindow);
        }

        private Window mainWindow;

        public Window CreateWindow()
        {
            // Create a window object and set its size to the
            // size of the display.
            mainWindow = new Window();
            mainWindow.Height = SystemMetrics.ScreenHeight;
            mainWindow.Width = SystemMetrics.ScreenWidth;

            Font font = Resources.GetFont(Resources.FontResources.NinaB);
```

```
        // Create a list box control and add text items
        ListBox listBox = new ListBox();
        for (int i = 0; i < 10; ++i)
        {
            string str = "Item " + i.ToString() + ". Hello World.";
            listBox.Items.Add(new Text(font, str));
        }

        // Add the text control to the window.
        mainWindow.Child = listBox;

        // Set the window visibility to visible.
        mainWindow.Visibility = Visibility.Visible;

        // Let the user select items with the up and down buttons.
        Buttons.Focus(listBox);
        // Get notified when the selected item was changed.
        listBox.SelectionChanged +=
                    new SelectionChangedEventHandler(listBox_SelectionChanged);
        // Get notified when a selected item was pressed
        // using the select button.
        listBox.AddHandler(Buttons.ButtonDownEvent,
                        new ButtonEventHandler(listBox_ButtonDown),
                        false);

        return mainWindow;
    }

    private void listBox_SelectionChanged(object sender,
                                    SelectionChangedEventArgs args)
    {
        Debug.Print("Item " + args.SelectedIndex + " was selected.");
    }

    private void listBox_ButtonDown(object sender, ButtonEventArgs args)
    {
        ListBox listBox = (ListBox)sender;
        if(args.Button == Button.Select)
            Debug.Print("Item " + listBox.SelectedIndex + " was pressed.");
    }
  }
}
```

Figure 11-38 show the text list box. The code in Listing 11-28 has one big drawback: you will not see which item was selected on the screen. Therefore, you need to change the visual appearance of the selected item to indicate the current item to the user; we'll discuss how in the next section.

```
Item 0. Hello World.
Item 1. Hello World.
Item 2. Hello World.
Item 3. Hello World.
Item 4. Hello World.
Item 5. Hello World.
Item 6. Hello World.
Item 7. Hello World.
Item 8. Hello World.
Item 9. Hello World.
```

Figure 11-38. *A text list box*

Highlighting Selected Items

The ListBox and ListBoxItem classes are designed for a very generic usage and, therefore, provide no built-in support for highlighting selected items. You need to implement this by yourself. The approach in this section allows a high level of flexibility.

You can change the appearance of the newly selected item and previously selected item in the SelectionChanged handler of the ListBox class. A better approach is to derive a custom list box item that is able to highlight itself. The ListBoxItem class provides a virtual OnIsSelectedChanged method that you can override to change the appearance of your item when it was selected or deselected.

Listing 11-29 shows the implementation of the custom HighlightableListBoxItem class. This item changes the background to blue when it is selected. When it is not selected, no background will be drawn, so that it is transparent and displays the background of the list box. The list box item will again accept any UIElement as its child content, so it provides a constructor that allows you to pass the content directly. You can use the custom list box item in Listing 11-29 with Listing 11-28, with minor code changes, to see highlighted selected list box items, as shown in Figure 11-39.

```
ListBox listBox = new ListBox();
for (int i = 0; i < 10; ++i)
{
    string str = "Item " + i.ToString() + ". Hello World.";
    ListBoxItem item = new HighlightableListBoxItem(new Text(font, str));
    listBox.Items.Add(item);
}
```

```
Item 0. Hello World.
Item 1. Hello World.
Item 2. Hello World.
Item 3. Hello World.
Item 4. Hello World.
Item 5. Hello World.
Item 6. Hello World.
Item 7. Hello World.
Item 8. Hello World.
Item 9. Hello World.
```

Figure 11-39. *Highlighting the selected item*

Listing 11-29. *A Generic, Highlightable List Box Item*

```
using System;
using Microsoft.SPOT;
using Microsoft.SPOT.Presentation.Controls;
using Microsoft.SPOT.Presentation.Media;
using Microsoft.SPOT.Presentation;

namespace Kuehner.SPOT.Presentation.Controls
{
    public class HighlightableListBoxItem : ListBoxItem
    {
        public HighlightableListBoxItem()
        {
            this.Background = null;
        }

        public HighlightableListBoxItem(UIElement content)
        {
            this.Child = content;
            this.Background = null;
        }

        protected override void OnIsSelectedChanged(bool isSelected)
        {
            if (isSelected)
            {
                Color selectionColor = ColorUtility.ColorFromRGB(0x00, 0x94, 0xFF);
                this.Background = new SolidColorBrush(selectionColor);
            }
            else
                this.Background = null;
        }
    }
}
```

We can add further improvements. First, it looks nicer to separate the list box items a little bit. To do so, you need to add a margin to the enclosed text content. Do not add the margin to the outer, parent list box item, because that would display a small, highlighted background. Another improvement is to change the text color to white when an item is highlighted.

Because displaying a list box with text items is a common scenario, it is a good idea to derive a custom HighLightableTextListBoxItem to do all this for us (see Listing 11-30).

Listing 11-30. *The HighlightableTextListBoxItem*

```
using System;
using Microsoft.SPOT;
using Microsoft.SPOT.Presentation.Controls;
using Microsoft.SPOT.Presentation.Media;
using Microsoft.SPOT.Presentation;

namespace Kuehner.SPOT.Presentation.Controls
{
    public class HighlightableTextListBoxItem : HighlightableListBoxItem
    {
        private readonly Text text;

        public HighlightableTextListBoxItem(Font font, string content) : base()
        {
            // create and remember a text element from the given
            // font and text content
            this.text = new Text(font, content);
            this.text.SetMargin(2); // set the margin for the text
            this.Child = this.text; // add as child content
        }

        protected override void OnIsSelectedChanged(bool isSelected)
        {
            if (isSelected)
            {
                Color selectionColor = ColorUtility.ColorFromRGB(0x00, 0x94, 0xFF);
                this.Background = new SolidColorBrush(selectionColor);
                this.text.ForeColor = Color.White;
            }
            else
            {
                this.Background = null;
                this.text.ForeColor = Color.Black;
            }
        }
    }
}
```

Now you have a reusable text list box item that creates a nice looking text list box (see Figure 11-40).

Item 0. Hello World.
Item 1. Hello World.
Item 2. Hello World.
Item 3. Hello World.
Item 4. Hello World.
Item 5. Hello World.
Item 6. Hello World.
Item 7. Hello World.
Item 8. Hello World.
Item 9. Hello World.

Figure 11-40. *Using HighlightableTextListBoxItem*

Displaying Separator Items

You might want to group your items into lists that are divided with a separator (see Figure 11-41).
A separator is a list box item that cannot be selected. The ListBoxItem class provides the
IsSelectable property to configure whether or not an item can be selected. You can easily add
a separator by adding a Rectangle shape with a height of 1 pixel to a list box item. You should
add a margin to either the rectangle shape or list box item. In this case, it does not matter which,
because the item will not be selectable and will never be highlighted. You should gray out the
separator to indicate that is not selectable. It is a good idea to pack all this in a custom list box
item called SeparatorListBoxItem (see Listing 11-31) to have a reusable component.

Listing 11-31. *A Reusable Separator List Box Item*

```
using System;
using Microsoft.SPOT;
using Microsoft.SPOT.Presentation.Controls;
using Microsoft.SPOT.Presentation.Shapes;
using Microsoft.SPOT.Presentation.Media;

namespace Kuehner.SPOT.Presentation.Controls
{
    public class SeparatorListBoxItem : ListBoxItem
    {
        public SeparatorListBoxItem()
        {
            Rectangle rect = new Rectangle();
            rect.Height = 1;
            rect.Stroke = new Pen(Colors.Gray);
            this.Child = rect;
            this.IsSelectable = false;
            this.SetMargin(2);
        }
    }
}
```

Item 0. Hello World.
Item 1. Hello World.
Item 2. Hello World.
Item 3. Hello World.
Item 4. Hello World.
Item 5. Hello World.
Item 6. Hello World.
Item 7. Hello World.
Item 8. Hello World.
Item 9. Hello World.

Figure 11-41. *A list with separators*

List Boxes with a Background

In the previous chapter, you learned how to create controls with a background and how to create transparent controls by setting the background to null.

The ListBox class is derived from ContentControl and provides its own background. In order to create a list box with a background, you need to add a background to the parent control of the list box (e.g., the window) and set the background of the list box to null or to set the background of the list box directly.

Further, you need to set the background of your list box items to null, because a ListBoxItem is a content control and, therefore, has its own background, which is set by default to white. The HighlightableListBoxItem element has a transparent background when it is not selected. It is important to make the background transparent in the OnIsSelectedChanged method and to do so at the beginning in the constructor.

But that's not enough. The ListBox class internally embeds a ScrollViewer control that holds all the list box items. A ScrollViewer is a content control and, therefore, provides its own white background by default. There are no properties for ScrollViewer, but you can get the ScrollViewer instance via the Child property of the list box.

Listing 11-32 demonstrates how to create a list box with a gradient color background, and Figure 11-42 shows how it looks.

Figure 11-42. *A list with a gradient color background*

Listing 11-32. *Creating a List with a Gradient Color Background*

```
using System;

using Microsoft.SPOT;
using Microsoft.SPOT.Input;
using Microsoft.SPOT.Presentation;
using Microsoft.SPOT.Presentation.Controls;
using Kuehner.SPOT.Presentation.Controls;
using Microsoft.SPOT.Presentation.Media;

namespace ListBoxBackgroundSample
{
    public class Program : Microsoft.SPOT.Application
    {
        public static void Main()
        {
            Program myApplication = new Program();

            Window mainWindow = myApplication.CreateWindow();

            // Create the object that configures the GPIO pins to buttons.
            GPIOButtonInputProvider inputProvider =
                                            new GPIOButtonInputProvider(null);

            // Start the application
            myApplication.Run(mainWindow);
        }

        private Window mainWindow;

        public Window CreateWindow()
        {
            // Create a window object and set its size to the
            // size of the display.
            mainWindow = new Window();
            mainWindow.Height = SystemMetrics.ScreenHeight;
            mainWindow.Width = SystemMetrics.ScreenWidth;
            // Add a gradient color background to the window
            mainWindow.Background = new LinearGradientBrush(Colors.White,
                                                Colors.Red,
                                                0, 0,
                                                mainWindow.Width,
                                                mainWindow.Height);

            Font font = Resources.GetFont(Resources.FontResources.NinaB);
```

```
    // Create a list box control and add text items
    ListBox listBox = new ListBox();
    // make the list box transparent
    listBox.Background = null;
    // make the enclosed scroll viewer transparent also
    // we get the scroll viewer via the child property but
    // need to cast it to Control in order to clear the background
    ((Control)listBox.Child).Background = null;
    for (int i = 0; i < 10; ++i)
    {
        string str = "Item " + i.ToString() + ". Hello World.";
        ListBoxItem item = new HighlightableTextListBoxItem(font, str);
        listBox.Items.Add(item);
        if (i > 0 && i % 4 == 0)
            listBox.Items.Add(new SeparatorListBoxItem());
    }
    // Add the text control to the window.
    mainWindow.Child = listBox;

    // Set the window visibility to visible.
    mainWindow.Visibility = Visibility.Visible;

    // Let the user select items with the up and down buttons.
    Buttons.Focus(listBox);
    // Get notified when the selected item was changed.
    listBox.SelectionChanged +=
                new SelectionChangedEventHandler(listBox_SelectionChanged);
    // Get notified when a selected item was pressed
    // using the select button.
    listBox.AddHandler(Buttons.ButtonDownEvent,
                    new ButtonEventHandler(listBox_ButtonDown),
                    false);

    return mainWindow;
}

private void listBox_SelectionChanged(object sender,
                                    SelectionChangedEventArgs args)
{
    Debug.Print("Item " + args.SelectedIndex + " was selected.");
}
```

```
        private void listBox_ButtonDown(object sender, ButtonEventArgs args)
        {
            ListBox listBox = (ListBox)sender;
            if (args.Button == Button.Select)
                Debug.Print("Item " + listBox.SelectedIndex + " was pressed.");
        }
    }
}
```

Full-Size List Boxes and Centered Text

If you add the following line to the code in Listing 11-32 after the list box is instantiated, you will see a list box that looks like the one shown in Figure 11-43 and fills the entire screen width:

```
listBox.Child.Width = mainWindow.Width;
```

You must set not the list box width but the width of the list box's child element, that is, the enclosed scroll viewer. The list box always calculates its desired size depending on the embedded scroll viewer.

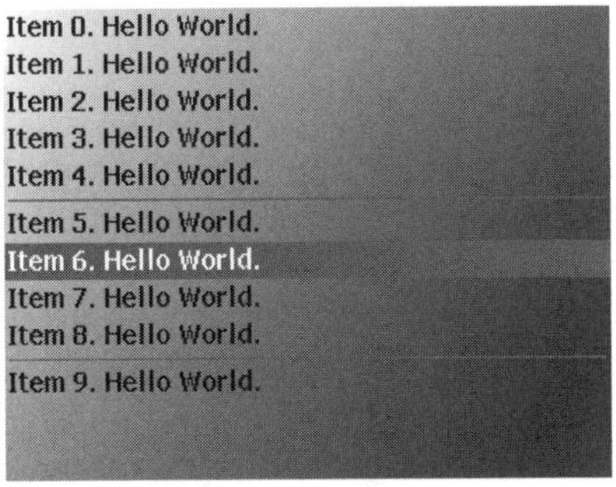

Figure 11-43. *A full-size list box*

If your list box needs to have center text like the one shown in Figure 11-44, you can add the following line to the constructor of HighlightableTextListBoxItem:

```
this.text.HorizontalAlignment = HorizontalAlignment.Center;
```

Instead of implementing this functionality in the constructor, you can set the alignment for each item individually. After you have created an item, you can set the horizontal alignment of its child. For a HighlightableTextListBoxItem instance, the text element is embedded as a child:

```
ListBoxItem item = new HighlightableTextListBoxItem(font, str);
item.Child.HorizontalAlignment = HorizontalAlignment.Center;
```

Item 0. Hello World.
Item 1. Hello World.
Item 2. Hello World.
Item 3. Hello World.
Item 4. Hello World.

Item 5. Hello World.
Item 6. Hello World.
Item 7. Hello World.
Item 8. Hello World.

Item 9. Hello World.

Figure 11-44. *A full-size list box with centered text*

Creating Items with Complex Content

Now that you have learned how to create and configure list boxes and derive custom list box items for general or special purposes, like highlighting selected items or special text items, you are able to create list boxes with complex content using all you learned about user interface elements in the previous sections.

To create multiple columns in a list box item, you should add a horizontal stack panel and populate it with different elements, such as text and images. You can set margins for the elements to separate them and use different alignments for each column.

The sample in Listing 11-33 builds a rather complex list box (shown in Figure 11-45). The first two items are simple text items followed by a separator. For the simple text items, we do not use the `HighlightableTextListBoxItem`; instead, we create the text manually to have full layout control, like setting a margin. We could also modify `HighlightableTextListBoxItem` to accept a `Text` element object. After the simple text items and one text item with icon, the list contains items with multiple columns using a vertical stack panel. The first column is right-aligned text, then an icon followed by left-aligned text. The next two items present a multiline text using a text flow element.

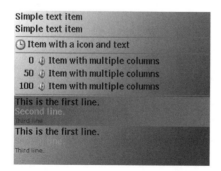

Figure 11-45. *Complex list box content*

Listing 11-33. *Building a Complex List Box*

```
using System;

using Microsoft.SPOT;
using Microsoft.SPOT.Input;
using Microsoft.SPOT.Presentation;
using Microsoft.SPOT.Presentation.Controls;
using Kuehner.SPOT.Presentation.Controls;
using Microsoft.SPOT.Presentation.Media;

namespace ComplexListBoxSample
{
    public class Program : Microsoft.SPOT.Application
    {
        public static void Main()
        {
            Program myApplication = new Program();

            Window mainWindow = myApplication.CreateWindow();

            // Create the object that configures the GPIO pins to buttons.
            GPIOButtonInputProvider inputProvider =
                                            new GPIOButtonInputProvider(null);

            // Start the application
            myApplication.Run(mainWindow);
        }

        private Window mainWindow;

        public Window CreateWindow()
        {
            // Create a window object and set its size to the
            // size of the display.
            mainWindow = new Window();
            mainWindow.Height = SystemMetrics.ScreenHeight;
            mainWindow.Width = SystemMetrics.ScreenWidth;
            // Add a gradient color background to the window
            mainWindow.Background = new LinearGradientBrush(Colors.White,
                                                    Colors.Red,
                                                    0, 0,
                                                    mainWindow.Width,
                                                    mainWindow.Height);
```

```
Font normalFont = Resources.GetFont(Resources.FontResources.NinaB);
Font smallFont = Resources.GetFont(Resources.FontResources.small);

// Create a list box control and add text items
ListBox listBox = new ListBox();
// set the width so that it fills the entire screen
listBox.Child.Width = mainWindow.Width;
// make the list box transparent
listBox.Background = null;
// make the enclosed scroll viewer transparent also
// we get the scroll viewer via the child property but
// need to cast it to Control in order to clear the background
((Control)listBox.Child).Background = null;

// Add simple text items
for (int i = 0; i < 2; ++i)
{
    string str = "Simple text item";
    Text text = new Text(normalFont, str);
    text.SetMargin(2);
    ListBoxItem item = new HighlightableListBoxItem(text);
    listBox.Items.Add(item);
}

// Add a separator
listBox.Items.Add(new SeparatorListBoxItem());

// Add a text item with icon
{
    // Create the stack panel to align the elements
    StackPanel stackPanel = new StackPanel(Orientation.Horizontal);

    // Icon
    Bitmap bmp = Resources.GetBitmap(Resources.BitmapResources.Clock);
    // Make the bitmap transparent using
    // the color of the top left corner pixel.
    // Therefore the image should not be in the Bitmap and Jpeg format
    // because that requires to create a copy in order to make it
    // transparent. Use Gif instead.
    bmp.MakeTransparent(bmp.GetPixel(0, 0));
    Image image = new Image(bmp);
    image.SetMargin(2); // set a margin to separate the image
    // vertically center the icon within the item
    image.VerticalAlignment = VerticalAlignment.Center;
    stackPanel.Children.Add(image);
```

```
    // Text
    Text text = new Text(normalFont, "Item with an icon and text");
    text.SetMargin(2); // set margin to separate the text
    // vertically center the icon within the item
    text.VerticalAlignment = VerticalAlignment.Center;
    stackPanel.Children.Add(text);

    // Create a highlightable list box item
    ListBoxItem item = new HighlightableListBoxItem(stackPanel);
    listBox.Items.Add(item);
}

// Add a separator
listBox.Items.Add(new SeparatorListBoxItem());

// Add two items with multiple columns
// use i to add a right aligned number to the first column
for(int i = 0; i <= 100; i += 50)
{
    //create the stack panel to align the elements
    StackPanel stackPanel = new StackPanel(Orientation.Horizontal);

    // Add right aligned text
    Text text1 = new Text(normalFont, i.ToString());
    text1.Width = 30;
    text1.SetMargin(2); // set margin to separate the text
    text1.TextAlignment = TextAlignment.Right;
    // vertically center the icon within the item
    text1.VerticalAlignment = VerticalAlignment.Center;
    stackPanel.Children.Add(text1);

    // Icon
    Bitmap bmp = Resources.GetBitmap(Resources.BitmapResources.Audio);
    // Make the bitmap transparent using
    // the color of the top left corner pixel.
    // Therefore the image should not be in the Bitmap and Jpeg format
    // because that requires to create a copy in order to make it
    // transparent. Use Gif instead.
    bmp.MakeTransparent(bmp.GetPixel(0, 0));
    Image image = new Image(bmp);
    image.SetMargin(2); // set a margin to separate the image
    // vertically center the icon within the item
    image.VerticalAlignment = VerticalAlignment.Center;
    stackPanel.Children.Add(image);
```

```
        // Text
        Text text = new Text(normalFont, "Item with multiple columns");
        text.SetMargin(2); // set margin to separate the text
        // vertically center the icon within the item
        text.VerticalAlignment = VerticalAlignment.Center;
        stackPanel.Children.Add(text);

        // Create a highlightable list box item
        ListBoxItem item = new HighlightableListBoxItem(stackPanel);
        listBox.Items.Add(item);
}

// Add a separator
listBox.Items.Add(new SeparatorListBoxItem());

// Add two multiline text items
for (int i = 0; i < 2; ++i)
{
    TextFlow textFlow = new TextFlow();
    textFlow.TextRuns.Add("This is the first line.",
                          normalFont,
                          Colors.Black);
    textFlow.TextRuns.Add(TextRun.EndOfLine);
    textFlow.TextRuns.Add("Second line.", normalFont, Colors.Green);
    textFlow.TextRuns.Add(TextRun.EndOfLine);
    textFlow.TextRuns.Add("Third line.", smallFont, Colors.Red);
    textFlow.SetMargin(2);

    ListBoxItem item = new HighlightableListBoxItem(textFlow);
    listBox.Items.Add(item);
}

// Add the text control to the window.
mainWindow.Child = listBox;

// Set the window visibility to visible.
mainWindow.Visibility = Visibility.Visible;

// Let the user select items with the up and down buttons.
Buttons.Focus(listBox);
// Get notified when the selected item was changed.
listBox.SelectionChanged +=
            new SelectionChangedEventHandler(listBox_SelectionChanged);
// Get notified when a selected item was pressed
// using the select button.
listBox.AddHandler(Buttons.ButtonDownEvent,
                new ButtonEventHandler(listBox_ButtonDown),
```

```
                                    false);

        return mainWindow;
    }

    private void listBox_SelectionChanged(object sender,
                                        SelectionChangedEventArgs args)
    {
        Debug.Print("Item " + args.SelectedIndex + " was selected.");
    }

    private void listBox_ButtonDown(object sender, ButtonEventArgs args)
    {
        ListBox listBox = (ListBox)sender;
        if (args.Button == Button.Select)
            Debug.Print("Item " + listBox.SelectedIndex + " was pressed.");
    }
  }
}
```

This section showed you how to build complex list boxes. You can expand on this example and even place several list boxes or other additional elements on your screen using stack panels.

The next section covers handling user input, such as button-click events, to build an interactive display that responds to user input.

Handling User Input and Events

The common way for the user to get in touch with a device is via GPIO hardware buttons on the device. The WPF controls can handle button events and respond to the input. You already saw all the built-in, ready-to-use interactive elements of the .NET Micro Framework such as ListBox, ScrollViewer, and TextFlow. This section describes how to bind hardware events to WPF elements and how event routing works.

If you create a fresh .NET Micro Framework WPF window application project, it will generate a GPIOButtonInputProvider class automatically. This class is instantiated in the main method of your program, right before main message loop starts and the main window is displayed.

```
public static void Main()
{
    Program myApplication = new Program();

    Window mainWindow = myApplication.CreateWindow();

    // Create the object that configures the GPIO pins to buttons.
    GPIOButtonInputProvider inputProvider = new GPIOButtonInputProvider(null);

    // Start the application
    myApplication.Run(mainWindow);
}
```

This class is responsible for mapping the GPIO input signals to button events and providing them for the WPF components (see Listing 11-34). The GPIO signals are caught with the InterruptPort class and mapped to buttons for the WPF and provided to the focused element. If the focused element does not handle the button event, the event bubbles up to each of its parents until one element handles it.

Listing 11-34. *A GPIO Button Input Provider*

```
using System;
using Microsoft.SPOT;
using Microsoft.SPOT.Input;
using Microsoft.SPOT.Hardware;
using Microsoft.SPOT.Presentation;

namespace ComplexListBoxSample
{
    // This class dispatches input events from emulated GPIO pins (0-4)
    // to Input.Button events. It is specific to the SDK's sample emulator;
    // if you use this code, please update this class to reflect the design
    // of your hardware.
    public sealed class GPIOButtonInputProvider
    {
        public readonly Dispatcher Dispatcher;

        private ButtonPad[] buttons;
        private ReportInputCallback callback;
        private InputProviderSite site;
        private PresentationSource source;

        private delegate bool ReportInputCallback(InputReport inputReport);

        // This class maps GPIOs to Buttons processable by
        // Microsoft.SPOT.Presentation
        public GPIOButtonInputProvider(PresentationSource source)
        {
            // Set the input source.
            this.source = source;
            // Register our object as an input source with the input manager
            // and get back an InputProviderSite object which forwards the
            // input report to the input manager,
            // which then places the input in the staging area.
            site = InputManager.CurrentInputManager.RegisterInputProvider(this);
            // Create a delegate that refers to the InputProviderSite
            // object's ReportInput method
            callback = new ReportInputCallback(site.ReportInput);
            Dispatcher = Dispatcher.CurrentDispatcher;
```

```
    // Allocate button pads and assign the (emulated) hardware pins as input
    // from specific buttons.
    ButtonPad[] buttons = new ButtonPad[]
    {
        // Associate the buttons to the pins as setup
        // in the emulator/hardware
        new ButtonPad(this, Button.Left  , Cpu.Pin.GPIO_Pin0),
        new ButtonPad(this, Button.Right , Cpu.Pin.GPIO_Pin1),
        new ButtonPad(this, Button.Up    , Cpu.Pin.GPIO_Pin2),
        new ButtonPad(this, Button.Select, Cpu.Pin.GPIO_Pin3),
        new ButtonPad(this, Button.Down  , Cpu.Pin.GPIO_Pin4),
    };

    this.buttons = buttons;
}

// The emulated device provides a button pad containing five buttons
// for user input. This class represents the button pad.
internal class ButtonPad
{
    private Button button;
    private InterruptPort port;
    private GPIOButtonInputProvider sink;

    // Construct the object. Set this class to handle the emulated
    // hardware's button interrupts.
    public ButtonPad(GPIOButtonInputProvider sink,
                     Button button,
                     Cpu.Pin pin)
    {
        this.sink = sink;
        this.button = button;

        // When this GPIO pin is true, call the Interrupt method.
        port = new InterruptPort(pin, true, Port.ResistorMode.PullUp,
                                 Port.InterruptMode.InterruptEdgeBoth);
        port.OnInterrupt += new GPIOInterruptEventHandler(this.Interrupt);
    }

    void Interrupt(Cpu.Pin port, bool state, TimeSpan time)
    {
        RawButtonActions action = state ?
                    RawButtonActions.ButtonUp : RawButtonActions.ButtonDown;

        RawButtonInputReport report = new RawButtonInputReport(sink.source,
                                                               time,
                                                               button,
                                                               action);
```

```
                    // Queue the button press to the input provider site.
                    sink.Dispatcher.BeginInvoke(sink.callback, report);
                }
            }
        }
    }
```

This `GPIOButtonInputProvider` class uses a button pad to associate the pins to buttons. By default, this class uses the pin configuration of the emulator. You need to associate the particular pins of your device as described in the device manual to buttons. The button pin associations for the emulator look like this:

```
ButtonPad[] buttons = new ButtonPad[]
{
    // Associate the buttons to the pins as setup
    // in the emulator/hardware
    new ButtonPad(this, Button.Left  , Cpu.Pin.GPIO_Pin0),
    new ButtonPad(this, Button.Right , Cpu.Pin.GPIO_Pin1),
    new ButtonPad(this, Button.Up    , Cpu.Pin.GPIO_Pin2),
    new ButtonPad(this, Button.Select, Cpu.Pin.GPIO_Pin3),
    new ButtonPad(this, Button.Down  , Cpu.Pin.GPIO_Pin4),
};
```

Your device might have more or fewer buttons on its surface than listed here; the buttons represented by the `Button` enumeration in Listing 11-35 are applicable.

Listing 11-35. *Possible Buttons*

```
namespace Microsoft.SPOT.Input
{
    public enum Button
    {
        None = 0,
        Menu = 1,
        Select = 2,
        Up = 3,
        Down = 4,
        Left = 5,
        Right = 6,
        Play = 7,
        Pause = 8,
        FastForward = 9,
        Rewind = 10,
        Stop = 11,
        Back = 12,
        Last = 13,
        Home = 13,
    }
}
```

The built-in scrollable components only respond to Up, Down, Right, and Left. You already learned how to register an event handler for the Select button to be notified if a selected list box item is pressed. Further, you can display a menu for your page if the Menu button is clicked; go to the previous menu page if the Back button is clicked; or use the Home button to go to your start screen. This requires you to provide the buttons on your device surface and connect them to GPIO input pins. It is up to you to map the GPIO input pins to the predefined button commands with your custom input provider. That means, with the WPF, you install event handlers not for particular pins but for the buttons, such as Button.Menu or Button.Up.

In order to get a notification when a button is clicked for your focused text flow element, you need to add the following lines:

```
textFlow.AddHandler(Buttons.ButtonDownEvent,
                new ButtonEventHandler(textFlow_ButtonDown),
                false // handledEventsToo
                );
```

You can also add the handler to your main window instead of to a particular element, in order to get the events regardless of which child has the focus. It is also possible to trigger to the ButtonUpEvent to be notified when a button is released. In the previous code, there is a boolean parameter called handledEventsToo. This flag indicates whether you want to get handled events too. If this paramter is false, you will not get the Up, Down, Right, and Left events for a TextFlow element, because this element handles these events (it marks these events as handled even if it did not need to scroll). The Select key is not handled, so you will get it all the time. If you want to get all events, set this parameter to true.

The following code shows an event handler for ButtonDownEvent:

```
private void textFlow_ButtonDown(object sender, ButtonEventArgs args)
{
    Debug.Print("Button: " + args.Button);
}
```

You can determine which button was clicked with args.Button. The sender parameter does not describe the focused element: it is the element to which the event handler was added, for example, the TextFlow object or main window. The element with the currect input focus can be determinded with Buttons.FocusedElement.

Creating Custom UI Elements

The following sections describe how to create custom WPF user interface elements tailored to your particular needs by extending the built-in elements or writing an element from scratch.

Choosing the Right Base Class

To create custom user interface elements, you can either extend existing ones or write custom elements from scratch. Before you start, you should be clear how your element should appear and behave, so that you can choose the right base class. You should derive owner-drawn elements from the most lightweight UIElement class possible; start at the top of the hierarchy to choose the class. If your owner-drawn element should render a background, select Control as the base class. If your element should have child elements, choose ContentControl if you do not require child element arrangement. Use the Panel class or a subclass of it to use or implement custom child positioning.

Measuring and Arranging Elements

During the layout process, the virtual MeasureOverride method is called for each element to tell an element the size that is available for it to occupy and to allow the element to request the dimensions that it desires. This method accepts the available width and height and returns the desired size of an element. A Text element implements this method to calculate and return the size needed to display its text, while an Image element returns the size of the image. A ContentElement object returns the desired size of its child element by calling the MeasureOverride method of its child element. To let your element fill the entire available space, set the desired size to the available size:

```
protected virtual void MeasureOverride(int availableWidth,
                                       int availableHeight,
                                       out int desiredWidth,
                                       out int desiredHeight);
```

After the system knows the desired sizes of the elements, it calls the virtual ArrangeOverride method to let the element know the final size allocated for this component. A Panel component, for example, will use this method to arrange its child elements. You can further allocate and initialize objects that depend on the element's size like so:

```
protected virtual void ArrangeOverride(int arrangeWidth, int arrangeHeight);
```

Rendering Owner-Drawn Elements

After all elements are measured and arranged, they need to be rendered on the display. This is done with the virtual method OnRender:

```
public virtual void OnRender(DrawingContext dc);
```

The method accepts a DrawingContext object (see Listing 11-36) that enables you to draw on the element's client area. The top-left corner of your element has the coordinates (0, 0). You can get the render size with the ActualWidth and ActualHeight properties or with the void GetRenderSize(out int width, out int height) method.

The following code shows an OnRender implementation that will render an ellipse in the element's client area:

```
public override void OnRender(DrawingContext dc)
{
    base.OnRender(dc);
    dc.DrawEllipse(null, // brush: filling not supported
                   new Pen(Colors.Blue),   // pen
                   this.ActualWidth / 2,   // x
                   this.ActualHeight / 2,  // y
                   this.ActualWidth / 2,   // x radius
                   this.ActualHeight / 2); // y radius
}
```

Listing 11-36. *The Microsoft.SPOT.Presentation.Media.DrawingContext Class*

```
using Microsoft.SPOT;
using System;

namespace Microsoft.SPOT.Presentation.Media
{
    public class DrawingContext : DispatcherObject
    {
        public DrawingContext(Bitmap bmp);
        public DrawingContext(int width, int height);

        public Bitmap Bitmap { get; }
        public int Height { get; }
        public int Width { get; }

        public void BlendImage(Bitmap source, int destinationX, int destinationY,
                               int sourceX, int sourceY,
                               int sourceWidth, int sourceHeight,
                               ushort opacity);
        public void Clear();
        public void DrawEllipse(Brush brush, Pen pen, int x, int y,
                                int xRadius, int yRadius);
        public void DrawImage(Bitmap source, int x, int y);
        public void DrawImage(Bitmap source, int destinationX, int destinationY,
                              int sourceX, int sourceY,
                              int sourceWidth, int sourceHeight);
        public void DrawLine(Pen pen, int x0, int y0, int x1, int y1);
        public void DrawPolygon(Brush brush, Pen pen, int[] pts);
        public void DrawRectangle(Brush brush, Pen pen, int x, int y,
                                  int width, int height);
        public void DrawText(string text, Font font, Color color, int x, int y);
        public bool DrawText(ref string text, Font font, Color color, int x, int y,
                             int width, int height,
                             TextAlignment alignment, TextTrimming trimming);
        public void GetClippingRectangle(out int x, out int y,
                                         out int width, out int height);
        public void PopClippingRectangle();
        public void PushClippingRectangle(int x, int y, int width, int height);
        public void SetPixel(Color color, int x, int y);
        public void Translate(int dx, int dy);
    }
}
```

Updating Element Properties

Your custom element might provide some properties for configuration. If you're assigning a new value to a property that requires the element to repaint, you need to call the Invalidate method to notify the element that it needs to be repainted.

```
public Color TextColor
{
    get{ return this.textColor; }
    set
    {
        this.textColor = value;
        Invalidate();
    }
}
```

If changing a property affects the size of the element, such as the font or text content properties, you need to call InvalidateMeasure to tell the component and its parents that the desired size has changed.

Properties that change the arrangement of a component need to call InvalidateArrange to tell the component and its child elements that the layout has changed, like you do, for example, with the HorizontalAlignment property.

Handling Events

The UIElement class provides two virtual methods that you can override in your custom element to handle button events from the user: OnButtonDown and OnButtonUp. If you handle an event, you should mark it as handled to avoid unnecessary further event routing and to let the parent elements know that it was handled.

```
protected override void OnButtonDown(ButtonEventArgs e)
{
    if(e.Button == Button.Left)
    {
        ...
        e.Handled = true; // mark as handled to avoid bubbling up
    }
}
```

Summary

This chapter was divided in two sections. The first section described how to obtain the screen resolution and how to use the Bitmap class to render common graphics primitives, bitmaps, and text with different colors, opacity, and fonts to the display.

The second section toured the WPF and described how to build rich user interfaces that respond to user input. This section of the chapter presented the various user interface elements, and you learned when and how to use, measure, and arrange the elements. You now know the differences between shapes, controls, content controls, and panels. This chapter showed you how to display elements with transparent or color gradient backgrounds, and we produced rich list box menus and derived custom list box items tailored for our needs. You also now know how to map GPIO buttons to button events and how to register button events to handle user input, and you understand how the event routing works. Finally, this chapter demonstrated how you can derive your custom elements, and you should be able to choose the right base class to meet your particular needs.

You are now able to write graphical user interfaces that run on the different .NET Micro Framework platforms with displays having different screen resolutions and color depths—although, currently, the two platforms provide display support only for the QVGA (320×240 pixels) resolution. The WPF especially helps you to write screen-resolution-independent applications that dynamically use all the available display size.

Now that you have a good understanding about the entire base class library of the .NET Micro Framework, we will proceed to the final chapter, which shows you how to use, configure, and extend the hardware emulator of the .NET Micro Framework for rapid prototyping in a way that was not possible with embedded programming until now.

CHAPTER 12

Hardware Emulation

In this chapter, you will learn how to describe your hardware platform to simulate physical hardware with software using the extensible emulator of the .NET Micro Framework. You will learn how to write and use custom emulators. We will configure the emulator using code and using XML emulator configuration files and compare these two methods. This chapter describes all the rich configuration features; it includes detailed configuration files, covers debugging custom emulators, and describes advanced configuration options.

Why Use Hardware Emulation?

The extensible hardware emulator is provided with the .NET Micro Framework and allows you to use software to simulate different hardware platforms on your development PC. This approach offers you a rapid prototype mechanism and the possibility to start developing your software a long time before the complete hardware becomes available. A prototype based on the extensible hardware emulator will surely influence the design of the final physical platform and peripheral components as well. The extensible hardware emulator for the .NET Micro Framework opens completely new possibilities for embedded development.

Which Hardware Can Be Emulated?

The emulator has built-in support for hardware components accessible with the .NET Micro Framework. You can simulate communication components such as GPIO ports, SPI devices, I^2C devices, and serial ports. In addition, you can simulate an LCD, RAM and flash memory, and a battery cell, as well as configure the processor speed and much more.

User Interfaces for Emulators

The emulator is a PC application, and its graphical user interface is arbitrary. Normally, an emulator has a graphical user interface for Microsoft Windows programmed with Windows Forms in .NET. Then again, an emulator might be a console application. The emulated hardware does not need to look the same as the real hardware and does not need exactly the same user interface as the original. You can also add several emulator components to the emulator's user interface that you might not want to include in the real device; for example, you can provide additional components for debugging purposes such as displaying information or data input.

The Extensible Emulator

A hardware emulator for the .NET Micro Framework consists, as I already said, of a .NET PC application for Microsoft Windows. This application creates the user interface, if necessary, and starts the emulator in its own thread. An emulator consists of various emulator components. The most necessary components are loaded automatically by the emulator, and you can configure them or replace the existing ones with custom components. Further, built-in and configurable components are provided with the .NET Micro Framework SDK. Your custom components can either extend the provided components or be created from scratch. The configuration and registration of custom components takes place via XML in an emulator configuration file; this configuration file is parsed by the configuration engine. Programmatic registration and config-uring components with code are also possible. However, the more flexible XML configuration is preferable, since you can easily make changes to the configuration file, without recompiling the emulator application.

An emulator is, preferably, developed as a .NET application with Visual Studio. When building an emulator application, the emulator is automatically registered in the registry. The emulator, instead of a real device, can be selected by other .NET Micro Framework applications in the project properties to execute and debug the applications on this emulator.

Getting Started with the Emulator

For a minimal emulator, you do not need much; a .NET Windows console application is enough. The project must reference the `Microsoft.SPOT.Emulator.dll` assembly to use the `Emulator` class that resides in the `Microsoft.SPOT.Emulator` namespace. In the `Main` method (the entry point) of the emulator application, the emulator will be created and started. That's all. The code of that minimal emulator is shown in Listing 12-1.

Listing 12-1. *A Minimal Emulator in a Console Application*

```
using System;
using Microsoft.SPOT.Emulator;

namespace MinimalConsoleEmulator
{
    class Program
    {
        static void Main()
        {
            new Emulator().Start();
        }
    }
}
```

You will get an error when running this project, as you would when executing a library project that requires an executable to run. The error message tells you that the emulator has no .NET Micro Framework application to run. When you select a registered emulator within Visual Studio for a .NET Micro Framework, Visual Studio starts the selected registered emulator to run the current .NET Micro Framework application project.

Later in this chapter, you will see how you can specify a .NET Micro Framework application to run on an emulator, an ability you will need to debug a custom emulator project.

Emulator Project Templates

Fortunately, the .NET Micro Framework SDK provides and installs a project template (see Figure 12-1) for an emulator for Visual Studio. This template creates an emulator project (see Figure 12-2) for a Windows Forms application with an empty main form and code to start the emulator, as shown in Listing 12-2.

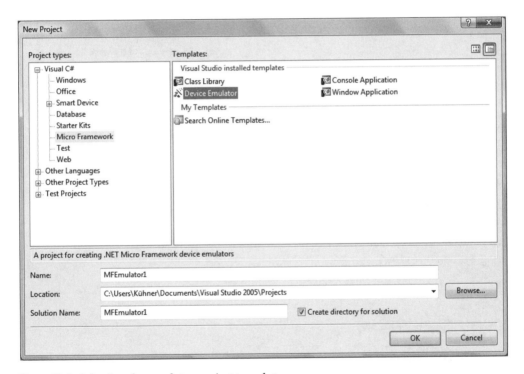

Figure 12-1. *Selecting the emulator project template*

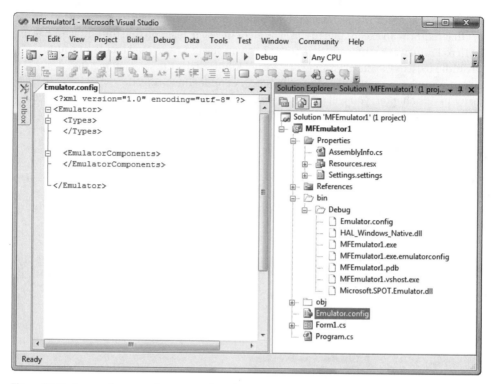

Figure 12-2. *An emulator project created with the emulator project template*

Listing 12-2. *The Emulator Class Created by the Emulator Project Template*

```
using System;
using System.Collections.Generic;
using System.Windows.Forms;
using System.Threading;

using Microsoft.SPOT.Emulator;

namespace MFEmulator1
{
    class Program : Emulator
    {
        public override void SetupComponent()
        {
            base.SetupComponent();
        }

        public override void InitializeComponent()
        {
            base.InitializeComponent();
```

```
        // Start the UI in its own thread.
        Thread uiThread = new Thread(StartForm);
        uiThread.SetApartmentState(ApartmentState.STA);
        uiThread.Start();
    }

    public override void UninitializeComponent()
    {
        base.UninitializeComponent();

        // The emulator is stopped. Close the WinForm UI.
        Application.Exit();
    }

    private void StartForm()
    {
        // Some initial setup for the WinForm UI
        Application.EnableVisualStyles();
        Application.SetCompatibleTextRenderingDefault(false);

        // Start the WinForm UI. Run() returns when the form is closed.
        Application.Run(new Form1(this));

        // When the user closes the WinForm UI, stop the emulator.
        Stop();
    }

    /// <summary>
    /// The main entry point for the application.
    /// </summary>
    static void Main()
    {
        (new Program()).Start();
    }
    }
}
```

A fresh emulator project contains the following files:

- `Program.cs`: Contains the entry point of the emulator application (`Main` method) and the Program class that extends the base `Emulator` class

- `Form1.cs` (and `Form1.Designer.cs`): Contains the graphical user interface for the emulator as a `System.Windows.Forms` form

- `Emulator.config`: The XML emulator configuration file

When building the project, the emulator is registered automatically in the registry with the project name and is then available for use by other .NET Micro Framework applications. How the registration exactly works and how you can customize it will be discussed later.

■**Caution**   The path of the compiled emulator executable is also stored in the registry. This executable path changes, for example, when you switch between Debug and Release compilation. Since the information of all registered emulators is collected when opening a .NET Micro Framework project, an already open .NET Micro Framework project must be closed and reopened when an emulator's registration has changed. That step is not necessary if the emulator in use is newly compiled, since the executable path and emulator name did not change.

Naturally, the emulator XML configuration file is taken into the emulator project as well. The file is called `Emulator.config`, and when building the project, the file is copied by the build process to the output directory as `<Emulator executable name>.emulatorconfig`.

Although implementing your own emulator class is not necessary, a custom emulator class allows additional configurations. Your own emulator class needs to inherit from the `Microsoft.SPOT.Emulator.Emulator` class. It is an emulator component and inherits from `Microsoft.SPOT.Emulator.EmulatorComponent`. Therefore, you can override the virtual methods `SetupComponent`, `InitializeComponent`, and `UninitializeComponent` to add custom code.

Emulator Components

A hardware emulator for the .NET Micro Framework is an emulator component and contains additional emulator components for the various hardware modules and system components. The emulator component approach makes the emulator modular, exactly the same as the physical hardware.

There are three ways to use emulator components:

Using and configuring existing components: If the hardware system that you want to emulate contains common hardware modules, you might use and configure an emulator component provided with the .NET Micro Framework. In that case, you describe the type name in the XML configuration file of the emulator, and you can specify, if necessary, further initialization and configuration information. The configuration file is then loaded and parsed by the emulator application. The indicated type names of the emulator components are read, and the appropriate components are loaded, created, and initialized according to the parameters in the configuration file.

Extending existing components: You can extend an existing component by simply deriving a subclass from it and implementing new functionality. The extended component is then added and parameterized with the XML configuration file like a built-in one.

Programming components from scratch: If no existing emulator component can be used or extended, you can write an emulator component from scratch. Your new custom emulator component inherits then from the `EmulatorComponent` class, and it can use services of existing built-in hardware components. For example, you might need an emulator component for a measuring device, which is interfaced via the serial port.

The EmulatorComponent Class

All emulator components are subclasses of the abstract EmulatorComponent base class (see Listing 12-3). An emulator component, which is loaded over the XML configuration file, must possess a parameterless default constructor. This constructor must perform all necessary initializations, so that the component is in a valid state, even if no further parameters are present in the configuration file for initializing the component.

An emulator component can be identified uniquely with its ComponentId property. This ID must be unique within the emulator. If this property is not specified in the configuration file for a component, it will be, by default, the class name of the component followed by a random global unique ID (GUID). The ID for an emulator component can be assigned only once. A second attempt to assign an ID to the ComponentId property would result in an exception.

The EmulatorComponent class possesses five virtual methods, which you can overwrite for further custom configuration. You can override the Configure method, if you require a complete custom parsing of the XML section for a component. The default implementation causes the data to be parsed by the configuration engine. Such an intervention is not necessary in most cases, since the configuration engine is already very efficient and provides a rich configuration mechanism.

The SetupComponent method of a component is called after the component is loaded, initialized, and added to the emulator.

The InitializeComponent method of a component is called as soon as *all* components are properly set up—that means loaded, initialized, and added to the emulator.

In the UninitializeComponent method, you can add clean-up code that will be executed when the component is no longer used, that is, after removing the component from the emulator when, for example, the emulator shuts down.

The IsReplaceableBy method controls whether an already existing component in the emulator can be replaced by another component. Components can be added manually before the analysis of the configuration file if the LoadDefaultComponents method of the Emulator class is overwritten. The standard implementation of IsReplaceableBy of the EmulatorComponent class returns the value false. Most of the components provided with the .NET Micro Framework SDK permit the respective component to be replaced by another component of the same type or a subclass of it. For example, an emulator can have only one memory manager, so the memory manager created in the default implementation of LoadDefaultComponents can be replaced via the XML configuration by any component that is a memory manager or a subclass of it.

Listing 12-3. *The Microsoft.SPOT.Emulator.EmulatorComponent Class*

```
using System;
using System.Xml;

namespace Microsoft.SPOT.Emulator
{
    public abstract class EmulatorComponent
    {
        public EmulatorComponent();
```

```
        public string ComponentId { get; set; }
        public Emulator Emulator { get; }
        public bool InvokeRequired { get; }

        public IAsyncResult BeginInvoke(Delegate method);
        public IAsyncResult BeginInvoke(Delegate method, params object[] args);
        public virtual void Configure(XmlReader reader);
        public object EndInvoke(IAsyncResult asyncResult);
        public virtual void InitializeComponent();
        public object Invoke(Delegate method);
        public object Invoke(Delegate method, params object[] args);
        public virtual bool IsReplaceableBy(EmulatorComponent ec);
        public virtual void SetupComponent();
        protected void ThrowIfNotConfigurable();
        protected void ThrowIfNotSetup();
        public virtual void UninitializeComponent();
    }
}
```

If you call the ThrowIfNotConfigurable method, an exception will be thrown if the emulator and all its components are already configured. With this method, you can ensure, in the setter method of a property, that the property value may not be further changed at runtime after the emulator was configured.

The overloads of the Invoke method enable you to synchronize data access of emulator components within different threads. With emulators that have a graphical user interface (GUI), the GUI and the emulator run in two different threads. You will see concrete samples when discussing the various emulator components.

Sharing Reusable Emulator Components

There are several locations to place shared emulator components. First, there are the built-in components provided with the .NET Micro Framework; these are in the Microsoft.SPOT.Emulator. dll assembly in the directory C:\Program Files\Microsoft .NET Micro Framework\v2.0.3036\ Tools (depending on the framework and Windows language version). Since this assembly must be referenced by each emulator, it is always automatically copied locally into the emulator directory.

Custom emulator components can be placed in shared library assemblies. Shared assemblies with emulator components are class libraries for Windows and compiled with the full .NET Framework. You need to place them either in the same directory as the emulator or into the Global Assembly Cache (GAC). In order to be able to put an assembly into the GAC, you must sign it with the strong name tool (sn.exe) with a key pair and copy it with the GacUtil tool into the GAC. Components in the GAC can be used widely.

Additionally, you can compile your custom components into the executable main assembly of your emulator, in which case they cannot be used with other emulators. This approach is recommended only if a component is strongly bound to a special emulator and need not be shared and distributed.

Creating a New Library Project for Emulator Components

A component library is a class library assembly for the full .NET Framework that contains one or more emulator components.

When creating a new project, you need to select Class Library for Windows as the project type (see Figure 12-3). Assemblies with emulator components are used with emulators, and emulators are Windows applications for the full .NET Framework. Therefore, the assemblies that an emulator references, such as the ones containing the emulator components, also need to be class libraries for Windows.

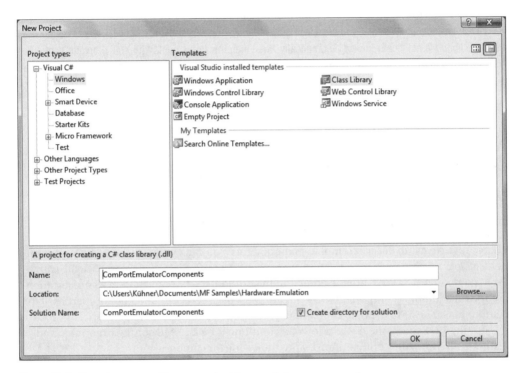

Figure 12-3. *Creating a new library project for emulator components*

In any case, the `Microsoft.SPOT.Emulator.dll` assembly in the `C:\Program Files\Microsoft .NET Micro Framework\v2.0.3036\Tools` directory (depending on the framework version and Windows language version) must be added as a reference to the project. In this assembly are all components that the .NET Micro Framework provides, which you can use as a base for your custom components. For each custom emulator component, you need to add a class that inherits either directly from `EmulatorComponent` or from a descendant of it.

```
using System;
using System.Threading;
using Microsoft.SPOT.Hardware;
using Microsoft.SPOT.Emulator;
using Microsoft.SPOT.Emulator.Time;
using Microsoft.SPOT.Emulator.Gpio;
```

```
namespace Kuehner.SPOT.Emulator
{
    public sealed class Oscillator : GpioPort
    {
    ...
    }
}
```

■**Note** A component library must always be in the same directory as an emulator or in the GAC. If the library is not referenced by an emulator, you need to ensure manually that it is in the correct directory or in the GAC, since the library is not locally copied automatically when the emulator is built. With XML emulator configuration, it is possible to use components from an assembly without having the emulator statically reference that assembly.

XML Configuration

In the following sections, we will explore XML configuration, and you will learn why and how to use XML configuration files to describe your emulator components.

Programmatic vs. XML Configuration

There are two ways to describe emulator components: you can configure the emulator components using program code or with an emulator configuration file, which is an XML file with a list of components to load into the emulator. In addition, the file can contain a configuration section for additional components, like pin numbers of GPIO ports and other properties of the components. The XML configuration is analyzed by the configuration engine.

Listing 12-4 shows the description of a component by an XML configuration file, and Listing 12-5 shows the configuration by program code for comparison.

Listing 12-4. *XML Configuration of Emulator Components*

```
<?xml version="1.0" encoding="utf-8" ?>
<Emulator>
  <Types>
    <GpioPort>Microsoft.SPOT.Emulator.Gpio.GpioPort</GpioPort>
    <ComPort>Kuehner.SPOT.Emulator.ComPortToPhysicalPcSerialPort,
            ComPortEmulatorComponents</ComPort>
    <MemoryManager>Microsoft.SPOT.Emulator.Memory.MemoryManager</MemoryManager>
    <RamManager>Microsoft.SPOT.Emulator.Memory.RamManager</RamManager>
  </Types>
```

```
<EmulatorComponents>

  <GpioPort id="myGpio">
    <Pin>5</Pin>
    <ModesAllowed>OutputPort</ModesAllowed>
    <ModesExpected>OutputPort</ModesExpected>
  </GpioPort>

  <ComPort>
    <ComPortHandle>Usart1</ComPortHandle>
    <Baudrate>9600</Baudrate>
    <PhysicalPortName>COM3</PhysicalPortName>
  </ComPort>

  <MemoryManager id="myMemManager">
    <RamManager type="RamManager" id="myRamManager">
      <Size format="HexNumber">200000</Size>
    </RamManager>
  </MemoryManager>

</EmulatorComponents>

</Emulator>
```

Listing 12-5. *Configuring Components with Code*

```csharp
using System;
using System.Windows.Forms;
using System.Threading;
using System.Globalization;

using Microsoft.SPOT.Hardware;
using Microsoft.SPOT.Emulator;
using Microsoft.SPOT.Emulator.Gpio;
using Microsoft.SPOT.Emulator.Com;
using Microsoft.SPOT.Emulator.Memory;
using Kuehner.SPOT.Emulator;

namespace MFEmulator1
{
    class Program : Emulator
    {
        public override void SetupComponent()
        {
            GpioPort gpioPort = new GpioPort();
            gpioPort.ComponentId = "myGpio";
            gpioPort.Pin = (Cpu.Pin)5;
```

```
            gpioPort.ModesAllowed = GpioPortMode.InputOutputPort;
            gpioPort.ModesExpected = GpioPortMode.InputOutputPort;
            RegisterComponent(gpioPort);


            ComPortToPhysicalPcSerialPort comPort =
                                            new ComPortToPhysicalPcSerialPort();
            comPort.ComPortHandle = new ComPortHandle(TransportType.Usart, 1);
            comPort.Baudrate = 9600;
            comPort.PhysicalPortName = "COM3";
            RegisterComponent(comPort);


            MemoryManager memoryManager = new MemoryManager();
            memoryManager.ComponentId = "myMemManager";
            RamManager ramManager = new RamManager();
            ramManager.ComponentId = "myRamManager";
            ramManager.Size = uint.Parse("200000", NumberStyles.HexNumber);
            memoryManager.RamManager = ramManager;
            RegisterComponent(memoryManager);


            base.SetupComponent();
        }
    ...
    }
}
```

You can see that, with the XML configuration, the superordinate elements refer to the respective type declarations and the subelements correspond to the public properties of the components. All components in a configuration file are loaded, configured, and registered when the emulator starts up. These components can be used in the same way as the components created by program code.

Configuration files offer a central place to describe the components of a system. Certain components can be easily replaced, or an emulator can behave differently with various configuration files, whereby each configuration can represent for example another stock keeping unit (SKU) of the hardware. Properties such as processor speed, memory capacity and layout, pin configuration, and so on can be easily changed without having several different emulator assemblies and without needing to recompile the emulator each time.

Registering Components

An XML file consists of two sections (see Listing 12-6). First, there is the Types section, which contains information to resolve types (the fully qualified type name and, optionally, an assembly name). In the EmulatorComponents section, the emulator components are listed and described.

Listing 12-6. *Sample XML Configuration File with the Section Types and EmulatorComponents*

```xml
<?xml version="1.0" encoding="utf-8"?>
<Emulator>
  <Types>
    <Display>Microsoft.SPOT.Emulator.Lcd.LcdDisplay</Display>
  </Types>

  <EmulatorComponents>
    <Display id="mydisplay">
      <Width>320</Width>
      <Height>240</Height>
      <BitsPerPixel>16</BitsPerPixel>
    </Display>
  </EmulatorComponents>
</Emulator>
```

In the configuration file in Listing 12-6, the `Types` section indicates that the emulator component class `Microsoft.SPOT.Emulator.Lcd.LcdDisplay` can be referenced and configured in the `EmulatorComponents` section as `Display`. The `Display` identifier is arbitrary—it is not necessary to name it like the type name of the component; it just must be the same in both sections, comparable to a local variable.

■Tip Ideally, the declaration of the component types in the `Types` section should contain no leading and trailing spaces and line breaks; they might prevent the type from being resolved.

In the `EmulatorComponents` section, a new emulator component is registered and configured with the `Display` tag. Even if there is no configurable property or you do not intend to specify further configurations, you must specify the tag so that the component will be created and registered. The empty `<Display/>` tag would create the component and initialize all the properties to the default values. The `id` parameter must be unique for all components. If this ID is missing, the component gets a random but unique ID that consists of the class name and GUID. You can address the component of Listing 12-6 with the known ID `mydisplay` after configuration from an emulator application.

Fundamental components, like a memory manager, are already registered by the default implementation of the emulator class in the `LoadDefaultComponents` virtual method, which ensured that the emulator will work properly even without a configuration file. When registering new components with a configuration file, the `IsReplaceableBy` method for each already registered component is called to check whether the existing component can be replaced by the new component. This guarantees that an emulator will not have several competing components that should exist only once, like memory managers.

Optionally, you can further configure a component in the XML file. In the previous example (Listing 12-6), the resolution and color depth of the LCD are specified. If you look at the `Microsoft.SPOT.Emulator.Lcd.LcdDisplay` class (see Listing 12-7) from the `Microsoft.SPOT.Emulator.dll` assembly, you can see that the configurable parameters (from Listing 12-6) exactly refer to the public properties, having read and write access. The default constructor of the class must ensure that the properties are initialized properly if the configuration is not specified in the XML configuration file, so the component is always in a valid state.

Listing 12-7. *The Microsoft.SPOT.Emulator.Lcd.LcdDisplay Class*

```
using Microsoft.SPOT.Emulator;
using System;

namespace Microsoft.SPOT.Emulator.Lcd
{
    public class LcdDisplay : EmulatorComponent
    {
        public LcdDisplay();
        protected LcdDisplay(int w, int h, int bpp);

        public int BitsPerPixel { get; set; }
        public int Height { get; set; }
        public int Width { get; set; }

        public event OnDevicePaintEventHandler OnDevicePaint;

        public override bool IsReplaceableBy(EmulatorComponent ec);
        public override void SetupComponent();
    }
}
```

■**Caution** You must not set the ID of an emulator component in the configuration file by its `ComponentId` property. You need to always set the component ID by the `id` parameter.

The Types section requires a deeper look; see Listing 12-8. This section is responsible for resolving the component types.

Listing 12-8. *Using Default Components from the Microsoft.SPOT.Emulator.dll Assembly*

```
<?xml version="1.0" encoding="utf-8"?>
<Emulator>
  <Types>
    <GpioPort>Microsoft.SPOT.Emulator.Gpio.GpioPort</GpioPort>
  </Types>
```

```
<EmulatorComponents>

<GpioPort id="Pin_Left">
  <Pin>0</Pin>
  <ModesExpected>InputOutputPort</ModesExpected>
  <ModesAllowed>InputOutputPort</ModesAllowed>
</GpioPort>

<GpioPort id="Pin_Right">
  <Pin>1</Pin>
  <ModesExpected>InputOutputPort</ModesExpected>
  <ModesAllowed>InputOutputPort</ModesAllowed>
</GpioPort>

</EmulatorComponents>
</Emulator>
```

As you can see in Listing 12-8, you can use and refer to a type defined in Types in the subsequent EmulatorComponents section several times. There, you can register and configure several components of the same type, so long as they have different IDs.

In both examples, already existing components from the Microsoft.SPOT.Emulator.dll assemblies were used. Therefore, indicating, in the Types section, only the fully qualified type name (including the namespace) was sufficient.

Now, if you need to load custom components, which are then obligatorily in another assembly or in the emulator assembly, you also need to specify the assembly name—even if a component is in the emulator application assembly. Listing 12-9 demonstrates how to load custom emulator components with a configuration file.

Listing 12-9. *Loading Custom Emulator Components with a Configuration File*

```
<Emulator>
  <Types>
    <TMP100>I2CTemperatureSensorSampleEmulator.TMP100Sensor,
            I2CTemperatureSensorSampleEmulator</TMP100>
  </Types>

  <EmulatorComponents>
    <TMP100 id="TMP100">
      <Address>72</Address>
    </TMP100>
  </EmulatorComponents>

</Emulator>
```

For the assembly name, you must not append the file extension (.exe or .dll). The assembly name mostly corresponds to the file name, but you can change it in the project properties on the Application page; see Figure 12-4.

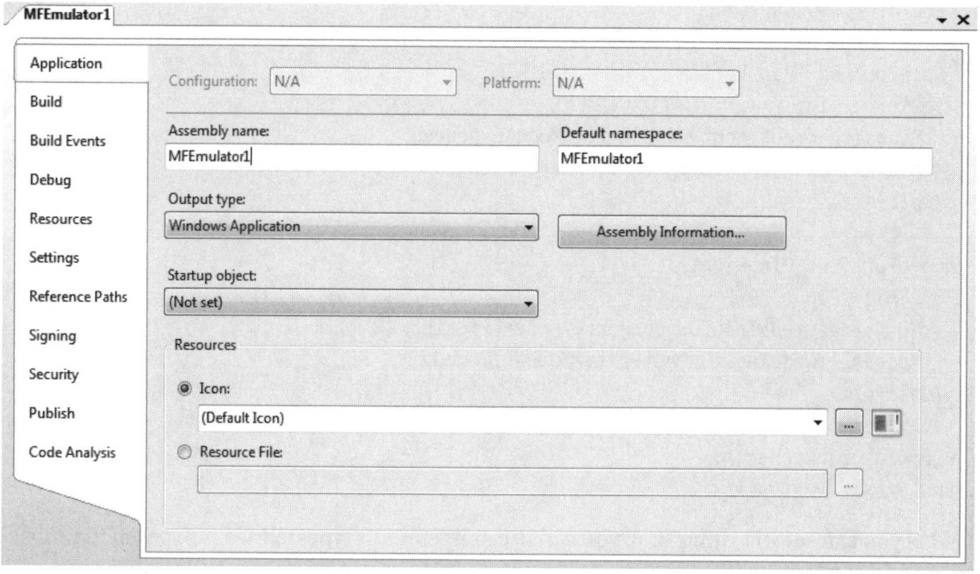

Figure 12-4. *Changing the name of an assembly*

The assembly can be described still more exactly by indicating the version number, culture, and public key token. Thus, the type information to load an emulator component type might look as follows:

```
<namespace>.<type name>, <assembly name>, [Version=1.0.0.0], [Culture=neutral],
[PublicKeyToken=1270f5f21e7f4192]
```

Finding and loading the data types and assemblies in the emulator take place with the standard .NET loading mechanism with the GetType method of the Type class and the GetType method of the loaded Microsoft.SPOT.Emulator assembly. The requirements for the physical memory location were already described in a previous section's discussion of sharing reusable emulator component libraries. A component, itself, can be placed in one of the following locations:

- The Microsoft.SPOT.Emulator.dll assembly

- The emulator's executable assembly

- A library assembly in the emulator directory

- An assembly in the GAC

For components provided in the Microsoft.SPOT.Emulator.dll assembly, which, therefore, do not require an assembly name indication in the Types section, you can also specify the data type directly. This allows you to omit the declaration in the Types section. For example, instead of the following lines

```xml
<?xml version="1.0" encoding="utf-8"?>
<Emulator>
  <Types>
    <GpioPort>Microsoft.SPOT.Emulator.Gpio.GpioPort</GpioPort>
  </Types>

  <EmulatorComponents>

  <GpioPort id="Pin_Left">
    <Pin>0</Pin>
    <ModesExpected>InputOutputPort</ModesExpected>
    <ModesAllowed>InputOutputPort</ModesAllowed>
  </GpioPort>

  </EmulatorComponents>
</Emulator>
```

this is also possible:

```xml
<?xml version="1.0" encoding="utf-8"?>
<Emulator>

  <EmulatorComponents>

  < Microsoft.SPOT.Emulator.Gpio.GpioPort id="Pin_Left">
    <Pin>0</Pin>
    <ModesExpected>InputOutputPort</ModesExpected>
    <ModesAllowed>InputOutputPort</ModesAllowed>
  </Microsoft.SPOT.Emulator.Gpio.GpioPort>

  </EmulatorComponents>
</Emulator>
```

Since the second example does not work for your custom components, only for components from the `Micosoft.SPOT.Emulator.dll` assembly, always declaring the types in the `Types` section is recommended.

Deleting or Updating Existing Components

In the previous section, you learned how components are registered with the emulator configuration file and in which cases they may replace an existing one. Now, you will learn how you can delete or update already existing components by specifying their IDs.

Components that were created programmatically in the `LoadDefaultComponents` method of the default emulator implementation each have a random, unique ID. The following samples demonstrate how to delete and update existing components using those IDs; therefore, you need to create and register components with a well known ID programmatically in the `LoadDefaultComponents` method. There is no difference between custom components or built-in components provided with the .NET Micro Framework. For registering components with a defined ID, you need to override the `LoadDefaultComponents` method in your own emulator class that inherits from the default Emulator class. For the following examples, a new battery component is registered. Do not forget to call the base implementation of LoadDefaultComponents so that the fundamental components will be loaded.

```
protected override void LoadDefaultComponents()
{
    base.LoadDefaultComponents();
    BatteryCell battery = new BatteryCell();
    battery.ComponentId = "myBattery";
    RegisterComponent(battery);
}
```

Now that the component is added to the emulator with program code, you will learn how to remove it using a configuration file:

```
<?xml version="1.0" encoding="utf-8" ?>
<Emulator>
  <Types>
    <Battery>Microsoft.SPOT.Emulator.Battery.BatteryCell</Battery>
  </Types>

  <EmulatorComponents>
    <Battery removes="myBattery" />
  </EmulatorComponents>

</Emulator>
```

Although the component is being removed, you need to specify a valid type. In this case, Battery is defined as Microsoft.SPOT.Emulator.Battery.BatteryCell, like the component that will be removed. A valid type is either the data type of the component to remove or a subclass of it.

The existing battery component can also be updated, and the properties of the component can be changed later using the configuration file without needing to register a new component. Properties not specified in the configuration file will keep their original values.

```
<?xml version="1.0" encoding="utf-8" ?>
<Emulator>
  <Types>
    <Battery>Microsoft.SPOT.Emulator.Battery.BatteryCell</Battery>
  </Types>

  <EmulatorComponents>
    <Battery updates="myBattery">
     <Voltage>5123</Voltage>
     <StateOfCharge>35</StateOfCharge>
    </Battery>
  </EmulatorComponents>

</Emulator>
```

It is also possible to change the ID of an already registered component in the configuration file. You can do this with the following XML snippet:

```
<EmulatorComponents>
  <Battery updates="myBattery" id="myUpdatedBattery">
    <Voltage>5123</Voltage>
    <StateOfCharge>35</StateOfCharge>
  </Battery>
</EmulatorComponents>
```

■**Note** Actually, you should also be able to replace an already existing component using the `replaces` attribute and specifying the ID of the existing component and a new one. This does not work currently, however, due to an error in the configuration engine.

Component Properties with Simple Types

As already demonstrated, all public properties of a component class are configurable using an XML configuration file. Therefore, the properties must be implemented as readable and writeable. In the following samples, you will get a close look at how the various data types of component properties are configured with XML.

String data is applied directly from the XML:

```
<MyComponent>
  <MyStringProperty>This is the text to assign to the property</MyStringProperty>
</MyComponent>
```

A Boolean property can be either `true` or `false`; whether the value is uppercase or lowercase does not matter.

```
<MyComponent>
  <MyBooleanProperty>true</MyBooleanProperty>
</MyComponent>
```

Integer properties of the `byte`, `sbyte`, `ushort`, `short`, `uint`, `int`, `ulong`, and `long` types are configured by default in decimal notation:

```
<MyComponent>
  <MyIntegerProperty>1234</MyIntegerProperty>
</MyComponent>
```

In addition, you can specify integers in hexadecimal notation:

```
<MyComponent>
  <MyIntegerProperty format="HexNumber">AAAA</MyIntegerProperty>
</MyComponent>
```

Contrary to conventional XML, the configuration engine parses the component properties in the emulator configuration file in accordance with the current culture. With the data types presented so far, the culture does not matter. But, for properties with floating point numbers, the decimal separator depends on the culture. By default, a .NET application refers to the culture of the underlying operating system as the current culture. Therefore, on a German Windows version the value 123,45 would be interpreted differently than on an English one.

■**Caution** When using floating point numbers in emulator configuration files, the emulator relies on the language version of the operating system.

To avoid conversion problems, you should avoid floating point numbers with properties. That's exactly what Microsoft does with the built-in components provided with the SDK. For example, for the battery component, the voltage is described as an integer in millivolts, instead of in volts.

There is an approach to solve the conversion issue when it can't be avoided. You need to override the Configure method of your emulator. Right before the analysis of the configuration file, you need to set the invariant culture, and right after the configuration, set it back to the original culture (see Listing 12-10). After that, your emulator will interpret the configuration file without variation for cultures; the invariant culture is equal to the US English culture.

Listing 12-10. *Culture Invariant Parsing of the Configuration File*

```
class Program : Emulator
{
    public override void Configure(System.Xml.XmlReader reader)
    {
        Thread.CurrentThread.CurrentCulture = CultureInfo.InvariantCulture;
        base.Configure(reader);
        Thread.CurrentThread.CurrentCulture = CultureInfo.InstalledUICulture;
    }
}
```

Enumeration properties are described directly as names of the enumeration values; whether they are uppercase or lowercase does not matter. For example, the enumeration MyEnum {NameA, NameB, NameC}; is used in the XML file as follows:

```
<MyComponent>
  <MyEnumProperty>NameB</MyEnumProperty>
</MyComponent>
```

In addition, you can specify the integer value of an enumeration member. This is used, for example, when describing a pin number for properties of the Cpu.Pin type for GPIO ports.

If you do not explicitly specify a particular integer value for an enumeration member, the successive numbering starts at 0 for the first member. NameA thus has the value 0, NameB the value 1, and NameC the value 2. Therefore, both of the following C# declarations are equal:

```
MyEnum {NameA, NameB, NameC};
MyEnum {NameA = 0, NameB = 1, NameC = 2};
```

In the XML configuration, you can specify the value 1 instead of writing NameB:

```
<MyComponent>
  <MyEnumProperty>1</MyEnumProperty>
</MyComponent>
```

For enumerations with the Flags attribute, you can combine several options with the OR operator. Imagine the following enumeration with the Flags attribute:

```
[Flags]
MyEnum {NameA = 1, NameB = 2, NameC = 4};
```

In the XML configuration, you can list several comma-separated members. You can use the previous enumeration in XML in the following way:

```
<MyComponent>
  <MyEnumProperty>NameB, NameC</MyEnumProperty>
</MyComponent>
```

This corresponds to the following program code:

```
myComponent.MyEnumProperty = NameB | NameC.
```

Also with Flag enumerations, you can directly specify an integer value, but comma-separated indication is not possible. You can only calculate and write the direct integer value of the combined flags. Thus, the following example results to the same as the previous one, because 2 | 4 (or also 2 + 4) gives the value six:

```
<MyComponent>
  <MyEnumProperty>6</MyEnumProperty>
</MyComponent>
```

Parsing Property Values

This section describes in detail how conversion of XML into the data types of the component properties works and how you can use that conversion for custom data types.

For string properties, no conversion is needed; the text is taken directly from the XML and assigned to the property.

Enumerations are parsed almost like all remaining data types, though not in exactly the same way. The Enum class possesses two overloads for the static Parse method. The configuration engine internally uses the following method for the conversion of XML with enumerations:

```
MyEnum myEnum = (MyEnum)Enum.Parse(typeof(MyEnum), "NameA", false);
```

All simple data types except strings and enumerations possess various static Parse methods. Among these overloads, one overload has exactly one string argument. This method interprets the string argument and returns an instance of that type. With the int and/or System.Int32 classes, the signature of the Parse method with the string argument looks as follows:

```
public static int Parse(string s);
```

The configuration engine looks for each property for this Parse method via reflection and calls it to convert the XML data and assign the value to the property. Microsoft uses this approach,

for example, with the ComPort class and its ComPortHandle property of the Microsoft.SPOT.
Emulator.Com.ComPortHandle type. There, from the string Usart1, the method extracts the
transport type and COM port number and creates and returns a ComPortHandle object. Because
this approach is very generic, you can use it also for your custom data types. The custom data
type, therefore, must implement only the static method with the String argument and return
an instance of the data type from the provided string data. This approach works for classes and
structures. The code snippet in Listing 12-11 demonstrates custom parsing.

Listing 12-11. *Custom Parsing*

```
public class MyType
{
    …
    public static MyType Parse(string s)
    {
        …
    }
    …
}

public class MyEmulatorComponent : EmulatorComponent
{
    private MyType myProperty;
    …
    public MyType MyProperty
    {
        get { return this.myProperty; }
        set { this.myProperty = value; }
    }
    …
}
```

Listing 12-12 shows an XML snippet of an emulator configuration file that demonstrates
the use of custom parsing.

Listing 12-12. *XML for Custom Property Parsing*

```
<EmulatorComponents>
  <MyEmulatorComponent id="myComponent">
    <MyProperty>ValueToParse</MyProperty>
  </MyEmulatorComponent>
</EmulatorComponents>
```

After the configuration engine reads the MyProperty tag in the XML configuration file (in
Listing 12-12), it looks via reflection for a property named MyProperty in the emulator component (the MyEmulatorComponent class in Listing 12-11). After that, it determines the property
type (the MyType class in Listing 12-11) and searches for a Parse method. Finally, it calls the found
MyType.Parse static method and passes the property value from the XML file (ValueToParse in

Listing 12-12). The `Parse` method returns a `MyType` object depending on the string argument. The new object will be assigned to the property `MyEmulatorComponent.MyProperty` (see Listing 12-11).

The format Specifier

You have already seen how integer properties can be configured in hexadecimal notation by using the `format = "HexNumber"` specifier in the configuration file; this is the only case I know where the `format` parameter is used. But this is a generic approach, again, so that you can implement custom parsing using the `format` attribute. Here's an example of using the `format` attributes:

```
<MyComponent>
  <MyIntegerProperty format="HexNumber">AAAA</MyIntegerProperty>
</MyComponent>
```

If you look at the simple integer data types like `byte`, `sbyte`, `ushort`, `short`, `uint`, `int`, `ulong`, and `long`, you can see that all types expose a static parse method with the following parameters:

```
public static int Parse(string s, NumberStyles style);
```

The `HexNumber` value for the format attribute in the previous XML configuration is a member of the `NumberStyles` enumeration. Therefore, the previous XML snippet corresponds to the following code:

```
myComponent.MyIntegerProperty = int.Parse("AAAA", NumberStyles.HexNumber);
```

In detail, this works as follows: if, in the XML configuration of a property, a format is specified, the configuration engine looks to see if the property type provides a static method with a string and an arbitrary enumeration parameter. For the interpretation, the same rules apply as with the configuration of enumeration properties.

Complex Data Types

Complex data types with several properties, as shown in Listing 12-13, or data types without a `Parse` method can also be configured as component properties per XML.

Listing 12-13. *A Class with a Complex Property*

```
using System;
using Microsoft.SPOT.Emulator;

namespace ConfigurationSampleEmulator
{
    public class MyClass
    {
        public bool B;
        private int i;
```

```
        public int I
        {
            get { return this.i; }
            set { this.i = value; }
        }
    }

    public sealed class MyComp : EmulatorComponent
    {
        private MyClass complexProp;

        public MyClass ComplexProp
        {
            get { return this.complexProp; }
            set { this.complexProp = value; }
        }
    }
}
```

The emulator component possesses the `ComplexProp` property of the `MyClass.MyClass` type. `MyClass.MyClass` contains a public property `I` and a public field `B`. The XML configuration file is shown in Listing 12-14.

Listing 12-14. *Configuring Complex Properties*

```xml
<?xml version="1.0" encoding="utf-8" ?>
<Emulator>
  <Types>
    <MyComp>ConfigurationSampleEmulator.MyComp, ConfigurationSampleEmulator</MyComp>
  </Types>

  <EmulatorComponents>
    <MyComp id="MyComp">
      <ComplexProp>
        <B>true</B>
        <I>5</I>
      </ComplexProp>
    </MyComp>
  </EmulatorComponents>

</Emulator>
```

In the configuration file in Listing 12-14, you can see the configuration of the `ComplexProp` component property and its public field `B` and public property `I`.

You can configure component properties only if they are exposed as public properties. On the other hand, you can configure the public properties and public fields of complex component properties with XML (see Listing 12-14). Exposing members as public, however, is not a good practice because of the possibility of missing validation.

If the data type of a component property does not possess a `Parse` method, an instance is created with the parameterless default constructor. In that constructor, the properties and fields need to be initialized with meaningful values so that the object is in a valid state. The configuration of the properties and the fields in XML is optional. In that case, the instance must be initialized properly with the constructor, so that it is also in a valid state without the specification of properties and fields. In C#, if no constructor is implemented, like in the `MyClass` class, the compiler adds an empty default constructor automatically.

The type Specifier

Usually, the data type of the component property to configure is determined, via reflection, based on the respective emulator component class. The configuration engine then looks to see if the property type has `Parse` methods. If none are present, it creates an object by calling the default constructor. With the XML configuration, you can additionally change the property type with the `type` attribute.

This means concretely that the `Parse` methods are searched in the new type (specified with the attribute). The specified new type does not have to be assignable to the original type, but the returned object from the `Parse` method must be assignable to the property.

If no `Parse` method is found, an instance of the new data type is created and assigned to the property, and the indicated data type must be assignable to the original property type.

If a property is an interface, a new data type must be indicated, since it is not possible to search in an interface for static `Parse` methods nor is it possible to create an instance of an interface. If the property type does not possess `Parse` methods and is defined as abstract, then a new assignable data type must be likewise indicated, so that an instance can be created.

A new data type for a property must be defined in the `Types` section of the XML file (see Listing 12-15), so the type can be resolved by the configuration engine. The same rules apply as those for valid component types. If a desired data type is in one of the two assemblies `mscorlib.dll` or `Microsoft.SPOT.Emulator.dll`, you can omit the declaration in the `Types` section and specify the fully qualified type name (including the namespace) in the `type` attribute.

Listing 12-15. *Using the type Specifier*

```
<?xml version="1.0" encoding="utf-8" ?>
<Emulator>
  <Types>
    <MyComp>ConfigurationSampleEmulator.MyComp, ConfigurationSampleEmulator</MyComp>
    <SomeType1>ConfigurationSampleEmulator.SomeType1,
            ConfigurationSampleEmulator</SomeType1>
    <SomeType2>ConfigurationSampleEmulator.SomeType2,
            ConfigurationSampleEmulator</Sometype2>
  </Types>

  <EmulatorComponents>
    <MyComp id="MyComp">
      <B type="System.Boolean">true</B>
      <ComplexProp type="SomeType1">
        <B type="SomeType2">true</B>
        <I>5</I>
```

```
    </ComplexProp>
   </MyComp>
  </EmulatorComponents>

</Emulator>
```

Listing 12-16 shows a commonly used application of the type attribute, and Listing 12-17 shows the same application with direct type specification.

Listing 12-16. *Practical Sample Application for the type Specifier*

```
<?xml version="1.0" encoding="utf-8"?>
<Emulator>
  <Types>
    <MemoryManager>Microsoft.SPOT.Emulator.Memory.MemoryManager</MemoryManager>
    <RamManager>Microsoft.SPOT.Emulator.Memory.RamManager</RamManager>
  </Types>

  <EmulatorComponents>

    <MemoryManager>
      <RamManager type="RamManager">
        <Size format="HexNumber">2000000</Size>
      </RamManager>
    </MemoryManager>

  </EmulatorComponents>
</Emulator>
```

The sample in Listing 12-17 works only because the RamManager class is a built-in component in the Microsoft.SPOT.Emulator.dll assembly. If you have custom components and types that are placed in other assemblies, you must use the first sample and specify the assembly.

Listing 12-17. *Practical Sample Application for the type Specifier with Direct Type Specification*

```
<?xml version="1.0" encoding="utf-8"?>
<Emulator>
  <EmulatorComponents>

    <MemoryManager>
      <RamManager type="Microsoft.SPOT.Emulator.Memory.RamManager">
        <Size format="HexNumber">2000000</Size>
      </RamManager>
    </MemoryManager>

  </EmulatorComponents>
</Emulator>
```

The `type` parameter can be used for properties of both an emulator component and a property.

Array Properties

It is possible to configure array properties of components and subordinated properties using XML. With each element, you need to specify the data type of the element. The specified type must be assignable to the array element's type. Valid types are the array element's type itself or a subtype of it. You can mix different types as long as they are all assignable to the array.

The example in Listing 12-18 shows how to populate an integer array with XML; the `System.Int32` data type is in the `mscorlib.dll` assembly, and therefore, you can specify it directly without declaring it in the `Types` section.

Listing 12-18. *Populating an Integer Array Using XML*

```
<?xml version="1.0" encoding="utf-8" ?>
<Emulator>
  <Types>
    <MyComp>ConfigurationSampleEmulator.MyComp, ConfigurationSampleEmulator</MyComp>
  </Types>

  <EmulatorComponents>
    <MyComp id="MyComp">
     <IntegerArrayProp>
        <System.Int32>1</System.Int32>
        <System.Int32>2</System.Int32>
        <System.Int32>3</System.Int32>
        <System.Int32>4</System.Int32>
     </IntegerArrayProp>
    </MyComp>
  </EmulatorComponents>
```

The example in Listing 12-19 demonstrates the use of custom data types as array elements. `SomeType1` and `SomeType2` must be assignable to the data type of the array elements. The array is filled with two elements that are of different types.

Listing 12-19. *Populating an Array of Different Custom Element Types*

```
</Emulator>
<?xml version="1.0" encoding="utf-8" ?>
<Emulator>
  <Types>
    <MyComp>ConfigurationSampleEmulator.MyComp, ConfigurationSampleEmulator</MyComp>
    <SomeType1>ConfigurationSampleEmulator.SomeType1,
            ConfigurationSampleEmulator</SomeType1>
    <SomeType2>ConfigurationSampleEmulator.SomeType1,
            ConfigurationSampleEmulator</SomeType2>
  </Types>
```

```
<EmulatorComponents>
  <MyComp id="MyComp">
    <ArrayProp>
        <SomeType1>data to parse</SomeType1>
        <SomeType2>
              <Prop>123</Prop>
        </SomeType2>
    </ArrayProp>
  </MyComp>
</EmulatorComponents>
```

The built-in `FlashManager` emulator component owns a `FlashSectors` array property that holds `FlashSector` items. The `FlashSector` class is in `Microsoft.SPOT.Emulator.dll`. Listing 12-20 shows how you can populate this array using the `Types` section, and Listing 12-21 uses direct specification of the type.

Listing 12-20. *Populating the FlashSectors Array Property Using the Types Section*

```
<?xml version="1.0" encoding="utf-8"?>
<Emulator>
  <Types>
    <MemoryManager>Microsoft.SPOT.Emulator.Memory.MemoryManager</MemoryManager>
    <FlashManager>Microsoft.SPOT.Emulator.Memory.FlashManager</FlashManager>
    <FlashSector>Microsoft.SPOT.Emulator.Memory.FlashSector</FlashSector>
  </Types>

  <EmulatorComponents>

    <MemoryManager>
      <FlashManager type="FlashManager">
        <FlashSectors>
          <FlashSector>
            <Length format="HexNumber">10000</Length>
            <Usage>Bootstrap</Usage>
            <Partition>Start</Partition>
            <Block>StartEnd</Block>
          </FlashSector>
          <FlashSector>
            <Length format="HexNumber">10000</Length>
            <Usage>Config</Usage>
            <Partition>None</Partition>
            <Block>StartEnd</Block>
          </FlashSector>
          <FlashSector>
            <Length format="HexNumber">10000</Length>
            <Usage>Code</Usage>
            <Partition>None</Partition>
            <Block>StartEnd</Block>
          </FlashSector>
```

. . .
```
            </FlashSectors>
          </FlashManager>
        </MemoryManager>


      </EmulatorComponents>
    </Emulator>
```

Listing 12-21. *Populating the FlashSectors Array Property Using Direct Type Specification*

```
<?xml version="1.0" encoding="utf-8"?>
<Emulator>
  <Types>
    <MemoryManager>Microsoft.SPOT.Emulator.Memory.MemoryManager</MemoryManager>
    <FlashManager>Microsoft.SPOT.Emulator.Memory.FlashManager</FlashManager>
  </Types>

  <EmulatorComponents>

    <MemoryManager>
      <FlashManager type="FlashManager">
        <FlashSectors>
          <Microsoft.SPOT.Emulator.Memory.FlashSector>
            <Length format="HexNumber">10000</Length>
            <Usage>Bootstrap</Usage>
            <Partition>Start</Partition>
            <Block>StartEnd</Block>
          </Microsoft.SPOT.Emulator.Memory.FlashSector>
          <Microsoft.SPOT.Emulator.Memory.FlashSector>
            <Length format="HexNumber">10000</Length>
            <Usage>Config</Usage>
            <Partition>None</Partition>
            <Block>StartEnd</Block>
          </Microsoft.SPOT.Emulator.Memory.FlashSector>
          <Microsoft.SPOT.Emulator.Memory.FlashSector>
            <Length format="HexNumber">10000</Length>
            <Usage>Code</Usage>
            <Partition>None</Partition>
            <Block>StartEnd</Block>
          </Microsoft.SPOT.Emulator.Memory.FlashSector>
...
        </FlashSectors>
      </FlashManager>
    </MemoryManager>

  </EmulatorComponents>
</Emulator>
```

In each of the previous examples, an array was created with exactly as many elements as were added with the XML. By using the `length` parameter, you can indicate for how many items the array is dimensioned, and no more than the indicated number of elements can be added with XML. If there are fewer items to be added than specified with the `length` attribute, the array is filled at the end with uninitialized elements having a `null` value.

In the configuration file in Listing 12-22, an integer array is created and dimensioned for ten elements, but only four will be added.

Listing 12-22. *Predimensioning Arrays with the length Parameter*

```
</Emulator>
<?xml version="1.0" encoding="utf-8" ?>
<Emulator>
  <Types>
    <MyComp>ConfigurationSampleEmulator.MyComp, ConfigurationSampleEmulator</MyComp>
  </Types>

  <EmulatorComponents>
    <MyComp id="MyComp">
     <IntegerArrayProp length="10">
        <System.Int32>1</System.Int32>
        <System.Int32>2</System.Int32>
        <System.Int32>3</System.Int32>
        <System.Int32>4</System.Int32>
     </IntegerArrayProp>
    </MyComp>
  </EmulatorComponents>
```

Component Collections

The `Microsoft.SPOT.Emulator.EmulatorComponentCollection` abstract class provides the base type for emulator component collections. A component collection is a list of other emulator components. This class inherits from `EmulatorComponent`, and therefore, it needs to be registered the same way as other emulator components. When deriving custom subclasses of it, you define the element type of your collection in the constructor. An example of a component collection is the `GpioCollection` class, which holds and manages all available GPIO ports.

The special feature of component collections is that the elements to be added can be registered and configured as emulator components in the configuration file in the `EmulatorComponents` section, on the highest level. After all components are registered, all components that are assignable to the element type of a collection are automatically collected and added to that collection.

The `GpioPortCollection` component collection of the `Microsoft.SPOT.Emulator.Gpio.` `GpioCollection` type in Listing 12-23 will finally contain the three indicated `GpioPort` components.

Listing 12-23. *Using Component Collections with the GpioPortCollection Example*

```xml
<?xml version="1.0" encoding="utf-8"?>
<Emulator>
  <Types>
    <GpioPort>Microsoft.SPOT.Emulator.Gpio.GpioPort</GpioPort>
    <GpioPortCollection>Microsoft.SPOT.Emulator.Gpio.GpioCollection
    </GpioPortCollection>
  </Types>

  <EmulatorComponents>

    <GpioPortCollection>
      <MaxPorts>128</MaxPorts>
    </GpioPortCollection>

    <GpioPort id="S4_PB9">
      <Pin>41</Pin>
      <ModesExpected>InputOutputPort</ModesExpected>
      <ModesAllowed>InputOutputPort</ModesAllowed>
    </GpioPort>

    <GpioPort id="S6_PB17">
      <Pin>49</Pin>
      <ModesExpected>InputOutputPort</ModesExpected>
      <ModesAllowed>InputOutputPort</ModesAllowed>
    </GpioPort>

    <GpioPort id="S7_PB16">
      <Pin>48</Pin>
      <ModesExpected>InputOutputPort</ModesExpected>
      <ModesAllowed>InputOutputPort</ModesAllowed>
    </GpioPort>

  </EmulatorComponents>
</Emulator>
```

The `EmulatorComponentCollection` abstract class is illustrated in Listing 12-24.

Listing 12-24. *The Microsoft.SPOT.Emulator.EmulatorComponentCollection Abstract Class*

```csharp
using System;
using System.ComponentModel;

namespace Microsoft.SPOT.Emulator
{
```

```
public abstract class EmulatorComponentCollection : EmulatorComponent
{
    protected EmulatorComponentCollection(Type collectionType);

    public Type CollectionType { get; }

    public event CollectionChangeEventHandler CollectionChanged;

    public override bool IsReplaceableBy(EmulatorComponent ec);
    public virtual void Register(EmulatorComponent ec);
    public virtual void Unregister(EmulatorComponent ec);
}
}
```

In derived subclasses of ComponentCollection, you need to pass the type of the elements in the collection to the base constructor. Elements are added to the collection with the Register method, and elements are removed with Unregister. You do not need to call these two methods or register components to the collection yourself. This is done by the configuration engine automatically after all components are configured. You can listen for changes to the collection by subscribing to the CollectionChanged event handler. Derived subclasses may provide and implement special access methods and indexers. These methods will be described in the next chapters when the individual classes are explained in detail.

In these sections concerning configuration files, you've learned that the XML configuration files offer versatile possibilities to describe the hardware components of your system. A configuration file is, in each case shown here, a better choice than the programmatic configuration with code. Some configuration features described in this chapter are very advanced, and you might not need them all with simple emulators. A good understanding of the configuration engine and its possibilities, however, will be very helpful in the next chapter, where you will learn to configure existing components and write custom emulator components for various hardware modules.

More About the Emulator

In the following sections, you will learn more about the emulator and how it works.

Members of the Emulator Class

The Emulator class (see Listing 12-25) inherits, as previously mentioned, from the EmulatorComponent class. In the next section, you will learn in which order the methods of the emulator are called when the emulator starts up.

Listing 12-25. *The Microsoft.SPOT.Emulator.Emulator Class*

```
using Microsoft.SPOT.Emulator.Battery;
using Microsoft.SPOT.Emulator.Gpio;
using Microsoft.SPOT.Emulator.I2c;
using Microsoft.SPOT.Emulator.Lcd;
using Microsoft.SPOT.Emulator.Memory;
```

```csharp
using Microsoft.SPOT.Emulator.Serial;
using Microsoft.SPOT.Emulator.Spi;
using Microsoft.SPOT.Emulator.Time;
using System;
using System.Threading;
using System.Xml;

namespace Microsoft.SPOT.Emulator
{
    public class Emulator : EmulatorComponent, IDisposable
    {
        public Emulator();

        //components
        public BatteryCell Battery { get; }
        public GpioCollection GpioPorts { get; }
        public I2cBus I2cBus { get; }
        public LcdDisplay LcdDisplay { get; }
        public MemoryManager MemoryManager { get; }
        public SerialPortCollection SerialPorts { get; }
        public SpiBus SpiBus { get; }
        public TimingServices TimingServices { get; }

        //component management methods
        protected virtual void LoadDefaultComponents();
        public void RegisterComponent(EmulatorComponent component);
        public void RegisterComponent(EmulatorComponent component,
                                      EmulatorComponent linkedBy);
        public void UnregisterComponent(EmulatorComponent component);
        public EmulatorComponent FindComponentById(string componentId);

        //inherited from emulator component
        public override void Configure(XmlReader reader);
        public override void SetupComponent();
        public override void InitializeComponent();
        public override void UninitializeComponent();

        //emulator control
        public void LoadAssembly(string asm);
        public virtual void Run();
        public void Start();
        public virtual void Start(string[] args);
        public void Stop();
        public ConfigurationEngine ConfigurationEngine { get; }
        public bool IsShuttingDown { get; }
        public Emulator.EmulatorState State { get; }
        public ManualResetEvent ShutdownHandle { get; }
```

```
        public enum EmulatorState
        {
            Configuration = 0,
            Setup = 1,
            Initialize = 2,
            Running = 3,
            ShutDown = 4,
            Uninitialize = 5,
        }
    }
}
```

The Emulator Start-up Process

When the emulator starts up, the following actions are performed:

- *Configuration emulator state*: The LoadDefaultComponents virtual method of the emulator is executed to create the fundamental default components. With the configuration file, you can configure, delete, or replace these components, and the Emulator class possesses properties to access these default components. The XML emulator configuration files are read, and the described emulator components are created, configured, and registered. The Configure virtual method of the emulator and components is called.

- *Setup emulator state*: All components of the system are now properly configured. The SetupComponent virtual method of the emulator and components is called. By overriding the SetupComponent method components, you can register their linked child components. At this point, for example, the MemoryManager component registers its RamManager and FlashManager components from its RamManager and FlashManager properties. Since the components are registered only now, you can replace these property values with your custom implementations per a configuration file. Also, at this stage, emulator components are sorted in the appropriate component collections. For example, GpioPort is sorted in GpioPortCollection.

- *Initialization emulator state*: After all components are properly set up, the InitializeComponent virtual method of the emulator and all its components is called. Here, you can make some last-minute initializations before the emulator is running.

- Also, all the .NET Micro Framework assemblies that were passed via the command line will be loaded now.

- *Running emulator state*: The emulator is running.

Linked Components

Programmatic registration using code is done via one of the two Register method overloads. The method with only one argument (the component to be registered) is used by the configuration engine. In addition to the component to be registered, the second variant expects that component's parent component as an argument. Components can possess child components, and child components need to be created and registered by the parent components. After registration, a child component is linked to its parent. When a component is removed with the UnregisterComponent method, all its linked child components are automatically removed also. The default MemoryManager component provided with the .NET Micro Framework SDK possesses, for example, RamManager and FlashManager components. Both child components are created programmatically by MemoryManager. When MemoryManager is removed, both child components are removed likewise. This is important, for example, if you replace the default memory manager with your custom one, because it ensures that no unneeded zombie components remain active.

Addressing Registered Components

Registered emulator components can be addressed via the FindComponentById method of the emulator.

```
GpioPort gpioDown = this.emulator.FindComponentyById("Pin_Down") as GpioPort;
```

The method returns null if the indicated component does not exist.

If an emulator uses and relies on certain components that are added using the configuration file, you should check for the presence of these components as soon as possible. A good place for that is in the InitializeComponent method of the emulator.

```
public override void InitializeComponent()
{
    base.InitializeComponent();

    if (FindComponentById("Pin_Down") == null)
        throw new Exception("The component 'Pin_Down' is required by the emulator.");

    // Start the UI in its own thread.
    Thread uiThread = new Thread(StartForm);
    uiThread.Start();
}
```

With the following code snippet, you can validate the type in addition to the presence— not only whether a component with the ID Pin_Down exists but also whether it is a GpioPort component:

```
if (FindComponentById("Pin_Down") as GpioPort == null)
    throw new Exception("The component 'Pin_Down' is required by the emulator.");
```

Debugging Emulators

If you write your own emulator, of course, it won't be error free from the beginning. Some errors can only be found and fixed using a debugger. To do so for an emulator, you must start a debugger and run a .NET Micro Framework application on the emulator. The two ways to debug an emulator will be discussed in this section.

To debug an emulator, you need to open the project that will be executed from the .NET Micro Framework application with Visual Studio. In the project properties, select the emulator that you want to debug as the emulator for the application (see Figure 12-5). The emulator must have been already built and registered for you to select it.

Figure 12-5. *Selecting an emulator to run the application on*

Next, run your application on the emulator. This step is necessary, since now, as shown in Figure 12-6, the necessary commands for starting the emulator and running an application appear in the output window of Visual Studio. Now, select all the text after /waitfordebugger, but not the final single quotation mark, and copy it into the clipboard.

```
Output                                                                        ▾ ą X
Show output from:  Debug            ▾ | 🔊 | 🔊 🔊 | 🔫 | 🔳
   Launching emulator with command line:  'C:\Users\Kühner\Documents\Visual Studio 2005\Projects\MFEmulator1\MFEmulator1\bin\Debug\MFEmulator1.exe "/waitfordebug ▲
   'MFEmulator1.exe' (Managed): Loaded 'C:\Program Files\Microsoft .NET Micro Framework\v2.0.3036\Assemblies\mscorlib.dll', No symbols loaded.
   'MFEmulator1.exe' (Managed): Loaded 'C:\Program Files\Microsoft .NET Micro Framework\v2.0.3036\Assemblies\Microsoft.SPOT.Native.dll', No symbols loaded.
   'MFEmulator1.exe' (Managed): Loaded 'MFConsoleApplication1', No symbols loaded.
   Hello World!
   The thread 0x5 has exited with code 0 (0x0).
   The program '[988] Process Name: Managed' has exited with code 0 (0x0).
◄ |                    ▥                                                        ►
```

Figure 12-6. *Text in the output window when building and debugging an application on the emulator*

For reference, here's the text you've copied to the clipboard:

```
Launching emulator with command line: ➡
'C:\Projects\MFEmulator\MFEmulator\bin\Debug\MFEmulator.exe "/waitfordebugger" ➡
"/load:C:\Projects\MFConsoleApplication\ ➡
MFConsoleApplication\bin\Debug\MFConsoleApplication.pe" ➡
"/load:C:\Program Files\Microsoft .NET Micro Framework\v2.0.3036\Assemblies\ ➡
Microsoft.SPOT.Native.pe" ➡
"/load:C:\Program Files\Microsoft .NET Micro Framework\v2.0.3036\Assemblies\ ➡
mscorlib.pe"'
```

Now, you need to switch to Visual Studio with the emulator project, and in the project properties on the Debug page, paste the copied text into the "Command line arguments" field (see Figure 12-7).

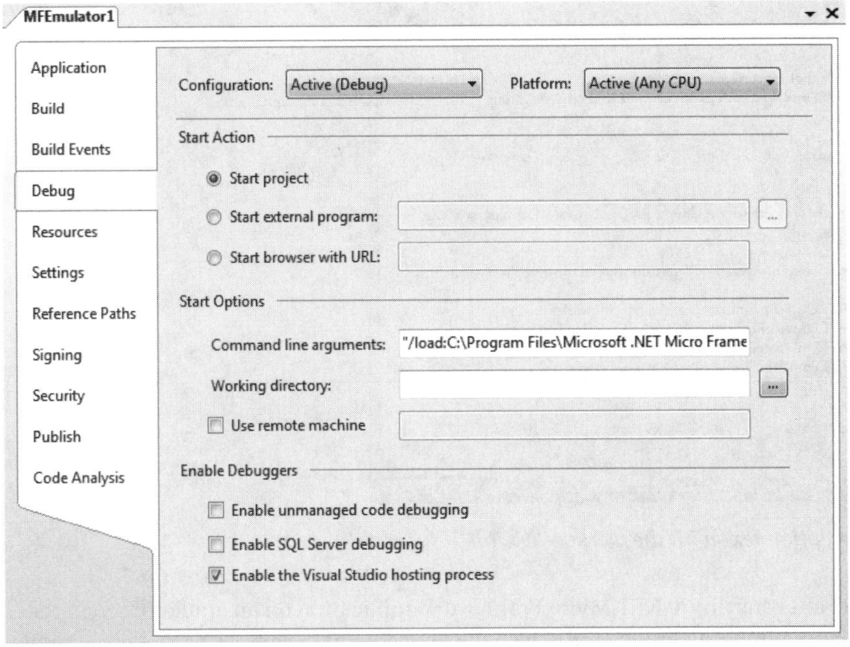

Figure 12-7. *Pasting the command-line arguments for debugging an emulator*

When starting the debug build for the emulator, the emulator is also started for debugging, and the desired .NET Micro Framework application runs on it.

If you add the /verbose option to the emulator's command line, you will see additional information for exceptions thrown and handled in the base implementation of the emulator where no source code is available; not only will the exception message property be printed but so will additional information like a stack trace. Without /verbose, only the message property of an exception is displayed (see Figure 12-8). With /verbose, more information is displayed with the ToString method of the exception (see Figure 12-9). This might be helpful to debug an emulator configuration file that is parsed by the configuration engine.

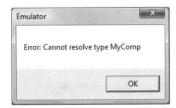

Figure 12-8. *Displaying exception information without the /verbose option*

The other approach to debugging an emulator is to execute a .NET Micro Framework application on an emulator first and then attach a debugger to the current emulator process. If the .NET Micro Framework application is executed in debug mode, you can debug the .NET Micro Framework application and the emulator at the same time.

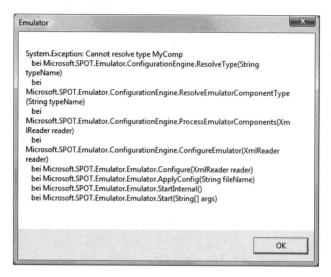

Figure 12-9. *Exception text with the /verbose option*

Therefore, after starting a .NET Micro Framework application on an emulator, open the emulator project with Visual Studio, and attach the debugger to the emulator process with the menu item Debug ➤ Attach to Process. In the list, find and select the executable of the emulator, as shown in Figure 12-10, and click the Attach button.

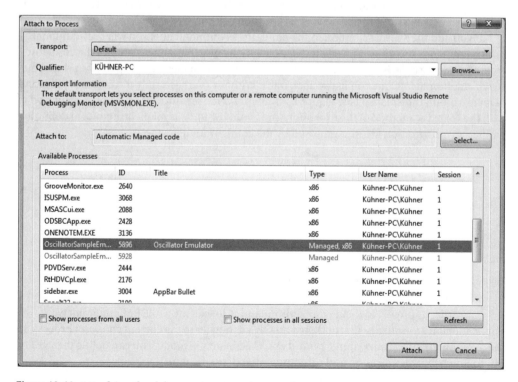

Figure 12-10. *Attaching the debugger to a running emulator process*

Command-Line Options

In the previous section, you learned how to debug an emulator with Visual Studio and how to specify command-line arguments, like /verbose, for the emulator. Other possible options follow:

- /waitfordebugger: This Boolean argument indicates whether the emulator should wait for a debugger before running; possible values are /waitfordebugger:true and /waitfordebugger:false. The default value, used when this argument is missing, is false. When debugging a .NET Micro Framework application with Visual Studio, this option is already set to true. When debugging an emulator, as described in the previous section, you need to remove this option or set it to false.

- /verbose: Use this option if you need more detailed information with error messages for exceptions, like a stack trace. When the emulator handles an exception and displays the error message, it displays the Message property of an exception by default if /verbose is not enabled. With /verbose, it displays more information obtained from the ToString method of the exception.

- /config: This option indicates the path and file name of an additional XML configuration file for the configuration engine, from which the described components are to be loaded. You can indicate this argument several times to load more than one additional configuration file. If this argument is specified one or more times, the configuration engine loads and analyzes all of the additional configuration files and merges their data with the main XML configuration file. With or without the specification of additional configuration files, the emulator always looks for a configuration file in the emulator directory that has the same file name as the emulator and the file extension .emulatorconfig.

- /nomessagebox: This Boolean option, if set to true, suppresses any message boxes in an error case, so the error message is traced only to the console. This option is helpful for any automated tasks with the emulator, for example, unit testing. By default, clickable message boxes are displayed (/nomessagebox:false), which is useful with interactive debugging with Visual Studio.

- /nodefaultconfig: The presence of this argument causes the emulator to load only the components described in the configuration files, not its default components. In other words, this argument will skip the LoadDefaultComponents virtual method. The default implementation of LoadDefaultComponents will load the default components Hal, ComPortCollection, GpioCollection, SpiBus, MemoryManager, TimingServices, I2cBus, SerialPortCollection, and NamedPipeServer. If you add this option, you need to create manually most of these vital or fundamental components.

- /load: With this option, you instruct the emulator to load additional .NET Micro Framework assemblies. When the emulator is started from Visual Studio to run a .NET Micro Framework application, all assemblies referenced from that application will be loaded. Possible files to load are .pe, .exe, .dll, .dat, and .manifest. But only .pe assemblies are officially supported; these assemblies are very compact assemblies especially for the .NET Micro Framework, which the metadata processor creates during the build procedure out of the compiled standard .NET assemblies. With file names containing spaces everything should be quoted, for example, "/load:C:\myassembly.pe".

- `/commandlinearguments`: Just like an emulator and every other Windows or smart device application, .NET Micro Framework applications also can accept command-line arguments. Passing a command line to a .NET Micro Framework application can be achieved either in Visual Studio, by entering the arguments at the "Command line arguments" field on the Debug page in the project properties exactly like it was described for the emulator earlier (see Figure 12-7), or by means of a command-line argument to the emulator, for example, `"/commandlinearguments:arg1 arg2 "arg with space" arg4"`. The entry point (the `Main` method) must be changed from `public static void Main()` to `public static void Main (string [] args)` to accept command-line arguments.

- `@filename`: If the first character of the first command line argument is "@", thereafter, a path and a file name are expected. With this option, you can let the emulator load all parameters from a separate text file. The option and the file name should be quoted: `"/load:C:\myargs.txt"`. The file with the options is a simple text file with one argument per line. Do not quote the arguments here. Remark lines start with the character "#".

When debugging a .NET Micro Framework application with Visual Studio on an emulator, Visual Studio automatically launches the emulator. Visual Studio generates and passes the command line for the emulator on the basis of information from the project (for example, referenced assemblies) and from the registry. What information the build process of an emulator writes into the registry will be discussed in the next section.

The Emulator and the Registry

When compiling an emulator project with Visual Studio, the emulator is registered automatically by the build process in the registry. After that, the emulator can be selected for other .NET Micro Framework applications.

During the build process, the information of an emulator is stored in its own and globally unique subkey in `Software\Microsoft\.NETMicroFramework\v2.0.3036\Emulators` under `HKEY_CURRENT_USER` (depending on the .NET Micro Framework version); see Figure 12-11.

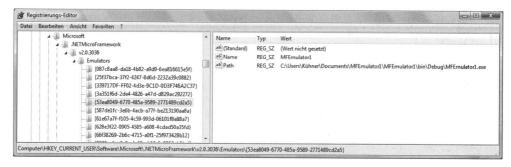

Figure 12-11. *An emulator automatically registered by the build process*

Furthermore, you are able to register an emulator under `HKEY_LOCAL_MACHINE` (see Figure 12-12). This is a good place for emulators that are installed with a setup program, for example, special emulators for development boards like the emulator of the Freescale i.MXS Development Kit (see Chapter 2). Wherever you register the emulator, both subkeys with GUID and friendly names are possible; they must just be unique.

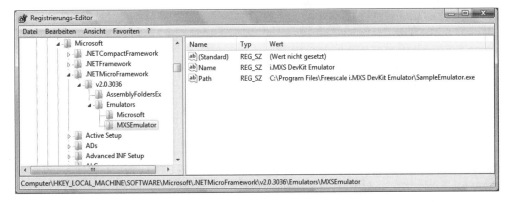

Figure 12-12. *Emulators registered by setup programs*

Now that you have learned where in the registry the information for an emulator is written, take a look at the information that can be written:

- `Path`: The directory and file name of the emulator executable.

- `Name`: The friendly name of the emulator, which appears with the emulator selection for a .NET Micro Framework application in the list.

- `Config`: A file path for an additional emulator configuration file. The value `c:\myconfig.emulatorconfig` would be added as `"/Config:c:\myconfig.emulatorconfig"` to the command line when starting the emulator from Visual Studio. Only one file can be specified here.

- `AdditionalCommandLineOptions`: With this value, you can add more command-line arguments, like `/verbose`.

During the build task, the `Path` and `Name` values are registered, but the path of a configuration file is not indicated. Therefore, by default, the emulator will look for the file `<Emulator name>.emulatorconfig` in the emulator directory. All modifications you made manually in a registry subkey for an emulator are overwritten by the build task when the emulator is compiled with Visual Studio.

To automatically let the build task write additional command-line arguments or an additional configuration file to the registry, you need to extend the global build file of the .NET Micro Framework SDK, `C:\Program Files\MSBuild\Microsoft\.NET Micro Framework\v2.0\Emulator.targets`, with the two bold lines in Listing 12-26.

Listing 12-26. *Emulator.targets*

```
<Project xmlns="http://schemas.microsoft.com/developer/msbuild/2003">
...
  <Target Name="RegisterEmulator" Condition=" '$(EmulatorId)' != '' " >
    <RegisterEmulator
       AddtionalCommandLineOptions="$(EmulatorCommandLineOptions)"
       Config="$(EmulatorConfig)"
       SubkeyName="$(EmulatorId)"
       Name="$(EmulatorName)"
       CurrentUser="$(EmulatorCurrentUser)"
       Path="$(OutDir)$(TargetFileName)" />
  </Target>
</Project>
```

> ■**Caution** Modifying the global build file for the .NET Micro Framework SDK is only advised for experienced users—you should really know what you are doing and have a good reason for doing it. Common scenarios will not require modifying the build file.

Now, a configuration file or additional command-line options can be added with the project file of an emulator (see Listing 12-27). In this way, each emulator can be configured separately, and the information will be added to the registry when building the emulator with Visual Studio.

Listing 12-27. *MFEmulator1.csproj*

```
<Project DefaultTargets="Build"
xmlns="http://schemas.microsoft.com/developer/msbuild/2003">
  <PropertyGroup>
    <Configuration Condition=" '$(Configuration)' == '' ">Debug</Configuration>
    <Platform Condition=" '$(Platform)' == '' ">AnyCPU</Platform>
    <ProductVersion>8.0.50727</ProductVersion>
    <SchemaVersion>2.0</SchemaVersion>
    <ProjectGuid>{8CFAAB2C-BCA4-4217-AA52-2FB2F48C11A9}</ProjectGuid>
    <OutputType>WinExe</OutputType>
    <AppDesignerFolder>Properties</AppDesignerFolder>
    <RootNamespace>MFEmulator1</RootNamespace>
    <AssemblyName>MFEmulator1</AssemblyName>
    <EmulatorId>{7273aa6c-3c7e-4a68-ab12-6a0953ab5baf}</EmulatorId>
    <EmulatorCommandLineOptions>/verbose</EmulatorCommandLineOptions>
    <Config>"c:\Documents\myconfig.emulatorconfig"</Config>
  </PropertyGroup>
...
</Project>
```

Summary

This chapter toured the complete extensible emulator mechanism. You learned how to write, use, and debug custom emulators, as well as a lot about the configuration engine.

You now know that the extensible emulator of the .NET Micro Framework is a powerful tool that can assist you to write and debug great embedded applications during the whole development life cycle.

A good understanding about how the emulator works and all the rich configuration features will help you with the next chapter, which explores all the built-in emulator components, and you will see how easy it is to extend existing components if they do not provide the desired functionality. Chapter 13 also describes many useful custom components to reuse with your custom emulators.

CHAPTER 13

■■■

Emulator Components

In this chapter, you will learn all about emulator components. I'll teach you how to use and configure the built-in emulator components, extend existing components, and write custom components from scratch for all the various hardware components described in Chapter 5.

GPIO Ports

This section describes how to simulate GPIO ports. GPIO ports are represented in the emulator by the `Microsoft.SPOT.Emulator.Gpio.GpioPort` emulator component. The `GpioPortSampleEmulator` project provides a complete emulator with GPIO ports, and you can find it in this chapter's directory.

For a GPIO port component, the `Pin`, `ModesAllowed`, and `ModesExpected` properties can be configured with the configuration file. `ModesAllowed` indicates whether the appropriate GPIO port can be used as input port, output port, or both. `ModesExpected` is actually never used and should be always set to the same value as `ModesAllowed`.

XML Configuration

The configuration of GPIO ports using XML might look like Listing 13-1.

Listing 13-1. *Configuring GPIO Ports*

```xml
<?xml version="1.0" encoding="utf-8"?>
<Emulator>
  <Types>
    <GpioPort>Microsoft.SPOT.Emulator.Gpio.GpioPort</GpioPort>
  </Types>

  <EmulatorComponents>

    <GpioPort id="GPIO0">
      <Pin>0</Pin>
      <ModesAllowed>InputOutputPort</ModesAllowed>
      <ModesExpected>InputOutputPort</ModesExpected>
    </GpioPort>
```

```
    <GpioPort id="StatusLED">
      <Pin>1</Pin>
      <ModesAllowed>OutputPort</ModesAllowed>
      <ModesExpected>OutputPort</ModesExpected>
    </GpioPort>

    <GpioPort id="ButtonLeft">
      <Pin>2</Pin>
      <ModesAllowed>InputPort</ModesAllowed>
      <ModesExpected>InputPort</ModesExpected>
    </GpioPort>

  </EmulatorComponents>
</Emulator>
```

Input Ports

With an input port for a .NET Micro Framework application, you can set the line state from within the emulator. For example, the emulator might change the state of a GPIO pin when you click a button on the emulator user interface (see Listing 13-2). You can change the state of a GPIO port emulator component with the Write method.

Listing 13-2. *Simulating Input Ports*

```
public partial class Form1 : Form
{
    private readonly GpioPort gpioInPort;

    public Form1(Emulator emulator)
    {
        if(emulator == null)
            throw new ArgumentNullException("emulator");
        InitializeComponent();
        this.gpioInPort = emulator.FindComponentById("GPIOIn");
    }

    private void gpioInButton_MouseDown(object sender, MouseEventArgs e)
    {
        this.gpioInPort.BeginInvoke(new MethodInvoker(delegate
                                        {
                                            this.gpioInPort.Write(true);
                                        }
                                    )
                        );
    }
```

```
    private void gpioInButton_MouseUp(object sender, MouseEventArgs e)
    {
        this.gpioInPort.BeginInvoke(new MethodInvoker(delegate
                                            {
                                              this.gpioInPort.Write(false);
                                            }
                                          )
                        );
    }
}
```

When you click the button, the high state is simulated, and when you release the button, the line state goes back to low.

The configuration file for the input port is shown in Listing 13-3.

Listing 13-3. *Describing an Input Port*

```
<?xml version="1.0" encoding="utf-8"?>
<Emulator>
  <Types>
    <GpioPort>Microsoft.SPOT.Emulator.Gpio.GpioPort</GpioPort>
  </Types>

  <EmulatorComponents>
    <GpioPort id="GPIOIn">
      <Pin>0</Pin>
      <ModesAllowed>InputPort</ModesAllowed>
      <ModesExpected>InputPort</ModesExpected>
    </GpioPort>
  </EmulatorComponents>
</Emulator>
```

Instead of defining the port only as an input port, you can actually define it for use as both an input and output port (with the ModesAllowed property). This enables applications using the port as output port to run in the emulator without errors.

Output Ports

With an output port for a .NET Micro Framework application, you can obtain the line state of the port from within the emulator. As an example, you can indicate the state of a status LED that is controlled from a .NET Micro Framework application directly on your emulator user interface, as shown in Listing 13-4. You can monitor changes on GPIO output pins made by a .NET Micro Framework application in the emulator by subscribing to an event handler of the GPIO port component.

Listing 13-4. *Simulating Output Ports*

```
public partial class Form1 : Form
{
    Private readonly GpioPort gpioOutPort;

    public Form1(Emulator emulator)
    {
        if(emulator == null)
            throw new ArgumentNullException("emulator");
        InitializeComponent();
        this.gpioOutPort = emulator.FindComponentById("GPIOOut");
        gpioOutPort.OnGpioActivity += new GpioActivity(gpioOutPort_OnGpioActivity);
    }

    private void gpioOut_OnGpioActivity(GpioPort sender, bool edge)
    {
        BeginInvoke(new MethodInvoker(delegate
                                        {
                                            this.gpioOutCheckBox.Checked = edge;
                                        }
                                    )
                );
    }
}
```

With each change on the output pin, the callback method is called. The somewhat awkwardly designated edge parameter immediately indicates the new level of the GPIO line.

The configuration file for the output port is shown in Listing 13-5.

Listing 13-5. *Describing Output Ports*

```xml
<?xml version="1.0" encoding="utf-8"?>
<Emulator>
  <Types>
    <GpioPort>Microsoft.SPOT.Emulator.Gpio.GpioPort</GpioPort>
  </Types>

  <EmulatorComponents>
    <GpioPort id="GPIOOut">
      <Pin>1</Pin>
      <ModesAllowed>OutputPort</ModesAllowed>
      <ModesExpected>OutputPort</ModesExpected>
    </GpioPort>
  </EmulatorComponents>
</Emulator>
```

Synchronizing the Emulator and GUI Thread

In the previous examples, you may have noticed the use of BeginInvoke. Since an emulator runs in a different thread than the GUI, you need to synchronize cross-thread data access.

In the first case (Listing 13-2), when the button is clicked, an emulator component (a GPIO input port) in the emulator thread is changed from the GUI thread. The code for changing the GPIO port must be executed, therefore, in the context of the emulator thread. You achieve this by calling the BeginInvoke method of the emulator component, as demonstrated with the code snippet in Listing 13-6.

Listing 13-6. *Synchronizing the Emulator and GUI Thread When Accessing Emulator Components*

```
this.gpioInPort.BeginInvoke(new MethodInvoker(delegate
                                                {
                                                  this.gpioInPort.Write(true);
                                                }
                            )
                           );
```

In the second case (Listing 13-4), a control on the user interface of the emulator is updated whenever the GPIO output port in the emulator thread changes. Any updates to the control to indicate the status must take place, therefore, in the context of the GUI thread. You also achieve this by calling the BeginInvoke method (see Listing 13-7) of the WinForms control.

Listing 13-7. *Synchronization of the Emulator and GUI Thread When Updating GUI Controls*

```
BeginInvoke(new MethodInvoker(delegate { this.gpioOutCheckBox.Checked = edge; }));
```

The signatures of the BeginInvoke method overloads for the emulator components are identical to the WinForms controls. In both prior examples, anonymous methods were used. MethodInvoker is already defined in the System.Windows.Forms namespace. In the first example, the following instruction was used:

```
this.gpioInPort.BeginInvoke(new MethodInvoker(delegate
                                                {
                                                  this.gpioInPort.Write(true);
                                                }
                            )
                           );
```

You can also specify the Write method directly:

```
this.gpioInPort.BeginInvoke(new PortWriteDelegate(this.gpioInPort.Write),
                            new object[] { true });
```

but, when specifying the method directly, an additional delegate is needed:

```
private delegate void PortWriteDelegate(bool state);
```

In my opinion, anonymous methods are easier to read, more type safe, more extensible, and require fewer extraneous delegate declarations than using the method directly with additional delegates and untyped arguments with the `BeginInvoke` call.

In all the examples so far, the actual operation was enclosed within a `BeginInvoke` method. Both emulator components and controls provide the following methods and properties concerning synchronization:

- `IAsyncResult BeginInvoke(Delegate method)`

- `IAsyncResult BeginInvoke(Delegate method, params object[] args)`

- `object EndInvoke(IAsyncResult asyncResult)`

- `object Invoke(Delegate method)`

- `object Invoke(Delegate method, params object[] args)`

- `bool InvokeRequired { get; }`

With `BeginInvoke`, the calling thread is not blocked, because the task to process is placed in the queue of the target thread. You need to call `EndInvoke` only if you need to evaluate a return value.

With `Invoke`, the calling thread is blocked until the task was processed. In addition, this method can provide a return value.

With the `InvokeRequired` property, you can determine whether synchronization is necessary or whether you're already operating in the context of the correct threads.

The MaxPorts Property of GpioCollection

If you assign a pin number greater than 127 (or 49 with SDK 2.0) to a GPIO port, the emulator outputs an error message:

```xml
<?xml version="1.0" encoding="utf-8"?>
<Emulator>
  <Types>
    <GpioPort>Microsoft.SPOT.Emulator.Gpio.GpioPort</GpioPort>
  </Types>

  <EmulatorComponents>
    <GpioPort id="GPIOOut">
      <Pin>150</Pin>
      <ModesAllowed>OutputPort</ModesAllowed>
      <ModesExpected>OutputPort</ModesExpected>
    </GpioPort>
  </EmulatorComponents>
</Emulator>
```

You can solve this issue with configuration of the `GpioCollection` class. The `GpioCollection` class is a component collection that holds and manages emulator components of the `GpioPort` type. It inherits from `ComponentCollection` and is shown in Listing 13-8.

Listing 13-8. *The Microsoft.SPOT.Emulator.Gpio.GpioCollection Class*

```
using Microsoft.SPOT.Emulator;
using Microsoft.SPOT.Hardware;
using System;
using System.Reflection;

namespace Microsoft.SPOT.Emulator.Gpio
{
    public class GpioCollection : EmulatorComponentCollection
    {
        public GpioCollection();

        public uint DebounceTime { get; }
        public bool HardwareDebounceSupported { get; set; }
        public uint MaxPorts { get; set; }

        public GpioPort this[Cpu.Pin pin] { get; }

        public override void Register(EmulatorComponent ec);
        public override void SetupComponent();
        public override void Unregister(EmulatorComponent ec);
    }
}
```

The class manages the GPIO ports on the basis of their pin numbers. You can determine a port with the indexer of the class by the pin number. If no port with the indicated pin exists, an exception is thrown.

By default, you can only address 128 (0 to 127) pin numbers. You can increase the maximum possible pin number by assigning a higher value to the MaxPorts property, as demonstrated in Listing 13-9.

Listing 13-9. *Increasing the Maximum Port Number*

```
<?xml version="1.0" encoding="utf-8"?>
<Emulator>
  <Types>
    <GpioPort>Microsoft.SPOT.Emulator.Gpio.GpioPort</GpioPort>
    <GpioPortCollection>
      Microsoft.SPOT.Emulator.Gpio.GpioCollection</GpioPortCollection>
  </Types>

  <EmulatorComponents>
    <GpioPortCollection>
      <MaxPorts>256</MaxPorts>
    </GpioPortCollection>
```

```
      <GpioPort id="GPIOOut">
        <Pin>150</Pin>
        <ModesAllowed>OutputPort</ModesAllowed>
        <ModesExpected>OutputPort</ModesExpected>
      </GpioPort>
    </EmulatorComponents>
</Emulator>
```

Now, you can add and address GPIO ports with pin numbers from 0 to 255. You do not need to assign an ID to the GpioCollection in the configuration file, because the emulator class possesses a GpioPorts property of the GpioCollection type, which you can easily use to address the class from the emulator program code. Obtaining the component with the FindComponentById emulator method of the class emulator can be omitted.

You should address GPIO ports by their IDs with the FindComponentById method, not by their pin numbers using the GpioCollection component—only then is your emulator code independent of the pin configuration of your hardware, and porting the emulator to a new hardware platform is limited to changes at the configuration file.

The Serial Port

You can emulate a serial port with subclasses of the ComPort class. Figure 13-1 shows the class hierarchy of the components provided with the .NET Micro Framework SDK.

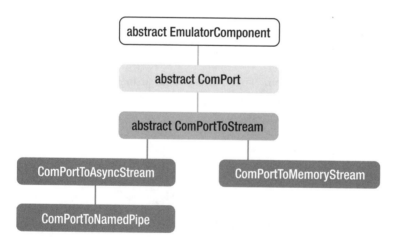

Figure 13-1. *Classes for serial port emulation*

ComPortToMemoryStream is a very useful component. With it, you can read and write data directly from within the emulator and exchange data with the .NET Micro Framework application. Use this component if you want communication between emulator and emulated application or if you want to write your own custom component for a device or sensor connected to the serial port. This component is also most useful if you want to provide and analyze the serial data from your own code, not just route it.

With the `ComPortToNamedPipe` component, you can communicate with a .NET Micro Framework application running on the emulator with a separate Windows application (outside of the emulator) running on the PC.

This section describes how to derive a custom subclass of `ComPortToStream` to route the data of a simulated COM port to sockets so that you are able to provide serial input for an emulated .NET Micro Framework application with the HyperTerminal tool or monitor the serial output of your application with HyperTerminal. In addition, you'll learn how a .NET Micro Framework application running on the emulator can communicate with real hardware over a physical serial port.

All COM port components, which only route the serial data (that is, all except `ComPortToMemoryStream`), are exchangeable. Exchanging them requires only small changes to the emulator configuration file, so the program code of an emulator remains untouched. That allows you to develop and debug a .NET Micro Framework application on an emulator first and, with HyperTerminal, send serial test data to your .NET Micro Framework application or verify the provided serial output. Afterward, you should test the emulated application with a real hardware component connected to a physical PC COM port by just replacing the socket emulator component with an emulator component for the physical COM port. Finally, your application should work fine with real hardware (the final hardware or a development board).

Communication Between Emulator and Application

An application simulating a serial port provides the direct data transfer between an emulator and a .NET Micro Framework application running on that emulator. You might display or enter serial data in any form on the user interface of the emulator (for example, a COM port monitor). Or you might want to provide your own emulator component that uses the serial port (for example, the simulation of a serial measuring instrument). In any case, data exchange is made directly with the RAM memory.

The emulator can provide simulated serial data with `ComPortToMemoryStream` for a .NET Micro Framework application running on the emulator to read it. The emulator writes the data into a stream, and a .NET Micro Framework application will be able to read the data over the serial port. The other direction works similarly. The emulator is able to read data from `ComPortToMemoryStream` that a .NET Micro Framework application sent over the serial port. Due to received commands or requests, the emulator can return simulated data in place of a sensor, for example. The configuration of a `ComPortToMemoryStream` component using XML is represented in Listing 13-10. This component is provided with the .NET Micro Framework SDK.

Listing 13-10. *Configuring the ComPortToMemoryStream Component*

```xml
<?xml version="1.0" encoding="utf-8"?>
<Emulator>
  <Types>
    <ComPort>Microsoft.SPOT.Emulator.Com.ComPortToMemoryStream</ComPort>
  </Types>

  <EmulatorComponents>
```

```
<ComPort id="COM1">
  <ComPortHandle>Usart1</ComPortHandle>
</ComPort>

</EmulatorComponents>
</Emulator>
```

The only property you can configure is `ComPortHandle`, which describes the serial port number to be simulated on the device. You need to specify the COM port as `Usart` (Universal Synchronous Asynchronous Receiver Transmitter) followed by the port number and describe the actual hardware module for the serial interface. Other transport types, such as `Debug` and `Messaging`, are reserved for internal use. The `ComPortHandle` property is of the `ComPortHandle` type. This class, by the way, implements its own static `Parse` method to interpret the XML information.

The example in Listing 13-11 demonstrates how the emulator can provide input data for the .NET Micro Framework to read.

Listing 13-11. *Providing Input Data from the Emulator for an Application to Read*

```
private void sendToAppButton_Click(object sender, EventArgs e)
{
    ComPortToMemoryStream comPort1 =
                this.emulator.FindComponentById("COM1") as ComPortToMemoryStream;
    byte[] bytes = Encoding.UTF8.GetBytes(this.com1ToAppTextBox.Text);
    comPort1.BeginInvoke(new MethodInvoker(delegate
                                    {
                                        comPort1.StreamOut.Write(bytes, 0, bytes.Length);
                                    }
                                    )
                        );
}
```

When clicking a button, the text of a text box is put on the serial port. The event handler for the button is called in the context of the GUI thread. Using the `BeginInvoke` method, the data writing will be done in the context of the emulator thread.

Next, you will learn how the emulator can read the data sent by a .NET Micro Framework application. Unfortunately, there is no callback method that signals the emulator when a .NET Micro Framework application has sent data to the serial port, so you need to poll whether any data is available to read. The example in Listing 13-12 creates a separate thread for polling the serial data.

Listing 13-12. *Using the Emulator to Read Serial Data Written from an Application to the Serial Port*

```
using System;
using System.Text;
using System.Threading;
using System.Windows.Forms;
using Microsoft.SPOT.Emulator;
using Microsoft.SPOT.Emulator.Com;
```

```csharp
namespace SerialPortSampleEmulator
{
    public partial class Form1 : Form
    {
        private readonly Emulator emulator;

        public Form1(Emulator emulator)
        {
            if (emulator == null)
                throw new ArgumentNullException("emulator");

            InitializeComponent();

            this.emulator = emulator;

            Thread comPortWatcherThread =
                new Thread(new ThreadStart(ComPortWatchThreadMethod));
            comPortWatcherThread.IsBackground = true;
            comPortWatcherThread.Start();
        }

        private void ComPortWatchThreadMethod()
        {
            ComPortToMemoryStream comPort1 =
                    this.emulator.FindComponentById("COM1") as ComPortToMemoryStream;
            byte[] buffer = new byte[1024];
            while (true)
            {
                int com1Count = 0;
                comPort1.Invoke(new MethodInvoker(
                            delegate
                            {
                              com1Count = comPort1.StreamOut.Read(buffer,
                                                                   0,
                                                                   buffer.Length);
                            }
                                       )
                            );
                if (com1Count > 0)
                 {
                     string text = Encoding.UTF8.GetString(buffer, 0, com1Count);
                     Invoke(new MethodInvoker(
                                      delegate
                                      {
                                        this.appToCom1TextBox.AppendText(text);
                                      }));
```

```
                }
                Thread.Sleep(25);
            }
        }
    }
}
```

■**Note** You can find a complete serial port emulator in the `SerialPortSampleEmulator` project located in the directory for this chapter.

Routing Data to and from Another Windows Application

You can also exchange data between a Windows application outside of the emulator and a .NET Micro Framework application running on the emulator.

For example, you can use this feature to write an external Windows application that provides simulated GPS data for an emulator. You can send the data through a named pipe, via the `ComPortToNamedPipe` emulator component, to a .NET Micro Framework application running on the emulator. The external Windows application writes the data into a named pipe, which then can be received by a .NET Micro Framework application over the serial port. Transferring data in the other direction is also possible: a Windows application reads data from a named pipe, which was sent by a .NET Micro Framework application over the serial port.

Listing 13-13 demonstrates how you can register and configure a `ComPortToNamedPipe` component. This component is provided with the .NET Micro Framework SDK. In most cases, an emulator does not have to address methods or properties of a `ComPortToNamedPipe` component, since the component routes only data between the emulator and external application, and vice versa. Therefore, the specification of an ID for this component can be omitted.

Listing 13-13. *Registering a ComPortToNamedPipe Component with the Configuration File*

```xml
<?xml version="1.0" encoding="utf-8" ?>
<Emulator>
  <Types>
    <ComPort>Microsoft.SPOT.Emulator.Com.ComPortToNamedPipe</ComPort>
  </Types>

  <EmulatorComponents>
    <ComPort>
      <ComPortHandle>Usart1</ComPortHandle>
      <Filename>\\.\pipe\SamplePipe</Filename>
    </ComPort>
  </EmulatorComponents>

</Emulator>
```

The `Filename` property describes the file name for the named pipe. The file names for named pipes always start with `\\.\pipe\`, followed by a unique name that needs to be known by both the emulator component and external application. The emulator component creates and opens a named pipe as soon as the .NET Micro Framework application on the emulator opens a serial port (the serial port opens when creating a `SerialPort` object). The named pipe is created from the emulator component as a client pipe in binary mode (that is, no-message mode). The other endpoint is a Windows application, which acts as server and waits until the emulator initiates a connection.

Further, you need the second communication endpoint—the external Windows application. Unfortunately, the full .NET Framework versions 2.0 and 3.0 do not support managed programming of pipes. Therefore, you need a few platform invoke (`PInvoke`) calls to the native Windows API. Fortunately, the full .NET Framework 3.5 possesses managed pipe classes.

Listing 13-14 demonstrates the initialization of a named pipe with the .NET Framework 2.0 and 3.0 using `PInvoke` calls. The initialization might seem a bit confusing. After successful initialization, however, you are able to comfortably address the pipe data via a stream. As before, the data that was written into the pipe can be read from the serial port with a .NET Micro Framework application running on the emulator, and in the other direction, the data sent to the serial port can be read from a pipe with the Windows application.

Using the managed pipe wrapper classes of the full .NET Framework 3.5 will simplify your program code, as shown in Listing 13-15. You must omit the prefix `\\.\pipe\` here; just specify the actual pipe name.

Listing 13-14. *Using Named Pipes with the Full .NET Framework 2.0 and 3.0*

```
using System;
using System.Text;
using System.Runtime.InteropServices;
using System.ComponentModel;
using System.IO;
using Microsoft.Win32.SafeHandles;
using System.Threading;

namespace PipeDesktopSample
{
    class Program
    {
        static void Main(string[] args)
        {
            const string pipeName = @"\\.\pipe\SamplePipe";
            const int inputBufferSize = 4096;
            const int outputBufferSize = 4096;

            IntPtr hPipe =
                NativeMethods.CreateNamedPipe
                        (
                        pipeName,
                        NativeMethods.PIPE_ACCESS_DUPLEX, // read/write access
```

```
                            NativeMethods.PIPE_TYPE_BYTE | // message type pipe
                            NativeMethods.PIPE_READMODE_BYTE | // message-read mode
                            NativeMethods.PIPE_WAIT, // blocking mode
                            NativeMethods.PIPE_UNLIMITED_INSTANCES, // max. instances
                            outputBufferSize, // output buffer size
                            inputBufferSize, // input buffer size
                            0, // default client time-out for WaitNamePipe Method
                            IntPtr.Zero // no security attribute
                        );
            SafeFileHandle safeHandle = new SafeFileHandle(hPipe, true);
            if (safeHandle.IsInvalid)
                throw new IOException("Could not open pipe " + pipeName + ".");

            Console.WriteLine("Waiting for client to connect.");
            bool connected = NativeMethods.ConnectNamedPipe(hPipe, IntPtr.Zero) ||
                            Marshal.GetLastWin32Error() ==
                            NativeMethods.ERROR_PIPE_CONNECTED;
            if (!connected)
                throw new Win32Exception(Marshal.GetLastWin32Error());
            Console.WriteLine("Connected to client.");

            Stream stream = new FileStream(safeHandle, FileAccess.ReadWrite, 4096);
            try
            {
                byte[] bytes = Encoding.UTF8.GetBytes("Hello World\n");
                while (true)
                {
                    stream.Write(bytes, 0, bytes.Length);
                    stream.Flush();//important to send immediately
                    Thread.Sleep(1000);
                }
            }
            finally
            {
                //proper disconnect before closing handle
                NativeMethods.DisconnectNamedPipe(safeHandle.DangerousGetHandle());
                stream.Dispose();
            }
        }
    }
}
```

Listing 13-15. *Using Named Pipes with the Full .NET Framework 3.5*

```
using System;
using System.IO.Pipes;
using System.Text;
```

```
using System.Threading;

namespace PipeDesktopSampleV35
{
    class Program
    {
        static void Main(string[] args)
        {
            using (NamedPipeServerStream serverPipeStream =
                new NamedPipeServerStream("SamplePipe"))
            {
                Console.WriteLine("Waiting for client to connect.");
                serverPipeStream.WaitForConnection();
                Console.WriteLine("Connected to client.");
                byte[] bytes = Encoding.UTF8.GetBytes("Hello World\n");
                while (true)
                {
                    serverPipeStream.Write(bytes, 0, bytes.Length);
                    serverPipeStream.Flush(); //to get sure it is sent immediately
                    Thread.Sleep(1000);
                }
            }
        }
    }
}
```

■**Note** You can find the emulator whose configuration file was shown in Listing 13-13 in the
`PipeSampleEmulator` project and the external Windows applications in the `PipeDesktopSample` and
`PipeDesktopSampleV35` projects (Listings 13-14 and 13-15). All three projects are in the directory for
this chapter.

Exchanging Serial Data with a Real Hardware Component

You might encounter the situation in which you need to start developing an application project,
but the target platform does not exist, or is not finished yet, and therefore, you need to use the
emulator to emulate your target platform to be able to start the programming of your application for the final, not-yet-available hardware. In addition, for example, a third-party sensor or
control unit that you want to connect to the final device may exist already for the serial port.

In the following example, a custom emulator component will be described that permits
you to access a real hardware module at a physical PC COM port with your .NET Micro Framework
application running on the emulator. The emulator component routes all serial data between
the emulator and Windows COM port (physical or virtual). Unfortunately, there is no built-in,
ready-to-use component provided with the .NET Micro Framework SDK. However, you can
easily create a custom emulator component, as shown in Listing 13-16.

Listing 13-16. *An Emulator Component to Access Real Hardware Connected to a Physical Serial PC Port*

```csharp
using System;
using Microsoft.SPOT.Emulator.Com;
using System.IO.Ports;

namespace Kuehner.SPOT.Emulator
{
    public class ComPortToPhysicalPcSerialPort : ComPortToStream
    {
        private SerialPort serialPort;
        private string physicalPortName = "COM1";
        private int baudrate = 9600;
        private int readTimeout = 1000;
        private Handshake handshake = Handshake.None;

        protected override void InitializeProtected()
        {
            base.InitializeProtected();
            if (this.Stream == null)
            {
                this.serialPort = new SerialPort(this.physicalPortName,
                                                 this.baudrate);
                this.serialPort.ReadTimeout = this.readTimeout;
                this.serialPort.Handshake = this.handshake;
                this.serialPort.Open();
                this.Stream = this.serialPort.BaseStream;
            }
        }

        protected override void UninitializeProtected()
        {
            base.UninitializeProtected();
            if (this.Stream != null)
            {
                this.serialPort.Close(); //also closes the underlying stream
                this.serialPort = null;
                this.Stream = null;
            }
        }

        #region properties
        public string PhysicalPortName
        {
            get { return this.physicalPortName; }
            set { this.physicalPortName = value; }
        }
```

```
        public int Baudrate
        {
            get { return this.baudrate; }
            set { this.baudrate = value; }
        }

        public int ReadTimeout
        {
            get { return this.readTimeout; }
            set { this.readTimeout = value; }
        }

        public Handshake Handshake
        {
            get { return this.handshake; }
            set { this.handshake = value; }
        }
        #endregion
    }
}
```

The custom emulator component extends the existing abstract ComPortToStream emulator component. The communication with the serial interface is realized with the System.IO.Ports. SerialPort class from the full .NET Framework. The custom emulator component possesses configurable properties for the serial port on your host PC, including the COM port name, baud rate, read timeout, and handshake.

The serial port object is not created and opened in the InitializeComponent virtual method of the EmulatorComponent class and not closed in the UninitializeComponent method; rather, it's opened and closed in the two virtual methods InitializeProtected and UninitializeProtected inherited from SerialPortToStream. This has the advantage that the serial port of the PC is only opened if necessary and remains open only as long as it is needed. InitializeComponent is called after initializing the emulator. UninitializeComponent is called when removing an EmulatorComponent, typically when terminating the emulator. InitializeProtected is called (in contrast to the InitializeComponent method) only if a .NET Micro Framework application running on the emulator opens the serial port (when a SerialPort object is created). UninitializeProtected is called if a .NET Micro Framework application releases the serial port (when the Dispose method of a SerialPort instance is called). If such an emulator component is registered with the emulator, but the executed .NET Micro Framework application does not use a serial port, no serial port will be opened on the PC.

After the serial port of the host PC is opened, in InitializeProtected, its BaseStream property is assigned to the Stream property of the emulator component, and the data is routed accordingly. Subclasses of SerialPortToStream are able to route all kind of streams, as the next sections will show.

The component can be configured as shown in Listing 13-17. All parameters for the configuration of the serial PC port are optional. If you do not describe the properties, they keep their default values.

Listing 13-17. *Configuration of the Custom ComPortToPhysicalPcSerialPort Component*

```xml
<?xml version="1.0" encoding="utf-8" ?>
<Emulator>
  <Types>
    <Com>Kuehner.SPOT.Emulator.ComPortToPhysicalPcSerialPort,
        ComPortEmulatorComponents</Com>
  </Types>

  <EmulatorComponents>
    <Com>
      <ComPortHandle>Usart2</ComPortHandle>
      <!--optional-->
      <RealPortName>COM1</RealPortName>
      <Baudrate>9600</Baudrate>
      <ReadTimeout>1000</ReadTimeout>
      <Handshake>None</Handshake>
    </Com>
  </EmulatorComponents>

</Emulator>
```

■**Note** You can find the source code for this component, as well as the following emulator components for COM ports, in the emulator component library project `ComPortEmulatorComponents`.

Exchanging Serial Data with HyperTerminal

Wouldn't it be nice to send serial test data to a terminal program like HyperTerminal or to monitor with HyperTerminal what an application running on the emulator transmitted to the serial port? Fortunately, HyperTerminal supports connections over TCP/IP sockets (see Figure 13-2), so you do not need a null modem cable or virtual serial ports. With sockets, data can be looped back within your host PC with the local host address 127.0.0.1.

Subclasses of the `ComPortToStream` emulator component are able to route serial data with any kind of stream. In this case, instead of a physical or virtual PC COM port, data is transmitted with a network socket (see Listing 13-18). Listing 13-19 demonstrates the configuration of this emulator component.

There is a small difference in the data flow compared to the previous emulator component in Listing 13-16. HyperTerminal acts as the client; that is, HyperTerminal initiates the connection, and the emulator component acts as the server that listens for a connection from HyperTerminal. Therefore, the emulator component pops up a message box with the instruction to create a connection from HyperTerminal as soon as the serial port is used by a .NET Micro Framework application. The .NET Micro Framework application is then blocked until you confirm the message box by clicking OK. If you still did not make a connection from HyperTerminal after confirmation, the emulator shows an error and terminates.

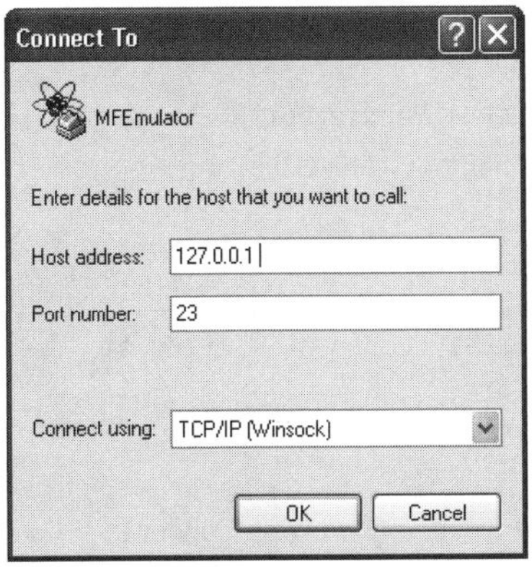

Figure 13-2. *Initiating a socket connection from HyperTerminal*

Listing 13-18. *The ComPortToServerSocket Custom Emulator Component*

```
using System;
using System.Net;
using System.Net.Sockets;
using System.Windows.Forms;
using Microsoft.SPOT.Emulator.Com;

namespace Kuehner.SPOT.Emulator
{
    public class ComPortToServerSocket : ComPortToStream
    {
        private Socket serverSocket;
        private IPAddress clientIpAddress = IPAddress.Loopback;
        private int ipPort = 23;
        private bool showWaitMessage = true;

        protected override void InitializeProtected()
        {
            base.InitializeProtected();
            if (this.Stream == null)
            {
                this.serverSocket = new Socket(AddressFamily.InterNetwork,
                                        SocketType.Stream,
                                        ProtocolType.Tcp);
                this.serverSocket.Bind(new IPEndPoint(this.clientIpAddress,
                                        this.ipPort)
                                );
                this.serverSocket.Listen(1);
                string message = string.Format(null,
                                        "The component {0} is waiting " +
                                        "for a client to connect at " +
                                        "port {1} for COM{2}.",
```

```
                                      this.ComponentId,
                                      this.ipPort,
                                      this.ComPortHandle.PortNumber);
        System.Diagnostics.Trace.WriteLine(message);
        if (this.showWaitMessage)
        {
            MessageBox.Show(message,
                        "ComPortToSocketServer Component waiting at " +
                        "Port " + this.ipPort,
                        MessageBoxButtons.OK);
        }
        //the emulator will block until a client eg. HyperTerm connects
        Socket clientSocket = this.serverSocket.Accept();
        this.Stream = new NetworkStream(clientSocket, true);
    }
}

protected override void UninitializeProtected()
{
    base.UninitializeProtected();
    if (this.Stream != null)
    {
        this.serverSocket.Close();
        this.serverSocket = null;
        this.Stream.Close();
        this.Stream = null;
    }
}

#region properties
public IPAddress ClientIpAddress
{
    get { return this.clientIpAddress; }
    set { this.clientIpAddress = value; }
}

public int IpPort
{
    get { return this.ipPort; }
    set { this.ipPort = value; }
}
```

```
        public bool ShowWaitMessage
        {
            get { return this.showWaitMessage; }
            set { this.showWaitMessage = value; }
        }
        #endregion
    }
}
```

Listing 13-19. *Configuring the ComPortToServerSocket Component*

```xml
<?xml version="1.0" encoding="utf-8" ?>
<Emulator>
  <Types>
    <ServerSocketCom>Kuehner.SPOT.Emulator.ComPortToServerSocket,
                     ComPortEmulatorComponents</ServerSocketCom>
  </Types>

  <EmulatorComponents>
    <ServerSocketCom>
      <ComPortHandle>Usart1</ComPortHandle>
      <!--optional-->
      <ClientIpAddress>127.0.0.1</ClientIpAddress>
      <IpPort>23</IpPort>
      <ShowWaitMessage>true</ShowWaitMessage>
    </ServerSocketCom>
  </EmulatorComponents>

</Emulator>
```

■**Note** HyperTerminal is not bundled with Windows Vista anymore. You can download a private edition from `http://www.hilgraeve.com/htpe/`, for personal use only. Or there are two *free* alternatives: TeraTerm Pro at `www.ayera.com/teraterm` and RealTerm at `http://realterm.sourceforge.net`.

Exchanging Data with Sockets Acting As a Client

This section describes a small variation to the previous socket component. The emulator component in Listing 13-21 will act as a client and connect with sockets to a server. With the component, the host IP address (127.0.0.1, if the server host is on the same PC as the emulator) can be specified (see Listing 13-20). As soon as a .NET Micro Framework on the emulator accesses the appropriate COM port, the component tries to connect with a server. Popping up a message box is not necessary here, since the other side must be already started and listening to a client. You can use this component with TeraTerm Pro, which has a built-in web server and can listen for incoming connections.

Listing 13-20. *Configuring the ComPortToClientSocket Emulator Component*

```xml
<?xml version="1.0" encoding="utf-8" ?>
<Emulator>
  <Types>
    <ClientSocketCom>Kuehner.SPOT.Emulator.ComPortToClientSocket,
                    ComPortEmulatorComponents</ClientSocketCom>
  </Types>

  <EmulatorComponents>
    <ClientSocketCom>
      <ComPortHandle>Usart1</ComPortHandle>
      <!--optional-->
      <HostIpAddress>127.0.0.1</HostIpAddress>
      <IpPort>23</IpPort>
    </ClientSocketCom>
  </EmulatorComponents>

</Emulator>
```

Listing 13-21. *The ComPortToClientSocket Emulator Component*

```csharp
using System;
using System.Net;
using System.Net.Sockets;
using Microsoft.SPOT.Emulator.Com;

namespace Kuehner.SPOT.Emulator
{
    public class ComPortToClientSocket : ComPortToStream
    {
        private IPAddress hostIpAddress = IPAddress.Loopback;
        private int ipPort = 23;

        protected override void InitializeProtected()
        {
            base.InitializeProtected();
            if (this.Stream == null)
            {
                Socket clientSocket = new Socket(AddressFamily.InterNetwork,
                                                 SocketType.Stream,
                                                 ProtocolType.Tcp);
                clientSocket.Connect(this.hostIpAddress, this.ipPort);
                this.Stream = new NetworkStream(clientSocket, true);
            }
        }
```

```
        protected override void UninitializeProtected()
        {
            base.UninitializeProtected();
            if (this.Stream != null)
            {
                this.Stream.Close();
                this.Stream = null;
            }
        }

        #region properties
        public IPAddress HostIpAddress
        {
            get { return this.hostIpAddress; }
            set { this.hostIpAddress = value; }
        }

        public int IpPort
        {
            get { return this.ipPort; }
            set { this.ipPort = value; }
        }
        #endregion
    }
}
```

The I²C bus

This section shows you how to use the I2cDevice and I2cBus emulator components to simulate devices connected to the I²C bus. You will also learn how to write a temperature sensor emulator component.

The I2cDevice Component

You can simulate devices connected to the I²C bus nearly as easily as serial devices. As a base class for all simulated I²C devices with the emulator, you need to extend the abstract emulator component class I2cDevice (see Listing 13-22). The I2cDevice class possesses only the Address property, which describes the address of the I²C module at the bus for the emulator.

Listing 13-22. *The Microsoft.SPOT.Emulator.I2c.I2cDevice Class*

```
using Microsoft.SPOT.Emulator;
using System;

namespace Microsoft.SPOT.Emulator.I2c
{
    public abstract class I2cDevice : EmulatorComponent
```

```
{
    protected byte _address;

    public I2cDevice();

    public byte Address { get; set; }

    protected virtual void DeviceBeginTransaction();
    protected virtual void DeviceEndTransaction();
    protected virtual void DeviceRead(byte[] data);
    protected virtual void DeviceWrite(byte[] data);
    public override bool IsReplaceableBy(EmulatorComponent ec);
    public static bool IsValidAddress(byte address);
    public override void SetupComponent();
}
}
```

The best and most flexible place to specify the address for a simulated I²C device is the configuration file. In order to create your own emulator component for an I²C module, you need to extend I2cDevice. Typically, you will override the two virtual methods DeviceRead and DeviceWrite. If a .NET Micro Framework application on the emulator has addressed and sent data to exactly this module, DeviceWrite is called. DeviceRead is called when a .NET Micro Framework application wants to read data from this module. The data parameter that is passed to DeviceRead is a byte array of the length of the requested data. That means if a .NET Micro Framework application wants to read, for example, 10 bytes from an I²C device, the DeviceRead method will be called with data dimensioned to ten elements. You do not need to allocate any memory yourself; just populate the dimensioned byte array with the appropriate data.

Both methods, DeviceBeginTransaction and DeviceEndTransaction, are called right before and after each time a .NET Micro Framework application calls the Execute method on a transaction. The base implementation does not do anything at all, but you can override the methods in your custom components. In a .NET Micro Framework application, the following code snippet

```
I2CDevice.I2CTransaction writeXAction = device.CreateWriteTransaction(outputData);
I2CDevice.I2CTransaction readXAction = device.CreateReadTransaction(inputData);
this.device.Execute(new I2CDevice.I2CTransaction[] { writeXAction, readXAction },
                    transactionTimeout);
```

would result in the following sequence of method calls:

1. BeginTransaction

2. DeviceWrite

3. DeviceRead

4. EndTransaction

The I2cBus Component

The I2cBus class is a component collection that contains and manages emulator components of the I2cDevice type. It inherits from the ComponentCollection class and has the members represented in Listing 13-23.

Listing 13-23. *The Microsoft.SPOT.Emulator.I2c.I2cBus Class*

```
using Microsoft.SPOT.Emulator;
using System;
using System.Reflection;

namespace Microsoft.SPOT.Emulator.I2c
{
    public class I2cBus : EmulatorComponentCollection
    {
        public I2cBus();

        public I2cDevice this[byte address] { get; }

        public override void Register(EmulatorComponent ec);
        public override void Unregister(EmulatorComponent ec);
    }
}
```

The I2cBus class manages the containing components based on their bus addresses. You can address and obtain the containing devices with the indexer of the class by specifying their bus addresses. If a device with the queried address does not exist, an exception is thrown.

You do not need to assign a unique ID to the I2cBus component in the configuration file. The emulator class possesses the I2cBus property of the I2cBus type, via which you can address the class in the program code directly. Therefore, you can omit obtaining the component with the FindComponentById method of the emulator class.

You should address I²C devices over their IDs with the FindComponentById method and not obtain them by their addresses with the I2cBus component. If you do so, your emulator code is independent of the address configuration, and porting the emulator to a new hardware platform requires you to only change the configuration file.

An Emulator Component for the TI TMP100 Temperature Sensor

In Chapter 5, you learned how to control the TI TMP100 temperature sensor with a custom managed driver; this chapter describes how to implement a custom emulator component for this sensor.

The custom emulator component for the sensor (see Listing 13-24) inherits, as expected, from I2cDevice and possesses only one public property, Temperature, of the float type, which lets you to set the measured temperature in degrees Celsius. You can either set this property once to a fixed value with the configuration file or change it at runtime with the emulator. So you could change the temperature, for example, with a track bar control on the emulator's user interface. When setting the temperature property with the XML configuration file, you need to pay attention to the correct decimal separator.

You need to override the DeviceWrite method to intercept the commands sent by a .NET Micro Framework application to the sensor—in this case, the command to trigger a new measurement or obtain the last measured temperature from the temperature register.

Listing 13-24. *The Emulator Component for the Temperature Sensor*

```
using System;
using System.Threading;
using Microsoft.SPOT.Emulator.I2c;
using Microsoft.SPOT.Emulator.Time;

namespace Kuehner.SPOT.Emulator
{
    public class TMP100Sensor : I2cDevice
    {
        private float temperature = 20.0f;
        private ushort temperatureRegister;
        private bool readTemperature;

        private const byte REGISTER_Control = 0x01;
        private const byte REGISTER_Temperature = 0x00;

        private const byte CONTROL_EnergyModeShutdown = 0x01;
        private const byte CONTROL_DataLengthTwelveBits = 0x60;
        private const byte CONTROL_OneShot = 0x80;

        protected override void DeviceWrite(byte[] data)
        {
            switch (data[0])
            {
                case REGISTER_Control:
                    if ((data[1] & CONTROL_OneShot) != 0) //make conversion
                    {
                        //only 12-bit conversion implemented
                        if ((data[1] & CONTROL_DataLengthTwelveBits) ==
                            CONTROL_DataLengthTwelveBits)
                        {
                            //conversion takes 600 ms for 12 Bit in the worst case
                            //temperature is available after this delay
                            new TimingServices.Timer(this.Emulator,
                                                new TimerCallback(Convert),
                                                null,
                                                600, //ms
                                                -1); //one shot
                        }
                    }
```

```
            }
            break;
        case REGISTER_Temperature: //read result of conversion from register
            this.readTemperature = true;
            break;
    }
}

private void Convert(object state)
{
    this.temperatureRegister = (ushort)(this.temperature * 256.0);
    this.temperatureRegister &= 0xFFF0; //keep only first 12 bit
}

protected override void DeviceRead(byte[] data)
{
    if(this.readTemperature) //if read command was received
    {
        data[0] = (byte)(this.temperatureRegister >> 8);
        data[1] = (byte)this.temperatureRegister;
        this.readTemperature = false;
    }
}

public float Temperature
{
    get { return this.temperature; }
    set
    {
        if (value < -128.0f || value >= 128.0f)
            throw new ArgumentOutOfRangeException("value", value, null);
        this.temperature = value;
    }
}
        }
    }
}
```

After triggering a 12-bit conversion, up to 600 milliseconds, in the worst case, may elapse before the measured temperature is converted and available in the temperature register for reading.

The extensible emulator is also able to simulate this behavior with the component. You can achieve this in the DeviceWrite method after you have received a OneShot command by starting a timer with a 600-millisecond interval. When the conversion time for the measurement expires, the measured temperature in the Temperature property is written into the temperature register. When reading the temperature register, the DeviceRead method is called, which provides the temperature register value to the .NET Micro Framework application. In this example, the special emulator timer Microsoft.SPOT.Emulator.Time.TimingServices.Timer is used. Timing and timers with the emulator will be discussed in detail later in this chapter.

The I2CTemperatureSensorSampleEmulator emulator project implements a complete emulator that uses the component in Listing 13-24, and you can find it in the directory for Chapter 13. With a track bar control, you can set the measurable temperature on the emulator's user interface. In Listing 13-25, you can see how to configure and register the component using XML. The component is registered with the TMP100 ID. With this ID, you can address and obtain the component with the emulator.

Listing 13-25. *Configuring the Temperature Sensor Component Using XML*

```xml
<?xml version="1.0" encoding="utf-8" ?>
<Emulator>
  <Types>
    <TMP100>Kuehner.SPOT.Emulator.TMP100Sensor,
            I2CtemperatureSensorSampleEmulator</TMP100>
  </Types>

  <EmulatorComponents>
    <TMP100 id="TMP100">
      <Address>72</Address>
    </TMP100>
  </EmulatorComponents>

</Emulator>
```

In the event handler of the track bar control, the measurable temperature is assigned to the component. Setting the Temperature property will store the temperature in the component, so that it can be returned when the temperature register is read from the .NET Micro Framework application the next time.

```
private void temperatureTrackBar_Scroll(object sender, EventArgs e)
{
    float temperature = this.temperatureTrackBar.Value / 1000.0f;
    this.temperatureSensor.BeginInvoke(new MethodInvoker(delegate
                            {
                                this.temperatureSensor.Temperature = temperature;
                            }));
    this.temperatureLabel.Text = temperature.ToString("F3") + " ° Celsius";
}
```

The SPI Bus

This section shows you how to use the SpiDevice and SpiBus emulator components to simulate devices connected to the SPI bus. You will also learn how to write an analog/digital converter emulator component.

The SpiDevice Component

Simulating a device connected at the SPI bus is also very straightforward. The base class for SPI devices in the emulator is the abstract SpiDevice class (see Listing 13-26). You need to indicate for the emulator only the Pin property, which describes the chip select line of a SPI component at the bus. All other configurable properties are optional; they will not be used by the emulator at all and are purely informative. Your custom components may, however, use the information.

Listing 13-26. *The Microsoft.SPOT.Emulator.Spi.SpiDevice Class*

```
using Microsoft.SPOT.Emulator;
using Microsoft.SPOT.Hardware;
using System;

namespace Microsoft.SPOT.Emulator.Spi
{
    public abstract class SpiDevice : EmulatorComponent
    {
        protected bool _chipSelectActiveState;
        protected uint _chipSelectHoldTime;
        protected uint _chipSelectSetupTime;
        protected bool _clockEdge;
        protected bool _clockIdleState;
        protected uint _clockRateKHz;
        protected Microsoft.SPOT.Hardware.Spi.SpiModule _spiModule;

        public SpiDevice();
        public SpiDevice(Cpu.Pin pin);
        public SpiDevice(Microsoft.SPOT.Hardware.Spi.Configuration configuation);

        public bool ChipSelectActiveState { get; set; }
        public uint ChipSelectHoldTime { get; set; }
        public uint ChipSelectSetupTime { get; set; }
        public bool ClockEdge { get; set; }
        public bool ClockIdleState { get; set; }
        public uint ClockRateKHz { get; set; }
        public Cpu.Pin Pin { get; set; }
        public Microsoft.SPOT.Hardware.Spi.SpiModule SpiModule { get; set; }

        public override bool IsReplaceableBy(EmulatorComponent ec);
        public override void SetupComponent();
        protected virtual byte[] Write(byte[] data);
        protected virtual ushort[] Write(ushort[] data);
    }
}
```

The chip select pin number is best specified with the configuration file. To write a custom emulator component for a SPI module, you need to derive and extend a subclass of SpiDevice. There is no separate read method, because for accessing SPI devices, a combination of write and read access is always necessary. Typically, you might override and implement one of the two overloads of the virtual Write method: one method processes data from a byte array, and the other expects an array with 16-bit integer values. You can use the most optimal method for the format in which the data to send and receive is provided. Write is called if a .NET Micro Framework application running on the emulator sends data (a command or request) to exactly this SPI module. The method returns the appropriate result depending on the received data (commands or requests) back to the .NET Micro Framework application.

The SpiBus Class

The SpiBus class (see Listing 13-27) is a component collection that contains and manages emulator components of the SpiDevice type. It extends ComponentCollection and looks as shown in Listing 13-27.

Listing 13-27. *The Microsoft.SPOT.Emulator.Spi.SpiBus Class*

```
using Microsoft.SPOT.Emulator;
using Microsoft.SPOT.Hardware;
using System;
using System.Reflection;

namespace Microsoft.SPOT.Emulator.Spi
{
    public class SpiBus : EmulatorComponentCollection
    {
        public SpiBus();

        public SpiDevice this[Cpu.Pin pin] { get; }

        public override void Register(EmulatorComponent ec);
        public override void Unregister(EmulatorComponent ec);
    }
}
```

The SpiBus class manages the containing components on the basis of the pin number of their chip select port. You can address and obtain the containing devices with the indexer of the class by specifying their chip select pin numbers. If a device with the queried chip select pin does not exist, an exception is thrown.

You do not need to assign a unique ID to the SpiBus component in the configuration file. The emulator class possesses a SpiBus property of the SpiBus type, via which you can address the class in the program code directly. Therefore, you can omit obtaining the component with the FindComponentById method of the emulator class.

You should address SPI devices by their IDs with the FindComponentById method and not by obtaining their chip select pin number with the SpiBus component. If you do so, your emulator code is independent of the pin configuration, and porting the emulator to a new hardware platform requires you to change only the configuration file.

An Emulator Component for the ADC124S101 AD Converter

In Chapter 5, you learned how to control the ADC124101AD converter with a custom managed driver; this chapter describes how to implement a custom emulator component for this AD converter. You can see the implementation in Listing 13-28.

The custom emulator component for the converter inherits, as you'd expect, from SpiDevice and possesses only one property, SupplyVoltage, of the uint type to set the power supply voltage. You should specify this property in the XML configuration file, because the maximum measurable voltage depends on the supplied voltage. You need to specify the voltage as an integer in millivolts. The voltage is specified as an integer to avoid a language- and culture-dependant decimal separator. So you could change the voltage to measure, for example, with a track bar control on the emulator's user interface.

You need to override the Write method to receive the commands sent from a .NET Micro Framework application to the module. In this case, an application needs to send the address (1–4) of the ADC channel it wants to read from.

Listing 13-28. *An Emulator Component for the AD Converter*

```
using System;
using Microsoft.SPOT.Emulator.Spi;

namespace Kuehner.SPOT.Emulator
{
    public sealed class ADC124S101 : SpiDevice
    {
        public enum AdcChannel { ADC1, ADC2, ADC3, ADC4 };

        private uint supplyVoltage = 5000;
        private readonly float[] voltages = new float[4];

        protected override ushort[] Write(ushort[] data)
        {
            //what was written to the bus is in data
            int channel = data[0]; //selected ADC channel
            float supplyVoltageVolt = this.supplyVoltage / 1000.0f;
            ushort rawValue = (ushort)(this.voltages[channel] /
                                supplyVoltageVolt *
                                4096.0f +
                                0.5f);
            return new ushort[] { rawValue }; //return what will be read
        }

        /// <summary>The supply voltage for the IC in Milli-Volts./// </summary>
        public uint SupplyVoltage
        {
            get { return this.supplyVoltage; }
            set { this.supplyVoltage = value; }
        }
    }
```

```
        /// <summary>
        /// returns the measured voltage in Volt of
        /// the specified ADC channel.
        /// </summary>
        public float this[AdcChannel channel]
        {
            get { return this.voltages[(int)channel]; }
            set
            {
                if (value < 0 || value >= this.supplyVoltage / 1000.0f)
                    throw new ArgumentOutOfRangeException("value", value, null);
                this.voltages[(int)channel] = value;
            }
        }
    }
}
```

The SpiAdcConverterSampleEmulator emulator project implements a complete emulator that uses the component in Listing 13-28, and you can find it in this chapter's directory. With a track bar control, you can set the measurable voltage on the emulator's user interface. In Listing 13-29, you can see how to configure and register the component using XML. The component is registered with the ADC ID. With this ID, you can address and obtain the component with the emulator.

Listing 13-29. *Configuring the ADC Emulator Component Using XML*

```
<?xml version="1.0" encoding="utf-8" ?>
<Emulator>
  <Types>
    <ADC124S101>Kuehner.SPOT.Emulator.ADC124S101,
                SpiAdConverterSampleEmulator</ADC124S101>
  </Types>

  <EmulatorComponents>
    <ADC124S101 id="ADC">
      <Pin>10</Pin> <!--chip select-->
      <SupplyVoltage>5000</SupplyVoltage>
      <!--SPI-->
      <ClockRateKHz>15000</ClockRateKHz>
      <ChipSelectActiveState>false</ChipSelectActiveState>
      <ChipSelectSetupTime>1</ChipSelectSetupTime>
      <ChipSelectHoldTime>1</ChipSelectHoldTime>
      <ClockIdleState>true</ClockIdleState>
      <ClockEdge>false</ClockEdge>
      <SpiModule>Spi1</SpiModule>
    </ADC124S101>
  </EmulatorComponents>

</Emulator>
```

In the event handler of the track bar control, the measurable voltage is assigned to the component as soon as the track bar is moved. Setting the voltage will just store the value with the emulator component to return the voltage when the .NET Micro Framework application reads from the AD converter the next time.

```
private void voltageTrackBar_Scroll(object sender, EventArgs e)
{
    float voltage = this.voltageTrackBar.Value / 1000.0f;
    this.adc.BeginInvoke(new MethodInvoker(delegate
                        { this.adc[ADC124S101.AdcChannel.ADC1] = voltage; }));
    this.voltageLabel.Text = voltage.ToString("F3") + " Volt";
}
```

Emulator Timing

This section covers the emulator timing and special emulator timers. For this, the .NET Micro Framework SDK provides the `Microsoft.SPOT.Emulator.Time.TimingServices` emulator component and its embedded classes. This section looks closely at these classes and shows how to simulate a certain processor speed. In addition, it explains how to put tasks asynchronously into the queue of the emulator to process. You will learn what continuations and completions are and how you can use special emulator timers to simulate correct time intervals. Finally, you will see how to implement a custom oscillator component for the emulator that toggles a GPIO pin periodically.

Simulating the Processor Speed

The `Microsoft.SPOT.Emulator.Time.TimingServices` class possesses only one configurable property—the `SystemClockFrequency` property for setting the clock rate of the processor in Hertz. To simulate a processor at 32 MHz, you need to use the XML configuration in Listing 13-30.

Listing 13-30. *Setting the Processor Speed*

```xml
<?xml version="1.0" encoding="utf-8" ?>
<Emulator>
  <Types>
    <TimingServices>Microsoft.SPOT.Emulator.Time.TimingServices</TimingServices>
  </Types>

  <EmulatorComponents>
    <TimingServices>
      <SystemClockFrequency>32000000</SystemClockFrequency>
    </TimingServices>
  </EmulatorComponents>

</Emulator>
```

Note that you do not need to specify a unique ID for the component, since the component can be obtained in the emulator code via the `TimingServices` property of the emulator class.

If you do not specify a system clock frequency, the default value 27 MHz is applied. The slowest processor on which the .NET Micro Framework is able to run is, by the way, exactly clocked at 27 MHz.

Continuations

Continuations are tasks that are placed into the queue of the emulator for processing. The program execution is continued immediately after placing a continuation into the queue. Continuations are always executed in the context of the emulator, and they are executed in the emulator thread even if they were placed into the queue by another thread. If several continuations are in the queue, they will be successively processed in the order they were placed there (first in, first out). Continuations are only processed when the emulator is not busy with other tasks (i.e., when it's in the idle state), when the emulator waits for events, or the program execution of an application was paused with `Thread.Sleep`. Continuations are suitable whenever the end of a task does not matter because the task does not return a result that needs to be evaluated, or if your task should be executed at the soonest possible time but not within a specific time.

Continuations are realized with the embedded abstract `Continuation` class of `TimingServices`. Fortunately, you do not have to use this class and do not need to derive a custom continuation class from it in order to use continuations. The mechanism for synchronizing the emulator and GUI thread using the `BeginInvoke` methods, as discussed earlier, internally uses continuations. Since the emulator is also an emulator component, just call one of the `BeginInvoke` methods of the emulator class.

Completions

Completions are similar to continuations. A `Completion` is a continuation, with the difference that a `Completion` is not executed as soon as possible but after a certain, given time period.

Completions are realized with the embedded abstract `Continuation` class of `TimingServices`. Fortunately, it is not necessary to use this class directly or to derive a custom completion at all. The next section describes a special timer class provided with the .NET Micro Framework SDK, which greatly simplifies working with completions and can be used like a common timer.

Timers

The embedded `Microsoft.SPOT.Emulator.Time.TimingServices.Timer` class can be used like the common timer from the `System.Threading` namespace. This emulator timer abstracts and simplifies handling time-critical tasks with continuations, as discussed earlier, on an emulator.

To realize time-critical tasks with an emulator, for example, periodically calling a method or implementing a one-shot timer to be called after a certain time, you should never use the Windows timer from the `System.Threading` namespace; always use the emulator-specific timer `Microsoft.SPOT.Emulator.Time.TimingServices.Timer`. For example, you may need to toggle a GPIO input port with the emulator to be read with a .NET Micro Framework application running on the emulator. Using an emulator timer will toggle the GPIO port for the application each second. If you're using a Windows timer, the accuracy depends on the speed of the PC processor. Then too, if the .NET Micro Framework application on the emulator is debugged and if it is interrupted by a break point, the timing of the emulator-specific timer is also paused.

In the earlier section about SPI, an emulator component for a temperature sensor was presented. After triggering a measurement, it takes up to 600 milliseconds until a new reading with 12-bit accuracy is converted and available. This time performance is simulated in the component by an emulator timer.

```
//conversion takes 600 ms for 12 Bit in the worst case
//temperature is available after this delay
new TimingServices.Timer(this.Emulator,
                        new TimerCallback(Convert),
                        null,
                        600, //ms
                        -1); //one shot
```

The next section shows how to use the emulator timer on a concrete example. It describes an oscillator component that periodically toggles a GPIO input pin.

An Oscillator Component

Now, an oscillator component is to be provided. The oscillator periodically toggles a GPIO input port and thus generates a square wave signal.

The component inherits from and extends the GpioPort component. The most important configurable properties are the pin number of the pin to toggle and the duration of a period in milliseconds. The GPIO port that can be used must be configured with ModesAllowed and ModesExpected in such a way that it can be used as an input port (by specifying InputPort or InputOutputPort). The timer method is executed in the context of the emulator; therefore, no synchronization is necessary to toggle the port. The emulator configuration of the oscillator component is shown in Listing 13-31 and the component in Listing 13-32.

Listing 13-31. *Configuring the Oscillator Emulator Component with XML*

```
<?xml version="1.0" encoding="utf-8" ?>
<Emulator>
  <Types>
    <Oscillator>Kuehner.SPOT.Emulator.Oscillator, OscillatorComponent</Oscillator>
  </Types>

  <EmulatorComponents>
    <Oscillator>
      <Pin>3</Pin>
      <ModesAllowed>InputPort</ModesAllowed>
      <ModesExpected>InputPort</ModesExpected>
      <Period>500</Period>
    </Oscillator>
  </EmulatorComponents>

</Emulator>
```

Listing 13-32. *The Oscillator Component*

```
using System;
using System.Threading;
```

```csharp
using Microsoft.SPOT.Hardware;
using Microsoft.SPOT.Emulator;
using Microsoft.SPOT.Emulator.Time;
using Microsoft.SPOT.Emulator.Gpio;

namespace Kuehner.SPOT.Emulator
{
    public sealed class Oscillator : GpioPort
    {
        private int period = 500;
        private TimingServices.Timer timer;

        public Oscillator()
        {
            this.ModesAllowed = GpioPortMode.InputPort;
            this.ModesExpected = GpioPortMode.InputPort;
        }

        public override void InitializeComponent()
        {
            base.InitializeComponent();
            this.timer = new TimingServices.Timer(this.Emulator,
                                                  new TimerCallback(OnTimer),
                                                  null,
                                                  0,
                                                  this.period);
        }

        public override void UninitializeComponent()
        {
            this.timer.AbortCompletion();
            base.UninitializeComponent();
        }

        private void OnTimer(object target)
        {
            bool status = Read();
            Write(!status);
        }

        /// <summary>
        /// The time interval between toggling the GPIO pin in milliseconds.
        /// </summary>
```

```
    public int Period
    {
        get { return this.period; }
        set
        {
            if (value <= 0)
                throw new ArgumentOutOfRangeException("value",
                                    "Period must be a positive number of ms.");
            this.period = value;
            if (this.timer != null)
                this.timer.Change(0, value);
        }
    }
  }
}
```

───

■**Note** You can find the oscillator component in the `OscillatorComponent` component library project. Also an emulator configured for using this component can be found in the `OscillatorSampleEmulator` project. The library assembly with the component must be either in the same directory as the emulator or in the GAC.

───

To try out the oscillator component, you can use an existing .NET Micro Framework application. In the directory for Chapter 5, you'll find the `GpioInterruptPortEdgeSample` project (see Listing 13-33). This application creates an interrupt port that is triggered on both edges of the GPIO input signal. In addition, it prints the current state of the input port and the current time in the interrupt handler. The oscillator component needs to be configured in such a way that it operates on GPIO pin 3, as the .NET Micro Framework application requires.

Listing 13-33. *A .NET Micro Framework Application for Use with the Oscillator Component*

```
using System;
using System.Threading;
using Microsoft.SPOT;
using Microsoft.SPOT.Hardware;

namespace GpioInterruptPortEdgeSample
{
    public class Program
    {
        public static void Main()
        {
```

```
            InterruptPort port = new InterruptPort(
                                    Cpu.Pin.GPIO_Pin3,
                                    false, //no glitch filter
                                    Port.ResistorMode.PullDown,
                                    Port.InterruptMode.InterruptEdgeBoth
                                    );
            port.OnInterrupt += new GPIOInterruptEventHandler(port_OnInterrupt);

            Thread.Sleep(Timeout.Infinite);
        }

        private static void port_OnInterrupt(Cpu.Pin port, bool state,
                                    TimeSpan time)
        {
            Debug.Print("Pin=" + port + " State=" + state + " Time=" + time);
        }
    }
}
```

The application in Listing 13-33 creates the following output when used with the oscillator from Listing 13-32. You can see clearly that the GPIO input port toggles every 500 milliseconds, as it was configured to do in Listing 13-31.

```
Pin=3 State=False Time=01:43:21.729
Pin=3 State=True Time=01:43:22.221
Pin=3 State=False Time=01:43:22.729
Pin=3 State=True Time=01:43:23.223
Pin=3 State=False Time=01:43:23.731
Pin=3 State=True Time=01:43:24.223
Pin=3 State=False Time=01:43:24.726
```

Memory Management

Each device possesses some kind of memory. With the MemoryManager class, you can describe and simulate random access memory (RAM) and flash memory. The MemoryManager class does not possess configurable simple properties; however, it serves as a container for the two components RamManager and FlashManager. RamManager and FlashManager are both emulator components, and the memory manager automatically creates them (like the linked components discussed earlier in Chapter 12). This allows you to configure the RAM and flash manager in the emulator configuration file as complex properties.

RAM

The MemoryManager has a RamManager property that is of the RamManager type. With RAM memory, there is only the one configurable property, Size, which indicates the size of the RAM memory in bytes. You can specify the number of bytes in hexadecimal notation with the format attribute in the XML file (see Listing 13-34). For the RamManager property, you must declare the data type

RamManager in the Types section to make it resolvable for the configuration engine. After the data type is declared, you need to indicate the data type with the type attribute. The details for configuration with the format and type attribute, as well as the configuration of complex properties, were already described in detail in Chapter 12, which covers the XML configuration.

Listing 13-34. *Configuring RAM Memory*

```
<?xml version="1.0" encoding="utf-8"?>
<Emulator>
  <Types>
    <MemoryManager>Microsoft.SPOT.Emulator.Memory.MemoryManager</MemoryManager>
    <RamManager>Microsoft.SPOT.Emulator.Memory.RamManager</RamManager>
  </Types>

  <EmulatorComponents>

    <MemoryManager>
      <RamManager type="RamManager">
        <Size format="HexNumber">2000000</Size>
      </RamManager>
    </MemoryManager>

  </EmulatorComponents>
</Emulator>
```

Flash Memory

Flash memory is exposed with the FlashManager property of the MemoryManager class, which is a FlashManager component. Flash memory is divided into sectors, partitions, and blocks; each block is intended for a certain purpose.

The flash manager is a container for flash sectors, and it possesses the following three configurable properties:

- bool IsReadOnly
- uint MaxSectorEraseTime
- uint MaxWordWriteTime

Note The FlashManager class possesses, exactly the same as RamManager, the public and configurable Size property, since this property is provided by the common base class MemoryManagerBase. For FlashManager, you do not need to set this property, because the memory capacity is calculated automatically on the basis of the flash sectors. A specified value in the configuration file will be overwritten in every case.

The FlashSectors property is a collection of FlashSector entries that describe the layout and purpose of the flash memory (see Listing 13-35).

Listing 13-35. *The Microsoft.SPOT.Emulator.Memory.FlashSector Class*

```
public struct FlashSector
{
    public uint Length;
    public FlashSectorUsage Usage;
    public FlashSectorPartition Partition;
    public FlashSectorBlock Block;
    public FlashSector(uint length,
                       FlashSectorUsage usage,
                       FlashSectorPartition partition,
                       FlashSectorBlock block);
    public FlashSector(uint length,
                       FlashSectorUsage usage,
                       FlashSectorPartition partition);
}
```

A sector is the smallest definable unit within the flash memory. Each sector describes a certain memory allocation by its length, which is indicated with the Length member.

A partition consists of one or more blocks, and a block contains one or more sectors.

The Block member defines the location of the sector within the superordinate block. For the FlashSectorBlock enumeration, the following values are possible:

- Start: The sector is at the beginning and defines the start of a block.

- End: The sector is at the end and defines the end of a block.

- None: The sector is somewhere in the middle of the superordinate block.

- StartEnd: The superordinate block consists only of this one sector.

The Partition member defines the location of the sector within the superordinate partition. For the FlashSectorPartition enumeration, the following values are possible:

- Start: The sector is at the beginning and defines the start of a partition.

- End: The sector is at the end and defines the end of a partition.

- None: The sector is somewhere in the middle of the superordinate partition.

- StartEnd: The superordinate partition consists only of this one sector.

The first sector of your flash memory must have Partition and Block set to Start (or StartEnd if there is only one definition). The last sector must set Partition and Block to End (or StartEnd if there is only one definition). An End definition must not occur before a Start, and a Start must be paired with exactly one End. The FlashManager component verifies these obvious rules and throws an exception when they are not obeyed.

The Usage member describes the purpose of this sector. This information is used by the system for optimization and validation. Possible values for the FlashSectorUsage enumeration are Application, Bootstrap, Code, Config, Deployment, Log, StorageA, and StorageB.

Listing 13-36 demonstrates a sample configuration of a flash memory layout.

Listing 13-36. *Configuring the Flash Memory*

```xml
<?xml version="1.0" encoding="utf-8"?>
<Emulator>
  <Types>
    <MemoryManager>Microsoft.SPOT.Emulator.Memory.MemoryManager</MemoryManager>
    <RamManager>Microsoft.SPOT.Emulator.Memory.RamManager</RamManager>
    <FlashManager>Microsoft.SPOT.Emulator.Memory.FlashManager</FlashManager>
    <FlashSector>Microsoft.SPOT.Emulator.Memory.FlashSector</FlashSector>
  </Types>

  <EmulatorComponents>

    <MemoryManager>
      <RamManager type="RamManager">
        <Size format="HexNumber">2000000</Size>
      </RamManager>
      <FlashManager type="FlashManager">
        <FlashSectors>
          <FlashSector>
            <Length format="HexNumber">10000</Length>
            <Usage>Bootstrap</Usage>
            <Partition>Start</Partition>
            <Block>StartEnd</Block>
          </FlashSector>
          <FlashSector>
            <Length format="HexNumber">10000</Length>
            <Usage>Config</Usage>
            <Partition>None</Partition>
            <Block>StartEnd</Block>
          </FlashSector>
          <FlashSector>
            <Length format="HexNumber">10000</Length>
            <Usage>Code</Usage>
            <Partition>None</Partition>
            <Block>StartEnd</Block>
          </FlashSector>
          ...
          <FlashSector>
            <Length format="HexNumber">10000</Length>
            <Usage>Code</Usage>
            <Partition>None</Partition>
            <Block>StartEnd</Block>
          </FlashSector>
          <FlashSector>
            <Length format="HexNumber">10000</Length>
            <Usage>Deployment</Usage>
            <Partition>None</Partition>
```

```
        <Block>StartEnd</Block>
      </FlashSector>
      ...
      <FlashSector>
        <Length format="HexNumber">10000</Length>
        <Usage>Deployment</Usage>
        <Partition>None</Partition>
        <Block>StartEnd</Block>
      </FlashSector>
      <FlashSector>
        <Length format="HexNumber">10000</Length>
        <Usage>Log</Usage>
        <Partition>None</Partition>
        <Block>StartEnd</Block>
      </FlashSector>
      <FlashSector>
        <Length format="HexNumber">20000</Length>
        <Usage>Log</Usage>
        <Partition>None</Partition>
        <Block>StartEnd</Block>
      </FlashSector>
      ...
      <FlashSector>
        <Length format="HexNumber">10000</Length>
        <Usage>Log</Usage>
        <Partition>None</Partition>
        <Block>StartEnd</Block>
      </FlashSector>
      <FlashSector>
        <Length format="HexNumber">10000</Length>
        <Usage>StorageA</Usage>
        <Partition>None</Partition>
        <Block>StartEnd</Block>
      </FlashSector>
      <FlashSector>
        <Length format="HexNumber">10000</Length>
        <Usage>StorageB</Usage>
        <Partition>End</Partition>
        <Block>StartEnd</Block>
      </FlashSector>
    </FlashSectors>
  </FlashManager>
 </MemoryManager>

 </EmulatorComponents>
</Emulator>
```

Emulating Persistent Flash Memory

Often, it is desirable to emulate the behavior and layout of a persistent flash memory to test and debug; for example, you might want to test the data storage in the flash memory using an ExtendedWeakReference reference. The built-in FlashManager component, unfortunately, does not offer this possibility. When the emulator is terminated, the data in the flash memory is lost. With the .NET Micro Framework SDK, a sample emulator named EWRSampleEmulator in the ExtendedWeakReferences solution is located in the Samples directory. This emulator writes the content of the flash memory, when terminating the emulator, into a file and recovers the data again with the emulator initialization from this file (if it's available). Unfortunately, this functionality is built into the emulator, so it can be used with only this emulator. It would be much more practical and flexible to derive a custom component from FlashManager and extend it with the functionality from the sample. In Listing 13-37, you can see the PersistentFlashManager component, which allows you to use persistent flash storage with any emulator. You can find this component in the PersistentFlashManagerComponent emulator component library in this chapter's directory.

Listing 13-37. *The Custom PersistentFlashManager Emulator Component*

```
using System;
using System.IO;
using System.Reflection;
using Microsoft.SPOT.Emulator.Memory;

namespace Kuehner.SPOT.Emulator
{
    public class PersistentFlashManager : FlashManager
    {
        private readonly string flashPath;

        public PersistentFlashManager()
        {
            //the file name of the flash file is the same as
            //the current emulator executable but with .flash extension
            //so every emulator has its own flash file
            string emulatorPath =
                    Assembly.GetEntryAssembly().GetModules()[0].FullyQualifiedName;
            this.flashPath = Path.ChangeExtension(emulatorPath, ".flash");
        }

        public override void InitializeComponent()
        {
            base.InitializeComponent();
            //reading from file
            if (File.Exists(this.flashPath))
            {
                using (FileStream stream = File.OpenRead(this.flashPath))
                {
```

```
                    //only read if file size matches size of flash
                    if (stream.Length == this._size)
                        stream.Read(this._memory, 0, (int)this._size);
                }
            }
        }

        public override void UninitializeComponent()
        {
            //writing to file
            using (FileStream stream = File.OpenWrite(this.flashPath))
                stream.Write(this._memory, 0, (int)this._size);
            //frees the memory so it needs to be called after persisting
            base.UninitializeComponent();
        }
    }
}
```

To use the `FlashManager` component without custom sector definitions but with the default sector definitions, just a simple configuration is necessary, as demonstrated in Listing 13-38.

Listing 13-38. *A Simple Configuration of the FlashManager Component*

```xml
<?xml version="1.0" encoding="utf-8" ?>
<Emulator>
  <Types>
    <MemoryManager>Microsoft.SPOT.Emulator.Memory.MemoryManager</MemoryManager>
    <FlashManager>Kuehner.SPOT.Emulator.PersistentFlashManager,
                  PersistentFlashManagerComponent</FlashManager>
  </Types>

  <EmulatorComponents>
    <MemoryManager>
      <FlashManager type="FlashManager">
      </FlashManager>
    </MemoryManager>
  </EmulatorComponents>

</Emulator>
```

To use custom sector definitions in Listing 13-36 with the flash manager, you need to replace the following line in the `Types` section:

```xml
<FlashManager>Microsoft.SPOT.Emulator.Memory.FlashManager</FlashManager>
```

with the following type declaration:

```
<FlashManager>Kuehner.SPOT.Emulator.PersistentFlashManager,
            PersistentFlashManagerComponent</FlashManager>
```

This functionality can be added with the help of your custom emulator component for the emulation of the persistent flash memory simply to any emulator.

Simulating a Battery Cell

It may be necessary to test the behavior of your application with certain battery configurations. Therefore, there is a configurable emulator component to simulate a battery cell. This emulator component is named BatteryCell and is provided with the .NET Micro Framework SDK in the Microsoft.SPOT.Emulator.dll assembly. With this component, you can directly set the charging state. Testing your application with various charging states using physical hardware would be much more complex. You can see the different configuration options in Listing 13-39.

Listing 13-39. *Configuring a Battery Cell*

```
<?xml version="1.0" encoding="utf-8"?>
<Emulator>
  <Types>
    <Battery>Microsoft.SPOT.Emulator.Battery.BatteryCell</Battery>
  </Types>

  <EmulatorComponents>
    <Battery>
      <Voltage>5123</Voltage>         <!--5.123 V-->
      <Temperature>234</Temperature> <!--23.4 °C-->
      <!--percent values (integer)-->
      <StateOfCharge>35</StateOfCharge>
      <BatteryLifeMin>10</BatteryLifeMin>
      <BatteryLifeLow>20</BatteryLifeLow>
      <BatteryLifeMed>30</BatteryLifeMed>
      <BatteryLifeFullMin>60</BatteryLifeFullMin>
      <BatteryLifeMax>98</BatteryLifeMax>
      <!--durations in milli seconds (integer)-->
      <BatteryLifeHysteresis>6</BatteryLifeHysteresis>
      <TimeoutCharging>30</TimeoutCharging>
      <TimeoutCharged>10</TimeoutCharged>
      <TimeoutCharger>5</TimeoutCharger>
      <TimeoutBacklight>5</TimeoutBacklight>
    </Battery>

  </EmulatorComponents>
</Emulator>
```

It is possible to configure the condition and behavior, as well as the current state of charge, with this component. You are able to change the public properties Voltage, Temperature, and StateOfCharge at runtime from the emulator code. You can access the component with the

BatteryCell property of the emulator class. The component does not have to be determined with FindComponentById and, therefore, does not need a unique ID to be specified with a configuration file.

```
BatteryCell battery = this.emulator.BatteryCell;
battery.StateOfCharge = 55;
battery.Voltage = 6000;
```

All other properties are static and can be initialized only during the configuration phase of the emulator. If you attempt to change such a property at runtime, you would get an exception.

When executing a .NET Micro Framework application on the emulator, the Battery. OnCharger method always returns true; in other words, an emulator always hangs on the battery charger. You cannot change or configure this.

When setting the properties at runtime, the component will not raise a battery event that notifies the system or the Battery.WaitForEvent method of a .NET Micro Framework application.

LCD Displays

The LcdDisplay component in the Microsoft.SPOT.Emulator.Lcd namespace is responsible for emulating an LCD display. With this component, you can configure the resolution (Width and Height) and color depth (BitsPerPixel), as demonstrated in Listing 13-40. Permitted values for the color depth are 1, 4, 8, and 16 bits per pixel. The emulator class possesses an LcdDisplay property to address this component.

Listing 13-40. *Configuring an LCD Display*

```xml
<?xml version="1.0" encoding="utf-8"?>
<Emulator>
  <Types>
    <LcdDisplay>Microsoft.SPOT.Emulator.Lcd.LcdDisplay</LcdDisplay>
  </Types>

  <EmulatorComponents>
    <LcdDisplay>
      <Width>320</Width>
      <Height>240</Height>
      <BitsPerPixel>16</BitsPerPixel>
    </LcdDisplay>

  </EmulatorComponents>
</Emulator>
```

The component provides an event handler, which is called each time a .NET Micro Framework application draws on the display. In this handler, you can implement your custom code to present the content of the display with your emulator user interface.

```
public event OnDevicePaintEventHandler OnDevicePaint;
```

This event handler of the OnDeviceEventHandler type can be implemented as follows:

```
public void OnDevicePaintEventHandler(object sender, OnDevicePaintEventArgs args)
{
...
}
```

The args parameter provides the contents of the display in form of a Bitmap object and the last updated rectangular area on the display. The method is called in the context of the emulator thread, and therefore, you need to synchronize it with the GUI thread when drawing to the emulator user interface.

With the .NET Micro Framework SDK, in the SampleEmulator project, a class named Lcd is provided, and it inherits from Control. You can place this control on the form of your emulator user interface. This control automatically manages updating and drawing the display content on your emulator surface (see Figure 13-3).

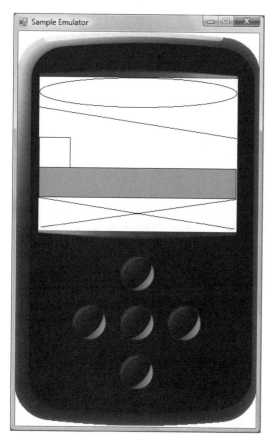

Figure 13-3. *An emulator with a display control*

Summary

In this chapter, you toured all the built-in emulator components, and you learned how to configure and extend them. The chapter covered emulator components for the following hardware components:

- GPIO ports

- Serial ports

- I²C bus

- SPI bus

- Emulator timing

- RAM and flash memory

- Battery cells

- LCD displays

You now know how to synchronize the emulator thread and UI thread to change emulator component properties or user interface elements.

You saw how easy it is to extend existing components if a desired functionality is not provided with the built-in components. The chapter described many useful custom components, such as components to connect HyperTerminal with your emulator, a temperature sensor, and an AD converter component to reuse with your custom emulators. Now, you are prepared to write rich and flexible emulators for your physical hardware.

Congratulations! This is the final chapter of this book, so you have completed your exciting tour through programming managed applications on embedded devices. All in all, you now know a lot about the .NET Micro Framework. This book started by introducing the .NET Micro Framework and went on to present available devices, tour the whole base class library, cover the extensible emulator and emulator components, and provide many practical and reusable samples and tips. You are now able to get as much as possible out of the .NET Micro Framework and write powerful and well performing embedded applications.

Index

You Need the Companion eBook

Your purchase of this book entitles you to buy the companion PDF-version eBook for only $10. Take the weightless companion with you anywhere.

We believe this Apress title will prove so indispensable that you'll want to carry it with you everywhere, which is why we are offering the companion eBook (in PDF format) for $10 to customers who purchase this book now. Convenient and fully searchable, the PDF version of any content-rich, page-heavy Apress book makes a valuable addition to your programming library. You can easily find and copy code—or perform examples by quickly toggling between instructions and the application. Even simultaneously tackling a donut, diet soda, and complex code becomes simplified with hands-free eBooks!

Once you purchase your book, getting the $10 companion eBook is simple:

❶ Visit **www.apress.com/promo/tendollars/**.

❷ Complete a basic registration form to receive a randomly generated question about this title.

❸ Answer the question correctly in 60 seconds, and you will receive a promotional code to redeem for the $10.00 eBook.

THE EXPERT'S VOICE™

2855 TELEGRAPH AVENUE | SUITE 600 | BERKELEY, CA 94705